Spotlight on Advanced

Student's Book

Second Edition

Carol Nuttall
Francesca Mansfield
age Testing 123

NATIONAL GEOGRAPHIC LEARNING

CENGAGE Learning

Australia • Brazil • Japan • Korea • Mexico • Singა

ngl.cengage.com/eltexampreparation

PASSWORD   spotlightadvance!D9#

NATIONAL GEOGRAPHIC LEARNING | CENGAGE Learning®

**Spotlight on Advanced Student's Book
(2nd Edition)**

Carol Nuttall and Francesca Mansfield
**This second edition has been updated for the revised
exam with some new material by a team led by
Michael Black from Language Testing 123.**
Ideas Generator spreads by Helen Stephenson

Publisher: Gavin McLean

Publishing Consultant: Karen Spiller

Project Manager: Karen White

Development Editor: Jennifer Nunan

Strategic Marketing Manager: Charlotte Ellis

Content Project Manager: Tom Relf

Manufacturing Buyer: Eyvett Davis

Head of Production: Alissa McWhinnie

Cover design: Oliver Hutton

Original page design: Keith Shaw

Additional text design and composition: Oliver Hutton

National Geographic Liaison: Wesley Della Volla

DVD-ROM: Tom Dick and Debbie Productions

ISBN: 978-1-285-84936-2

National Geographic Learning
Cheriton House, North Way, Andover, Hampshire, SP10 5BE
United Kingdom

Cengage Learning is a leading provider of customized learning solutions
with office locations around the globe, including Singapore, the United
Kingdom, Australia, Mexico, Brazil and Japan. Locate your local office at:
international.cengage.com/region

Cengage Learning products are represented in Canada by Nelson
Education, Ltd.

Visit National Geographic Learning online at **ngl.cengage.com**

Visit our corporate website at **www.cengage.com**

CREDITS

Although every effort has been made to contact copyright holders before publication, this has not always been possible. If contacted, the publisher will
undertake to rectify errors or omissions at the earliest opportunity.

Text

We are grateful to the following for permission to reproduce copyright material:

Guardian News & Media Ltd for an extract in unit 2 from "Pioneer nursery stays open – in all weathers" by Severin Carroll *The Guardian*, 30 October 2006,
copyright © Guardian News & Media Ltd 2006; Headline Publishing Group and Perseus Books Group for an extract in unit 3 from *Close to the wind* by Pete
Goss, copyright © 1998, 1999 Pete Goss. Reprinted by permission of Headline Publishing Group and Da Capo Press, a member of The Perseus Books Group;
Tribune Content Agency for extracts in unit 4 from 'The Cretaceous World' edited by Peter Skelton reviewed by Douglas Palmer. *New Scientist*, news service;
'Dinosaurs of the air' by Gregory Paul reviewed by Jeff Hecht, New Scientist, Issue 2349; 'Chasing monsters' by Michael Benton and the Dinosaur Hunters by
Deborah Cadbury, *New Scientist*, Issue 2259; 'There be dragons' by Christopher McGowan reviewed by Simon Knell, *New Scientist*, Issue 2293; and 'A field guide
to Dinosaurs: The essential handbook for travelers' in the Mesozoic by Henry Gee and Luis V. Rey reviewed by Jeff Hecht, New Scientist, Issue 2387, copyright
© Reed Business Information – UK. All rights reserved. Distributed by Tribune Content Agency; Guardian News & Media Ltd for an extract in unit 5 from 'Of
worms and woodpeckers: the changing world of the virus-busters fighting rise in internet crime' by Bobbie Johnson, *The Guardian*, 6 February 2006, copyright
© Guardian News & Media Ltd 2006; Straw Works for an extract in unit 8 adapted from *Straw Bale Futures, Introduction, Information guide to straw Bale Building*,
"http://www.strawworks.co.uk" www.strawworks.co.uk. Reproduced with permission; Tribune Content Agency for an extract in unit 8 from 'Easter Island:
A monumental collapse' by Emma Young, New Scientist, Issue 2562, copyright © Reed Business Information – UK. All rights reserved. Distributed by Tribune
Content Agency; Guardian News & Media Ltd for an extract in unit 10 from 'Nice week at the office, darling?' by Joanna Moorhead, *The Guardian*, 13 January
2007, copyright © Guardian News & Media Ltd 2007; The Random House Group Ltd and Simon & Schuster for an extract in unit 11 from Brick Lane by Monica
Ali, published by Transworld, copyright © 2003 by Monica Ali. Reprinted by permission of The Random House Group Limited and Scribner Publishing Group. All
rights reserved; and Peter Bradshaw for extracts in unit 12 from 'Casablanca review', 'The Truth about love review', 'Rocky Balboa review', 'The Simpsons Movie
review' and 'Casino Royale review' by Peter Bradshaw, "http://film.guardian.co.uk/ews_Story/Critic_Review/Guardian_review/0,,2013773,00.html" http://film.
guardian.co.uk/. Reproduced with permission; Fauna & Flora International for an extract in the Practice Test adapted from 'Conservation challenge: Our depleted
oceans – what lies beneath...' by Dr Abigail Entwistle, http://www.fauna-flora.org/initiatives/our-depleted-oceans/, copyright © Fauna & Flora International;
Guardian News & Media Ltd for extracts in the Practice Test from 'Review: To the Letter by Simon Garfield' by Kathryn Hughes, and 'Mountain rescue: ski
co-operatives blazing a trail in Canada' by Susan Greenwood, *The Guardian*, 15/16 November 2013, copyright © Guardian News & Media Ltd 2013; and John
Wiley & Sons Ltd for an extract in the Practice Test adapted from *Managing Teams For Dummies* by Marty Brounstein, copyright © 2002 by Wiley Publishing, Inc.
Reproduced with permission of John Wiley & Sons Ltd.

In some instances we have been unable to trace the owners of copyright material and we would appreciate any information that would enable us to do so.

Printed in China by RR Donnelley
Print Number: 04   Print Year: 2015

CONTENTS

Unit	Vocabulary	Grammar	Use of English	Reading
1 **Beginnings**	Starting again Key word *make*	Review of tenses (past and present)	Part 4: key word transformation	Reading for specific informa
2 **A child's world**	Parts of the body idioms Phrasal verb: *pick up* Key word *run*	Passive forms Passive form with *have* and *get*	Part 1: multiple-choice cloze	*Pioneer nursery stays outdoo* Part 7: gapped text
3 **Are you game?**	Phrases with *up* and *down* Phrasal verbs with *take* Phrases with *take* Key word *game*	Modal auxiliaries (1)	Part 4: Key word transformation Part 2: open cloze	*A close encounter* Part 5: multiple choice
4 **Eureka!**	Colourful language Key word *tell* Prefixes	The future	Part 3: word formation	*Dinosaur books* Part 8: multiple matching
5 **Safe and sound?**	Crimes Phrasal verbs with *turn* Key word *law*	Verbs followed by infinitive or *-ing*	Part 4: key word transformation Part 2: open cloze	*Of worms and woodpeckers* Part 7: gapped text
6 **Hale and hearty**	Expressions with food Key word *life*	Conditionals	Part 4: key word transformation Identifying collocations Part 1: multiple-choice cloze	*Superfoods: are they really so super?* Part 6: cross-text multiple matching
7 **Wish you were there …**	Describing places Phrasal verbs and phrases with *look* Key word *road*	Inversion	Part 3: word formation Part 2: open cloze	*City reviews* Part 8: multiple matching
8 **Making our mark**	Phrases with *bring* Key word *that*	Relative pronouns Defining and non-defining relative clauses Reduced relative clauses	Part 3: word formation	*Straw bale futures* Part 5: multiple choice

Listening	Speaking	Writing	Video / Review
Short extracts; interpreting context from vocabulary	Talking about new experiences	Part 2: a letter	Video: Profiles in exploration Ideas generator: structuring spontaneous answers
Language development in children Part 2: sentence completion	Part 3: using visual prompts	Part 2: a review	
An interview with an explorer Part 3: multiple choice	Part 3: interacting	Part 2: a formal letter	Video: Frozen search and rescue Ideas generator: brainstorming and selecting
Inventions Part 4: multiple matching	Part 4: three-way task	Part 1: an essay – using the notes provided	Review 1 Reading and Use of English, Part 4: Key word transformation Reading and Use of English, Part 2: Open cloze
DNA analysis Part 2: Sentence completion	Part 1: giving personal information	Part 2: a report	Video: The world in a station Ideas generator: interpreting pictures
The benefits of eating raw food Part 3: multiple choice	Part 2: comparing pictures	Part 1: an essay – developing an argument	
Commercial space travel Part 4: multiple matching	Part 4: discussing	Part 2: a proposal	Video: Our ATM is a goat Ideas generator: focusing your ideas to talk about abstract topics
Working life Part 1: multiple choice	Part 3: reaching a decision through negotiation	Part 2: a review	Review 2 Reading and Use of English, Part 3: Word formation Reading and Use of English, Part 4: Key word transformation

Listening	Speaking	Writing	Video / Review
Interview about an artist Part 3: multiple choice	Part 3: suggesting solutions, justifying ideas	Part 1: an essay – supporting your ideas	Video: Aboriginal rock art Ideas generator: making a decision
(1) *Identifying feelings* Part 4: multiple matching (2) *Freecycling* Note-taking	Part 2: organising a larger unit of discourse	Part 2: a proposal	
The history of credit Part 2: sentence completion	Parts 3 and 4: disagreeing with someone else's opinion	Part 2: a report	Video: Rainy day flea market Ideas generator: alternative viewpoints
Film makers Part 1: multiple choice	Parts 3 and 4: exchanging ideas	Part 2: a review	Review 3 Reading and Use of English, Part 3: Word formation Reading and Use of English, Part 4: Key word transformation
Communication skills Part 4: multiple matching	Part 3: sustaining interaction	Part 2: a proposal	Video: The Braille Hubble Ideas generator: making your responses relevant to the discussion
Atmospheric conditions in the Earth's past Part 2: sentence completion	Part 3: evaluating	Part 1: an essay – discussing issues that surround a topic	
The origin of kissing Part 3: multiple choice *Living abroad* Part 4: multiple matching	Part 1: talking about your country, culture and background	Part 2: a report	Video: The Hadzabe tribe Ideas generator: explaining familiar topics
Three short extracts Part 1: multiple choice	Part 2: individual long turn	Part 2: a letter	Review 4 Reading and Use of English, Part 4: Key word transformation Reading and Use of English, Part 2: Open cloze

Introduction

Spotlight on Advanced is a new preparation course for students intending to take the *Cambridge English: Advanced* (CAE) examination. The course is based on the new Cambridge exam guidelines for January 2015 and onwards.

Approach of the book

Spotlight on Advanced consists of 16 stimulating units covering a wide range of themes that will take you from *Cambridge English: First* through to an advanced level of English. For those hoping to continue with *Cambridge English: Proficiency* it will act as an essential stepping stone. For others it is a valuable certificate in its own right.

Preparing for the exam

The student's book will help you to develop the skills you need to be successful in the exam. You will learn how to approach the exam and each paper with confidence, while building essential skills that will enable you to use the English language at an advanced level.

Spotlight features

The Exam Spotlight boxes provide valuable information and advice on different parts of the exam, and they help you to focus on key skills and techniques that you will need to develop in order to pass the exam. Most Spotlights are 'active', which means that you are required to do something to consolidate the skills being focused on.

Language development

Each unit includes a Language Development section which focuses on important language areas such as phrasal verbs, idiomatic expressions, key words, vocabulary groups, collocations and word formation exercises.

'Key word' feature

Each unit includes a key word feature, which focuses on one common word or a word that has already appeared in the unit. This feature analyses the different uses that the specific word has, either grammatically, or lexically, or both.

Vocabulary organisers

At the back of the book there is a Vocabulary Organiser for each unit. This will help you to organise, develop and consolidate vocabulary as you learn it through the course of each unit. Ideally, each exercise should be completed alongside the tasks in the unit as you complete them.

'In other words' feature

This feature focuses on useful ways you can develop your vocabulary when using the English language actively (that is, when speaking or writing).

Phrasal verbs and expressions

Each unit focuses either on phrasal verbs or idiomatic expressions or both. In order to pass the *Cambridge English: Advanced* exam, you'll need to be aware of a wide range of idiomatic expressions and their correct usage.

Approach to grammar

If you're taking the *Cambridge English: Advanced* exam you will already be familiar with the main areas of English grammar covered up to *Cambridge English: First* level. The *Spotlight on Advanced* student's book revises and consolidates what you should already know, and develops certain areas to a more advanced level.

Each grammar section is linked to the Grammar Reference section on pages 208–221, which should be consulted as you do each section.

Reading

There are a wide variety of reading texts from a number of sources such as you will find in the *Cambridge English: Advanced* exam. As well as giving you plenty of exam practice, the topics covered in the reading sections should create plenty of opportunities for discussion and help you develop your vocabulary and language skills.

Writing

The writing sections cover each of the writing task types that may appear in the exam and give guidelines and practice at writing for both Part 1 and Part 2 of the Writing paper. This section looks in detail at how to analyse a question, brainstorm ideas, use input material where required, draw up a detailed writing plan, and improve vocabulary and paragraph structure, before attempting a similar task by yourself, either during the lesson or for homework.

You can also refer to the Writing Guide on pages 222–230 to see samples of model pieces for each task type and guidelines for approaching the task, as well as additional task questions for extra practice.

Use of English

Spotlight on Advanced includes an in-depth section on the Use of English parts of the Reading and Use of English paper, with detailed guidelines and tasks to help you approach each part of the paper with confidence. Each section will also help you improve your level of English and develop further skills for reading, writing and speaking.

Listening

The listening sections throughout the student's book cover all four parts of the Listening paper and are designed to help you develop the necessary skills required for each part. Each section also includes useful advice and tips.

Speaking

Spotlight on Advanced provides innumerable opportunities to discuss the subjects and topics raised in each unit. In addition to this, there is a focused Speaking section in each unit that looks at a different part of the Speaking test so that all four parts are covered. The Speaking sections present useful functions and expressions which you will use in real life but which are also practised in the context of an exam-type task.

The Speaking Reference Files on pages 231–240 contain extra practice and useful expressions.

Finally, don't forget to use the *Exam Booster* workbook which provides further practice in all these areas and includes an audio CD which you can use at home.

Have fun with your course, and good luck!
Francesca and Carol

Overview of the exam

The *Cambridge English: Advanced* examination consists of four papers. The Reading and Use of English paper carries 40% of the marks, while Writing, Listening and Speaking each carry 20%. A candidate achieving Grade A will receive a certificate stating that they demonstrated ability at C2 (proficiency) level; for Grades B and C candidates will receive a certificate at C1 level, and a candidate whose performance is at B2 will receive a certificate stating this. It is not necessary to achieve a satisfactory grade in all four papers in order to receive a particular grade.

Reading and Use of English

1 hour 30 minutes

- There are eight parts with 56 questions in total.
- Parts 1 and 3 mainly test vocabulary, Part 2 mainly tests grammar, Part 4 tests both grammar and vocabulary, and Parts 5 to 8 test reading skills.
- Parts 1, 2, and 3: each correct answer receives 1 mark. Part 4: each correct answer receives up to 2 marks. Parts 5–7: each correct answer receives 2 marks. Part 8: each correct answer receives 1 mark.

Part 1: Multiple-choice cloze
A modified cloze test containing eight gaps and followed by eight four-option multiple-choice items. You must choose the option that correctly fills the gap from options A, B, C and D.

Part 2: Open cloze
A modified open cloze test containing eight gaps. You must write one word to fill each gap.

Part 3: Word formation
You must read a text containing eight gaps. Each gap corresponds to a word. The stems of the missing words are given beside the text and you must change the form of the word to fill the gap.

Part 4: Key word transformation
There are six separate questions, each with a lead-in sentence and a gapped second sentence to be completed in three to six words, including a given 'key word'. The second sentence must have the same meaning as the lead-in sentence.

Part 5: Multiple choice
A longer text followed by six four-option multiple choice questions. The emphasis is on understanding a long text, including detail, opinion, tone, purpose, main idea, implication, attitude, and text organisation.

Part 6: Cross-text multiple matching
You have to read four short texts and answer four questions that require you to read across texts. The emphasis is on comparing and contrasting opinions and attitudes across texts.

Part 7: Gapped text
Six paragraphs have been removed from a longer text and placed in a jumbled order, together with an additional paragraph. You have to choose the missing paragraph for each gap. Emphasis is on understanding how texts are structured and following text development.

Part 8: Multiple matching
A text or several short texts is preceded by ten multiple-matching questions. Emphasis is on locating specific information, detail, opinion and attitude in texts.

Writing

1 hour 30 minutes

The writing paper is divided into two parts. You must answer both parts (a compulsory one in Part 1, one from a choice of three in Part 2).

Part 1: One compulsory question
You will be asked to write an essay based on two points given in the input text, and to explain which of the two points is more important and why. You must use the input material and write 220–260 words.

Part 2: One from a choice of writing tasks
You must write one task from a choice of three questions. You may be asked to write any of the following: a letter, a proposal, a report or a review. You must write 220–260 words.

Listening

Approximately 40 minutes

You listen to each part twice and write your answers on an answer sheet.

- Four parts
- Each part contains a recorded text or texts and corresponding comprehension tasks.
- Each part is heard twice.
- There are 30 questions in total.

Part 1: Multiple choice
Three short extracts, from exchanges between interacting speakers. There are two four-option multiple-choice questions for each extract.

Part 2: Sentence completion
A monologue with a sentence completion task which has eight items. You must complete each sentence with information that you hear in the recording.

Part 3: Multiple choice
A longer dialogue or conversation involving interacting speakers, with six multiple-choice questions.

Part 4: Multiple matching
Five short, themed monologues, with ten multiple-matching questions. There are two tasks to complete.

Speaking

15 minutes

- Four parts
- There will be two examiners: one who is both interlocutor and assessor, and one who is an assessor.
- There will be two or three candidates per group.
- You will be expected to respond to questions and to interact in conversational English.

Part 1: Introductory questions
A conversation between the interlocutor and each candidate (spoken questions).

Part 2: Individual 'long turn'
An individual 'long turn' for each candidate with a brief response from the second candidate (visual stimuli, with spoken instructions).

Part 3: Two-way conversation
A two-way conversation between the candidates (written stimuli, with spoken instructions).

Part 4: Extension of discussion topics
A discussion on topics related to Part 3 (spoken questions).

BEGINNINGS

GETTING STARTED

1 Work in pairs. This picture shows a beginning. What other types of beginnings can you think of?

2 The verbs in the box can mean a beginning but are used in different contexts. Match the verbs with the contexts (1–3).

activate   bring about   conceive   embark on
engender   establish   found   generate
inaugurate   incite   initiate   inspire   instigate
launch   launch into   originate   produce   prompt
provoke   set about   set off   set up   spawn
stimulate   trigger

1   cause something to begin or happen
2   create something
3   start doing something

READING reading for specific information

3 Read text A and find out when Charlie Chaplin first performed on the stage and why he had to work so hard as a boy.

Text A

HUMBLE BEGINNINGS

Charlie Chaplin remains to this day one of the world's most famous and best-loved comedians. Born in London in 1889, to parents who were music hall performers, he inherited their talent and was taught to sing and dance from the moment he could walk. He made his debut appearance on stage at the age of five when his mother became hoarse and was unable to perform. This was a highly auspicious start to his career: he was a resounding success, and from then on secured several engagements as a child actor. He had little contact with his father, who left home when Charlie was about a year old and died of alcoholism in 1901. Charlie's mother suffered a mental breakdown, which led to her being placed in a psychiatric institution. He and his half-brother Sydney were sent to a home, and for a while, Charlie lived on the streets.

Between the ages of 12 and 14, Chaplin worked in various establishments to make ends meet, including a barber shop, a stationer's, a doctor's surgery, a glass factory and a printing plant. His experiences in these places no doubt provided him with invaluable material for the films he would eventually make. Charlie began performing in earnest, and after making a name for himself in vaudeville, travelled to the United States, where his real career began.

4 Look at the following pair of sentences about Charlie Chaplin, and decide whether they convey the same information (S) as that which appears in text A, or different (D).

1 Charlie's first performance occurred when his mother was taken ill.   S / D
2 Charlie made a living as a child actor between the ages of 12 and 14.   S / D

5 Decide whether the following statements are true (T) or false (F).

1 Charlie Chaplin first went on stage as soon as he could walk.   T / F
2 Charlie was successful as a child actor.   T / F
3 Charlie was homeless for a period after his mother became mentally ill.   T / F
4 Charlie acted in a film about a barber shop when he was 12.   T / F
5 The writer suggests that Charlie's films were inspired by the jobs he undertook as a teenager.   T / F

6 Text B is about someone who returns to an interest she abandoned as a child. Read the text and find out:

1 why she gave it up originally.
2 how her new interest is similar/different.

Text B
Back to the Drawing Board

When I was at school, I loved painting and drawing. I used to create beautiful illustrations for the covers of all my exercise books and I dreamt of being an illustrator. But when I mentioned the possibility of going to art college to my art teacher, Miss Wright, she shook her head, saying that in such a competitive, creative field, only the most talented would succeed and advised me to focus on my academic studies instead. Disheartened, I put away my pencils and paints and buried my head in my books.

Many years later, after a life and career well away from the art world, my creative spirit was reawakened when I went along to a beginner's photography class. I was starting from scratch and wanted to learn about all the buttons and settings on my camera, but instead my interest was piqued by the composition element of the course. In our first class, the teacher told us to explore the grounds of the college for something that caught our eye. She said that we weren't to snap away, but to spend time choosing our subject, framing the shot and filling the frame. We were to come back with no more than a handful of pictures from which we chose our favourite three. As she put each shot up on the screen, we had to say why we'd chosen it and what we liked about it. The results were amazing! Everyone had such a different take on what seemed like a simple task; the photos reflecting the unique view of each photographer. I feel like I've made a fresh start in an exciting new medium and I can't wait to learn more!

7 Quickly read through this text about talent and what can impact on its development. How could you sum up the writer's opinion?

Text C
IS TALENT ENOUGH?

It is sometimes assumed that painters, actors and other artists, armed with natural talent and an innate drive to develop that talent, can achieve excellence (though not necessarily commercial success) through their own efforts alone. That, however, is a somewhat simplistic view.

Nurture, too, plays a significant role in artistic progress. Growing up in a musical household, for example, is likely to develop at least an interest in music. Take the Bach family, whose members over two centuries included 50 or more performers and composers. Being born into a family like this must at the very least have meant there were few obstacles to developing a Bach child's musical talent.

However, not all life experiences benefit the would-be artist. Their first tentative steps can easily falter in the face of unsupportive, even if well-meant, reactions from others. On the other hand, while poverty might necessitate a way of life that hinders artistic development, even poverty can be put to good use: close observation of human nature in difficult situations can help the painter, sculptor or actor to convincingly portray a wide range of human behaviour.

8 Consider all three texts and answer the questions.

1 Which text illustrates the writer of text C's opinion about motivation coming from within?
2 Which text illustrates the writer of text C's opinion about a possible benefit of hardship?
3 Which text gives an example of the positive effect of family background that is mentioned in text A?
4 Which text illustrates the writer of text C's opinion about how talent can be discouraged?

9 Discuss. What feelings do you experience when you start something new?

LANGUAGE DEVELOPMENT starting again

1 **Discuss. The title of text B on page 11, *Back to the Drawing Board*, has a double meaning. What is it? Find other phrases in the text which mean 'to start again'.**

2 **Complete the phrases with the words in the box. There is one extra word.**

fresh   leaf   scratch   slate   source   square

1 to make a _____ start
2 to turn over a new _____
3 back to _____ one
4 to start from _____
5 to wipe the _____ clean

3 **What similar meaning do the expressions in exercise 2 all convey?**

4 **Complete the sentences with the correct form of an expression from exercise 2.**

1 The cake was a complete disaster, so I threw it in the bin and _____ _____ scratch.
2 We've had too many arguments recently. Let's _____ _____ _____ clean and see if we can get on better.
3 Billy's attempt to get an income by setting up his own business failed, and he was back _____ _____ _____ .
4 Jenny found it easy to _____ _____ _____ start when she moved to the city.
5 Having _____ _____ a new leaf, Gillian felt it was unfair for anyone to hold her past mistakes against her.

5 **The phrases in the box all appeared in text A on page 11. Use them to complete the sentences.**

make (one's) debut   make ends meet   make a name for oneself

1 Leonardo di Caprio _____ in the film *What's Eating Gilbert Grape* but didn't become famous until he appeared in *Romeo and Juliet*.
2 Although Roald Dahl wrote several books for adults, he _____ as a writer of children's books.
3 While she was writing her first novel, Helena worked as a waitress to _____ .

KEY WORD make

6 **These sentences all use an expression with *make*. Explain what it means in each sentence.**

1 Everyone was yelling so much that I found it hard to make myself heard.
2 'I haven't got a clue what this question is asking us to do.'
   'That makes two of us.'
3 'A small packet of crisps, please. No, make it a large one.'
4 News of the flooding made the national papers.
5 He made me stay in and do my homework even though I had been invited to a party.

7 **Complete the sentences with the correct form of one of the phrases in the box.**

make a go of   make do with   make it   make out   make-or-break   make the best of

1 He grabbed hold of the rock and pulled himself up. He was exhausted, but he'd finally _____ !
2 She _____ that she was searching for something on the ground, so the boy wouldn't notice she'd been staring at him.
3 David realised that he was in a _____ situation. Success would mean certain promotion, while failure would result in the loss of his job.
4 Jim and Sally have had their problems, but they've decided to _____ their marriage.
5 The rain spoiled their plans for a picnic, but they _____ it by playing games indoors.
6 I can't afford to buy a new car this year, so I'll have to _____ my old one.

GRAMMAR review of tenses (past and present)

8 **Discuss. How did the universe begin or has it always existed? What do you think will happen to it in the future?**

9 **Read text A. Find examples of the following tenses:**

1 Present simple
2 Present perfect
3 Past simple
4 Present continuous
5 Present perfect continuous

Text A

THE ULTIMATE BEGINNING

Throughout history we have been searching for answers to explain how the universe began. While there have been countless theories, much of what we know is still only speculation, and many people are still questioning and re-evaluating most of the information we have collected. However, through the revelations of modern science, we have been able to offer firm theories for some of the answers we once called hypotheses. True to the nature of science, a majority of these answers have only led to more intriguing and complex questions. It seems to be inherent in our search for knowledge that questions will continue to arise and maybe there will never be any definite answers.

10 **Which of the tenses in exercise 9 is used in text A to talk about:**

1 an activity that started in the past but has not yet ended
2 a present state
3 a finished past event
4 an event that began in the past but relates to the present
5 an activity happening in the present

11 **Read text B. Name the past tenses that have been underlined.**

Text B

The Expanding Universe

Until Edwin Hubble <u>proposed</u> that the universe <u>was expanding</u>, it <u>had been assumed</u> by the majority of scientists that the universe <u>existed</u> in a constant state, that it <u>had</u> no past or future and simply 'was'. Yet, although Hubble <u>had not been trying</u> to explain the universe's beginning, his discovery would seriously challenge this notion. Hubble <u>knew</u> that all the galaxies <u>were moving</u> away from each other, but he <u>noticed</u> that the speed they <u>were travelling</u> was proportional to their distance from Earth. This could only mean one thing: the universe <u>was expanding</u> and therefore in a state of flux. It clearly <u>had</u> a past, a present, and it was logical to assume, a future.

▶ GRAMMAR REFERENCE (SECTION 1) **PAGE 208**

12 **Rewrite the following sentences so that the tenses are used correctly.**

1 He had been looking at the stars but he wasn't finding any new planets.
2 He realised that the universe was growing for 13 billion years.
3 It all was starting with a big bang, according to some scientists.
4 We searched for answers and we are still looking.
5 The universe has been starting to expand a very long time ago.

13 **What 'notion' would Hubble's discovery challenge? Why was this? Answer in your own words.**

14 **Complete text C with the correct form of the verbs in brackets. In some places more than one answer may be possible.**

Text C

The Big Bang

Hubble's discovery that the universe (1) _____ (expand) lent weight to a hypothesis that (2) _____ (put forward) in 1927 by a Belgian priest, Georges Lemaître. He (3) _____ (postulate) that all the matter in the universe (4) _____ (spring) from a single source, now called a 'singularity' – a point so small it (5) _____ (have) no dimensions – and that at some indefinably minuscule slither of time approximately 13.7 billion years ago, all this matter (6) _____ (explode) outwards from its source in a massive blast – so massive in fact that it (7) _____ (still / go on), and the universe (8) _____ (expand) ever since. The term 'The Big Bang' (9) _____ (coin) some time later by scientist Fred Hoyle, who, at the time (10) _____ (try) to criticise the hypothesis, but it (11) _____ (stick), and now this (12) _____ (be) the idea that most scientists seem to favour.

▶ GRAMMAR REFERENCE (SECTION 1) **PAGE 208**

15 **Work in pairs.**

Student A: Describe the process mentioned in *The Big Bang* in your own words.

Student B: Ask questions about anything you don't understand.

LISTENING short extracts

1 Look at the words in the box. Are they associated with books, cinema or the Internet?

> animation chapter download excerpt extract
> first edition front cover online paperback
> print out scene soundtrack special effects surfing
> trailer web page

2 You are going to hear someone talking about an advert. Before you listen, look at the questions below and underline the key words.

1 The advertisement is for
   a an arts and crafts book.
   b a design to make something.
   c a do-it-yourself kit.

2 The speaker is reading from
   a a magazine.
   b a mail order catalogue.
   c the Internet.

3 ◎1 Listen to the conversation and answer the questions in exercise 2. Turn to the audioscript on page 242 and underline the key words that helped you find the answers.

4 Read the questions for the second conversation and complete the rubric in your own words.

You are going to hear _____ .
Read the questions and then listen to the conversation.
1 What is the couple's main reason for moving?
2 How does the main speaker feel about the move?

5 ◎2 Listen and check your answer. Then answer the questions in exercise 4.

6 Turn to the audioscript on page 242 and underline any words or phrases that tell you how the speaker feels. Listen again, paying attention to her intonation.

7 Decide whether the following statements are true (T) or false (F).
1 The couple are moving to another country.   T / F
2 The man is worried that the sheep farm may not work.   T / F
3 The woman is used to a lot of noise.   T / F
4 She thinks that the move will be good for them.
                                              T / F

8 Read the rubric for the third conversation. Which of the words from exercise 1 might you hear?

You are going to hear two people discussing plans to make a film based on a book.

9 ◎3 Listen to the conversation and complete the sentence.

The woman expresses concern about
a the proposed lack of special effects in the film.
b the complex nature of some of the drafted scenes.
c the film potentially being too superficial in its approach.

USE OF ENGLISH key word transformation

10 For each of these sentences, decide which of the options that follows is closest in meaning. Explain why the other two sentences don't mean the same thing.

1 I've had enough of teaching, and would like a change.
   a I've been doing quite a lot of teaching, and I need a holiday.
   b I'm tired of teaching, and would like to make a fresh start.
   c I've had a lot of experience of teaching, and am looking for a new post.

2 He was doing well at work, but he suddenly decided to pack it all in and go to live on an island.
   a Although he was successful, he gave it all up and went to live on an island.
   b Due to his success, he decided to give it all up and live on an island.
   c Despite going to live on an island, he was successful.

11 Reading and Use of English, Part 4

For questions 1–6, complete the second sentence so that it has a similar meaning to the first sentence, using the word given. Do not change the word given. You must use between three and six words, including the word given.

1 I urgently need to give Simon a message about where to meet Jane.
   DELIVER
   I have to _____
   Simon about where to meet Jane.

2 Please hurry up and decide which film to watch.
   MIND
   I wish you would _____
   about which film to watch.

3 I found it quite hard to get this place at university.
   EASY
   It has _____ get
   this place at university.

4 I'd been worrying about the test, but it was easy.
   EXPECTED
   I _____ be so easy.

5 The police suspect that he killed his wife.
   OF
   He _____ his wife.

6 She's taking karate lessons, and kickboxing as well.
   IS
   Not only _____ , she's
   also doing kickboxing.

Reading and Use of English, Part 4
Key word transformation

In Reading and Use of English, Part 4, you might have to do several things.

Look at the checklist below and decide whether the points are true (T) or false (F), based on exercise 11.

1 Both sentences should have the same meaning. T / F
2 Both sentences should be in the same tense. T / F
3 An idiom, phrasal verb or fixed phrase could replace a verb or noun. T / F
4 One or more words in the sentence may change form. T / F
5 The key word must be put into the appropriate form. T / F
6 Inverted sentences may not be used. T / F
7 An active sentence could be transformed into a passive sentence. T / F
8 A positive sentence cannot be transformed into a negative sentence. T / F

SPEAKING talking about new experiences

12 Work in pairs and describe the pictures. What do they have in common?

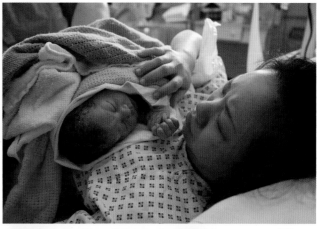

13 A friend of yours has just told you the following:

Guess what! I've taken up hang-gliding! I had my first lesson this morning.

What questions would you ask her about this to gain more information?

In Speaking Part 1 the examiner asks each candidate something about themselves. This is an opportunity for candidates to show their ability to talk socially. It's important to give detailed answers to the questions in this section.

14 **Discuss. The following statements are answers to the question:** *Tell me about a new experience you have had recently.* **What else could you say to expand on them?**

> Last week I went to the Natural History museum and I found it very interesting.

> I took an English exam two months ago, and I was anxious about the Speaking test!

> I went to Spain on holiday this summer.

15 **Match the sentences (1–7) with the more detailed descriptions (a–g).**

<table>
<tr><td rowspan="16" style="writing-mode: vertical-rl">IN OTHER WORDS</td></tr>
<tr><td>1</td><td>It was fun.</td><td>5</td><td>It did me good.</td></tr>
<tr><td>2</td><td>I felt scared.</td><td>6</td><td>I quit too easily.</td></tr>
<tr><td>3</td><td>I won't forget it.</td><td>7</td><td>I was given a chance.</td></tr>
<tr><td>4</td><td>I would do it differently.</td><td></td><td></td></tr>
<tr><td>a</td><td colspan="3">I can still clearly remember every moment.</td></tr>
<tr><td>b</td><td colspan="3">It was a long time ago but I still remember how terrified I felt.</td></tr>
<tr><td>c</td><td colspan="3">If only I hadn't given up so easily.</td></tr>
<tr><td>d</td><td colspan="3">If I could relive the experience, I would try to change the way I reacted.</td></tr>
<tr><td>e</td><td colspan="3">Despite what happened to me, I benefited in a number of ways.</td></tr>
<tr><td>f</td><td colspan="3">I realised that I had been given a unique opportunity.</td></tr>
<tr><td>g</td><td colspan="3">It was probably the most enjoyable experience I have ever had.</td></tr>
</table>

16 **Work in pairs.**

Student A: You are the examiner. Ask Student B to describe a significant experience that changed his/her life, and to say in what way it changed it.

Student B: Listen to the question carefully, and give a detailed answer. Use the In Other Words box to help you.

Student A: Make sure that Student B answers your question fully.

Swap roles.

WRITING a descriptive or narrative piece of writing (letter)

PLANNING YOUR WORK

Planning is always important and should take up a good part of your allotted writing time.

1 **Put the planning stages in the correct order (1–5).**

> brainstorming   checking   outlining   selecting vocabulary   writing

Use this five-point plan for any piece of writing you do.

2 **Read the announcement in a student magazine. What are you being asked to write? What two things are you being asked to include in it?**

> ## WE ARE OFFERING READERS A FREE HOLIDAY WEEKEND FOR THE BEST DESCRIPTIVE ACCOUNT OF A NEW OR UNUSUAL EXPERIENCE.
>
> *Write a letter describing the experience and explaining what made it so memorable or significant.*

EXAM SPOTLIGHT

Writing, Part 2 Descriptive or narrative writing

In Writing Part 2, you may be asked to write a piece that has descriptive or narrative elements, or outlines a personal experience. This could be in the form of a letter or a review. You therefore need to familiarise yourself with the structures and vocabulary relevant to describing, narrating and explaining, and you should know how to express levels of formality. A letter to a newspaper or magazine may include a narrative element which details personal experience. If you haven't had any relevant experiences that you think are worth writing about, it doesn't mean you can't attempt the task: you can always invent one.

3 **Write down three ideas for an unusual experience, either from your own life or invented.**

4 **4 Listen to a class brainstorming session. What new or unusual experiences did the students think up?**

Check your answers with the audioscript on page 242.

5 **5 Listen to the same class discussing the paragraph structure. Then complete the structure that they agree on.**

First paragraph:
Next paragraph or paragraphs:
Final paragraph:

6 A friend of yours submitted the letter on the right to the magazine. Read it and decide what structural problems it has.

Dear Editor,

I had always dreamed of going up in a hot-air balloon, so when I was offered the chance last year, I jumped at it. It was my mother's fiftieth birthday, and as a special treat, my dad decided to take the whole family up. I think it must have been quite expensive but it was well worth it. It was a beautiful summer's day with a fresh crisp wind blowing from the east – ideal weather for a balloon ride. Nevertheless, we wrapped up warm and equipped ourselves with hats, sunglasses, cameras and binoculars. I had expected to be frightened but as the balloon rose gently into the air I was amazed at how safe I felt. We could see the airfield getting smaller and the horizon expanding as we ascended over the nearby village. It was amazing to see how quickly it started to look like a toy town. Before long, everything below was just a patchwork of fields and roads. We were floating effortlessly in a blue sky with only the sound of the wind buffeting round the balloon itself. It was breathtaking. We each took turns regulating the amount of hot air needed to keep us at just the right height until it was time to begin our descent. Naturally, we were reluctant to return to earth.

Yours faithfully,
Anneka Johansson

DESCRIPTIVE VOCABULARY

A descriptive account needs the right vocabulary to make it easy for the reader to picture what you are describing. This means carefully selecting appropriate words and phrases. You should do this before you start writing.

7 Look back at Anneka's letter and underline the words and phrases she uses to describe:
1 the weather.
2 the view from the air.
3 the writer's feelings about the experience.

8 Write a suitable ending to Anneka's letter. Make sure you answer the second part of the question.

9 Work in pairs. Read your partner's ending to Anneka's letter and check it for mistakes.

Writing, Part 2 letter

10 Read the exam question and write your letter. Use between 220–260 words. Make sure you follow all the planning stages.

We are offering three months' free subscription to our magazine to the reader that sends in the best account of an important turning point in their life. This will be published in a special supplement entitled *A Fresh Start*. Write a letter and tell us how you turned your life around and what made it happen.

VIDEO profiles in exploration

1 **This photo shows explorer Johan Reinhard at one of the most important moments in his career. Work in pairs and discuss the questions.**

1   Where do you think he is?
2   What kind of an explorer might he be?
3   What might be important about the pile of stones?

2 **In the video, you will hear Johan Reinhard and two more National Geographic explorers describe experiences in their work.**

1   Read the information in the table below and match A with B.
2   Watch the video and match the information in A and B with the names in C.

A	B	C
an archaeologist	spends a lot of time underwater, finding connections between the living systems in the ocean	Alexandra Cousteau
an environmental advocate	explores the unknown in the natural world and shares the resulting discoveries and stories with other people	Johan Reinhard
an oceanographer	discovers and interprets ancient sites to understand the past, for example, Inca mummies and their burial grounds	Sylvia Earle

3 Read the notes for each person. Then watch the video again and complete the notes.

Part 1 Alexandra Cousteau

family influence: comes from a family of (1) _____ , learnt to dive with her (2) _____

a key aspect of her experiences: the excitement of (3) _____ places + creatures

how other people feel about her job: people are excited + (4) _____

Part 2 Johan Reinhard

a personal achievement: best known for his (5) _____ of the Ice Maiden + (6) _____ perfect Inca mummies

a key moment in his work on the Ice Maiden: when he saw her (7) _____ – confirmed it was a mummy

the importance of the Ice Maiden: the body was (8) _____ – able to do DNA studies on it

Part 3 Sylvia Earle

the best part of her job: joy of (9) _____

an example of animal behaviour she studies: how (10) _____ spend their days + nights

what she says about discovery: everybody should try to (11) _____ the natural world

4 Watch the video and make a note of at least one question you would like to ask each explorer.

5 Work in groups of three. Compare your questions and speculate on possible answers, based on what you have learnt about the explorers.

6 Work in groups of three explorers. You are going to meet at a social event. Prepare questions to ask the other two. Use your notes and the ideas below to help you.

| a typical day | family | leisure time | travel | work |

SPEAKING Part 1 interview

IDEAS GENERATOR

STRUCTURING SPONTANEOUS ANSWERS

In Part 1 of the Speaking test, the examiner will ask you questions about yourself and about general topics. The questions are simple and open: it's up to you to give complete and spontaneous answers. You can prepare for this by thinking about typical topics in advance, and by practising a simple structure for your answers:

1 respond   2 expand   3 example / focus

This is similar to the structure that the explorers use in the video. Imagine that the question the interviewer asked them was *What do you enjoy about your job?*

Alexandra **responds** with *So there's nothing I would rather be than a National Geographic explorer, and I'll tell you why.*

She **expands** her answer to talk about her family's influence.

She **focusses** her answer by talking about what excites her.

How does Sylvia Earle structure her answer?

7 How would you answer the question *What do you enjoy about your job/studies?* Make notes.
1 respond
2 expand
3 example / focus

8 Work in pairs. Ask and answer the question in exercise 7. Try not to look at your notes.

9 As well as work and studies, topics that may come up in the interview include leisure, daily life, travel, holidays, where you live and your future plans. Repeat exercise 7 using *respond, expand, example / focus* for questions 1–5.
1 What do you enjoy doing in your free time?
2 What's your favourite time of day?
3 Where would you choose to go on holiday?
4 What's your home town like?
5 What do you think you'll be doing this time next year?

10 Look at the Useful Expressions box. It includes some of the ways the people in the video talk about their experiences. Complete the sentences for you. Write as many as you can in five minutes.

11 Work in groups of three. Take turns to be the interlocutor. Ask and answer the questions from exercise 9.

12 Think about your performance in exercise 11. Were your answers complete and well structured? Did you sound spontaneous or rehearsed? Repeat <u>one</u> of the question and answer exchanges and try to improve on your first performance.

VIDEOSCRIPT 1 is on page 253.

2 A CHILD'S WORLD

GETTING STARTED

1 Work in pairs. Use the verbs in the box to talk about what you liked doing when you were young.

> bound   clamber   heave   hop   leap   march
> paddle   skip   slide   stride   swing   tiptoe
> wade   wander   wrestle

READING gapped text

2 Read the headline and predict the subject of the text that follows.

> **PIONEER NURSERY STAYS OUTDOORS – IN ALL WEATHERS.**
> **ENTHUSIASTIC PARENTS SEE KINDERGARTEN**
> **AS ANTIDOTE TO SEDENTARY LIFESTYLE.**

3 Work in pairs. Read the two paragraphs that follow. The middle paragraph is missing. What information would you expect it to contain?

> Freddie and Alastair clambered around their childminder's garden snugly dressed in their unofficial uniform: chest-high waterproof trousers, rainbow braces, thick jumpers and welly boots. Blond and ruddy, the pair, aged two and three, earnestly heaved stones about and wrestled with a wooden wheelbarrow before bounding off for their daily session on the open-air trampoline.

> Their childminder, Cathy Bache, is planning to open Britain's first outdoors nursery, a lottery-funded kindergarten where the children will be taught and entertained in a wood. All day, every day. Whatever the weather.

4 Look closely at the paragraphs before and after the gap. There are several factors that could link them to the missing paragraph. Find the following in the first paragraph:

1   the names of two boys
2   a noun that refers to them
3   another person

5 Find the following in the second paragraph:

1   the name of a person
2   a possessive pronoun referring to the boys
3   a plural noun referring to the boys
4   two synonymous words that refer to a place where the children are

6 Information File 1, page 241. Read the three paragraphs on page 241 and decide which would best fit between the two paragraphs in exercise 3.

7 Read the rest of the article. Six paragraphs have been removed and replaced with two headings. Choose the headings which you think best summarise the missing paragraph.

> Ms Bache, 46, has been given £10,000 by the lottery-based 'Awards for All' scheme to help create an open-air nursery for up to 24 children alongside Monimail Tower, a recently restored medieval tower that once formed part of a palace used by the ancient bishops of St Andrews.

1   a   Ms Bache wins the lottery
    b   Monimail Tower

When the Secret Garden nursery opens next autumn, the children will have none of the games and equipment seen in a normal suburban nursery: plastic see-saws, cushioned vinyl floors and sterilised building blocks. Their curriculum will be devoted to nature walks, rearing chickens, climbing trees, 'mud play' and vegetable gardening. Their playground will be the forest, and their shelter a wattle and daub 'cob' building with outdoor toilets. The children Ms Bache cares for are oblivious to the weather, she said, even sub-zero temperatures.

2 a The children and the weather
  b The school curriculum

'When it gets particularly cold we light a bonfire and play running around games. In February we were out all day in minus six and the children were perfectly happy. I thought: "If I can stay out in this, we can stay out in anything". It's us that imagine they're not going to like the weather. It's a cultural attitude, but if you're warm and dry, you don't notice.'

3 a Scottish winters
  b What it is hoped the school will do for the children

Ms Bache borrowed the idea for the Secret Garden, which will cost at least £100,000 to open, from Norway. 'It's embedded in their cultural life, being outdoors, in the same way it's embedded in ours to stay indoors,' she said. The Childcare Commission, Scotland's childcare regulator, 'think it's fantastic. They're 100% in support of what I'm doing.'

4 a How Ms Bache got started
  b Schools and attitudes in Norway

After six months keeping the children indoors, with a few hours' play in the garden, she realised the kids thrived outdoors. So, like Alastair and Freddie, they stayed there. 'In a normal nursery you might have to learn about shapes, but these children know the difference between an oak tree and a birch tree, which is a lot more complex than a square and a circle,' she said.

5 a A parent's view
  b The dangers of school illnesses

'The risks can be exaggerated,' added Alastair's mother. 'With the best will in the world, all children will pick up things even when I'm watching them,' she said. 'But I do think they're probably too protected in a lot of environments. No one wants them to come to any harm, but they've got to learn – in as safe an environment as is possible. The most important thing is that it is a real confidence builder. Strangely, it can be pouring with rain all day, but when they get home they don't even mention the weather.'

6 a The children's reactions
  b After-school activities

8 **Look again at the heading you chose for missing paragraph 1 in exercise 7. Find the paragraph from A–G below that matches it. Underline the key words in the paragraph.**

9 **Reading and Use of English, Part 7**

Read the paragraphs A–G below and choose the one which fits each gap (1–6). There is one extra paragraph which you do not need to use.

A A primary school and drama teacher for 20 years, Ms Bache left teaching to run a small childminding business from her home on the edge of Letham, about 15 miles west of St Andrews.

B Katie Connolly, a graphic designer, said her sons, Freddie and Magnus, four, preferred it to their other nursery. 'There isn't much outdoor space there and they get frustrated. They talk about the things they do here a lot more, and they bring home bits of fungus or a rosehip necklace and tell me all about it.'

C When they graduate to primary school, alumni of the Secret Garden can expect to be expert in poisonous fungi and able to spot dangerous yew berries or foxgloves, the flowers that contain the toxin digitalis, at a hundred paces. 'They know what poisonous means, and they really do avoid it. They learn so quickly.'

D 'We've recently had two full days with seven hours of solid rain, and the kids don't bat an eyelid. As soon as it rains heavily here, there's a stream comes down the wee road outside – they built dams on it. They loved it.'

E Ms Bache looks after 17 children during the week. Their parents are enthusiastic about her approach. Kirsty Licence, 40, a doctor and Alastair's mother, believes the nursery will be an antidote to Britain's increasingly sedentary, over-protective culture. 'Childhood obesity is a big problem, and one of the things is that children spend too long inside.'

F Their sedentary lifestyle clearly was not helping with their academic progress. As the pounds went on, the marks began to decline and the children showed no enthusiasm about becoming involved in physical activities, preferring to stay in and battle it out with the TV games from the couch.

G Monimail, which sits in a sheltered dip in the hills just south of the Firth of Tay, was bought in ruins in 1985 by a group of Edinburgh psychotherapists as a therapeutic retreat. Now owned by a trust, it is home to environmentalists running a 'sustainable living' commune. Another donor, who has asked to remain anonymous, has pledged £20,000, the first big sum raised by the Secret Garden's well-connected local parents and supporters.

10 **Discuss. What are your views about this kind of kindergarten? Do you think it would be successful in your country?**

LANGUAGE DEVELOPMENT parts of the body idioms

1 **Discuss.** *The kids don't bat an eyelid* (missing paragraph D, page 21). What does this phrase mean?

2 **Use a dictionary to find the meaning of the body idioms in these sentences.**

   1 Jemma's just had a brainwave! Listen to her great idea.

   2 I saw Andrea in town. She really gave me the cold shoulder even though I said I was sorry!

   3 You look a bit down in the mouth. Have you had a bad day?

3 **Complete the sentences with idioms from the box.**

all fingers and thumbs	didn't bat an eyelid
pain in the neck	see eye to eye
tongue in cheek	wet behind the ears

   1 Bill doesn't like his new boss. They never
     _____ .

   2 My chemistry practical exam was a disaster! I was
     _____ and spilt the liquid all over the floor!

   3 Nick's little brother is a real _____ !
     He wouldn't let us listen to music, and kept interrupting us!

   4 I think the teacher's remark about punishing the whole class was _____ ! She didn't mean it, did she?

   5 When I told William I was going to marry his sister, he _____ .

   6 James will make a great businessman one day but at the moment he's completely
     _____ .

PHRASAL VERB *pick up*

4 *All children will pick up things …* **Which of the definitions below matches the meaning of *pick up* in this sentence?**

   1 to get someone and go somewhere in your car
   2 to be arrested
   3 to learn a skill without much effort
   4 to catch an illness
   5 to receive or detect a signal
   6 to refer to a subject already mentioned
   7 to increase or improve
   8 to get more interesting
   9 to lift someone or something up from a surface

5 **Match the definitions in exercise 4 with these example sentences.**

   a They picked him up trying to leave the country.
   b You probably picked it up at school – there's something going round at the moment.
   c To begin with it was so boring I nearly fell asleep, but fortunately the second half picked up a bit.
   d I'll pick you up at seven.
   e Trade picked up slowly over the next six months.
   f Can I pick up on the point you raised earlier …
   g Dogs can pick up sounds well beyond the range of our own hearing.
   h Even though Julia had only heard the song once, she managed to pick it up right away.
   i She picked up the phone and called him.

KEY WORD *run*

6 *Ms Bache left teaching to run a small childminding business.* **Which six things in the box are NOT used in an expression with *run*? Use a dictionary if necessary.**

a bus   a business   a conversation   a message
a party   a race   a risk   a road
a story in a newspaper   a temperature   an errand
an idea   counter to someone   for cover somewhere
for office   politics   the bath   water

7 **Match each definition (a–e) with an expression with *run* from exercise 6.**

   a to do a task for someone
   b to go against or in opposition to something or someone
   c to publish an article
   d to become a political candidate
   e to do something that is dangerous or uncertain

GRAMMAR passive forms

8 **Underline the passive structures in each sentence.**

> ... Cathy Bache is planning to open Britain's first outdoors nursery, a lottery-funded kindergarten where the children will be taught and entertained in a wood.

> Their curriculum will be devoted to nature walks, rearing chickens, climbing trees, 'mud play' and vegetable gardening.

9 *The risks can be exaggerated.* **Which of these sentences has the same meaning?**

1 People are able to exaggerate the risks.
2 It is possible the risks have been exaggerated.
3 The risks are sometimes exaggerated.

10 **Read sentences 1–4. Match them with the active sentences (a–d).**

1 The outdoor curriculum will be regarded with suspicion.
2 The outdoor curriculum may / might be regarded with suspicion.
3 The outdoor curriculum can be regarded with suspicion.
4 The outdoor curriculum should be regarded with suspicion.

a People sometimes express their doubts about the outdoor curriculum.
b It is possible that people will express their doubts about the outdoor curriculum.
c It is a good idea to doubt the value of the outdoor curriculum.
d People will certainly express their doubts about the outdoor curriculum.

VERBS WITH PASSIVE FORMS

Verbs such as *consider, believe, think, assume, suppose, report,* etc. have two passive constructions. Consider:
People think he is the troublemaker.
Construction 1: He is thought to be the troublemaker.
Construction 2: It is thought that he is the troublemaker.

---

11 **Rewrite the following sentences using both forms of the passive.**

1 There have been reports of children stealing from the school cafeteria.
2 They believe that a dolphin rescued the baby.

12 **Complete the sentences using the correct passive form.**

1 People consider the five-year-old boy to be too young to have a mobile phone.
   The five-year-old boy _____ to have a mobile phone.
2 There have been rumours that the children's playground is going to become a car park.
   It _____ to become a car park.
3 The public think that the laws against underage drinking are too strict.
   The laws _____ too strict.
4 They suspect that a nine-year-old boy broke into his aunt's home and stole money.
   A nine-year-old boy _____ his aunt's home and stealing money.
5 The government has estimated a 10% increase in the number of children under 14 who smoke.
   The number of children under 14 who smoke _____ by 10%.
6 People say that the missing boy was a loner and didn't have many friends.
   It _____ many friends.
7 Police believe she went missing somewhere between the bus stop and Walvern Road.
   It _____ and Walvern Road.

passive form with *have* and *get*

13 **Match the sentences (1–2) with the explanations (a–b).**

1 We had our house painted last month.
2 We had the roof of our house torn off in the storm.

a Replacement of a passive verb when talking about an accident or misfortune.
b Causative form, when someone else does something for the speaker.

14 **Some verbs cannot be changed into the passive, or they require other changes to be made. Make these sentences passive. What needs to change or be added?**

1 My mum lets me have friends to stay at the weekend.
2 My mum made me do my homework before I could go out.

▶ GRAMMAR REFERENCE (SECTION 2) **PAGE 209**

LISTENING sentence completion

Listening, Part 2 Predicting information

In Listening, Part 2, you will need to write down words or short phrases that best complete a number of sentences. By studying the sentences before you listen, you can often identify important information that will help you complete the exercise.

Read the sentence. How many words can you think of to complete it?

By keeping his eye on the _____ , Jack is able to choose the right equipment for the task.

Without hearing the audioscript, it will not normally be possible to guess the answer as several words may fit, but you can limit the options by following the points below:

- Read the other sentences in this part of the paper to help you focus on the theme of the extract.
- Try to visualise the speaker and the situation and imagine what information they might be giving.
- Decide what part of speech (noun, verb, adjective, etc.) and quantity (singular, plural) is required in the gap. Is the word positive or negative in meaning?

1 Read the sentences. How many words or short phrases can you think of to complete them?

1 Some people think my methods are not _____ , but I don't let that put me off.
2 Linda is staying with Simon _____ , until her roof gets fixed.
3 Scientists have been analysing the effects of _____ on the local area.

2 ◉ 6 Listening, Part 2

You will hear an anthropologist talking about the way language developed in children. For questions 1–8, complete the sentences with a word or short phrase.

Most meat-eating animals find that it is more effective to hunt in (1) _____ .

The first languages may not have had much (2) _____ because they lacked refinement.

Deaf children may have problems learning to speak if they have never been (3) _____ language.

Children under (4) _____ don't need to make much effort to learn a language.

Most young mammals can (5) _____ their basic needs to their mother.

Children in different (6) _____ are likely to produce different kinds of babble.

The child's (7) _____ voluntary syllable may be a result of imitating the sounds around him.

The (8) _____ between mother and child may have contributed to the development of language.

SPEAKING using visual prompts

3 Discuss. Look at the first set of pictures on page 231.

1 Do you think the activities shown in the photographs are popular with young children?
2 Do you think young children spend too much time playing computer games?

EXPRESSING OPINIONS

In the Speaking test, you'll be given the chance to express your opinions. You'll need to show that you can organise your thoughts and ideas coherently. There is no right or wrong answer to the questions you will be asked, so just concentrate on getting your views across. You will need to talk on your own for about a minute in Part 2.

4 Work in groups of three: an interlocutor, Student 1 and Student 2.

Interlocutor: Read this task. Student 1, it's your turn first. Look at the first set of photographs on page 231. They show children doing different activities. I'd like you to compare two of the pictures, and say whether you think these activities are suitable for young children, and how they might be feeling about doing them.
(Allow approximately one minute.)

Interlocutor: Thank you. Student 2, at what age do you think children should be allowed to do these activities and why?
(Allow approximately 30 seconds.)

Interlocutor: Thank you. Look at the second set of photographs on page 231. Student 2, here are your pictures. They show young people doing different activities. I'd like you to compare two of the pictures, and say how the people might be feeling.
(Allow approximately one minute.)

Interlocutor: Student 1, when do you think a young person is mature enough to do these activities and why?
(Allow approximately 30 seconds.)

Change roles so that the interlocutor can talk about the pictures.

USE OF ENGLISH multiple-choice cloze

EXAM SPOTLIGHT

Reading and Use of English, Part 1
Recognising option types

In Reading and Use of English, Part 1, you may be presented with any of the following multiple-choice options.

Words that appear similar in meaning, but may be used in quite different contexts.

1 What do the these words mean?
  a unsuspecting   c unaware
  b unconscious   d unwitting
2 Which of the words above cannot be used in the following sentence?
  He was totally _____ of the fact that I had lied to him.
3 Which of the above options can be used in the following sentence?
  He was an _____ accomplice to the crime.

Words that appear to be similar but whose meanings are quite different.

1 Which of the words below can be used in the following sentence?
  His _____ of the events that occurred that night are still a little hazy.
  a conception   c perception
  b deception   d recollection
2 What do the other words mean? Write example sentences.

Words that are all similar in meaning but are used in different contexts.

Use these words to complete the sentences that follow:
  a means   c tool
  b method   d aid
1 Downloadable apps can be a useful _____ to language learning.
2 John has his own _____ for making soup.
3 Dancing can be an important _____ of emotional expression.
4 A dog's tail is an important _____ for communication.

Words that have similar meanings but may follow a different grammatical context.

1 Which three words would fit into the sentence below?
  a findings   c reports
  b studies   d research
  _____ *have shown that populations tend to increase during long spells of mild weather.*
2 Why could the other word not be used?

5 Reading and Use of English, Part 1

For questions 1–8, read the text below and decide which answer (A, B, C or D) best fits each gap.

Children and colour

Parents tend to assume that the choices they make for their offspring are the right ones. Take the (1) ____ of colour, for example. Parents are likely to choose the colours for young Jimmy or Jenny's bedroom or clothes, thereby conditioning their child's (2) ____ of colour from a very early age. (3) ____ choosing a pair of pink trousers for their six-year-old son, for example, (4) ____ counter to most parents' idea of how to dress a boy.

However, psychologists believe that allowing children to choose their own colours increases their self-confidence and their ability to express themselves. They use colour as a (5) ____ of helping children to identify their feelings and discuss them. For instance, (6) ____ have shown that after listening to a sad story, children tend to draw in dark brown, black or grey, whereas one with a happy ending will (7) ____ a response in yellow or orange. (8) ____ children free rein to choose colours for themselves may help parents to understand them better.

1 A question   C theme
   B type   D view
2 A conception   C consideration
   B observation   D perception
3 A Intentionally   C Enthusiastically
   B Willingly   D Energetically
4 A plays   C goes
   B runs   D comes
5 A means   C process
   B tool   D device
6 A conclusions   C studies
   B recommendations   D statements
7 A lead   C reveal
   B evoke   D envisage
8 A Giving   C Displaying
   B Letting   D Passing

WRITING a review

Writing, Part 2

1 **Read the exam question. Underline the two things you need to include in your answer.**

> Your local newspaper has invited its readers to send in a review of one of the museums in your area. You decide to write about a museum you recently visited, describing what there is to see and do there and saying whether or not you recommend it to other people and why.
>
> Write your **review** (220–260 words).

2 **You are a teacher. One of your students submitted the following answer to the question. Read it and report to the rest of the class, commenting on its organisation and use of language. Does it answer the question fully?**

My family and I recently visited a toy museum. They have dedicated it to a local family who were among the earliest toy makers in my country, and they have built the museum on the site of the family's factory. They made toys mainly out of wood or metal, but the [museum shows the developments in toy making, from then until now.]

The Bryant Toy Museum is a new, interactive playground for children. When we arrived, they gave us a notebook called 'My Toy Scrapbook'. The cover shows a photograph of the original factory. As we [walked around] the museum, people encouraged us to fill it with pictures, stamps and notes, if we wanted. They designed each room to look like scenes from particular periods in history.

For example, they have created one room to look like a scene from a Charles Dickens novel, another from around the time of the Second World War, and then suddenly, you're in a room filled with all kinds of electronic games. [My brother and I liked this.] In every room, they encourage children to play with some of the toys, and when they come to the final room in the museum, some people show the children how to [make] their own toys, if they want.

SENTENCE DEVELOPMENT

In the Writing paper you should aim to vary your sentence structures. Using the passive voice enables you to:

- make your style more formal
- emphasise an action rather than the agent
- talk about an action when you do not know or care who did it

3 **Look at the museum review again, and replace the underlined structures with a suitable passive structure. You may need to make some other changes to the sentences.**

4 **The conclusion is an important part of any piece of writing. Choose the most suitable concluding paragraph for the student's museum review.**

1

> The Bryant Toy Museum is believed to be informative and inspiring. It certainly was for me.

2

> *At the end of the tour, we showed everyone the toys we had designed, and people commented on them. It was great!*

3

> *I came away from the museum inspired by the things I had seen and learnt. The Bryant Toy Museum is well worth a visit, and I would recommend it to anyone who enjoys playing, irrespective of age.*

5 Make the student's review on page 26 more descriptive, by varying the language presented in brackets [ ].

Use some of the words and expressions in the In Other Words box to help you.

5 Make the student's review on page 26 more descriptive

IN OTHER WORDS

exhibits
innovative
revolutionary
let their imaginations run wild
design / create / build / construct
encourage / stimulate / inspire / fire someone's imagination
stroll around / through; make one's way around; wander
amusing / fascinating / delightful / imaginative
cleverly designed / attractive / well designed
inspiration / creativity

6 Imagine you are on a day out with your family. Comment on what you see. Add to the list of words to describe your reaction to things.

dull	mundane	_____
fascinating	nondescript	_____
imaginative	old-fashioned	_____
innovative	poorly designed	_____
inspirational	well designed	_____

7 Read the exam question and write your review. Use between 220–260 words.

The local tourist board website has invited users to send in a review of a place that represents a day out for all the family. You decide to write about a place that is special to you. Describe the place, say what there is to see and do there, and state why you would recommend it.

GETTING STARTED

1 ⊙ 7 **Listen to three people describing their feelings about doing sports. Match what each speaker says with one of the activities in the box.**

> bodyboarding cycling hang-gliding
> ice skating kite landboarding mountaineering
> paragliding rowing running skiing
> snorkelling swimming triathlon
> white-water rafting yacht racing

2 **Now listen again and circle any of the words in the box that you hear.**

> adrenalin rush amazing awesome
> determined exhausted exhausting exhilarating
> fantastic frightening incredible loneliness
> petrified reassuring relaxed relaxing
> terrifying tiredness wild

3 **Discuss. Talk about an experience you have had that was exhilarating or frightening. Use some of the words from exercise 2.**

4 **Information File 2, page 241. How game are you? Complete the questionnaire to find out how daring you are!**

READING multiple choice

UNDERSTANDING THE WRITER'S / NARRATOR'S ATTITUDE

Some questions require an understanding of the writer's (or their narrator's) attitude to the subject they're discussing. By this, we mean their opinion or feeling about it.

5 **Read *A Close Encounter*. How does the narrator feel about what he has to do?**

a frightened
b determined
c reluctant
d complacent

DIFFICULT WORDS IN A READING TEXT

Sometimes when we read we encounter words which are technical or very specific to the topic. It doesn't matter if we don't understand every word as we can usually get a sense of meaning from the context.
It isn't usually necessary to understand all the words in a text.

6 Reading and Use of English, Part 5

You are going to read an extract from an autobiographical account. For questions 1–6, choose the answer (A, B, C or D) which you think fits best according to the text.

1 In what way did the writer misinterpret the distress call at first?
   A He thought that it came from an Australian yacht.
   B He believed the yacht in question was close by.
   C He couldn't believe that anyone was in trouble.
   D He didn't think it came from anyone he knew.

2 When he refers to 'one of us', we can infer that the writer is talking about
   A a member of his team.
   B another Australian.
   C a fellow competitor.
   D a fellow naval officer.

3 According to the writer, he decided to view the rescue mission as 'a fight',
   A so as to dispel his fear and increase his determination to succeed.
   B because he was angry about the situation in which he found himself.
   C because he wanted to think of the wind and waves as enemies.
   D in order to shake off his feelings of anger and fatigue.

4 As he turned the Aqua Quorum around, the writer was amazed by
   A the boat's resistance.
   B the force of the wind.
   C the height of the waves.
   D his feelings of anger.

5 Which of the following does the writer imply helped him face the task ahead?
   A his faith in the boat
   B his desire to win
   C his previous military training
   D his knowledge of the sea

6 Which word best describes the writer's attitude towards his rescue mission?
   A horrified   C resigned
   B resolute   D concerned

A CLOSE ENCOUNTER

There was a tremendous crash and Aqua Quorum was knocked down again. I was thrown across the cabin as the boat groaned under the strain. Through the din I heard the satcom system bleeping away. I couldn't believe it was still able to work on what had practically become a yellow submarine. I struggled across to the chart table and called up the message. Mayday! Mayday! Mayday! It was a distress call being passed on by Marine Rescue and Control Centre (MRCC) Australia. The vessel in trouble was the yacht Algimouss. I wondered who they were and hoped I wouldn't be joining them. I assumed that she was somewhere near the Australian coast. I extricated a chart from the mess, plotted their position and did a double take. They were about 160 miles away. Who the hell would be daft enough to be down here? It never occurred to me that it might be one of us. The name Algimouss meant nothing to me as race communications had used the name of the skipper rather than the name of the boat.

The satcom bleeped again. This time the message was from Philippe Jeantot. The mayday was from one of us. Algimouss was Raphael Dinelli's boat and he was in trouble. Philippe asked if I could help. I took another look at the chart and realised that things were pretty bad: not only was Raphael 160 miles away from me but he was also to windward in atrocious conditions. But I had to go, I knew that. It was that simple; the decision had been made for me a long time ago by a tradition of the sea. When someone is in trouble, you help. However, I needed a minute to grasp the enormity of it. I thought about what I was about to put on the line: my family, my boat, my life. I knew I had to stand by my morals and principles. Not turning back, whatever the stakes, would have been a disservice to myself, my family and the spirit of the sea. I fired off a quick fax to Philippe and expressed my doubts as to our ability to make our way back to Raphael – but I was going anyway.

I ventured on deck and the fight began. I had to think of it as a fight. I shouted at the wind and the waves, and the anger helped to strengthen my resolve. We had to jibe. Oddly it was easy and went like clockwork. I brought Aqua Quorum up to face the wind, feeling the full force of the hurricane, as the wind across the deck immediately increased by the 25 knot speed that I had been travelling downwind. The gust put the guard-rail under and the lower spreaders touched the water. I couldn't believe the energy that was whistling past. I winched in the storm jib hard, put the helm down again and waited to see what would happen. Aqua Quorum was game, it was as if she knew what was at stake. The mast slowly came upright and she began to move to windward. I couldn't believe that she was making about eight knots – sometimes more – as she climbed steeply to the wild, topping crests at the apex of each huge wave, before accelerating down the 50 foot slope on the other side and into the next trough. It wasn't quite the course I needed – 80 degrees to the wind was the best we could do – but it was a start and the wind would ease soon. It had to.

Meanwhile it screamed deafeningly through the rigging, sounding like a jet taking off, as Aqua Quorum gamely struggled away. It was impossible to breathe if I faced windward – the breath was sucked from my lungs – and I couldn't open my eyes.

Now that we were committed, I knew that we would do it somehow. The things I learnt with the Royal Marines took over: be professional at all times, never give up and make intelligent use of everything to hand. I had asked a lot of my boats in the past, but never this much. I decided to take no prisoners. Aqua Quorum would do it or she would break up in the attempt; a man was out there and there could be no half measures. Night closed and we struggled on. The huge breaking seas and the waves were horrifying.

LANGUAGE DEVELOPMENT phrases with *up* and *down*

1 *What if I wasn't up to it?* Explain what this question means.

2 **Work in pairs. Discuss the meanings of these sentences, and rephrase them without using *up* or *down*.**
 1 What are you up to nowadays?
 2 We must get down to some work.
 3 It's up to you what you do.
 4 The cancellation is down to Brian.
 5 I'm down to my last few pennies.
 6 The children get up to all sorts at their grandmother's house!
 7 What's up?
 8 I'm feeling down at the moment.
 9 Great! Finished that thank you letter! Five down, four to go!
 10 That film wasn't up to much, was it?

phrasal verbs with *take*

3 *The things I learnt with the Royal Marines took over.* **What does the writer mean here?**

4 **Complete the phrasal verbs in these sentences with a particle from the box.**

| after apart back down for on out |
| over to up |

 1 You say you're working in the shop, and now at the restaurant as well? You've taken _____ too much.
 2 Have you heard? George Brown has taken _____ from Bill Coles as managing director!
 3 You're absolutely right. I shouldn't have said that. I take _____ everything I said against him.
 4 I've taken _____ a year's subscription to the *National Geographic* magazine.
 5 Sam took the DVD player _____ to see what was wrong with it, and found a piece of cheese stuck inside it!
 6 Your mum and mine seem to have taken _____ each other. They haven't stopped talking all afternoon!
 7 The lecture was really useful, and Helena took _____ a lot of notes.
 8 Oh! I'm terribly sorry, Madam! I took you _____ a friend of mine!
 9 Nick really takes _____ his father. He's so like him!
 10 I've just taken _____ snowboarding. It's great fun!

phrases with *take*

5 **Work in pairs. In the reading text on page 29, the writer *did a double take*, and decided to *take no prisoners*. Choose the best explanation for these phrases.**
 1 *do a double take* means
  a look at something again in surprise
  b do something again because you doubt it
 2 *take no prisoners* means
  a show no fear in the face of danger
  b fight to succeed, or die trying

KEY WORD *game*

6 **Match the phrases (1–10) with their meanings (a–j).**
 1 Are you game?
 2 fun and games
 3 the name of the game
 4 give the game away
 5 beat somebody at their own game
 6 play games with somebody
 7 What's (your) game?
 8 the game's up
 9 game plan
 10 big game

 a someone's intended actions in order to achieve something
 b used when asking somebody what their true intentions are
 c used when asking somebody if they are willing to do something dangerous, new or difficult
 d used to tell someone that their secret plan or activity has been discovered
 e used to describe large wild animals that are hunted
 f spoil a surprise or secret by letting someone know about it
 g win against somebody by using the same methods as they do
 h used in a humorous way to describe a situation that you don't enjoy dealing with
 i behave in a dishonest or unfair way towards somebody to get what you want
 j the most important thing in an activity or situation

7 **Use phrases from exercise 6 to complete sentences a–e.**
 a Right, team! Let's get to work, and remember, _____ is 'efficiency'!
 b We were planning a surprise party for Mum, but Jonas _____ by asking her if his best friend could come!
 c Sam, we're going to St. Moritz to do some extreme snowboarding. _____ ?
 d OK, Kathy. _____ . I know it's you making those noises, so you can stop now!
 e Don't _____ me! I know you're not really my friend, so go away!

GRAMMAR modal auxiliaries (1)

8 Work in pairs. What can you see in the photo above? Use the following structures to make suggestions:
It could be a … / It might be … / It must be … / It can't be …

SPECULATION AND SUGGESTION

We use *may*, *could* and *might* to talk about possibility, speculate, or make suggestions.
We use *must* when we are fairly certain that something is true. We use *can't* when we are fairly certain that something is not true.
We use *could have*, *might have*, *must have* and *can't have* to speculate about the past.

DEDUCTION

We use *must* to talk about deduction, when we are certain that something is true.
We use *can't* and *couldn't* to talk about negative deduction when we are certain that something is not true.

ASSUMPTION

We use *will* or *would* to make an assumption when we think something is true without having evidence.

▶ GRAMMAR REFERENCE (SECTION 3) **PAGE 210**

9 Do these statements show speculation, suggestion, assumption or deduction?
1 You could try phoning her to apologise.
2 You may find it works better if you turn up the volume.
3 I was wearing my glasses during the history lesson, so I must have left them in the classroom.
4 The phone's ringing, Mum! That will be Sarah. She said she'd call today.
5 He never thought she might leave him.
6 Mr Newton said he'd be wearing a black raincoat and hat, so that must be him over there!
7 It can't be Sally's husband! He's on a business trip in Spain.
8 You might go to the library tomorrow if you want a quiet place to work.

10 🔘 8 Listen to a conversation between a man and his wife and answer the questions.
1 What does the man say is a possible reason for Jane's lateness?
2 What assumptions does the woman make?
3 What deduction does she make?

11 We use *may / might … but* to refute someone else's comment, or qualify someone's criticism of us. Complete the comments. Do they refute or qualify?
1 'You don't know much about the Middle Ages!'
   'I might have studied history, but _____ .'
2 'You're a real chatterbox!'
   'I _____ , but at least I've got something to say.'

12 Reading and Use of English, Part 4

For questions 1–6, complete the second sentence so that it has a similar meaning to the first sentence, using the word given. Do not change the word given. You must use between three and six words, including the word given.

1 James hasn't called. It's possible he's forgotten my birthday.
   HAVE
   James _____ , because he hasn't called.
2 I definitely didn't write that note, Lyn! That's not my handwriting!
   WRITTEN
   I _____ , Lyn, because that's not my handwriting!
3 Paul said he would call April to tell her he's not going to the party, and I'm sure he has.
   WILL
   Paul _____ April he's not going to the party, because he said he would.
4 'Has Anthea gone to Dubai yet?' 'I don't think so, because she hasn't called me to say goodbye.'
   WOULD
   'Has Anthea gone to Dubai yet?' 'I don't think so. She _____ goodbye.'
5 It's true that I lost the match, but I played well.
   NOT
   I _____ the match, but I played well.
6 Although he's good with animals, he's not very comfortable with people.
   MAY
   He _____ animals, but he's unable to relax around people.

LISTENING multiple choice

EXAM SPOTLIGHT

Listening, Parts 3 and 4
Understanding the speaker's attitude

In Parts 3 and 4 of the Listening paper it's often necessary to understand the speaker's attitude towards the subject they are talking about. This can be done by listening to the tone of their voices, and the language they use.

1 **Work in pairs. Practise saying the following phrase using the various tones of voice below.**
How did you manage to do that?

amazed   angry   sarcastic   excited

2 🔘 9 **Listen to four people. Choose the attitude A–E which best matches each speaker's feelings towards their subject. There is one extra option you do not need to use.**

A   critical
B   dismissive   Speaker 1 ☐
C   frustrated   Speaker 2 ☐
D   noncommittal   Speaker 3 ☐
E   philosophical   Speaker 4 ☐

3 🔘 10   **Listening, Part 3**

You will hear part of a radio interview with the mountaineer and explorer Tom Masefield. For questions 1–6, choose the answer (A, B, C or D) which fits best according to what you hear.

1   For most of the year, Tom works
    A   at a school.
    B   for the local authority.
    C   at a sports centre.
    D   privately.

2   While kayaking, Tom and his group were surprised by the sight of
    A   an unusual animal.
    B   a school of dolphins.
    C   a sunken ship.
    D   the local people.

3   According to Tom, mountaineers
    A   often misunderstand each other's intentions.
    B   experience friction under extreme conditions.
    C   form close bonds with the surrounding environment.
    D   appreciate the importance of trust in the team.

4   Regarding the problem with frostbite on Everest, Tom is
    A   philosophical.
    B   frustrated.
    C   indifferent.
    D   dismissive.

5   The team's first attempt to climb Carstensz Pyramid failed due to
    A   mechanical problems with their helicopter.
    B   disagreements with their sponsors.
    C   disturbances caused by local dissidents.
    D   a lack of sufficient time and funding.

6   Tom's conquest of Carstensz Pyramid was special because it was
    A   the first time anyone had done this.
    B   the second time he had climbed it.
    C   a dream he had had since childhood.
    D   his second historic achievement for his country.

4 **Discuss. Do you do any kinds of adventure sports? Why or why not?**

SPEAKING interacting

Speaking, Part 3 Collaborative task

In Part 3 of the Speaking paper, you'll be given instructions and some written prompts which form the basis for a collaborative task that you will carry out with your partner. The written prompts consist of a question and ideas for answers to the question. You will be expected to discuss each idea, sustaining interaction with your partner, expressing and justifying opinions, agreeing / disagreeing, suggesting, evaluating and speculating, and working towards a negotiated decision.

5 Work in pairs. Turn to page 232 and answer the question.

USE OF ENGLISH open cloze

Reading and Use of English, Part 2
Sentence structure

In this part of the Reading and Use of English paper you are asked to fill in missing words. The task is mainly grammatical, so it's important to think carefully about sentence structure. Always read the passage through first, before filling in any gaps, because some of the missing words may be:

- time reference words
- introducing a secondary or relative clause
- text reference words
- prepositions and particles

What is the missing word in the following sentence?

_____ 1856, there has been an Oxford and Cambridge boat race almost every year.

6 **TIME REFERENCE WORDS Complete the sentences with one suitable word. Explain your choice.**

1 _____ she left university, Marcia got a job in advertising.
2 _____ going to university, Kevin had worked as a waiter in Rome for a year.

SECONDARY OR RELATIVE CLAUSES What is the missing word in these sentences?

3 Diana did not do well in the maths test, _____ upset her.
4 The party was a great success, with lots of people _____ to music from the 80's until three in the morning.

TEXT REFERENCES Remember to think of the meaning of the whole text. One word may refer back to a previous sentence. What is the missing word in these sentences?

5 Annette is terrified of dogs. Her mother says _____ is probably because she was bitten by one at the age of five.
6 Peter was terrified of heights. _____ , he climbed the tree.

PREPOSITIONS AND PARTICLES Complete the sentences with a suitable preposition.

7 Roberto has given up skiing to concentrate _____ his studies.
8 Scientists have been conducting research _____ the potential health benefits of drinking tea.

7 **Reading and Use of English, Part 2**

For questions 1–8, read the text below and think of the word which best fits each gap. Use only one word in each gap.

Beyond the pain barrier

Endurance sports are gaining in popularity. Since making (1) _____ debut at the 2000 Olympic Games, the triathlon has become (2) _____ of the world's fastest developing 'multi-sport' endurance challenges, with thousands of races (3) _____ held every year. Usually, races consist of a swimming section, followed by a cycling stretch, culminating (4) _____ a run. The individual legs of each course depend on the level of the event. For instance, the Olympic event includes a 1.5 km swim, a bike ride of 40 km, with a 10 km run to finish. This is known (5) _____ the 'standard course'. For those masochists who really want to push (6) _____ beyond the pain barrier, there are the Ironman long-distance triathlons, requiring competitors to swim 3.8 km, cycle a gruelling 180 km and then run 42 km. However, (7) _____ athletes have the stamina to endure such distances. Most find the Olympic course more accessible. (8) _____ the reasons for its popularity might be, the triathlon now constitutes a major multi-sport event in many parts of the world.

WRITING a formal letter

1 **Discuss. Should schools be allowed to take students on activity holidays, or holidays abroad, or should they be restricted to day trips to museums and galleries? Explain your reasons.**

2 **Read the exam question from Part 2 of the Writing paper. Is it asking you to write a formal or informal letter?**

> You are a teacher. After a school skiing trip in which two teenagers were badly injured, an article appeared in your local newspaper criticising all school trips of this nature. You have decided to write a letter to the newspaper, expressing your views. Read the extract from the article below. Then write a letter to the newspaper.
>
> > This skiing accident highlights the problem of supervision on such school trips. Were those pupils properly catered for? Is it realistic to expect a group of 50 students to be safe in the care of a handful of teachers? Should school trips perhaps be restricted to educational visits to museums and places of interest?

EXAM SPOTLIGHT

Writing, Part 2 Writing a formal letter

In Part 2 of the Writing paper you may be required to write a letter. It is important to read the instructions and the input material carefully and decide:

• who you are writing to
• why you are writing – to complain, request information, etc.
• what information you need to include
• what outcome you expect from your letter

3 **Work in pairs. Read the question in exercise 2 again and make notes to cover the three questions in the letter.**

4 **Read the letter written in response. Has the writer considered the points in the Spotlight? Is the letter well organised? Is the language appropriate for the intended reader?**

> Dear Newspaper,
> I am a teacher. I read your article about the recent skiing accident, and I want to give my view of what happened.
> First, those students were properly catered for, but disobeyed strict instructions to stay with the rest of the group. Something like this had never happened before! There were five teachers in charge – one for every ten students – so, I suppose there could have been more, but the teachers were with them the whole time. After all, do parents watch their teenage children 24 hours a day?
> In my opinion, school trips should not be restricted to educational visits to museums and places of interest, as your article suggests, because this is often boring. Not everyone likes history! Skiing holidays give students and teachers the chance to relax together, and improve relations between them.
> So, I think you're wrong to suggest that such trips should be banned and I don't think this skiing accident highlights the problem of supervision on school trips. Please print my letter to show readers another view of the situation.
> Yours,

5 The writer fails to use the correct register consistently in their answer, and several phrases are rather informal. Decide which phrases are inappropriate, and use suitable phrases from the In Other Words box to improve the register of the letter.

IN OTHER WORDS

FORMAL LETTERS

Dear Sir / Madam, …
To whom it may concern, …
I would like to present an account of the situation from my own point of view.
I would like to present my own account of the occurrence.
This event was unprecedented, and occurred as a result of …
This occurrence was the first of its kind …
Unfortunately, these activities do not always interest students …
Therefore, I feel it would be a mistake to suggest …
In my view, this incident is not typical of most school trips.
I would be grateful if my letter could be published in the next issue …

USING YOUR OWN WORDS

The writer of the letter above also 'lifts' many phrases directly from the question, and doesn't vary her language. She will lose marks for this.

6 Rewrite the sentences in your own words.
1 I am a teacher.
2 First, those students were properly catered for …
3 In my opinion, school trips should not be restricted to visits to museums and places of interest …
4 I don't think this skiing accident highlights the problem of supervision on school trips.

7 Discuss. The letter of response in exercise 4 is too short. What is missing?

8 Writing, Part 2

You are a PE teacher. Recently, one of your students broke her leg during a lesson. Read the extract from a letter you received from the girl's parents below, and write a reply, explaining why the accident happened.

We are very dissatisfied with the way the school's sports training programme is run. The equipment is not well maintained, and it is the teacher's responsibility to ensure that the safety mat is in place before each pupil attempts to use it, which did not happen on the day in question. We feel that there was insufficient supervision of the students during the gymnastics session, resulting in our daughter being injured, …

Write your letter in 220–260 words in an appropriate style.

VIDEO frozen search and rescue

1 Work in pairs. Look at the photo and discuss the questions.

1 What sport do you think this is?
2 How would you describe the place and the weather conditions?
3 What kind of thing could go wrong in this situation?

2 Work in pairs. Decide how dangerous these winter sports are on a scale of 1 to 10, where 1 = not dangerous.

- cross-country skiing
- dogsled racing
- ice climbing
- kite skiing
- mountaineering
- skiing
- snowboarding
- snowmobiling

3 You are going to watch a video about a search and rescue mission in Alaska. Read three alerts that the state troopers received from the rescue base. Then watch the first part of the video (up to 2.20) without sound and choose the correct alert.

1
'A group of climbers has been injured following an avalanche this morning. The helicopter rescue is on-going and only two climbers still need to be taken out of the area.'

2
'A man is in difficulty after breaking his leg while dogsled racing. Whiteout weather conditions are making flying extremely hazardous. Time is of the essence.'

3
'Two men have been lost since yesterday when they set off to go snowmobiling. We located one man this morning but the second is still missing in an area of forest and mountain ridges.'

4 Watch the rest of the video with sound. How does the mission end?

5 Watch the whole video with sound. Decide whether the statements are true (T) or false (F).

1 The man has been lost overnight. T / F
2 The helicopter crew have no information about the man's location. T / F
3 There have been no snowstorms in the last few days. T / F
4 It should be easy to spot the man. T / F
5 The helicopter crew see a set of tracks leading to a mountain ridge. T / F
6 They locate an abandoned snow machine. T / F
7 The helicopter lands near the sighting of the man. T / F
8 The man asks about his companion. T / F
9 He had camped under some trees the previous night. T / F

6 How dangerous did you say snowmobiling was in exercise 2? Have you changed your mind after watching the video?

7 Work in pairs. You are the two men in the video at the moment that they first become lost, but before they get separated. Discuss what different courses of action you can take and decide on the best one.

SPEAKING Part 3 collaborative task

IDEAS GENERATOR

BRAINSTORMING AND SELECTING

In Part 3 of the Speaking test you discuss different ideas related to a single topic with your partner, then you come to a decision. In both parts of the discussion (discussing and deciding), it's important to link your discussion with the key characteristic in the written instruction. During the Speaking test you can brainstorm ideas around the central question and discuss them with your partner – during the discussion stage the interlocutor will be listening to how well you talk about your ideas, keep the conversation going, express opinions and agree or disagree. When you are asked to come to a decision you must negotiate with your partner briefly, and choose one of the options presented to you. This is similar to the tasks you did in exercises 2 and 7.

8 Work in pairs. Look again at the sports in exercise 2 and the 'danger' points you gave them. Decide which sport or sports are the most appropriate for a group of school children aged 16.

USEFUL EXPRESSIONS

MAKING A DECISION

What do you think about … ?
My opinion is that … . What's yours?
How do you think … compares with …?
I'm not sure I agree that …
How strongly do you feel about … ?
I wonder what you think of …

9 Look at the suggestions for raising money for a winter sports challenge for teenagers. Brainstorm ideas for the following:

- how to organise the activities
- who they would appeal to
- the amount of money they could raise

pay to wear fancy dress day at school

sell your old childhood toys

hold a sponsored talent show

raising money for a charity

sports trip

have a pay-to-sing karaoke evening

get sponsored to give up social media for a week

bake cakes to sell

10 Work in pairs. Talk about each question for one minute. Then decide which is the most effective way of fundraising.

1 How easy is it to organise these activities?
2 Who would most enjoy these activities?
3 Which activities generate a lot of money for a small cost?

11 Think about your performance in exercise 10. Did you have enough to say about each question? Were there any gaps in your vocabulary?

VIDEOSCRIPT 3 is on page 253.

EUREKA!

GETTING STARTED

1 Put the subjects in the box into categories.

> archaeology astronomy biology chemistry
> electronics forensic science genetics geology
> inventions IT mathematics medicine
> palaeontology physics prehistory

READING multiple matching

SCANNING TEXTS FOR INFORMATION

Sometimes you have to read a number of texts to
search for a particular piece of information. It's not
necessary to fully understand everything you read,
but it's important to be able to identify the theme
and the main points.

2 Read the sentences and reviews A and B. Decide
which of the reviews each sentence refers to, or if
it refers to both.

1 This book examines the link between dinosaurs
and modern animals.   A / B / BOTH
2 This book documents the events of a period of
ancient history.   A / B / BOTH
3 This book is visually interesting.   A / B / BOTH

3 Reading and Use of English, Part 8

You are going to read an article containing five
reviews of dinosaur books. For questions 1–10,
choose from the reviews (A–E). The reviews may
be chosen more than once.

In which review are the following mentioned?

1 A book that illustrates evolutionary progress
with artwork _____

2 A book that is meant to be taken lightly
_____

3 The possible cause of the dinosaurs'
extinction _____

4 A book that is informative and visually
appealing _____

5 A book that conjures up a colourful
portrayal of dinosaurs _____

6 An explanation for the creation of a
legendary creature _____

7 Related animals that exist in contrasting
environments _____

8 A description of dinosaurs that still exist
today _____

9 People who made an impact on a particular
scientific field _____

10 Evidence that early humans shared an
interest in fossils _____

DINOSAUR BOOKS

Some of the latest books recommended for dino fans

A The Cretaceous World

edited by Peter Skelton
Reviewed by Douglas Palmer

If the Cretaceous period conjures up anything at all, it is probably some vague association of chalk, school blackboards and big white cliffs on both sides of the English Channel. Bright sparks might also know that Cretaceous times were brought to an abrupt end by a bolt from the blue, a big bang and a sticky end for the dinosaurs. But do you know what chalk is actually made of? What was going on globally between 142 and 65 million years ago? If you don't know, then you ought to, and *The Cretaceous World* is the book for you. OK, it is a textbook but it's how a textbook should be. To begin with it is actually a joy to look at. Now, if only the same team could address themselves to the remaining dozen or so periods of geological time ...

B Dinosaurs of the Air

by Gregory Paul
Reviewed by Jeff Hecht

Dinosaurs no longer thunder across the land, but they do flutter among the trees and paddle around the pond. Evolutionarily speaking, modern birds from hawks to hummingbirds are avian dinosaurs, descended from swift two-legged predators like the velociraptors of *Jurassic Park*. Gregory Paul's title, *Dinosaurs of the Air* symbolises the compelling links that he documents. A sparrow perched on a twig is far from our usual view of the elephantine Apatosaurus (better known as Brontosaurus) or the terrifying Tyrannosaurus rex. Yet under the skin they share the same anatomical kinship as bats and whales, two mammals that evolved into profoundly different forms. The similarities among dinosaur and bird fossils are striking. Paul includes his own careful drawings that show how anatomical features shade gradually from dinosaur into bird.

C Chasing Monsters

by Michael Benton

and The Dinosaur Hunters

by Deborah Cadbury
Reviewed by Douglas Palmer

People have always been fascinated by fossils, attracted by their curious shapes and rarity. A hand axe from the early Stone Age contains a fossil in its side. The ancient Greeks based their mythical giants on dinosaur skulls exposed in eroding cliffs. Fossil finds inspired dragons for the Chinese and suggested griffins to the Scythians.
These days, of course, we can unpick such myths and often identify some of the species that gave rise to them. Common fossils even acquired folk tales and names to match: thunderstones, or ammonites, were supposedly lightning-struck serpents, coiled in a spiral and bound in stone by the force of the shock. There's also a fossil mollusc whose shell resembles a large, ugly, claw-like nail. To early discoverers, these were obviously the devil's toenails.

D The Dragon Seekers

How an extraordinary circle of fossilists discovered the dinosaurs and paved the way for Darwin

by Christopher McGowan
Reviewed by Simon Knell

Does every science have its heroic age? Geologists certainly think so: theirs spanned the first 50 years of the 19th century, when geology was born as a rigorous and essentially modern science. And historians agree. Of course, the science had really been gestating for more than a century, but extraordinary characters suddenly threw their energies into exploring the past. In the 1810s a coincidence of scientific and social circumstances turned this proto-science into a social phenomenon. Soon the most fashionable science in England, knowledge of geology was sought by the gentry, the scientific literati and provincial philosophers. Geology did not lose its appeal, even when it became preoccupied with the arcane details ...

E A Field Guide to Dinosaurs

by Henry Gee and Luis V. Rey
Reviewed by Jeff Hecht

'This is a work of fiction,' says the introduction, but author Henry Gee and artist Luis Rey didn't make all of it up. They began with the facts known from dinosaur fossils, then extrapolated other details that aren't evident from the bones. In one sense, that's not a dramatic step beyond painting colour portraits of dinosaurs, since fossils preserve no clue of colour. Yet it is also a daring move because the casual reader won't know immediately what is based on solid science and what comes from the fertile imaginations of Gee and Rey. Your best bet is to relax and enjoy *A Field Guide to Dinosaurs* in the playful spirit the authors intended.

LANGUAGE DEVELOPMENT
colourful language

1 *Cretaceous times were brought to an abrupt end by a bolt from the blue …*
What does this expression mean?

2 **Choose the best option (a, b or c) to complete the sentences with the correct idiomatic expression.**

1 You can complain about it until you go _____ – it won't make any difference at all.
   a blue moon
   b blue in the face
   c blue around the gills

2 If you don't pay your debts promptly, you could end up on someone's _____ and then you'll find it hard to get credit anywhere.
   a black mark
   b black card
   c black list

3 You'd better not spend any more money or you'll end up _____ again.
   a in the red
   b seeing red
   c in red tape

4 My grandmother used to have such _____ – her garden always looked so beautiful.
   a green fingers
   b green hands
   c green gloves

5 Stop complaining! You know the grass always looks _____ on the other side!
   a golder
   b greener
   c yellower

KEY WORD *tell*

3 **Match the sentences (1–7) with the definitions (a–g).**

1 I told myself it would be all right in the end.
2 I could tell that she was lying.
3 Did she tell you the one about the turkey and the fox?
4 I can't tell the twins apart.
5 What this tells us is that she was here at 8 o'clock.
6 The pressure began to tell the night before the exam.
7 Michael was told off for talking in the lesson.

a to communicate a joke
b to put something into words in your own mind to give encouragement or persuade yourself about something
c if facts or events tell you something, they reveal information
d if an unpleasant experience begins to tell, it has a serious effect
e to reprimand someone for something
f to judge a situation correctly based on evidence
g to differentiate between two or more things

4 ⊙ 11 **Listen and complete the conversation with expressions with *tell*.**

Kate: Hi Sally. I wanted to tell you about what happened to me yesterday, but I don't want you to think I'm being (1) _____ .

Sally: (2) _____ , why don't you tell me about it and I promise I won't (3) _____ .

Kate: I'll try. But I don't want you to say (4) '_____ !'

Sally: Well, (5) _____ …

Kate: I (6) _____ how much it means to me that you're my friend.

Sally: (7) _____ you're my friend too!

Kate: Yes, but (8) _____ .

GRAMMAR   the future

5 **Underline the future forms.**

1 The icebergs will melt within the next 40 years.
2 By the end of this week I will have been working here for ten years.
3 This time next week we'll be flying to Mexico.
4 The match starts at 2 p.m. so you'd better hurry.
5 I'm going to visit Julie after I've picked up my son.
6 James will be here for another hour.
7 I won't forget to write to you.
8 By the time you're ready, everyone else will have left.
9 It looks like it's going to be one of those days!
10 I'm meeting Mark outside the cinema.

6 **Match the future forms in exercise 5 to these uses.**

a programmed or scheduled events
b statements of fact
c predictions
d promises
e prearranged events
f intentions or plans
g statements based on present evidence
h actions in progress at a certain time in the future
i actions which will be finished by a given future time
j the duration of an action or state at a given future time

▶ GRAMMAR REFERENCE (SECTION 4.1) **PAGE 210**

7 Rewrite the sentences in two different ways using the words provided.

1 I very nearly picked up the phone.
   I was just _____ up the phone.
   ABOUT
   I was on _____ up the phone.
   POINT
2 John is sure to pass his exam.
   John is _____ his exam.
   BOUND
   It is _____ his exam.
   CERTAIN
3 He is due for a promotion.
   He _____ promoted.
   SHOULD
   It's _____ promoted.
   TIME
4 I think it's very likely that everyone will have a computer.
   In my opinion there's a good _____ have a computer.
   CHANCE
   I very much _____ have a computer.
   DOUBT

FUTURE TIME IN SUBORDINATE CLAUSES

With certain time reference words, a different tense is sometimes used in the subordinate clause to the one used in the main clause.

8 Look at sentences 1–4 in exercise 9 and underline the time references. What tense is the verb in the main clause? What tense is used in the subordinate clause?

9 Match the sentences (1–4) with the explanations (a–d).

1 I'll walk the dog while you load the dishwasher.
2 By the time Peter gets here, the show will have started.
3 As soon as they arrive, I'll take the cake out of the oven.
4 I won't leave until I've received a phone call from Dad.

a one action happening after another action has happened
b two actions happening simultaneously
c one action happening immediately after another
d one action that will be completed before another one happens

▶ GRAMMAR REFERENCE (SECTION 4.2) **PAGE 211**

10 Complete the sentences with the correct form of the verbs in brackets.

1 Once the roof _____ (be) fixed, I _____ (move) back to my house.
2 I _____ (not / leave) until you _____ (tell) me where you put my keys.
3 When you _____ (decide) to tell him the truth, he _____ (stop) bothering you.
4 I _____ (phone) you as soon as the results _____ (arrive).
5 By the time you _____ (get) this message, I _____ (leave) the country.

11 Read the text below and underline all the future forms. Correct any which are wrong.

Predictions for a new century

In December 1900 a magazine called *The Ladies' Home Journal* contained an article which featured a variety of predictions about life in the 20th century. Here are a few of the predictions that were made.

1 There will have been almost 500 million people in America, and countries in Central America and South America are wanting to join the American Union.
2 The letters C, X and Q will be disappearing from the English alphabet due to lack of use and spelling will have been phonetic. English will have become the most extensively spoken language in the world and Russian will have come second.
3 Automobiles are cheaper and more common than horses. Even ambulances, hearses, police patrols, hay wagons, ploughs and street sweepers are going to be becoming automobiles.
4 Giant guns will be able to shoot 25 miles or more and destroy whole cities. Aerial warships and submarine boats are to be used in warfare.
5 Cameras will have been connected electronically with screens at the end of circuits thousands of miles away, enabling audiences in one part of the world to view something happening in another part of the world at the same time it happens. Giant telephones are going to provide the sound at the same time.
6 Strawberries will be being as large as apples and it won't not be necessary to eat more than one at each meal.

12 Discuss. Which of the above predictions have come true?

13 Write a list of predictions of your own describing how you believe things will have changed 100 years from now.

SPEAKING three-way task

1 **Discuss. In the future, do you think that to get a job in your country it will be essential to know how to use a computer?**

2 **Work in pairs and discuss the following question.**

How far do you agree that the computer is the greatest invention of modern times?

When you have finished making your point, prompt the second candidate, using expressions such as *What do you think? Do you agree? How about you?*

3 **Work in pairs and discuss the following question. Try to speak equally on the subject and prompt each other if necessary.**

Some people say that computers are helping to create a generation of people without social skills. What's your opinion?

LISTENING getting the gist

4 **Discuss. In your opinion, what is the most important item that has ever been invented? What would life be like today without it?**

5 **◉ 13 Listen to short extracts of five different people talking about inventions and make brief notes of key words to help you focus on the gist. The first one has been done for you.**

Speaker 1: *to get around, stress, pollution, driving, city*
Speaker 2:
Speaker 3:
Speaker 4:
Speaker 5:

6 **◉ 14 Listening, Part 4**

Now listen to the whole extracts, including the parts you have just heard.

TASK ONE
For questions 1–5, choose from the list (A–H) what each speaker is describing.

TASK TWO
For questions 6–10, choose from the list (A–H) each speaker's attitude towards the invention.

While you listen you must complete both tasks.

A a centrally installed vacuum cleaning system	
B the bicycle	Speaker 1 ☐
C the wheel	Speaker 2 ☐
D the radio	Speaker 3 ☐
E the mobile telephone	Speaker 4 ☐
F the Internet	Speaker 5 ☐
G computer software	
H satellite TV	

A believes it has greatly simplified a domestic chore	
B feels it enables them to do something environmentally friendly	Speaker 1 ☐
C considers that its advantages outweigh its disadvantages	Speaker 2 ☐
D wants to have the opportunity to use it more	Speaker 3 ☐
E thinks it has enabled society to progress	Speaker 4 ☐
F is disappointed that more people don't use the invention	Speaker 5 ☐
G admits to having had a change of heart about it	
H regrets the loss of certain things that it has replaced	

USE OF ENGLISH prefixes

PREFIXES

A prefix is a letter or group of letters which is added to the beginning of a word in order to form a different word. Here are some examples.

agree → **dis**agree
legible → **il**legible
develop → **re**develop
dress → **un**dress
regular → **ir**regular
possible → **im**possible
arrange → **pre**arrange
adequate → **ina**dequate

7 **Add a prefix to each of the word groups.**

1 ___logical; ___literate; ___legal
2 ___balance; ___mutable; ___proper
3 ___able; ___gender; ___list
4 ___correct; ___decision; ___sane
5 ___responsible; ___resolute; ___rational
6 ___cultural; ___millionaire; ___lingual
7 ___conscious; ___likely; ___necessary
8 ___new; ___name; ___locate
9 ___violet; ___marine; ___sound
10 ___marine; ___conscious; ___directory
11 ___meditated; ___historic; ___fixed
12 ___associate; ___appear; ___arm

EXAM SPOTLIGHT

Reading and Use of English, Part 3
Forming words from stems

In a word formation task, you may have to make more than one change to a word. What changes need to be made to complete these sentences?

1 He was sentenced to eight years' _____ . PRISON
2 The road had to be _____ after the floods. SURFACE
3 I'm afraid to say they were _____ married for many years. HAPPY

8 **Reading and Use of English, Part 3**

For questions 1–8, read the text below. Use the word given in capitals at the end of some of the lines to form a word that fits in the gap in the same line.

Mysteries of computer from 65BC are solved

A 2,000-year-old mechanical computer salvaged from a Roman shipwreck in 1900 has astounded scientists who have finally unravelled its secrets. The ship carrying the device sank off the coast of the Greek island of Antikythera in 65BC. Since its discovery, scientists have been trying to (1) _____ the device, which is now known to be an (2) _____ calendar capable of tracking with remarkable (3) _____ the position of the sun and other heavenly bodies, and even recreate the irregular orbit of the moon.

It consists of a wooden and bronze casing bearing ancient Greek (4) _____ , enclosing gear wheels and other mechanical elements. (5) _____ , scans showed the device uses a type of gear previously believed to have been invented in the 16th century. The level of miniaturisation and (6) _____ of its parts is (7) _____ to that of 18th century clocks. No one knows why the technology invented for the machine seems to have (8) _____ for well over 1,000 years.

CONSTRUCT

ASTRONOMY

PRECISE

INSCRIBE

ASTONISH

COMPLEX
COMPARE

APPEAR

WRITING an essay – using the notes provided

1 **Discuss. How do you think people's lives will change in the future? What trends or developments will have the greatest impact on our lives? Will the changes they bring be positive or negative?**

EXAM SPOTLIGHT

Writing, Part 1 What is an essay?

In Part 1 of the Writing paper you will be asked to write an essay. Essays need to present an argument and give reasons for it. Therefore, an essay needs to be well organised with an introduction, clear development and an appropriate conclusion. The main purpose of an essay is to develop an argument and / or discuss the issues surrounding a certain topic. You should give reasons for your views.

2 **Read the question below and the notes. Underline key words or phrases in the question (not the notes).**

Writing, Part 1

A research scientist has given a lecture at your college entitled *How we see the future*. The lecture included some statistics drawn from a survey of people's views. You have made the notes below:

Areas that the lecture focused on:

- automation
- medical advances
- improved life expectancy

Some views and statistics from the survey:
'Robots will get all the best jobs in the future – 40% of people agree'
'Couples should be allowed to choose the sex of their babies – 20% of people agree'
'Society cannot support increasing numbers of old people – 65% of people agree'

Write an essay for your tutor discussing two of the areas in your notes. You should explain which future development you think will benefit humans most and provide reasons to support your opinion. You may, if you wish, refer to the views expressed in the survey, but you should use your own words as far as possible.

USING THE NOTES PROVIDED

You will be given some notes in the essay question and it's essential that you make good use of these. Make sure you understand what you have to write about, and then organise the notes in a way that will help you.

3 **Work in pairs. Match the views and statistics to the areas that the lecture focused on. Select two of the views and say whether you agree or disagree with them. Explain your reasons why.**

4 **Discuss. Read the two paragraphs. How do the arguments in the paragraphs differ? Which argument do you agree with most? Why?**

Scientists are working very hard to help human beings live longer but, like the majority of people, I believe that an ageing population is going to result in a number of problems for society. The most significant of these will be the difficulties health services will face in their efforts to care for elderly people with dementia and Alzheimer's. Even today, there are numerous reports in the media about the poor quality of care for people with these conditions. By the middle of the century, this problem will have become much worse.

People often talk about the 'ageing population' in negative terms, yet most people would like to live longer if they had the choice. In fact, life expectancy is improving all the time and that is not going to change. The good thing is that people will be healthier in their old age and fewer resources will be needed. So, although a considerable number of people feel that an ageing population will be a burden on society, I think this view is short-sighted and fails to take into account people's wishes and the impact of scientific progress.

5 **Look back at the paragraphs and underline the ideas that support each argument.**

6 Read the essay. Discuss which paragraph highlights the future development that will benefit humans most. What are the reasons given?

Without a crystal ball, it is difficult to predict how our lives will change in the future, but one thing is certain: there will be changes and technology will play a major role in these.

One area that continually moves forward is medicine. However, I think governments need to think carefully about how money is allocated to medical research. In my view, finding a cure for diseases such as malaria and cancer would be more advantageous to humans than any other aspect of scientific progress because it would save so many lives. On the other hand, not many people believe it is desirable for couples to be able to choose whether they have a boy or a girl because this type of medical intervention diverts resources from more critical areas of research.

Like medicine, automation is another area that is continually developing. Science fiction films have been describing scenes in which robots do the jobs of humans for many years. With the technological revolution, huge advances have been made in this field: workers have been replaced by robots and soon robots will be cleaning people's homes. Yet robots still cannot interact well with humans and, contrary to what quite a few people think, until they can, they will only be able perform routine tasks. Some areas of life will progress faster than others and it is likely that some changes will be for the good, while others will have drawbacks. Ultimately, it is up to us to ensure that we manage these changes in the best way possible.

7 Underline the future forms that the writers have used in the paragraphs and the essay. What do you notice about them?

IN OTHER WORDS

In both essays the writers use phrases instead of statistics to introduce other people's views. These phrases can be useful in general to present different opinions in an essay and show how popular you think the opinions are.

8 Find the phrases used in exercises 4 and 6 to replace these percentages.
1   65%   (two phrases)
2   40%
3   20%

9 **Writing, Part 1**

Your class has attended a panel discussion about the impact of technology on the future of primary school education. You have made the notes below:

> Features of primary education that the panel discussed:
> * learning on the Internet
> * the role of the teacher
> * classroom organisation

> Some comments from parents in the audience:
> 'Young children cannot be expected to use the Internet without a lot of help and supervision.'
> 'The traditional school teacher will become redundant as cyber-teachers fill their roles.'
> 'There'll be no need for a classroom at all, and children will just be sectioned off into computer cubicles to get on with it alone.'

Write an essay for your tutor discussing two ways that you think primary education will change in the future. You should explain whether you think the changes will be negative or positive and provide reasons to support your opinions.
You may, if you wish, refer to the parents' comments, but you should use your own words as far as possible.

Write your answer in 220–260 words in an appropriate style.

REVIEW 1

1 Choose the best option to complete the sentences.

1 I don't really see David any more, but once in a _____ he phones me and we talk of old times.
   A red sunset
   B blue moon
   C green field
   D purple heart

2 He was _____ to finish the race, despite being so tired.
   A exhausted
   B petrified
   C relaxed
   D determined

3 Joe, you'd better lie down. You're _____ a temperature!
   A making
   B running
   C taking
   D raising

4 I _____ when I saw how they'd destroyed my plants.
   A saw red
   B went red
   C was green
   D went yellow

5 That was mean and unfair! I want you to take _____ everything you just said about me!
   A out
   B off
   C back
   D down

6 That was fantastic! Your raft travels so fast, it's really _____ !
   A exhausting
   B terrifying
   C reassuring
   D exhilarating

7 I made a real mess of my presentation! I was _____ , kept dropping my notes, and knocked over the microphone twice!
   A wet behind the ears
   B all fingers and thumbs
   C a pain in the neck
   D down in the mouth

8 Until I find work as an actress, I'm working as a child minder to make _____ .
   A it
   B my debut
   C ends meet
   D a name for myself

9 Nick really takes _____ his uncle. They even laugh in the same way!
   A after   B for   C apart   D in

10 They thought of selling up and moving to Australia, but decided to stay and try to make _____ the business.
   A do with   B out   C a go of   D up for

2 Complete the dialogues with the correct form of the verbs in brackets.

1 A: How are Ann and Tim, by the way? Do you hear from them?
   B: Oh, they _____ (move) to Spain! They _____ (go) last year, actually. Tim _____ (not be) happy at work for a long time, so they _____ (decide) to pack it all in and leave. Apparently, they _____ (open) a hotel in Alicante, and I believe it _____ (do) really well!

2 A: Right! I must dash! I _____ (go) to pop in and see my gran on the way home, but I don't want to miss *Lost*.
   B: I thought you said Mike _____ (come) round for a meal tonight.
   A: Oh no, I _____ (forget)! I _____ (have to) go shopping! I've no idea what we _____ (eat)!
   B: How about making him a chilli? I _____ (really like) that one you _____ (make) for me last week.
   A: Good idea! Thanks! Bye!

3 A: So, how _____ (it happen)?
   B: Well, I _____ (ride) my bike along Price Street. It _____ (be) dark, but the moon _____ (shine), so I _____ (can) see fairly well. Then this car just _____ (come) from nowhere, and _____ (crash) into me!

3 Complete the sentences with the correct form of a verb from the box. There are more verbs than you need.

activate   bound   bring about   clamber   embark on
generate   hop   initiate   instigate   launch into
leap   march   paddle   prompt   provoke   skip
stride   trigger   wade

1 The two little girls _____ happily off down the road to buy an ice cream.

2 The Mayor's speech _____ an angry reaction from the crowd.

3 A couple of Chelsea fans were accused of _____ the fight that had broken out after the match on Saturday.

4 The lead singer _____ off the stage into the crowd.

5 You have to stand on one leg and _____ towards the finish line, carrying an egg on a spoon!

6 His kind words _____ her to ask him if he was married.

7 My father doesn't walk along the street, he _____ as if he were still in the army!

8 Before _____ such a dangerous journey, it would be a good idea to pack a first aid kit.

9 When Andy goes salmon fishing, he _____ into the middle of the river before casting his rod.

10 The new headmistress has _____ discussions with the student council regarding the question of bullying in the school.

4 **Complete the sentences with a future form of the verb in brackets.**

1. We're so late, that by the time we _____ (get) there, they _____ (finish) their meal!
2. In a few years, almost all university coursework _____ (conduct) online.
3. As soon as John _____ (finish) painting, I _____ (be able) to work on that project.
4. 'So, what have you decided to do?' 'I _____ (tell) him the truth, and I hope he _____ (believe) me.'
5. By this time next week, we _____ (trek) across the Gobi desert!
6. By 2020, people _____ (no longer use) landline phones.
7. I _____ (see) Anika later, and we _____ (think) of going to the cinema. Do you want to come?
8. 'Fiona _____ (take) her driving test this afternoon.' 'She _____ (be bound to) fail, as she's hardly had any practice!'

5 **Reading and Use of English, Part 4**

For questions 1–6, complete the second sentence so that it has a similar meaning to the first sentence, using the word given. Do not change the word given. You must use between three and six words, including the word given.

1. She learnt how to dance the tango ten years ago.
   ABLE
   She _____ the tango for ten years.
2. Although we've been friends for a long time, I don't always understand her.
   HAVE
   We _____ a long time, but I don't always understand her.
3. There have been rumours that Peter and Jane are getting married.
   HAS
   It _____ Peter and Jane are getting married.
4. They finally got married last year, after being engaged for 12 years.
   BEEN
   When they finally got married last year, _____ 12 years.
5. It is likely that local residents will be suspicious of the company's plans for development in the area.
   MAY
   The company's plans for development _____ with suspicion by local residents.
6. It definitely wasn't Paul you saw with that girl, because he's in Glasgow on business!
   SEEN
   You _____ that girl, because he's in Glasgow on business!

6 **Reading and Use of English, Part 2**

For questions 1–8, read the text below and think of the word which best fits each gap. Use only one word in each gap.

Sunshine and showers during dinosaurs' heyday

Dinosaurs might have known an astonishing amount about what we think of (1) _____ a quintessentially contemporary problem: global warming. Fossilised vegetation from 65 million years (2) _____ , in the Cretaceous period, reveals that central Siberia and other cold regions were actually a lot (3) _____ present-day Florida, with lush ferns and lots of rain. Academics from various universities examined fossilised fern leaves to estimate temperatures at the time. (4) _____ of the zero degrees centigrade that climate models had led them to expect, the average temperature was far higher. Based on this study, (5) _____ are at least two possible reasons for the results being different from their expectations.

Occurrences such as continental drift, differences (6) _____ atmospheric chemistry or the shape of the Earth's orbit round the sun might have made the world (7) _____ different then that the models we use for today's atmosphere cannot mimic it. However, some academics argue that these explanations don't adequately explain the results. An alternative explanation is that the fossil evidence (8) _____ have been misunderstood, and needs to be re-examined.

7 **Choose the correct options in italics to complete the sentences.**

1. The children had a great morning, but as soon as their friends left, they got *up to / down* to work tidying up their room.
2. Kevin didn't bat *an eyelid / a finger* when Sara told him she was leaving, but just said, 'Oh, OK then.'
3. After the disastrous meeting, they agreed to wipe *a new leaf / the slate clean*, and start again with a different approach.
4. Give your child free *will / rein* to express herself, and you will help her build self-confidence.
5. I did a double *take / look* when I saw Jill – she's lost so much weight.
6. The change of plan is *up to / down to* Tom. If he'd come home earlier, we wouldn't have missed the train.
7. Take a paintbrush and some colours, and let your imagination run *wild / free*.
8. I didn't like the design, so I tore it up and started from *square one / scratch*.

GETTING STARTED

1 **Look at the photo. Which of the crimes in the box does it show?**

arson	computer hacking	drug trafficking
fraud	kidnapping	murder

READING gapped text

2 **Read part of a headline from a newspaper article. What do you think the article is about?**

OF WORMS AND WOODPECKERS:
THE CHANGING WORLD OF THE VIRUS-BUSTERS

3 **Scan the first paragraph of the article to find out who the woodpeckers are. Who or what do you think are worms?**

EXAM SPOTLIGHT

Reading and Use of English, Part 7
Following a line of argument in a text

In Reading and Use of English, Part 7, you have to read a text from which paragraphs have been removed, and decide where they fit. If you find that more than one option seems to fit a particular gap, be careful to read the whole preceding paragraph and the one that follows the gap. Make sure that your option fits both.

Read the opening paragraph of the article more carefully. Turn to page 241 and decide which two of the three paragraphs there could follow it. (gap 0)

4 **Read the second paragraph of the article and decide which of the paragraphs on page 241 is correct. Explain your choice.**

SUPPORTING POINTS IN AN ARGUMENT

There are a number of different ways to support an opinion in an article. For example:
a Statistical examples e.g. *35% of the population said …*
b Background / historical information e.g. *This would not have been possible ten years ago, when …*
c Comments from experts e.g. *'You see this kind of thing often in urban environments', says Dr. Brown.*

5 **Read the sentence. What kind of information would you expect to follow it?**

They examine and create antidotes to more than 200 pieces of code every day, but it is a task that is proving increasingly difficult.

6 **Look at the gaps between the paragraphs in the text. Try to predict which of the support points in the box above (a, b or c) you would expect to see in the missing paragraphs.**

TEXT ORGANISATION FEATURES: COMPARISON

When writers make a point, they often compare the present situation with the past.
The modern computer is very different from Charles Babbage's invention. He envisaged a sophisticated mathematical tool, and could not have imagined how this would develop into today's tool.

Look back at the article and find a similar example of this kind of comparison.

OF WORMS AND WOODPECKERS:
THE CHANGING WORLD OF THE VIRUS-BUSTERS FIGHTING THE RISE IN INTERNET CRIME

Inside a gloomy tower block on the north-western outskirts of Moscow a team of young computer programmers is deep in concentration.

0 [...]

Each day a dozen team members at the anti-virus firm Kaspersky Lab – mostly in their late teens or early 20s and nicknamed 'woodpeckers' – work in 12-hour shifts to crack, decode and eradicate some of the world's most malicious computer viruses, or 'crimeware'. They examine and create antidotes to more than 200 pieces of code every day, but it is a task that is proving increasingly difficult.

1 [...]

The danger of crimeware and hackers is being recognised by authorities and law enforcement around the globe. Last week Britain unveiled plans to stiffen its computer crime laws, doubling the maximum jail sentence for hacking to ten years and making it illegal to own 'hacking tools' such as password-cracking software. And with good reason, say experts.

2 [...]

Eugene Kaspersky knows the mind of a cyber-criminal better than most. For 15 years he has worked on understanding viruses and their creators. His company is one of a host of anti-virus and internet security companies fighting to keep their customers secure. It is a battle that is getting bigger. According to figures released by the FBI last week, around 90% of people have experienced computer security problems recently. Research published last year suggested that the global cyber-crime industry is now worth more than the international illegal drugs trade.

3 [...]

It is all a far cry from the earliest days of hacking, when viruses were created by bored teenagers. It is 20 years since the first widespread PC virus, *Brain*, which was created by brothers Amjad and Basit Farooq Alvi. *Brain* was a piece of trickery that began as a benign experiment but left corporate America shaking. Although there had been viruses before, business simply didn't understand the concept of security. As a result, *Brain* caused panic.

4 [...]

But the days of playing for fun are long gone. According to research, just 5% of malicious programs are now written by bored teenagers. The rest are produced by ever-increasing numbers of professional criminals and fraudsters. 'A lot of people are stuck in the 1990s, with their image of a virus writer as a kid eating pizza in their bedroom,' said Graham Cluley, an expert with Sophos. 'In fact, they are now much more serious, and much nastier.'

5 [...]

The hackers' change in attitude has also had other side effects. 'There are no global epidemics like there were in the past,' said Mr Kaspersky. 'Just local ones.'

Several years ago virus epidemics regularly hit the headlines. Now the smarter focus from criminals means they don't get as much coverage, despite being more successful. Some experts say this creates a sense of complacency.

6 [...]

Back in his Moscow laboratory, Mr Kaspersky directs his woodpeckers as they cope with a new influx of crimeware. Outside is winter, but inside the chill is warded off by the banks of screens. He knows that his job will never be over. 'Sometimes when you feel ill you can go to the chemist, and sometimes you need to go to hospital,' he shrugged. 'But people will never stop getting sick.'

---

7 Reading and Use of English, Part 7

You are going to read an extract from a magazine article. Six paragraphs have been removed from the extract. Choose from the paragraphs A–G the one which best fits each gap (1–6). There is one extra paragraph which you do not need to use.

A Mr Viveros agrees. 'Now that there's money involved, the threats have become a lot greater. The widespread adoption of broadband internet means that hackers have targets they can always access.'

B 'Hackers don't want to damage computers any more, they want to own them,' said Eugene Kaspersky, the founder of Kaspersky Lab. 'They've started to run direct attacks where just one business, or even just one computer, is infected.'

C 'If the guys on the News at Ten aren't talking about viruses, then the guy on the street doesn't think about it,' said Mr Cluley. 'But we're seeing fewer massive outbreaks, because actually clever criminals don't want access to 200,000 bank accounts at once, because they can't cope with that many. Instead they get access to 200, and just keep going back for more. The problems are less likely to get headlines,' he says, 'but that makes them more dangerous.'

D Over the weekend thousands of computers worldwide were crippled by the latest virus, Kama Sutra. The worm, which spread through emails and inside computer networks over the past month, was estimated to have caused tens of thousands of pounds of damage as it attempted to erase files on infected computers. Last week the Russian stock exchange, a short distance from Kaspersky Lab, shut down for an hour after a virus attack.

E A harmless but annoying virus which contained the names of its creators, *Brain* spread worldwide in just a few months, making it the first widespread PC virus. Then in 1992, the infamous *Michelangelo* came on the scene. One of the first viruses to get widespread media coverage, the reach of *Michelangelo* – at one point predicted to hit 5 million machines – turned out to be far smaller than anticipated.

F 'What we saw 20 years ago was really technical enthusiasts, and people creating proof of concept viruses,' said Sal Viveros, a security specialist with the anti-virus company McAfee. 'For the first seven or eight years that was really who made these things.'

G Through viruses and worms, hackers can control thousands of computers – turning them into 'zombies'. After that, they can steal people's identities, engage them in complex fraud or blackmail, send spam, attack websites, or run an cyber-protection rackets. The Internet security firm Sophos estimates that an unprotected computer connected to the Internet has a 50% chance of being infected within 12 minutes.

LANGUAGE DEVELOPMENT phrasal verbs

1 Work in pairs. Complete the newspaper report with particles from the box.

for	in	of	to	with

JILTED LOVER'S PLOT FOR REVENGE

There may be an element of truth in the saying that 'hell hath no fury like a woman scorned', if the case heard recently at the Old Bailey* is anything to go by.
A top businesswoman was convicted (1) _____ inciting her new boyfriend to kill her former partner and his wife. Amy Hynde was furious when her lover of 22 years, Clive Layne, told her he'd found someone else. Unable to cope (2) _____ the rejection, Hynde resorted (3) _____ repeatedly sending Layne hate mail, accusing him (4) _____ abuse and unfair treatment. A year later, she began a relationship with another man, Adrian Lewis, and confided (5) _____ him about her feelings. When Layne changed his will, leaving everything to his new wife, Hynde and Lewis decided to act.
Lewis contacted an acquaintance in search of an assassin, but the police were informed (6) _____ his plans, and this led to an undercover officer being sent to pose as the 'hitman'. He met with Hynde, taped their conversation and subsequently arrested her. She was charged (7) _____ soliciting murder. At first, Hynde tried to blame her boyfriend (8) _____ forming the plan, but then admitted (9) _____ going along with the idea. Lewis confessed (10) _____ the crime, claiming he was 'blinded by love', and the jury found both guilty (11) _____ soliciting murder. They were sentenced (12) _____ 15 years' imprisonment.
*Note: The Old Bailey is the central criminal court in London.

phrasal verbs with *turn*

2 In paragraphs E and G on page 49, the phrasal verbs *turn out to be* and *turn into* appeared. Match them to their definition below.

1 was discovered to be
2 made someone become

3 Complete the sentences with particles from the box.

down	in	to	out	over	on	in	off

1 I'm exhausted from studying all day. I think I'll turn _____ and have an early night.
2 When his business went bankrupt, Ken turned _____ his brother for help.
3 This company's doing very well, and turned _____ a profit of $4 million last year.
4 I know all about his illegal activities. I have decided to turn him _____.
5 David asked Sarah to marry him, but she turned him _____.
6 As Simon walked up the garden path, his neighbour's dog suddenly turned _____ him, and bit his arm.
7 They turned _____ the water supply for a while to repair the boiler.
8 Sam's landlord turned him _____ of his flat because he hadn't paid his rent for three months.

KEY WORD *law*

4 Use a dictionary to find the meanings of the phrases in the box.

be above the law	be against the law
break the law	by law	enforce the law
law-abiding	law and order	law enforcement
lawsuit	lay down the law	obey the law
take the law into your own hands	within the law

5 Complete the sentences with phrases from exercise 4 in a suitable form.

1 The problem of the Queen's missing dog has been keeping _____ agencies busy in London.
2 But officer, I wasn't _____ . I was only driving at 40 miles an hour!
3 Politicians sometimes make the mistake of thinking they _____ , and can do what they want.
4 Kelly has decided to bring a _____ against her next door neighbours, regarding the noise they make.
5 All owners of a television are required _____ to have a TV licence.
6 Police have difficulty maintaining _____ in some inner-city areas.
7 It _____ to drive after you have been drinking alcohol in many countries.
8 Joe's dad was really angry, and we could hear him _____ through the closed door!

GRAMMAR verbs followed by infinitive or -ing

6 Put the verbs in the box into the correct category.

a followed by infinitive with *to*
b followed by infinitive without *to*
c followed by -*ing*

> advise agree appreciate arrange ask
> attempt avoid choose contemplate dare
> decide deny encourage enjoy expect
> face fail invite involve let make order
> persuade practise pretend refuse remind
> threaten

7 Choose verbs from exercise 6 to complete the sentences. In some cases more than one answer may be possible.

1 You must _____ playing the piano for two hours a day.
2 Tom _____ to break his brother's train set if he didn't shut up.
3 I've _____ to have the kitchen painted next week.
4 Ann _____ going to Switzerland for Christmas, but changed her mind at the last minute.
5 Claire _____ having an affair with her boss, but Kevin didn't believe her.

8 Some verbs can be followed by either -*ing* or the infinitive with *to* (*like, remember,* etc). Read the pairs of sentences. How do the verb forms in italics change the meaning?

1 I don't *like listening* to my teacher's stories.
   I don't *like to disturb* my teacher at home.
2 She *remembered seeing* Patrick at the beginning of the party, but not later on.
   She *remembered to see* John on his way home.
3 Oliver *went on talking* for an hour, and some people fell asleep!
   Trixie *went on to thank* the teacher for all his help.
4 Sorry, I *meant to tell* you about the meeting!
   Sorry, but this *means having* a meeting at 7 o'clock in the morning!
5 Helen *stopped to talk* to her neighbour.
   Will you *stop talking* for five minutes!

▶ GRAMMAR REFERENCE (SECTION 5) **PAGE 211**

9 **Reading and Use of English, Part 4**

For questions 1–6, complete the second sentence so that it has a similar meaning to the first sentence, using the word given. Do not change the word given. You must use between three and six words, including the word given.

1 'Give me your money or I'll shoot you!' said the thief to the old lady.
   THREATENED
   The thief _____ if she didn't give him her money.
2 'I didn't take the wallet from your bag, Sir, honest!' cried Ronald.
   DENIED
   Ronald _____ from his teacher's bag.
3 'When you went into the room, Mrs Smith, did you notice anything unusual?' asked the police officer.
   REMEMBERED
   The police officer asked if _____ when she went into the room.
4 I can't phone her at this time of the night, it's too late!
   LIKE
   'I _____ so late.'
5 Diane told the police she hadn't intended to burn her ex-husband's house down.
   MEAN
   'I _____ fire to my ex-husband's house, Officer. Really!'
6 Bill succeeded in convincing his wife that she should tell the police what she had noticed.
   PERSUADED
   Bill _____ tell the police what she had noticed.

LISTENING sentence completion

1 Discuss. What do you know about forensic science and DNA analysis?

2 Work in pairs. A lot of specialised terms are referred to by initial letters. For example, *DNA* stands for deoxyribonucleic acid. Choose the correct full- length phrase for these well-known initials.

   1 CIA stands for
     a Central Investigation of Advertising
     b Central Intelligence Agency
   2 CSI, from the American television series about forensics, stands for
     a Criminal Science Institute
     b Crime Scene Investigation

3 🔘 15 Listen to someone talking about DNA analysis. The speaker mentions *RFLP testing*, *STR testing* and *PCR testing*. As you listen, match each abbreviated phrase with the correct description (1–3).

   1 Requires only a very small sample of DNA, which may be slightly degraded. However, this form of testing is highly susceptible to contamination.
   2 Requires a small sample of DNA, but this must be recent, as degraded DNA is unsuitable for testing using this method.
   3 Requires large amounts of DNA from recent samples.

4 Listen to the extract again, and summarise the main point the speaker makes in one sentence. Is it necessary to understand all the terminology to answer the question?

DISTINGUISHING KEY INFORMATION

In Part 2 of the Listening paper you have to complete eight sentences which summarise information you have heard. When you listen, you need to isolate the key word or phrase needed to complete each sentence.

5 🔘 16 Read the following sentence. It is a completed sentence from a Listening, Part 2 exercise.

According to the speaker, a national DNA database would act as a strong deterrent to potential criminals.

Now listen to the extract. Which word or phrase do you think has been filled in to complete the sentence above?

6 Read questions 1–8 in exercise 7. What kind of information is each one asking for?

7 Listening, Part 2

🔘 17 Listen to a criminologist giving a talk about DNA profiling. For questions 1–8 complete the sentences.

DNA analysis

According to Daniel, before the advent of DNA testing (1) _____ was the main source of forensic evidence.

Thanks to technological developments in DNA testing, one man was recently convicted of crimes he committed between (2) _____ and 1986.

Daniel thinks the (3) _____ is responsible for creating an unrealistic image of DNA profiling.

He regards the view that DNA testing alone can prove that a person is guilty as (4) _____ .

A number of scientists have expressed concern that forensic evidence presented in the case of Barry George was (5) _____ .

DNA analysis can now be carried out on a (6) _____ sample, which enables cases from years ago to be solved.

Today, the odds of more than one match being found are approximately one in (7) _____ .

Daniel says that despite technological advances, DNA is not (8) _____ , and mistakes are made.

---

8 Work in groups. Read the statement and brainstorm arguments for and against it.

A national DNA database containing DNA samples from every citizen is the best way to ensure our country becomes a safer place to live.

USE OF ENGLISH gapped sentences

EXAM SPOTLIGHT

Reading and Use of English, Part 2
Finding the right preposition

In Part 2 of the Reading and Use of English paper you have to decide which word fits into each gap. In some cases, the missing word is a preposition that is normally used with the word preceding or following it. When you learn new words used with a preposition, make sure you learn them as a phrase.

9 **Which preposition can follow all verbs in each set?**

1 to believe _____ always telling the truth
   to succeed _____ an attempt to do something
   to invest _____ something
2 to hear _____ someone
   to translate _____ one language into another
   to save someone _____ drowning
3 to laugh _____ something funny
   to shout _____ someone
   to smile _____ someone
4 to admit _____ having done something wrong
   to refer _____ what somebody else has said
   to devote time _____ something
5 to accuse someone _____ a crime
   to cure someone _____ an illness
   to remind someone _____ of somebody else

10 **Which preposition follows these adjectives?**

1 to be grateful _____ someone
2 to be jealous _____ someone
3 to be absorbed _____ what you're doing
4 to be hopeless _____ something
5 to get married _____ someone

11 **Complete the phrases with a preposition from the box. There are two extra prepositions.**

by	in	on	to	of	over	for

1 a reason _____ doing something
2 to do something _____ mistake
3 to go somewhere _____ business
4 to have authority _____ someone
5 to have access _____ something

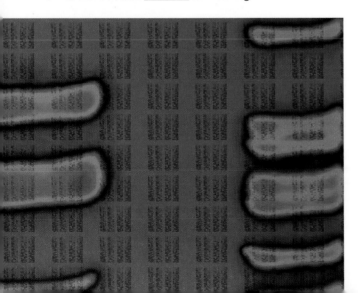

12 **Reading and Use of English, Part 2**

For questions 1–8, read the text below and think of the word which best fits each gap. Use only one word in each gap.

Improving road safety in the town

Road safety varies a great deal around the country, and locally our record is among the best. In fact, in the past five years, the number of accidents has fallen faster here than anywhere else. This is something we can be proud (1) _____ .

But (2) _____ good our record may be, there are no grounds (3) _____ complacency. Much more needs to be done, both locally and nationally, to improve road safety. Changes are planned to safety education (4) _____ drivers, cyclists and motorcyclists. This will reduce various costs, including those of the emergency and health services, and the personal cost to people affected by road accidents.

When it (5) _____ to speed limits, it is surely unnecessary to point (6) _____ that nobody should exceed these, apart (7) _____ the emergency services. Yet they are ignored all too often. Some limits have been lowered in the district, in (8) _____ to reduce speeds in residential roads and particularly in the vicinity of schools. Further measures are currently under consideration.

SPEAKING giving personal information

13 **⊙ 18** Listen to the first part of a *Cambridge English: Advanced* examination interview, where the examiner asks two candidates about themselves. Compare the answers given by the two candidates.

EXAM SPOTLIGHT

Speaking, Part 1 Talking about yourself

In this part of the Speaking paper candidates have to talk about themselves. Listen to the questions carefully, and try to give as many details about yourself and why you like or dislike something. Do not answer with one word or a short phrase.

14 Listen again and make notes on how Beret expands her answers to include more detail.

15 Look at some of Juan's answers below. Try to expand them, in a similar way to Beret.

Spain. *I'm working, and trying to improve my English.*

I play football every Saturday, and I train twice a week.

I'd like to play water polo. *… because I like swimming.*

WRITING a report

Writing, Part 2

1 Discuss the following.

1 Is there a lot of traffic in your area?
2 Is your area safe for pedestrians?
3 What about cyclists?

2 Read the exam question and plan an answer by creating four paragraph headings.

> A research group from your local council has asked you to write a report on road safety in your area. You should consider the amount of traffic, the presence and location of traffic signals and pedestrian crossings and cycle lanes. Make recommendations for improvements.

1 _____
2 _____
3 _____
4 _____

3 Read these three opening paragraphs in answer to the question above. Which is the most appropriate?

a The question of road safety in our area is a controversial issue, due to the fact that the level of traffic has increased drastically in the last few years, whereas the need for corresponding safety measures has largely been ignored.

b In this report, I'm going to examine the amount of traffic in the area, and look at how effective traffic signals, pedestrian crossings, etc, are. I will also suggest some ways of improving the present situation.

c The aim of this report is to evaluate road safety in this area, by examining the level of traffic, and the provision of traffic signals, pedestrian crossings and cycle lanes. It will consider their effectiveness, and make recommendations for improvements.

4 What is wrong with the other two paragraphs?

WRITING A REPORT

Reports require formal language. Their purpose is usually to assess a current situation, and make recommendations for improvement. The opening paragraph outlines the aim of the report and the points it will address, and so its style is fairly standard. Make sure you build up a bank of useful words and expressions for your introductory paragraph.

IN OTHER WORDS

Use a dictionary to add formal equivalents to these words.

look at – *examine*, …
consider – *assess*, …
suggest – …

Notice the use of nouns rather than verbs in formal language. Write the noun forms of these words.

evaluate
provide
consider
effective
scarce
recommend
improve

5 Look at paragraph b in exercise 3. Rewrite it using some of the formal language you have found.

6 Read the rest of the report below. Does it answer the question? If not, make recommendations for improvements.

7 Give each paragraph a suitable heading.

8 Work in pairs. Read the exam question, then brainstorm ideas for your response. Plan your paragraph headings, 1–4.

You work as a teacher, and the principal has asked you to write a report on the standards of safety in your school. You should consider the presence of fire escapes, fire doors and fire-fighting equipment, in relation to the fact that class sizes have increased, and make recommendations for improvement.

9 🔘 19 Listen to a school safety inspector giving a talk on fire prevention, and write down any points and vocabulary which are useful for writing an answer to the question above.

10 Write your report. Use 220–260 words.

Heading: _____

The level of traffic in the area has increased dramatically during the last three years, as a result of the construction of a new industrial park on the edge of the town. Not only are there more cars on the roads, but also an increased number of heavy goods vehicles travelling through the town centre. A lack of parking facilities means that cars park on the roadside in the centre, often blocking the road for large vehicles. This causes congestion and delays, and has given rise to complaints from local shop owners and business people.

Heading: _____

Despite the rise in traffic, little has been done to improve road safety. The town centre itself is fairly well catered for, with a sufficient number of traffic lights and pedestrian crossings. The main problem lies in the residential areas of the town, particularly those in the direction of the industrial park, such as Rookwood, where there are several schools, yet traffic signals and pedestrian crossings are scarce. Several accidents involving schoolchildren have been reported on Hampton Road in the last few months, and local residents are extremely concerned about the fact that there are no cycle paths near the schools.

Heading: _____

There are several ways in which the situation could be improved. One would be to construct a by-pass for heavy goods vehicles to travel to the industrial park without having to pass through the town. Also, the construction of a multi-storey car park in the town centre would help reduce congestion in the streets, while the creation of more pedestrian crossings with warning signals near the schools in Rookwood would reduce the risk of accidents occurring.

VIDEO the world in a station

1 **Which of these statements about DNA is not true?**

1 All living organisms contain DNA.
2 DNA is passed from generation to generation.
3 DNA is found in special cells in the body.
4 Each individual person has a unique DNA profile.
5 The DNA profiles of people who are related are similar.

2 **Read the first paragraph of a newspaper item about a project involving DNA. Then watch the first part of the video and find four factual errors in the text.**

National Geographic joined forces with IBM in April 2005 to study important questions about people in the United States. The study, called the Genographic Project, aimed to trace human DNA back to ancestors in South Asia. The project created a huge database of DNA by taking samples from several hundred people around the world. How did they get the samples? Well, one method was to ask travellers in New York's Grand Central Station to give blood samples. While most of the sampling was anonymous, four people were given the chance to find out about their heritage.

3 **In the video, Dr Spencer Wells invites people to take part in the study. How would you feel if you were asked? What would you say to him? What questions would you ask him?**

4 **Watch the rest of the video. Choose the correct options in italics to complete the sentences.**

Dee Dee lives in (1) *Minnesota / Michigan*. Her ancestors moved from Africa to (2) *Europe / the Middle East*.

Frank lives in Southern (3) *Colorado / California*. He might have had (4) *Aztec / African* ancestors. He feels he is a (5) *survivor / southerner*.

Cecile's ancestors were from (6) *the South Pacific / South East Asia*. She lives in (7) *New York City / New Jersey*. When she thinks about her roots, she feels (8) *proud / privileged*.

JW is a (9) *police officer / fire officer* in New York City. He feels (10) *confused / connected* because of everyone's common origin.

5 **Watch the whole video. Then use the words in the box to summarise the Genographic Project.**

analysis   ancestors   connect   database   origin
results   sample   species

6 Work in pairs. Why do you think the four people featured in the video were in Grand Central Station? Think of at least two reasons for each person.

SPEAKING Part 2 long turn

IDEAS GENERATOR

INTERPRETING PICTURES

In Part 2 of the Speaking test you talk about two pictures from a set of three. You also make a short comment on your partner's pictures. It's important to express what you think might be happening in the pictures. You can prepare for this by identifying key things in photos and speculating on several different 'scenarios' for each one. This is similar to the task you did in exercise 6.

You should also show you have a wide range of vocabulary in this task. You can prepare for this by learning synonyms for words you already know. Think of different ways of expressing the words in exercise 5, either with a word or an expression.

7 Work in pairs. Look at the people labelled 1–4 in the photo opposite. What do you think they are doing in Grand Central Station? Why? Use the expressions in the Useful Expressions box at least once in your answers.

VIDEOSCRIPT 5 is on page 254.

USEFUL EXPRESSIONS

SPECULATING ABOUT PHOTOS

It looks to me as if …
It looks as though …
I suppose they might …
I think they could feel …
I would imagine that …
I would say that …

8 Work with a new partner. Tell them about the people in the photo in a long turn of about one minute.

9 Look at the photos on this page. For each one, spend one minute doing the following.
1 Write six words connected with what you see.
2 Think of synonyms or alternative ways of saying your six words.
3 Think of at least two possible interpretations of what you see.

10 Work in pairs. Choose one photo each. Talk for about 30 seconds and answer these questions about the photo.
1 Why might these people be in this situation?
2 What might they be thinking?

11 Think about your performance in exercise 10. How well did you:
• use more than 'basic' vocabulary?
• keep talking without long pauses or hesitation?
• speculate about the photos rather than simply describe what they show?

12 Use the other photos in this book to practise the tasks in exercise 9.

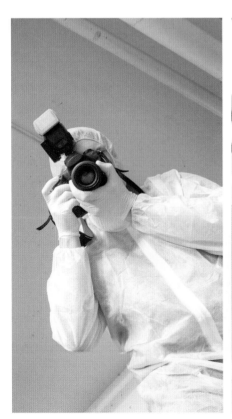

6 HALE AND HEARTY

GETTING STARTED

1 **Discuss. Which of the following factors are the most important for a healthy life? Put them in order of priority, giving your reasons.**

1 Consuming plenty of fresh fruit and vegetables
2 Avoiding stress and tiredness
3 Eating organically grown food
4 Not watching too much TV
5 Developing a strong immune system and exercising regularly
6 Not using chemicals in the home
7 Doing yoga and meditation
8 Going to the doctor and taking medication

2 🔘 **20** **Listen to three people discussing some of the topics above. Which topic (1–8) is each speaker talking about?**

READING identifying opinions

UNDERSTANDING WRITTEN TEXTS

The following techniques will help you to gain a better understanding of a written text.

a Work out the meaning of new vocabulary from the context.
b Read parts of the text several times if necessary in order to understand it.
c Underline key words or phrases that seem to answer the question.

3 **Number the methods in the tip box in order of usefulness to you.**

4 **Read the text on page 59. As you do, try to use techniques a and b in the tip box.**

EXAM SPOTLIGHT

Reading and Use of English, Part 6 Text analysis

In Reading and Use of English, Part 6, you will read four short texts with a common theme. You must compare and contrast opinions and attitudes across the texts, and answer four questions relating to this. To do this, you will need to identify the main ideas or arguments presented in the texts.

Answer the questions about identifying ideas and opinions in the texts about superfoods.

a Look at the title and sub-title. Do you think the tone of the four texts will be generally positive or generally sceptical about superfoods?
b The main theme of the texts is superfoods. Can you identify four ideas that are discussed across the four texts? All four ideas may not necessarily appear in each text.
c Find and underline language which indicates the writers' opinions or attitudes in each text. For example, the use of first person I/ adverbs, e.g. *convincingly*; or conjunctions which signal comparison and contrast, e.g. *However*.
d Which of the stated opinions are positive and which are negative? You could keep track of these as you read by putting '+' or '–' in the margin next to the opinion.

5 Reading and Use of English, Part 6

You are going to read four newspaper articles. For questions 1–4, choose from the articles A–D. The articles may be chosen more than once.

Which article

1 expresses a similar opinion to article C with regard to the credibility of scientific research?
2 expresses a different attitude from the others towards the motives of food companies in marketing superfoods?
3 takes a similar view to article A with regard to modern and traditional advice about eating?
4 shares the opinion expressed by the writer in article C about having personally accepted the idea that some foods are better than others?

ANALYSING UNKNOWN WORDS

It is often possible to work out the meaning of unknown words by trying the following techniques:

• look closely at the words in context
• identify the part of speech
• look at the positive or negative meaning of the sentence
• use other lexical clues around the word

6 Read the text again. Match the italicised words in the text with the definitions (1–6). What part of speech are the italicised words?

1 accepted as normal by most people
2 very unpleasant
3 cleverly planned
4 very effective
5 very attractive
6 very small in amount

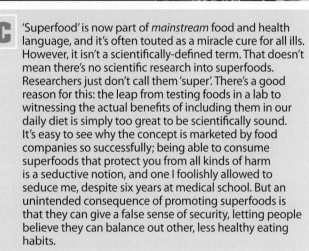

Superfoods: Are they really so super?
Four critics of the superfood phenomenon give their views

A Natural food communities have long stressed the value of eating whole grains, vegetables, nuts and fruit. Now, we've added the word 'super' to some foods, elevating them to a special status that companies are simply using as a means to more profit. Whether the food has special nutrient value seems barely relevant to them, aware as they are that as a result of living in an environment bombarded by toxins, we've come to the conclusion that foods with high nutrient density are our best hope of staying healthy. Hardly a new approach, but rather a resurrecting of ancient wisdom from cultures that paid attention to the effects of nature on health. The theory is that any nutritionally-dense food qualifies as a 'superfood'. Research indicates such foods are *powerful* allies in our fight to hold onto our health, but no one food provides everything: variety is the key to staying healthy and living a long time.

B Every Tuesday for years, I've forced down a meal of oily fish, despite the fact I find its taste and smell *repulsive*. So new official guidance suggesting that the role of oily fish in preventing disease 'could be *minimal*', is far from welcome. We all know certain foods are better for us than others, but the idea that some possess mystical properties is *seductive*, and something that suppliers and manufacturers understandably continue to promote in *ingenious* ways. Yet research into the benefits of many of these foods is often based on preliminary studies open to multiple factors that can skew the results, and few claims that a food has a miracle benefit live up to scrutiny. I don't see anything wrong in seeking out new ways to improve our diets, and we're already outliving previous generations. Until a cure-all food is found, however, I'll just look forward to a decent Tuesday dinner.

C 'Superfood' is now part of *mainstream* food and health language, and it's often touted as a miracle cure for all ills. However, it isn't a scientifically-defined term. That doesn't mean there's no scientific research into superfoods. Researchers just don't call them 'super'. There's a good reason for this: the leap from testing foods in a lab to witnessing the actual benefits of including them in our daily diet is simply too great to be scientifically sound. It's easy to see why the concept is marketed by food companies so successfully; being able to consume superfoods that protect you from all kinds of harm is a seductive notion, and one I foolishly allowed to seduce me, despite six years at medical school. But an unintended consequence of promoting superfoods is that they can give a false sense of security, letting people believe they can balance out other, less healthy eating habits.

D Every week new research comes to light about another berry, grain or unusually-named compound that the marketing world claims is a key to better health and longer life. No doubt there's something in these claims, but do these 'superfoods' really deserve the enormous amount of hype they get? Nutritionists and scientists don't have a definition for superfood. What might deserve the label 'super', though, is food with high nutrient density. Some of the foods making headlines boast high antioxidant contents. Others promote good digestive health, or are known for their mineral content. The problem with them is that people may overestimate their power. They do have some health benefits, but they're not magical. General dietary research shows that consuming a variety of foods, including lots of fruits and vegetables, gives a person the best chance of obtaining the full spectrum of nutrients: a balanced diet, just like mother always said.

LANGUAGE DEVELOPMENT expressions with food

USING IDIOMS IN SPEECH

Native speakers tend to use idiomatic expressions a lot in speech but only in very informal situations and not very often in written form. An idiom used appropriately and wisely can add emphasis or description to what you say, but be careful! Do not overuse idioms – especially if you're not sure of the correct meaning or the appropriate situation, as it could sound rather odd.

However, you may well come across idiomatic expressions in the Reading and Use of English and the Listening papers, and it's therefore important to build up your passive knowledge of English idioms.

1 ⊙ 21 Listen to four short conversations and note down any food idioms that you hear.

1 Turn to the audioscript on page 245 and underline the idioms.
2 Work in pairs. Explain what each idiom means and in what context it could be used.

2 Choose the correct word to complete the sentences.

1 Have you two been plotting something again? Something certainly smells _____ around here!
   a greasy   b meaty   c stale   d fishy
2 Gregory threatened to spill the _____ if we didn't tell him where the car keys were kept.
   a biscuits   b eggs   c milk   d beans
3 I know I said it was a good idea to take on some extra work, but now I think you've bitten off more than you can _____ .
   a chew   b swallow   c digest   d gnaw

3 Discuss. In what situations do you think you might use the expression *You can't make an omelette without breaking eggs*?

4 Use a dictionary to find further expressions with the words in the box. Then write example sentences.

bacon   butter   cake   egg   salt

KEY WORD *life*

5 Answer questions 1–7.

1 Which of the following expressions may be used to talk about a car's engine suddenly starting?
   a bring to life
   b spring to life
   c come to life
   d roar into life
2 It could be said that growing old is …
   a a fact of life.
   b true to life.
3 If we say that someone was the 'life and soul of the party', we mean he or she was …
   a a lot of fun.
   b very healthy.
4 If something gives you 'a new lease of life', it …
   a cures you from a serious illness.
   b fills you full of optimism or energy to start again.
5 Which of the following expressions is the odd one out?
   a a matter of life and death
   b to risk life and limb
   c to lay down one's life
   d to have the time of your life
6 Arnold and Graham are _____ friends.
   a lifetime
   b lifestyle
   c lifelike
   d lifelong
7 She had a small, _____ model made of her cat, Hugo, after he died.
   a lifesize
   b lifeless
   c lifelike
   d lifetime

6 Which of the words in the box cannot follow the word *life*?

achievement belt blood boat cycle dream expectancy force form guard history imprisonment insurance jacket killer line raft sentence support vision

GRAMMAR conditionals

7 **Look at audioscript 20 on page 245. Underline one conditional sentence that each speaker uses. Which one is a …**

a likely situation in the present with a possible solution?

b hypothetical situation in the present with a definite consequence?

c usual or habitual situation in the past?

8 **Read the sentences (1–6) and match them with the rules (a–f) that follow.**

1 If it rained we took the bus, but if the sun came out we always walked.

2 If I didn't love chicken so much, I would become a vegetarian.

3 If you look after your immune system, it will look after you.

4 If the core body temperature drops by a few degrees, the immune system shuts down.

5 If I hadn't been to that yoga class, I would never have learnt what it could do for me.

6 If I hadn't smoked when I was younger, I'd be far healthier now.

a what is always true – present facts [present + present]

b real situations in the present and future [present + future]

c hypothetical present situations [past + would]

d what used to always be true – past facts [past + past]

e past events with results in the present [past perfect + would]

f hypothetical past situations and regrets [past perfect + would have + past participle]

9 **Which of the sentences (1–6) in exercise 8 is an example of the …**

a zero conditional   d third conditional

b first conditional   e mixed conditional

c second conditional f false conditional

▶ GRAMMAR REFERENCE (SECTION 6) **PAGE 212**

10 **In addition to *if* sentences, there are other forms of conditionals.**

Underline the conditional phrases in sentences 1–9.

Match the sentence beginnings (1–9) with the endings (a–i).

1 Unless I go on a diet,

2 If I should give up eating hamburgers,

3 Provided you exercise regularly,

4 As long as you eat all your vegetables,

5 Even if it rains,

6 If you were to cut out the junk food,

7 Had it not been for Judy,

8 Supposing you gave up coffee,

9 But for Helen's advice,

a I would never have tried Chinese food.

b I'll have to start eating vegetables.

c I'll have to buy some new clothes.

d you'll be fit enough to take part in the games.

e what would you drink instead?

f I'm still going to go for a walk.

g I'll let you have some ice cream.

h I would still be taking antibiotics.

i you'd feel so much better.

11 **Reading and Use of English, Part 4**

For questions 1–6, complete the second sentence so that it has a similar meaning to the first sentence, using the word given. Do not change the word given. You must use between three and six words, including the word given.

1 If his temperature increases, I'm going to call the doctor.
   INTEND
   Unless his temperature _____ the doctor.

2 I didn't have time today so I didn't have any lunch.
   HAD
   If I _____ had lunch today.

3 If William hadn't advised me to continue, I would have given up.
   ADVICE
   But _____ I would have given up.

4 Drop in and see us if you ever come to Manchester.
   HAPPEN
   Should you _____ Manchester, drop in and see us.

5 I was so short that I couldn't reach the top shelf.
   WOULD
   If I _____ been able to reach the top shelf.

6 You wouldn't have to visit the dentist so often, if you ate fewer sweets.
   CUT
   Were _____ sweets, you wouldn't have to visit the dentist so often.

LISTENING multiple-choice questions

1 **Underline the key words in this question.**

According to the speaker, why are enzymes essential in our diet?

2 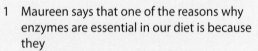 22 **Listen to a woman answering the question. She explains what enzymes are. What is the main point she makes?**

3 ◉ 23 **Listening, Part 3**

You will hear an interview with a food writer about the benefits of eating raw food. For questions 1–6, choose the answer (A, B, C or D) which fits best according to what you hear.

---

1 Maureen says that one of the reasons why enzymes are essential in our diet is because they
   A stop us consuming poisonous substances.
   B are the main cause of chemical changes.
   C increase our resistance to disease.
   D prevent us contracting harmful diseases.

2 Maureen recommends reducing our intake of cooked food because
   A it cannot supply us with all the nutrients we need.
   B too much cooked food makes us feel heavy.
   C cooked food can cause health problems.
   D raw food tastes so much better.

3 The experiment with the cats showed that
   A each generation of cats responded differently to the foods offered.
   B there was a mixed reaction in the first group of cats.
   C the majority of cats developed health problems after starting the diets.
   D the fourth generation of cats eating cooked food had the most problems.

4 If we don't consume enough enzymes in our food
   A we force our bodies to use their own store of enzymes.
   B we will not be able to process any of the vitamins it contains.
   C our bodies will be forced to manufacture inferior enzymes.
   D we are likely to suffer from digestive problems.

5 Cooking food may cause some proteins to
   A break up into amino acids.
   B fail to function efficiently.
   C attack our bodies by mistake.
   D become damaged and dangerous.

6 The presence of too much cooked food in our bodies may
   A change the colour of our blood.
   B attract invasive organisms.
   C put our immune system on a state of alert.
   D set off an unusual chemical reaction.

SPEAKING comparing pictures

EXAM SPOTLIGHT

Speaking, Part 2 Comparing pictures

In the Speaking test, Part 2, you will be shown three pictures, and asked to compare two of them. That means you need to say how the pictures are similar or mention the different ways they deal with the same theme. It isn't enough to just describe each picture separately. Your response needs to go beyond the level of pure description – you should speculate about the pictures. You'll also be asked a specific question about the pictures. There are written prompts to help you with this. You should try to talk for about a minute.

4 Turn to page 233 and look at the pictures. Find two things that each set of three pictures has in common. Describe the different ways in which they deal with those themes.

5 In groups of three, practise the speaking tasks that follow. One person should be the interlocutor and read the questions to the other students, who take turns to answer.

> Interlocutor: [Student 1], here are your pictures. They show people eating different types of food. I'd like you to compare two of the pictures and say how food can affect people's mood and why the people might have chosen to eat this food.

Student 1: …

> Interlocutor: [Student 2], which type of food do you prefer to eat?

Student 2: …

> Interlocutor: [Student 2], here are your pictures. They show people engaged in different types of physical activity. I'd like you to compare two of the pictures and say how doing physical activities can help people stay healthy, and how these people may be feeling.

Student 2: …

> Interlocutor: [Student 1], which activity would you prefer to do?

Student 1: …

USE OF ENGLISH identifying collocations

IDENTIFYING COLLOCATIONS

In the exam, your knowledge of collocations may be tested, particularly in Reading and Use of English, Part 1. You need to be able to recognise different kinds of collocation.
For example:
- verb + verb: *let someone know*
- verb + noun: *take offence*
- adj + noun: *miniature railway*
- noun + prep + noun: *matter of fact*

Whenever you come across a new collocation, make a note of it in your vocabulary notebook.

6 Use a dictionary. How many collocations can you find for the word *stand*?

7 Which of the following noun phrases cannot be used with the verb in bold?

1 **take** offence / the initiative / fault / into account
2 **do** harm / luck / good / wonders for
3 **run** a process / a risk / its course / for government
4 **make** fun of / a mistake / an effort / justice
5 **give** rise to / credit / fortune / notice
6 **fall** to pieces / into disrepair / from grace / off power

8 Reading and Use of English, Part 1

For questions 1–8, read the text below and decide which answer (A, B, C or D) best fits each gap.

Naturopathic medicine philosophy

Illness is the body's way of letting us know that something is wrong, and according to believers in Naturopathic Medicine we should listen to the messages. This form of medicine treats disease by stimulating, enhancing and supporting a person's own healing (1) _____ .

One of the main underlying (2) _____ of naturopathic healing is to trust in the healing power of nature. The body has the inherent ability to establish, maintain, and (3) _____ health by itself. Furthermore, no illness (4) _____ without a reason, so without identifying and treating the underlying causes of that illness, a person cannot recover completely. A further directive that naturopathic doctors must consider is to do no (5) _____ to the body. Symptoms are an expression of the healing process and therapeutic actions should allow them to (6) _____ their course. Obstructing a symptom, or (7) _____ it, will only force it to reappear later, perhaps in a more damaging form. (8) _____ forms of treatment, which allow the body to heal itself, are encouraged.

1	A facility	C	aptitude
	B gift	D	capacity
2	A codes	C	moralities
	B principles	D	ethics
3	A restore	C	reinstate
	B remake	D	renovate
4	A transpires	C	instigates
	B establishes	D	occurs
5	A hurt	C	impairment
	B harm	D	destruction
6	A go	C	run
	B do	D	make
7	A demolishing	C	suppressing
	B oppressing	D	restraining
8	A Balancing	C	Matching
	B Corresponding	D	Complementary

WRITING developing an argument in an essay

1 Discuss. *You are what you eat.* How important do you think diet is to our health? Explain your reasons.

2 Read the exam question and the beginning of one student's attempt to answer it. Does it meet the requirements for the introduction?

> Your class has attended a lecture entitled *You are what you eat*. You have made the notes below:
>
> **Main ideas of lecture**
> * The body's response to healthy eating
> * The body's response to unhealthy eating
> * The effect of food on how we feel
>
> **Questions raised during lecture by students:**
> 'What is meant by 'healthy eating'?'
> 'What happens if we eat too much junk food?'
> 'How can food affect our minds?'
>
> Write an essay for your tutor on two of the main ideas in the lecture. You should explain how important you feel diet is to human health and provide reasons to support your opinion.

You are what you eat. The importance of diet to our health.

You are what you eat because if you eat good food then you feel good, but if you eat bad food then you feel awful. If you eat lots of junk food you will get fat and you won't be able to go out and exercise because you'll feel heavy and you'll be tired all the time, so you'll just sit on the couch and watch even more TV and eat lots of pizzas and drink lots of fizzy drinks and get even fatter. But if you eat lots of healthy food like fruit and vegetables and beans and rice then you will have lots of energy and it won't all turn into fat so you'll have more energy to do the things you want to do and then you'll feel really great.

DOING AN ESSAY PLAN

Follow these steps when writing an essay:

1 Brainstorming: Write down your ideas or a list of points that would answer the question.
2 Plan the paragraphs: Remember there should be a clear development between your ideas, so keep your paragraph organisation simple.
3 Write an introduction: Introduce the topic of the essay to the reader. Often the easiest way to write an introduction is to rephrase the question using your own words.
4 Write the main body paragraphs: Clearly state your main points. Use examples if necessary. Explain your reasons. Link your paragraphs appropriately.
5 Write a conclusion: A conclusion sums up your main message in the essay.

3 In which paragraphs would you write points 1–4? Match them to the list (a–d) that follows.

1 The physical benefits of eating good food
2 The effects of eating a lot of sugar and fat
3 Summary of main points (importance of paying attention to our diet in order to be healthy)
4 Analysis of main statement (the fact that diet affects our health and makes us who we are)
a Opening paragraph – introduction
b Main paragraph 1
c Main paragraph 2
d Closing paragraph – conclusion

4 Look at the following introductory paragraphs. Which one would you choose for the exam question in exercise 2? Why wouldn't you choose the others?

1
> *We are what we eat and therefore diet is very important to our health. This is for a number of reasons.*

2
> *It goes without saying that good health is dependent on the food we eat as well as a number of other factors. Our diet not only contributes to our physical health but also to the way we feel our overall sense of wellbeing. This essentially means that we are what we eat.*

3
> *If people eat well they will be healthy and happy. If people eat badly, they will be unhealthy and therefore unhappy. For this reason it is clear that what we eat makes us who we are.*

5 Using the notes below, write the main body of your essay (b and c in exercise 3).

> **nutrients (vitamins, minerals, protein, carbohydrates, fats, enzymes)**
>
> repair tissues and cells, maintain healthy organs, provide energy, strong immune system, fight off illness, feel great ...

> **nutrient deficiency**
>
> too much fat / salt / sugar, overweight or obese, bad health, lack of energy so limited physical exercise, weak immune system, illness and disease, feel bad psychologically ...

6 Show the development between your arguments by using examples. Look at the statements below and notice how examples point towards a clear conclusion.

	Statement	Example	Conclusion
1	Vitamins / minerals = healthy organs / repair tissues / cells	Vitamin C = healthy skin / immune system	Protects against illness / makes us look better
2	Too much junk food = feeling bad about yourself	Too much junk food = overweight = lack of exercise	Exercise releases endorphins = a sense of wellbeing and happiness

The first statement could be written like this:

> We need vitamins and minerals to maintain healthy organs and repair tissues and cells. For instance, vitamin C is essential for healthy skin and boosts our immune system, as a result protecting us from illness and making us look better at the same time.

Rewrite the second statement in the same way:

> Eating ....

7 Look back at the student's writing in exercise 2. How many times have the words *and*, *but*, *because* and *so* been used? Replace as many as possible with a suitable word or phrase from the box below. Make other changes if they help.

> **LINKING DEVICES**
>
> also   another point is that   as a result of this / which   ... but on the other hand
>
> consequently   despite the fact that   finally   for which reason   furthermore
>
> however   in that   in view of this   moreover   nevertheless   on the one hand ...
>
> secondly   subsequently   therefore   whereas   while   which is why

8 Read the student's conclusion. It says the right things but it is one long sentence. This makes it sound clumsy. Rewrite it as two shorter sentences.

> And so therefore, if we want to live long healthy lives we should follow a number of general guidelines, like for example not smoking and exercising more, but also we must be aware of the food we eat and we should aim to eat more of the right foods and less of the wrong ones because good health is fundamental to our sense of wellbeing and feelings of happiness and as good food equals good health, we should make every effort to eat well – because we are what we eat.

9 **Writing, Part 1**

Read the exam question. Write your answer in 220–260 words in an appropriate style.

> Your seminar group has attended a talk by a nutritionist about the effects of diet on different groups of people. You have made the notes below:
>
> > **Groups**
> > - children
> > - college students
> > - adults at work
>
> > **Speaker's opinions:**
> > 'well-fed children work harder in school'
> > 'too much coffee at night can keep students awake'
> > 'how much you eat depends on what work you do'
>
> Write an essay for your tutor discussing two of the groups in your notes. You should say which group is most at risk of eating unhealthily, giving reasons in support of your answer.

GETTING STARTED

1 🔘 24 **Listen to a tour operator making predictions about the future of travel. Which type(s) of travel does he think will be accessible to the masses?**

2 **Which of these types of travel appeal to you? Why?**

READING multiple matching

3 **Work in pairs. Think of a city you have visited that you really like, or the one you live in. Tell your partner about it.**

4 🔘 25 **Listen to Fiona and Nick talking about a city they visited recently. Answer the questions using F for Fiona, N for Nick or B for both. Who ...**

1 thinks the architecture was impressive?
2 talks about the city in terms of smell?
3 is enthusiastic about the local people?

5 **Read texts A and B about two cities that are special to the writers, and find one thing they like about their chosen city.**

A St. Petersburg

I was brought up in London by an English mother and a Russian father, so I guess Russia has always been in my blood. It wasn't until I visited my father's home city of St Petersburg though that I felt an unexpected surge of belonging. It was 1986 and the Soviet Union was only just starting to open up. I was rather nervous about the visit and I'd expected Leningrad, as it was still called back then, to be a grey and dreary place. I couldn't have been more wrong.

It was mid-summer, a period known as the White Nights, when the sun never quite sets below the horizon. I wandered the streets in the romantic twilight, the sky tinged in pinks and purples, coming across beautiful church domes, towering arches and the most spectacular historic buildings. On that first visit, I remember being completely overawed by the vast Hermitage Museum and its never-ending galleries of treasures. Each time I've been back since, I make a point of visiting it again and on each visit, I discover some new gem.

B I lost my heart in ... Dublin

I recently moved back to Dublin, my childhood home, after more than a decade living and working across the water in England. The place welcomed me back with open arms and I realised just how much I feel at home here. It was as if I'd been on my best behaviour all the time I'd been in England and now I could just relax and be myself again!

Of course, the city's changed enormously while I've been away. It's a much more cosmopolitan place than it used to be. You're as likely to hear a French or a Polish accent as you are an Irish lilt. I'm finding that lots of my old haunts have had a makeover, often for the better. Although I do worry that the city's starting to lose its character. People come to Dublin for a taste of Irish culture, but now many of the shops and bars have been bought up by chains that you'd find in any European city.

Reading and Use of English, Part 8
Interpreting the question speaker's main points

In this part of the Reading and Use of English paper, read each question very carefully, and underline the key words, showing what information you need to find in the text.

6 **Read the two statements. What is the difference in their meaning? Which one is true for texts A and B?**

1 Both writers are connected by birth with the place they write about.

2 Both writers were born in the place they write about.

7 **Decide whether the following statements are true (T) or false (F).**

1 The writer was surprised by their reaction when they first arrived in Russia.   T / F

2 The writer mentions their favourite place in Dublin.   T / F

3 The writer expresses concern about future developments in Dublin.   T / F

4 The second writer has a more pragmatic view and appreciation of their city than the first.   T / F

8 **Reading and Use of English, Part 8**

You are going to read a magazine article in which four people write about a city they love. For questions 1–10, choose from the writers (A–D). The writers may be chosen more than once.

Which writer

1 mentions the warmth and resilience of the local people? _____

2 shows concern about the city retaining its identity? _____

3 talks about an earlier change of mood in the city? _____

4 found their initial fears about the city to be groundless? _____

5 mentions two events which had a great impact on the city? _____

6 talks about the mix of architectural styles in the city? _____

7 is pleased how an area of the city has developed? _____

8 mentions the risk of developing misconceptions about the city? _____

9 is a frequent visitor to the city? _____

10 mentions how the population of the city has changed? _____

C Kolkata

One of the things I love most about Kolkata is the eclectic mix of faded colonial-era grandeur alongside exotic temples and modern glass skyscrapers. People imagine the city as a sprawl of poverty-stricken slums and it's true, there are some incredibly deprived areas, but there's so much more to it than that if you're prepared to see beneath the surface and keep an open mind.

When I was first posted here, my family were a bit concerned about security. And I have to admit that I started flat-hunting with some trepidation. Kolkata is a huge and rather bewildering city to the visitor, but once you get to know your way around, you soon settle in. We found an apartment in a really friendly neighbourhood where everyone was incredibly welcoming.

I can't pretend that life here is always easy, just getting about can be endlessly frustrating and when the rainy season comes, everywhere floods. But people look out for each other, they muddle through together. People take things in their stride that would bring a city like London or Paris to a standstill.

D Barcelona

Barcelona has always had its own unique culture and style, with the amazing architecture of Gaudí and Domènech i Montaner. When I was growing up though, it was a rather neglected, run-down sort of a city.

Catalonia regained its status as an autonomous region within Spain in 1978 and as the region's capital, Barcelona rediscovered a sense of identity. After years of decline, the city reawakened and recovered some of its heart and passion; it was an exciting time. Then in 1992, the coming of the Olympic Games really revitalised the city with the complete redevelopment of the harbourside area. It's now transformed into a beautiful bustling hub for locals and tourists alike. There's nothing quite like sitting out in a waterfront café on a warm summer's evening, enjoying a paella with friends and soaking up the buzz of the place.

9 **Find words or phrases in texts A–D that match the definitions (1–9).**

1 sudden strong feeling (text A)

2 feeling both impressed but slightly afraid (text A)

3 companies which own a number of shops in different towns (text B)

4 a place that you visit and spend time at regularly (text B)

5 a large urban area that spreads in an untidy way (text C)

6 worry about what is going to happen (text C)

7 to stop all activity or movement (text C)

8 independence (text D)

9 busy and full of activity (text D)

LANGUAGE DEVELOPMENT describing places

1 **Which of the words and phrases in the box could you use to talk about the following in a town or city?**

a   buildings
b   atmosphere
c   personal reaction

> amazing   appealing   breathless   crumbling
> disgusting   dusty   eerie   gothic   grandeur
> horrible   industrious   it has it all   like home
> lovely fresh air   magical   old   open mind
> passion   threatening   remarkable   run down
> shoddy   slums   sober   sparkling   snow
> the essence of   touristy   unique

phrasal verbs and phrases with *look*

2 *But people look out for each other, they muddle through together.*

What does *look out for* mean here?

3 **Match the phrasal verbs (1–8) with their meanings (a–h).**

1   look forward to
2   look ahead
3   look someone up
4   look up to someone
5   look into
6   look to someone
7   look down on someone
8   look out for each other

a   visit someone when you go to their town
b   investigate, try to learn the truth
c   be excited and pleased about something
d   try to ensure the other person is treated well
e   think about what might happen in the future
f   think you are better than another person
g   respect and admire someone
h   depend on someone to provide help or advice

4 **Decide whether the following sentences are true (T) or false (F).**

1   To *look something up* means to find out what a word or phrase means in the dictionary.   T / F
2   If you *look through someone* you don't understand what they are really like.   T / F
3   If you *look on someone with affection*, you watch them tenderly.   T / F
4   If you say that someone is *not much to look at*, you don't find them attractive.   T / F
5   If you say you'll *look in on someone*, you promise to make them a short visit, while you are going somewhere else.   T / F

5 **Match the sentence beginnings (1–7) with the endings (a–g).**

1   Look me in the eye and
2   If you see someone being attacked,
3   I can't believe anyone could
4   Mrs Brown looked Jenny
5   By the looks of it,
6   The situation's getting worse, and I
7   She just stood there

a   overlook such an important detail!
b   up and down coldly.
c   you won't be going on that trip tomorrow.
d   don't like the look of it.
e   with a strange look on her face.
f   tell me you didn't break that window!
g   don't just look the other way!

KEY WORD *road*

6 **Choose the best ending to complete the sentences.**

1   If you are *on the road to recovery*, you are
   a   making new plans for the future.
   b   becoming well after an illness.
2   If you are *on the road* you
   a   are travelling for a while.
   b   have no fixed home.
3   Someone says *we've come to the end of the road* when
   a   they've exhausted all possible solutions, and don't know what to do next.
   b   they've finished a process.
4   Someone tells you not to *go down that road* when they
   a   want to harm you.
   b   think a course of action is wrong.
5   If you say *one for the road* you
   a   are leaving.
   b   are asking for one more alcoholic drink before you leave.

7 **Which of these words can follow *road*?**

> back   block   blog   credible   hog   house
> map   rage   side   sign   show   value
> wise   works   worthy

8 Reading and Use of English, Part 3

For questions 1–8, read the text below. Use the word given in capitals at the end of some of the lines to form a word that fits in the gap in the same line.

Hi Jeanette!

How are you? Another teacher and I took our classes on an (1) _____ to Blackpool yesterday, and the students had a great time. **OUT**

Blackpool is a (2) _____ town, **SEA**
and so it's really (3) _____ . **TOUR**
It used to be very popular, and if you ignore the run-down places, many of the houses along the sea front have kept an air of
(4) _____ from when the town **GRAND**
was booming. It's making a comeback now, though, with the help of
(5) _____ from some local **INVEST**
businesses.

We took our classes to the Pleasure Beach fairground, and they went on all the rides. A boy won a prize in an Elvis
(6) _____ contest and everyone **LOOK**
teased him.

We had some (7) _____ **FORSEE**
problems on the way home, caused by roadworks on the motorway, but that didn't dampen the kids' spirits. All in all it was one of the most
(8) _____ school trips I've ever **MEMORY**
been on.

Take care, and let me know when you're coming.

Love, Sally

USE OF ENGLISH open cloze

EXAM SPOTLIGHT

Reading and Use of English, Part 2 Contrast and negative ideas in the text

In this part of the Reading and Use of English paper you're sometimes presented with a gap that requires a negative word. This can usually only be understood by looking carefully at the context and tone of the passage.
E.g. *We had a barbecue on Saturday, but (1) nobody turned up, because it was raining.*
Similarly, you may be required to fill a gap with a linking word that shows an opposing idea (contrast).
E.g. *The TV can be a wonderful source of information.*
(2) nevertheless, we need to monitor the programmes children watch.

9 Complete the sentences with the words in the box.

despite	few	however	hardly	often
many	with	without		

1 Although she likes watching films, she _____ ever goes to the cinema.
2 There are _____ ways in which you can enjoy yourself in Blackpool, as there is so much to do and see.
3 _____ his fear of heights, Adam went up the Eiffel Tower.
4 Most people find it difficult to be _____ a mobile phone nowadays.
5 It was a beautiful sunny day. _____ , she decided to stay in and do her homework.
6 The beach was crowded, _____ colourful umbrellas and sunbeds covering almost every inch of sand.
7 David _____ visits his grandmother, even though she lives 50 miles away.
8 _____ people I know have ever visited Alaska, because they prefer going somewhere hot.

10 Reading and Use of English, Part 2

For questions 1–8, read the text below and think of the word which best fits each gap. Use only one word in each gap.

New worlds

Until relatively recently, the word 'travel' conjured up visions of packed bags, the open road, and the idea of escape. Holidays were planned well (1) _____ advance, and regarded with eager anticipation. The Internet, however, has changed all that – just as it has so (2) _____ else. Not (3) _____ can you now travel to another country, but you can visit another 'world', (4) _____ even leaving home.

Interactive simulated worlds on the Internet go far (5) _____ showing you reality; they offer visitors the ultimate form of escapism, the ability to reinvent (6) _____ and live their dream life. By creating a proxy, called an avatar, you can choose to be whoever you like, and travel anywhere. For many, the attraction of these simulated worlds is being able to fly, and watch that world change before your very eyes.

There is also scope (7) _____ a whole range of social activities as you interact with other avatars. Never before (8) _____ travel offered so many options!

LISTENING multiple matching

1 **Discuss. Would you like to travel in space? Why or why not?**

2 **Read the comment on space travel. Does the speaker approve or disapprove of it?**

> *The best spaceship is the one we live on. It's fully equipped with food, water and the natural resources necessary to sustain human life. Anyone who studies outer space for a living as I do can tell you that we have yet to discover a planet that comes close. So why pay extortionate sums of money to leave it, when we'd be better off protecting it from destruction?*

EXAM SPOTLIGHT

Listening, Part 4
Interpreting context to identify the speaker

In this part of the Listening paper you're presented with distractor options which may use similar words to those in the audioscript. It is important to listen to the whole extract before making your choice.

3 **Answer the questions.**

1 Who is making the comment in exercise 2?
   a   an astronomer
   b   a political activist
2 Which words or phrases helped you choose your answer?
3 What is the speaker expressing?
   a   fears that space travel will destroy the Earth's environment
   b   concern that human beings fail to appreciate what they've got

4 🔘 26 **Listening, Part 4**

You will hear five short extracts in which people talk about commercial space travel.

GRAMMAR inversion

5 **Sentence 1 below has been inverted. Compare it with sentence 2. What effect does it have?**

1 Not only can you now travel to another country, but you can visit another 'world', without even leaving home.
2 You can now travel to another 'world', as well as another country, and not leave home.

USING INVERSION

We tend to use inversion:
*   in formal situations
*   to emphasise a point, especially in official / political speeches
*   to make a statement more convincing or interesting
*   to make a recommendation more persuasive
*   to make a narrative more dramatic

TASK ONE		**TASK TWO**	
For questions 1–5, choose from the list (A–H) the occupation of the person who is speaking.		**For questions 6–10, choose from the list (A–H) what each speaker is expressing.**	
		While you listen you must complete both tasks.	
A a future 'space tourist'		A dismissal of the idea of space travel	
B a medical expert	Speaker 1 ☐	B ignorance of the ethical problems	Speaker 1 ☐
C a spaceflight representative	Speaker 2 ☐	surrounding space travel	Speaker 2 ☐
D a journalist	Speaker 3 ☐	C a desire to fulfil a lifelong ambition	Speaker 3 ☐
E a professor of science	Speaker 4 ☐	D medical advice on travelling in space	Speaker 4 ☐
F an environmentalist	Speaker 5 ☐	E pride in personal involvement in	Speaker 5 ☐
G a businessman		developments in space	
H a university student		F an explanation of spaceflight procedure	
		G fears about safety in spaceflights	
		H concern that important issues are being ignored	

6 Invert the sentences, beginning with the phrases given.

1 This tough cleaning gel will clean your kitchen surfaces, and also make your pans shine!
Not only _____ .

2 As soon as she opened the door, flames swept into the room.
No sooner _____ .

3 'This is the first time anything like this has happened in this town!' said the Mayor.
'Never before _____ ',
said the Mayor.

4 Visitors must not take photographs inside the museum under any circumstances.
Under no circumstances _____ .

5 This is the only opportunity you will have to buy our product at this price!
Never again _____ !

7 For each of the contexts, choose the sentence you would be most likely to hear.

1 Politician at a press conference:
a 'Never before has the country been more in need of positive action!'
b 'The country really needs some positive action to be taken!'

2 Four-year-old child to mother:
a 'Not once have you let me watch TV this week!'
b 'You haven't let me watch TV once this week!'

3 Newsreader:
a 'Rarely has a politician had such a dramatic effect on opinion polls.'
b 'A politician doesn't often have such a dramatic effect on opinion polls.'

4 Friend to friend:
a 'On no account am I going to Paul's party!'
b 'I'm not going to Paul's party, and that is final!'

8 Turn to audioscript 26 on page 246, and underline the inverted phrases. In which extract does the speaker NOT use inversion?

9 Make the speech in audioscript 26 sound more persuasive by inserting some inverted phrases where appropriate. Make any necessary changes to the sentence structure.

10 Complete the second sentence in these pairs of sentences.

1 This is the first time a game has offered players so many options.
_____ a game offered players so many options.

2 As soon as the President began his speech it started to rain.
_____ the President begun his speech than it started to rain.

3 Students must not talk during the exam.
_____ students talk during the exam.

11 Make the statement more persuasive.

> Commercial space travel is now available to the public, and you can book tickets for the first flight. This is an opportunity for anyone who is interested in space.

▶ GRAMMAR REFERENCE (SECTION 7) **PAGE 213**

SPEAKING discussing possible future developments

12 Discuss. Read the statements and decide whether you agree with them or not. Give reasons for your opinions.

> One day, people will be going on virtual holidays in the comfort of their own home. It could become the only kind of holiday they'll be able to afford!

> Future weekends away will include trips to space station hotels.

> We could soon be coming to Earth 'on holiday'.

> We spend too much time rushing around, and speed in travel seems to be a constant issue. I think people will veer towards the 'go slow' idea of pony trekking, as a reaction to all this.

Speaking, Part 4

13 Discuss. Use the phrases in the Useful Expressions box to express your views about this statement.

> Future weekends away will include trips to space station hotels.

USEFUL EXPRESSIONS

EXPRESSING A VIEW

We can't say for certain how things will be, but …
It's very likely that …
There's a strong possibility that …
Contrary to popular opinion, I think that …
I disagree with the belief that things will …
One day, you may see …
There will still be people who …

WRITING a proposal

Writing, Part 2

1 One of the options in Writing, Part 2, may be a proposal. You will have to write your answer in 220–260 words in an appropriate style. Read this exam question and note some ideas that you might include in an answer. Will your writing be formal or informal in style?

> You work at an art gallery. The number of people visiting the gallery has fallen, and the director has sent you the following email, asking you to help.
>
> > Following our telephone conversation, I raised the matter of improving the gallery in order to attract a wider range of visitors at the Town Council meeting last Friday. They are interested in helping, so could you draw up a proposal outlining your suggestions, so that I can present it to the council?
> > Thanks.
> > Marcia Bond,
> > Gallery Director
>
> Write a **proposal** suggesting the best ways to attract more visitors to the gallery.

2 Compare the two answers (A and B). Look at whether the style and register are appropriate, and how effectively the writers have addressed the request made by the director.

Introduction
Following the Town Council meeting last Friday, here are some suggestions to help us attract a wider range of visitors to the gallery.

Exhibitions
One method we can use is to exhibit a more varied display of artistic work. I think we should include work from a range of contemporary local artists, but we should also vary the art medium, by featuring photography, pieces of sculpture and different tile or textile designs. Perhaps some graphic design could also be featured if we can find some good local examples. To enhance the exhibits, we need to spend some money on improving the lighting in some of the Exhibition Halls.

Workshops for schools
To attract more visits from schools, one thing we could do is to hold painting workshops, with experts displaying their skills and techniques. This may turn out to be rather expensive, however, as extra staff would have to be employed. Another possibility we could consider would be to encourage students of all ages to join our Art Club. A painting competition could be held every term for different age groups, and the winners' work could be displayed in the gallery.

Conclusion
All in all, I feel that the various suggestions that I have mentioned above are practical, and would, over time, bring more visitors to the gallery and thus solve our problems.

B

Introduction
The aim of this proposal is to suggest some practical ways to attract more visitors to the Terrigal Art Gallery.

Exhibitions
First of all, we need to vary the range of artistic work on display in the gallery. Until now, exhibitions have been restricted almost exclusively to paintings, and so have attracted a relatively small group in the community. A good idea would be to offer stimulating alternative art forms. For example, we could hold a photographic exhibition, then one of sculpture, followed by fabric design or possibly graphic design. Not only would this cater for a broader range of contemporary specialist tastes, but the variety would also arouse the interest of the general public.

Workshops for schools
Another idea is to target local schools and hold art workshops on a regular basis. The workshops should be related to a specific exhibition being held in the gallery, with artists demonstrating some of their techniques and giving students an opportunity to practise these in the museum. The costs to the gallery could be kept to a minimum by charging participants a nominal fee. The workshop feature could be further developed by the creation of an Art Club for young people. Through this, painting and photography competitions could be held, with sponsorship from local businesses.

Conclusion
Only by developing a broader range of exhibits, more in line with contemporary interests, can we make the gallery successful once more.

PERSUASIVE LANGUAGE

In a proposal, your answer needs to contain an element of persuasion. You may have to persuade your reader to follow a particular course of action, or you may need to convince them that your idea is a good one.

3 **Discuss. Look back at proposal B. How does the writer make their ideas sound convincing?**

4 **Compare these pairs of sentences. Which pair sounds more persuasive? Why?**

1. a If we implemented these ideas, we would improve museum facilities.
   b This would attract more visitors, and also encourage businesses to invest in the area.
2. a The implementation of such ideas would dramatically improve museum facilities.
   b Not only would this attract more visitors, but it would also encourage businesses to invest in the area.

5 **Use some of the words and structures in the In Other Words box in appropriate ways to make proposal A on page 72 more persuasive.**

6 **Writing, Part 2**

You are a representative of the student union of your college. You have received the email below from the union president, regarding the end-of-year college outing.

As you know, last year's summer trip to the Museum of Antiquities was not popular. Students generally feel this last trip of the year should be fun! Suggestions included a trip to the coast, an adventure theme park and a sightseeing trip around one of the nearby cities. Could you draw up a proposal, outlining the merits of these suggestions, so that I can present it to the college principal?

Thanks,

Peter

Write your proposal in 220–260 words.

IN OTHER WORDS

Displaying … would arouse interest among …

For example, modern innovations in … could be exhibited.

Not only would this … but also …

This would certainly attract …

Costs could be kept to a minimum by …

Only if …

attractive   inspirational   stimulating   innovative   effective

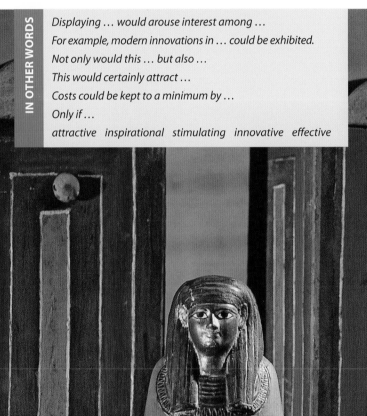

VIDEO our ATM is a goat

1 **Work in two groups. You are visiting a new place for the first time. Make a list of ten things you might find unusual.**

  Group A: You are from New York and you are visiting Kenya for the first time.

  Group B: You are from Kenya and you are visiting New York for the first time.

2 **Work in pairs. Explain to your partner why you would find the things on your list unusual.**

3 **You are going to watch a video about two Kenyans, Boni and Lemarti, on a trip to New York, where they are going to run in the New York marathon. Their guide is a musician, Rene Lopez. Watch and see if the things they find surprising are on your list.**

4 **Watch the video again. Tick the things you see happening.**

  1 Rene shows Boni and Lemarti around his neighbourhood.
  2 The Kenyans are surprised at the high-rise apartment buildings.
  3 The three men take a yellow taxi cab to a bank.
  4 Rene gets some cash from an ATM.
  5 A group of Kenyans take a cow to market.
  6 The three men go to Washington Square park.
  7 People are jogging and running in the park.
  8 Boni and Lemarti are confused by the food at the hot dog stand.

5 Boni and Lemarti ask Rene about different things they see. How would you answer these questions?

1 Why do people live on top of each other?
2 Why do people use ATMs?
3 What's inside a hot dog?

6 Work in pairs. Read the things Boni and Lemarti say. What do they mean?

> 1 Our ATM is a goat.

> 2 You have no dollar, you have no voice.

> 3 People graze like cows here.

7 Work in pairs. Read the statements (a–c) about things that can happen as a result of the comments in exercise 6. Match a–c with the comments (1–3) above. Do you agree that these are possible consequences? Why / Why not?

a People eat more than they need to.
b If you haven't got any money, it's hard to do things.
c People can't spend cash so easily.

SPEAKING Part 4 discussion

IDEAS GENERATOR

FOCUSING YOUR IDEAS TO TALK ABOUT ABSTRACT TOPICS

In Part 4 of the Speaking test the examiner asks several related questions which you discuss with your partner. The questions are about more general or abstract ideas than other parts of the test and might be things you haven't thought about before. One way of preparing for this type of question is to think of some specific consequences of the general point in the question. This is similar to the task you did in exercise 7. This gives you a focus for expressing your opinion. For example:

> *general idea*
>
> people eat non-stop

⬇

> *specific consequence*
>
> people eat more than they need to

⬇

> *opinion*
>
> ?

8 Work in groups. Read the statements below.
Student A: state a possible consequence of the first statement.
Student B: add another consequence.

1 People eat too much processed food.
2 City life is very expensive.
3 Space travel is only for people who have too much money.
4 Budget airlines make air travel easy.
5 People have to move away from their home towns to find work.
6 More people than ever live in a 'virtual' world.

9 Work in groups of three: A, B and C. Read your questions below and write an additional, related question for each one. Then take turns to be the interlocutor and two candidates and discuss the questions.

A
1 Some experts say that people eat too much processed food these days. Do you agree with that statement?
2 What kinds of problems are associated with living in a big city?

B
1 In the future, do you think space travel will become popular with ordinary people?
2 What are some of the advantages or disadvantages of budget air travel?

C
1 These days, people move away from their homes and families to find work. Do you think this is a good idea?
2 What do you think are the advantages and disadvantages of virtual reality?

10 Each person should think about the discussion when they were in the role of the interlocutor. Give feedback to your partners on their performance.

- Could they improve the way they answered the questions? How?
- Could they improve the way they stated their opinions? How?
- Could they improve the way they interacted with their partner? How?

USEFUL EXPRESSIONS

ASKING FOR OPINIONS

Why do you think … ?
What is it about … that makes you say that?
Have you got an opinion about … ?
Do you think … is a good idea?
Do you agree that … ?
What do you think about … ?
I think … . What's your opinion?

VIDEOSCRIPT 7 is on page 255.

MAKING OUR MARK

GETTING STARTED

1 Work in pairs. Think of a world-famous landmark. Use your own words and adjectives from the box to describe it to your partner.

> ancient   awe-inspiring   beautiful
> breathtaking   curious   dominating
> fascinating   grand   imposing   impressive
> massive   modern   mysterious   peculiar
> revealing   stunning   unusual   (un)attractive

READING   understanding opinion

2 Which of the following criteria should be considered by architects planning to build an eco-house? Number a–j in order of importance.

a   aesthetics (appearance)
b   building materials (ecological impact, sustainability)
c   cost (materials, labour)
d   design features (modern or traditional)
e   durability (lifespan of the building)
f   efficiency (insulation, energy costs)
g   environment (surroundings)
h   energy (for construction, pollution)
i   health (toxicity of materials)
j   safety (fire risk, structural reliability)

3 Look at the photo of a house made out of bales of straw. What do you think would be the advantages and disadvantages of building a house like this?

4 ⊙ 27 Listen to somebody listing the benefits of a straw bale house and check your answers to exercise 3. What are the seven main advantages?

UNDERSTANDING OPINION

In the Reading and Use of English paper candidates are expected to show understanding of the writer's opinion, even if the writer's view contradicts other information. You should aim to read the text carefully to understand the main points the writer is making before you read the multiple-choice questions.

5 Read the extract from an information leaflet about straw bale buildings and answer the questions below according to the writer's view. Underline the parts of the text which answer the questions.

1   Why does the writer think that straw bale houses are at 'a pivotal point'? (Para 1)
2   What's the atmosphere like on a straw bale house construction site? (Para 2)
3   What does the writer think are the two main practical advantages of a straw bale house? (Para 3)
4   According to the writer, what kinds of houses are ideally built out of straw? (Para 4)
5   What kind of attitude does the writer think you should adopt when working with straw? (Para 5)
6   Why does the writer think straw bale houses are better for our health? (Para 6)

6 Reading and Use of English, Part 5

For questions 1–6, choose the answer (A, B, C or D) which you think fits best according to the text.

STRAW BALE FUTURES

Straw bale building is a smart way to build. It's more than just a wall building technique that has yet to come into its own. It's a radically different approach to the process of building itself. Like all innovative ideas, it has been pioneered by the passionate, and used experimentally by those with the vision to see its potential. Its background is grassroots self-build; it is firmly based in that sustainable, 'green building' culture that has brought to the construction industry many new and useful ideas about energy efficiency and responsibility towards the environment. It is now at a pivotal point in its development, ready to be taken on by construction firms who see its value in terms of cost-effectiveness, sustainability, ease of installation and energy efficiency. The building method itself is based on a block system, making the designs very easy to adapt from one project to another, and giving great flexibility in its use.

The accessible nature of straw means that people unfamiliar with the building process can now participate in it. This opens the door for interest groups to work together on joint projects. Local authorities and housing associations, for example, are ideal managers for self-build straw projects that won't take years to complete, and which will engender an excitement and motivation that gets the job done. The atmosphere on a straw bale building site is qualitatively different to that found on the vast majority of other sites. It is woman-friendly, joyful, optimistic and highly motivated. Knowledge and skills are freely shared, and co-operation and teamwork predominate, all of which has a positive effect on health and safety on site.

Straw as a building material excels in the areas of cost-effectiveness and energy efficiency. If used to replace the more traditional wall-building system of brick and block, it can present savings of around £10,000 on a normal three-bedroomed house. Of interest to the home owner is the huge reduction in heating costs once the house is occupied, due to the super-insulation of the walls. Here the potential savings are up to 75% compared to a conventional modern house.

One of the biggest attributes of straw bale building is its capacity for creative fun, and its ability to allow you to design and build the sort of shape and space you'd really like. It lends itself very well to curved and circular shapes, and can provide deep window seats, alcoves and niches due to the thickness of the bales. It's also a very forgiving material, can be knocked back into shape fairly easily during wall-raising, doesn't require absolute precision, and can make rounded as well as angular corners. Partly due to its great insulation value and partly because of its organic nature, the inside of a straw bale house feels very different to a brick or stone one, having a cosy, warm quality to it and a pleasing look to the eye.

Straw is a flexible material and requires us to work with it somewhat differently than if it was rigid. Accurate measurement and precision is impossible and unnecessary with straw, but working without these aids can be worrying to the novice, and threatening if you're already used to 21st century building techniques. You have to develop a feel for the straw. You have to give it time, absorb its flexibility. More than any other material (except perhaps cob and clay) it is susceptible to your own spirit and that of the team. Straw bale building is not something to do alone. It requires co-operation, skill-sharing and common sense. Many of the inspirational and artistic features occur in this atmosphere. It is empowering, expanding the world of opportunities for you and making possible what you thought to be impossible!

The atmosphere and environment in which we live is becoming increasingly a matter of concern to homeowners and designers alike. There is a growing body of knowledge on the harmful effects of living long-term with modern materials that give off minute but significant amounts of toxins, the so-called 'sick-building syndrome'. Living in a straw house protects you from all that. It is a natural, breathable material that has no harmful effects. Hay fever sufferers are not affected by straw, as it does not contain pollens. Asthmatics too find a straw bale house a healthier environment to live in. Combined with a sensible choice of natural plasters and paints, it can positively enhance your quality of life.

---

1 According to the first paragraph, straw bale building
- A is a novel variation of standard wall building techniques.
- B developed from experiments to build houses out of grass.
- C is favoured by people who have radically different views.
- D is about to be taken seriously by designers and builders.

2 What does the writer say about building straw bale houses in the second paragraph?
- A Building projects should be managed by authorised groups.
- B A straw bale house can be erected quickly by people working together.
- C There are more women builders on a straw bale site than men.
- D It is only possible to build your own house if you join a co-operative.

3 What does the writer claim about heating costs?
- A Straw bale buildings use far less energy to keep warm than conventional houses.
- B The majority of brick houses do not have super-insulated walls.
- C A conventional family house can cost £10,000 a year to heat.
- D A move from a brick to a straw bale house can reduce heating bills by up to a quarter.

4 What is said about building with straw in the fourth paragraph?
- A It can only be used to build houses that do not need a precise design.
- B It is an ideal material for a variety of organic designs.
- C It has to be used in a particular rounded style of house.
- D It makes traditional stone or brick houses appear colder.

5 The writer insists that when building with straw,
- A it is easy to make mistakes if you don't know the material.
- B novice builders should seek expert advice about building techniques.
- C a good team effort and sense of logic is essential.
- D you are given the power to do anything you want.

6 What does the writer say about air quality?
- A More people are becoming affected by the atmosphere inside their houses.
- B All modern building materials emit poisonous contaminants.
- C A straw bale house can remove the toxins in the air and walls.
- D People with breathing problems would be better off in a straw bale house.

LANGUAGE DEVELOPMENT phrases with *bring*

1 **Complete the sentences with the particles in the box. There is one extra particle.**

> about   back   down   forward   out   on   up

1 Brian always manages to bring _____ the best in his boys, doesn't he?
2 All those industrial strikes in the '70s finally managed to bring _____ the government.
3 It's funny you should bring that _____ – I was just thinking of mentioning it myself.
4 Jackson managed to bring _____ a complete change in the way we worked.
5 Mr Johnson has brought _____ the meeting to this morning at 11 o'clock.
6 They think his illness was brought _____ by all the stress and anxiety in his work.

2 **Match the sentences (1–8) with the definitions (a–h).**

1 They were hoping for a good review; they hadn't expected to bring the house down.
2 Against all the odds, she managed to bring three healthy boys into the world.
3 He added a few jokes to the telling in order to bring it alive.
4 Her tone of voice brought it home to me that we were no longer friends.
5 Listening to that song again brought it all back to me.
6 The smaller children marched in front and Tim and George were told to bring up the rear.
7 Doing a university degree while raising four children nearly brought her to her knees, but she did it!
8 He couldn't bring himself to tell her the truth.

a to make somebody realise something
b to make somebody remember something
c to be the last person in a moving line
d to give birth to
e to make oneself do something difficult
f to make something more interesting
g to greatly impress an audience or critic
h to defeat someone

KEY WORD *that*

> **THAT CAN BE USED:**
>
> 1 as a relative pronoun (instead of *who* or *which*)
> 2 to introduce reported speech
> 3 as a reference device (to refer back to something previously mentioned)
> 4 to refer to something the speaker is physically distant from or not involved in
> 5 after adjectives, to introduce a clause

3 **Match the sentences to the rules in the box above.**

a That smells delicious. What is it?
b They announced that they were going to resume excavations in the spring.
c It's obvious that they will never approve of his house plans.
d We've been invited to a house-warming party by the woman that moved in next door.
e For that reason, we decided it was time to move out.

4 *That* **can often be omitted altogether. Put brackets around the instances of *that* that can be omitted in exercise 3.**

5 **Look back at *Straw Bale Futures* on page 77. Underline the instances of *that*.**

1 How many times can *that* be replaced by *which*?
2 How many times can *that* be replaced by *who / whom*?
3 How many times can *that* be omitted altogether?
4 How many times is *that* used as a reference device?
5 How many times is *that* used to introduce speech?

SPEAKING reaching a decision through negotiation

> **REACHING A DECISION THROUGH NEGOTIATION**
>
> In the Speaking test, Part 3, first you have two minutes to talk about the task with your partner. Then the interlocutor will tell you that you have one minute to make your decision. It can be a good idea to try to persuade your partner to agree with you by giving reasons for your opinion or reasons why you don't agree with their opinion. Be flexible and listen to your partner's ideas too.

6 Read the Student A statements and choose the most suitable response as Student B. Give reasons for your choice.

1 Student A: I think the Parthenon in Athens is the most impressive monument.
   a I don't think it is the most impressive monument. I think the Colosseum is the most impressive monument.
   b I don't disagree with you completely, but personally I prefer the Colosseum because …

2 Student A: I would like to visit the Pyramids in Egypt.
   a Yes, I would too, but actually I think that Machu Picchu has much more to offer because …
   b No, I would like to visit Machu Picchu because it has more to offer.

3 Student A: I would probably choose the Great Wall of China – it has to be the biggest human-made structure on Earth. What about you?
   a No. Stonehenge. It's older.
   b You're definitely right about that, but I'm not sure it would be as fascinating to see as Stonehenge, which …

Speaking, Part 3

7 Work in pairs. Look at the task on page 234. Read the instructions given by the interlocutor in an exam and follow the instructions.

Now, I'd like you to talk about something together for about two minutes. Here are some reasons people give for visiting monuments. Talk to each other about how valid these reasons might be for visiting monuments. You now have some time to look at the task.
(Allow 15 seconds) All right?
(Allow 2 minutes)
Now you have a minute to decide which reason would have the most educational value.

LISTENING interpreting context

> **EXAM SPOTLIGHT**
>
> **Listening, Part 1** Interpreting context
>
> In Listening, Part 1, you may be required to interpret the context of the pieces you hear in order to answer the questions correctly. You may not actually hear the answer in the dialogue, but there will be other verbal clues to help you identify it.

8 ⊙ **28** Listen to a man being interviewed.

The man is
a an architect. b a fine artist. c a philosopher.

Write down three phrases or clues which give away his occupation.

9 You may also hear words or phrases that lead you towards an incorrect answer. Listen to the dialogue again and write down any words or phrases which may lead you to think the other options may be correct. Explain why they are wrong.

10 ⊙ **29** **Listening, Part 1**
You will hear three different extracts, including the one you have just heard. For questions 1–6, choose the answer (A, B or C) which fits best according to what you hear. There are two questions for each extract.

Extract One
You hear a man being interviewed about his work.
1 In connection with his work, the man is proud that
   A it is of use to other people.
   B few other people can do what he does.
   C it has been compared with the work of great artists.
2 He thinks it is important to
   A keep his clients satisfied.
   B make a mark on the landscape.
   C maintain harmony between his work and the landscape.

Extract Two
You hear two people discussing a significant moment in the woman's career.
3 The woman is probably
   A a student.
   B an archaeologist.
   C an explorer.
4 She is describing
   A the moment she made a significant discovery.
   B the main motivations behind the project.
   C an Egyptian artefact excavated 10,000 years earlier.

Extract Three
You hear part of an interview with the rock star Angel Jacobs.
5 Angel is talking about
   A her childhood.
   B her education.
   C her main reason for becoming a rock star.
6 What does Angel regret most about being famous?
   A that she can't be left alone when she wants to be
   B that she can't totally disappear from the public eye
   C that reporters follow her wherever she goes

GRAMMAR relative pronouns / defining and non-defining relative clauses

1 Complete the sentences with *which, who, whose, when* or *where*.

1 That's the man _____ dog keeps following me home.
2 It was almost dark _____ Sam got here.
3 Isn't that the expedition _____ you wanted to go on?
4 If I ever go back to the place _____ I was born, I'll let you know.
5 Is that the man _____ bought your car?

2 In which of the sentences in exercise 1 can the pronoun be replaced by *that* or be omitted altogether?

3 Complete the sentences with one of these phrases.

> all of whom   as a result of which
> at which point   both of whom   by which time
> in which   neither of whom   some of which
> the person whom

1 We arrived at the station at 3.10, _____ the train had left.
2 Julian is _____ I was telling you about.
3 We missed the train, _____ we were both late for work.
4 That's the church _____ my grandparents were married.
5 Two hundred immigrants, _____ were looking for a better life, had fled their homes.
6 Mike and Jill, _____ had ever eaten asparagus before, thought it was delicious.
7 The houses, _____ were still unfinished, were put up for sale.
8 Andy and Karen, _____ are unemployed, have offered to look after my house next summer.
9 We spread out the rug and opened the picnic basket, _____ the rain came pouring down.

▶ GRAMMAR REFERENCE (SECTIONS 8.1 AND 8.2) **PAGE 214**

4 Read the pairs of sentences. Decide which sentence contains a defining relative clause and which contains a non-defining relative clause. What's the difference in meaning between each sentence in the pair?

1 a The Indians, who lived in these parts, respected the land.
   b The Indians that lived in these parts respected the land.
2 a Petra, the architect who built this house, studied in London.
   b The architect that built this house studied in London.
3 a The trees that had been growing for over a century were cut down.
   b The trees, which had been growing for over a century, were cut down.

5 Why are commas used in some of the sentences in exercise 4? What other differences are there between the sentences in each pair?

6 Rewrite each of the following sentences twice, so that the information in brackets is clear in the meaning.

1 The exhibits were in the Egypt section. They were very old.
   (All of them / Some of them)
2 The students got part-time jobs. They wanted some extra money.
   (Some of them / All of them)
3 The girls were waiting for the bus. They were wearing a school uniform.
   (Only one girl / All the girls)
4 The house is going to be knocked down. It has a beautiful garden.
   (There are many houses / Only one house)

reduced relative clauses

7 It is quite usual to alter or reduce sentences which contain a relative clause. Look at the following sentences. What changes have been made?

1 Many species which are growing in the rainforest have not yet been discovered.

   Many species growing in the rainforest have not yet been discovered.

2 The box, which was broken in the accident, was a family heirloom.

   The box, broken in the accident, was a family heirloom.

3 Neil Armstrong was the first man who walked on the moon.

   Neil Armstrong was the first man to walk on the moon.

▶ GRAMMAR REFERENCE (SECTION 8.2) **PAGE 214**

8 Read the sentences and underline the relative clauses. Rewrite each sentence with a reduced relative clause.

1 The tunnel, which was weakened by years of neglect, was no longer considered safe.
2 Children who are attending that school have all their lessons in French.
3 Gillian was the only person who volunteered to help organise the event.
4 Rebecca, who was embarrassed by what she had done, decided not to tell anyone.
5 Adrian, who was expecting to be paid that week, offered to buy drinks for everyone.

USE OF ENGLISH word building (noun groups)

9 Transform the words in the box into nouns using the suffixes below.

combine	cosmic	deliver	dependent
develop	encourage	inhabit	naughty
obsessed	persuade	racist	redundant
sensitive	stupid	tense	tired

-ant -ation -cy -ism -ity -ment -ness
-ology -ry -sion

COMPILING NOUN GROUPS

Be careful! Some nouns have more than one form.

10 Discuss. What do you know about the statue in the photo? Who do you think made it? Why?

11 Reading and Use of English, Part 3

For questions 1–8, read the text below. Use the word given in capitals at the end of some of the lines to form a word that fits in the gap in the same line.

Easter Island – a monumental collapse?

It is a familiar tala of greed, stupidity and self-destruction. For hundreds of years the (1) _____ of one of the most remote islands on Earth vied with each other to build ever more impressive statues, pillaging their resources to feed their obsession. (2) _____ disaster was inevitable. As the island's last tree was (3) _____ , the society collapsed into war, starvation and (4) _____ . Armed with deadly spears, the workers rose up against their rulers. The vanquished were either (5) _____ or eaten.

INHABIT

ECOLOGY

FELL

CANNIBAL

SLAVE

This version of events on Easter Island has become not only received wisdom, but a dark warning about a possible fate for our entire planet. 'The parallels between Easter Island and the whole modern world are (6) _____ obvious,' writes Jared Diamond of the University of California. 'Easter's (7) _____ makes it the clearest example of a society that destroyed itself by overexploiting its own resources.' But is it true or, in our (8) _____ to think the worst of our species, have we been seduced by mythologies?

CHILL

ISOLATE

EAGER

---

12 Discuss. Do you think the people of Easter Island really brought about their own destruction? What else could have happened that led to their disappearance?

13 🔘 30 Listen to the extract and answer the questions. Turn to the audioscript on page 247 and underline the key words that helped you find the answers.

1 The islanders may have _____ with each other by trying to build the biggest statues.

2 There is a lack of _____ to prove that the people of Easter Island brought about their own destruction.

3 The island was 'discovered' on _____ by a Dutch explorer called Jacob Roggeveen.

4 The island had once been home to around _____ palm trees.

5 Due to _____ the trees were all gone by the year 1500.

6 It is thought that _____ , introduced by colonisers, may have eaten the palm nuts.

7 Many of the oral stories contain contradictory information and are therefore considered to be _____ .

8 Missionaries may have _____ the idea that the islanders were cannibals.

9 What some people consider to be spearheads may in fact have been made for _____ purposes.

WRITING a review

1 Discuss. What type of buildings can you see in your home city? Do you prefer old buildings or modern buildings? What's the most memorable building you have visited and how did you feel when you were there?

THE PURPOSE AND STRUCTURE OF A REVIEW

The main purpose of a review is to tell readers something about the subject of the review and give an opinion on it. Your readers may use your review to decide whether or not they wish to visit a certain place or see a certain film, etc. A review should be written in paragraphs so that it is easy for the reader to follow. Use the information in the task to decide what aspects you need to include in your review, then organise your paragraphs around these.

Writing, Part 2

2 Read the exam question and answer the questions.

1. What topic should you write about?
2. What information should you give about it?
3. How could you organise your paragraphs?

You read this announcement in your college magazine.

Interesting buildings

People differ in their views about the age of the buildings they like to visit and the different types of architecture that interest them. We have decided to publish a collection of reviews of 'interesting buildings' and we are inviting you to participate. Send in a review describing the most interesting building you know. Tell us about the age and appearance of the building, and explain why you think it is so interesting.

---

3 Read the review that was written by someone from Spain, describing a well-known building there. Have they included all the information and dealt with the task in the same way that you planned in exercise 2?

Even for Spanish people, a trip to the famous Sagrada Familia in Barcelona is a special treat. It is incredibly tall and very impressive and, if you go to Barcelona, it is the one place that I would recommend you see.

This enormous temple was built by the famous architect Gaudi and is over 100 years old. In fact, Gaudi died in 1926 before he had finished his remarkable construction, so if you do go, don't be surprised to see that architects and builders are still working on its completion and there is some scaffolding around parts of it.

From a distance, it looks unreal – rather like a fairy castle, with its astonishingly tall, conical towers that seem to disappear into the skyline. Once you get a closer look, you see that the whole façade is covered in a range of intricate sculptures of religious scenes and figures. But nothing will prepare you for the view inside, which is absolutely spellbinding. The internal columns rise up to the roof forming a geometrical design and a dazzling array of colours.

The Sagrada Familia is unique – there is nothing like it anywhere else in the world, and this is what makes it so special. You may see a picture of it and gasp, but when you are actually there, it is an astonishing experience that you will always remember.

4 In what ways is a review different from an essay?

BRAINSTORMING VOCABULARY

Examiners will be looking for good use of descriptive language, so think carefully about the words you use. Before you start writing it's a good idea to brainstorm descriptive adjectives and phrases that you could use.

5 Read the review again and underline all the descriptive adjectives and phrases.

6 Brainstorm. Write down three or four adjectives or phrases to describe the following in your country, town or city.

1 houses
2 apartment blocks
3 places of worship
4 public buildings
5 schools and universities
6 shops and restaurants

AVOIDING REPETITION

In order not to sound repetitive, it's a good idea to substitute synonyms for a particular word that you may be using repeatedly. The following words can all mean 'the place / area or building where someone or something lives'.

abode   dwellings   habitat
housing   lodgings   place   residence

7 Use a dictionary to compare differences in meaning between the words in the In Other Words box. Then complete these sentences using the words in the box.

1 The _____ provided by the council was in very poor condition.
2 The natives live in hut _____ made from natural materials.
3 In its natural _____ the elephant lives for over 70 years.
4 Buckingham Palace is the Queen's formal place of _____ in London.
5 He claimed he had no telephone and no fixed _____ .
6 He invited me back to his _____ but told me to be quiet so as not to disturb his landlady.

Writing, Part 2

8 Read the exam question and write your review in 220–260 words. Spend time planning the paragraph layout and headings, and brainstorm vocabulary before you begin.

One of your professors is writing a book on the architecture of different types of home around the world. She has asked your class to contribute to her book.
Write a review of the oldest or the newest homes in your city. Describe the buildings themselves and explain why they are architecturally interesting.

REVIEW 2

1 Complete the sentences with one of the verbs from the box. There are two extra words you do not need to use.

> confess   confide   consume   convict
> contemplate   digest   enhance   erect
> incite   overlook   run   sustain

1 The man they were holding in custody eventually _____ to the crime.
2 If you eat fruit after a meal it will be harder for the stomach to _____ it.
3 The temple was probably _____ in honour of a goddess.
4 A number of essential nutrients are needed to _____ life.
5 Their relationship had _____ its course so they parted as friends.
6 Taking up some form of exercise will _____ your quality of life.
7 In the West we _____ far too much junk food.
8 Lillian promised to _____ her secret to me if I told her mine.
9 The police don't yet have enough evidence to _____ him.
10 A few people tried to _____ the crowd to start shouting.

2 Complete the sentences with a correct form of a verb from the box, and one or more particles to form a phrasal verb that means the same as the word in brackets.

> bring x 3   look x 2   turn x 3

1 Harold has proposed to Madge six times but she keeps _____ him _____ . (refuse)
2 We can't _____ _____ a change if no one is prepared to adapt their working styles. (create)
3 I have always really _____ _____ Grant. (admire)
4 It would be great if they _____ _____ sixties fashions! (revived)
5 This has _____ _____ to be one of the happiest days of my life! (become)
6 I promised Michael I would _____ _____ the mystery of what's been eating his lettuces! (investigate)
7 I'm absolutely exhausted. I think I'll _____ _____ . (go to bed)
8 It was tactless of Augusta to _____ _____ the subject of her wedding. (mention)

3 Replace the underlined parts of the sentences with an expression using the word in capitals.

1 If you don't tell me what you did with the money I'm going to tell someone your secret.
   BEANS
2 Even though we are all aware of the suffering that exists in the world, most of us choose to ignore it.
   LOOK
3 I wouldn't do something that might lead to trouble if I were you.
   ROAD
4 Martha would do absolutely anything at all for Robbie.
   LIFE
5 Seeing that photo of the children made me realise how quickly they grow up!
   BROUGHT
6 Sam is getting better after his operation.
   ROAD
7 Slow down! I think you've taken on a larger burden than you can cope with!
   CHEW
8 Just because his father owns the company, it doesn't mean that Julian can do whatever he likes!
   ABOVE

4 Choose the best word from the options A, B, C or D to complete the sentences.

1 The most _____ moment of my life was when I stood on the top of Everest!
   A appealing
   B awe-inspiring
   C unusual
   D stunning
2 The view from the top of the Empire State Building is _____ !
   A breathtaking
   B sparkling
   C revealing
   D threatening
3 Despite its history, Cairo is a fascinating, _____ modern city.
   A breathless
   B shoddy
   C crumbling
   D industrious
4 There was a / an _____ air of mystery surrounding the Inca temple.
   A mysterious
   B eerie
   C unique
   D remarkable
5 I felt so small and insignificant, standing under the _____ structure of the Eiffel Tower.
   A peculiar
   B curious
   C imposing
   D impressive

5 Complete the sentences with one of the verbs from the box and a particle. There are two extra words you do not need to use.

accuse	bring	charge	deter	resort	turn

1 Miriam tried to _____ Rupert _____ going to the police.
2 Arnold _____ Ethel _____ eating the last cookie.
3 The plumber had to _____ _____ the the water supply before he fixed the leaking bath.
4 Police have not _____ Liam _____ burglary, but they are holding him for further questioning.
5 I've _____ _____ paying my teenagers to help with the housework.
6 The police are _____ _____ the date of Bobby Dazzler's trial.

6 Reading and Use of English, Part 3

For questions 1–8, read the text below. Use the word given in capitals at the end of some of the lines to form a word that fits in the gap in the same line.

What should we eat?

A good diet is crucial for our health. Yet it seems we have a number of (1) _____ about   PRECONCEIVE
what's good for us and what isn't. Most people assume that the
(2) _____ of great   CONSUME
quantities of fish and meat will provide us with plenty of protein. The truth is that cooking meat and fish all the way through results in the (3) _____ of   DESTROY
up to 95% of its protein content. In fact, most plant foods can provide us with all the protein we need. We also believe that our (4) _____ systems were   DIGEST
designed for large heavy meals high in animal protein. Actually, our very long intestine is ideal for breaking down plant foods, but not animal proteins.

Eating plenty of raw fruit and vegetables allows for the
(5) _____ of our immune   RESTORE
system, and can (6) _____   STRONG
it after illness or stress. This in turn ensures the body receives proper (7) _____ , protects   MAINTAIN
us from disease and reduces the number of times we have to rely on (8) _____ drugs.   PRESCRIBE

7 Reading and Use of English, Part 4

For questions 1–6, complete the second sentence so that it has a similar meaning to the first sentence, using the word given. Do not change the word given. You must use between three and six words, including the word given.

1 'I didn't burn the house down!' said June.
   ON
   June _____ fire.
2 Alison continued to talk for hours about her children.
   WENT
   Alison _____ her children for hours.
3 If Jasper hadn't warned me about the dog, I would have stroked it.
   WARNING
   But _____ touch the dog, I would have stroked it.
4 No matter what happens, you mustn't open this door.
   ACCOUNT
   On _____ open this door.
5 This is the best opera I have ever seen.
   HAVE
   Never _____ a good opera.
6 Timmy and Paul have started a business even though they don't have any experience.
   WHOM
   Timmy and Paul, _____ any experience, have started a business.

8 Write the verb that collocates with each word or phrase.

1 _____ offence / the initiative / into account
2 _____ harm / good / wonders for
3 _____ a risk / its course / for government
4 _____ fun of / a mistake / an effort
5 _____ rise to / credit / notice
6 _____ to pieces / into disrepair / from grace

BRUSHSTROKES AND BLUEPRINTS

GETTING STARTED

1 **What styles of art and design do you particularly like? Why?**

READING understanding tone and implication in a text

UNDERSTANDING TONE AND IMPLICATION

At first glance, a writer's attitude towards what they are writing about is not always clear. Below are three of the main ways in which a writer may express their views indirectly.

1 Use of positive or negative vocabulary to describe something
2 Presenting an opposing point or opinion in order to refute it
3 Leaving something unexpressed when describing feelings in a narrative

2 **Match the extracts (A–C) to one of the techniques (1–3) in the tip box.**

A Wellington boots, and the people who wear them, are the subject of many a comedian's funny stories. After all, they're not very stylish, and certainly don't show off the shape of your legs. Yet put yourself in the middle of a muddy field on a wet Sunday afternoon, and you'll soon feel differently about them.

B 'I'm leaving you, Petunia,' he said. Words momentarily failed her, but she quickly recovered her composure. 'If that's what you want, Geoffrey,' she replied simply.

C This eyesore of a building, a blot in an otherwise attractive urban landscape, is said to be at the cutting edge of architectural design.

3 Answer the questions.

1 In extract A, does the writer think that wellington boots are
  a funny?
  b useful?

2 In extract B, how does Petunia react?
  a She is indifferent to the man's revelation.
  b She tries to conceal her feelings.

3 In extract C, the writer
  a likes the building.
  b dislikes the building.

4 Reading and Use of English, Part 6

You are going to read four reviews of an art exhibition. For questions 1–4, choose from the reviews A–D. The reviews may be chosen more than once.

Which reviewer

1 shares reviewer A's opinion about the interest value of Daniels's paintings?

2 has a different opinion from the others about the visual impact of the size of the paintings?

3 takes a similar view to reviewer C on the matter of how well Daniels puts his artistic abilities to use?

4 expresses a different view from the others regarding Daniels's use of a particular medium?

William Daniels Four reviewers comment on William Daniels's solo exhibition

TEXT A William Daniels's solo exhibition of paintings is almost too tedious to write about. He has created a series of eight irritatingly tiny oil paintings based on classical arches, the only slight differences between them being their colour and whether the foreground or background is emphasised. Each motif is composed of dozens of different but related colours. In one arch alone, red, blue and green fold into each other yet don't compete. The guy's got skill. Too bad it's employed to such redundant ends. Maybe it's a question of misplaced methods. More interesting is the process Daniels uses to make the work. First, he forms a kind of sculpture out of foil. Taking a picture of the scene, he then paints sections of the photographs onto board. Photographs of his creations are more alluring than the resulting flat canvases, which raises the question of why Daniels is painting at all.

TEXT B William Daniels's latest solo show is based on making a non-referential aluminium setup which is photographed and then painted. His works are highly intricate renderings of the shapes and colours reflected in and created by the folds of the foil. They are all untitled and very small, yet each one becomes a monument on the wall it occupies – perhaps even a commentary on the blankness of the wall itself. Each piece is a wonder of astounding colour and shape relationships, revealed through careful and extensive examination. Every square inch is afforded the same attention as the next. Far from dull, this endless array is precisely what makes the work so appealing. The colours seem to emerge from another, unknown dimension, expressing the fact that they have been observed, not directly but through reflection.

TEXT C 'I thought they'd be bigger!' exclaimed one visitor to William Daniels's solo show of oil-on-board paintings, none bigger than 33 centimetres square. In reproductions, Daniels's images of angular metallic surfaces grab attention. In person, the tiny pieces dotting the walls of the main gallery seem shallow, evoking nothing deeper than shiny candy wrappers or coloured lights glinting off a polished surface. Despite the pretty hues, the subject matter is monotonous; a style that's especially frustrating when the objects are hard to distinguish from their backgrounds and merge into shallow planes of crinkly foil. Daniels rejects references to the outside world, creating little models of light and colour, calculated to break boundaries between abstraction and representation, painting and sculpture, by being all these at once. Undoubtedly, this show proves Daniels's painterly ability and experimental creativity. But his latest work is, unfortunately, literally reflective, and not metaphorically so. Ultimately, while Daniels's paintings connect with contemporary fashion, they have disappointingly little to say.

TEXT D William Daniels's recent work is his most compelling to date. Each of his small, understated paintings is a depiction of a lightly crumpled bit of tin foil on a stage-like setting, illuminated by indirect coloured lights. More than a mere struggle between abstraction and realism, the result is a rich blend of painting, sculpture, photography and theatre. Daniels knows how to work the brush, how to fit its movement to the task at hand. At close range, his surfaces swarm with tinted greys and flashes of strong colour. In the flattened canvas, the object's irregular, meandering outline is difficult to pick out. Only at a distance does one detect a slight softening of contours in the areas outside the crumpled form. Is Daniels critiquing current art practice with these alluring surfaces that possess no colour of their own but merely reflect their surroundings?

LANGUAGE DEVELOPMENT compound words

1 Join words from group A with words from group B to make compound nouns. In some cases, more than one combination may be possible.

A
paper   roof   wind   desk   finger   foot

B
print   top   nail   top   mill   clip

COMPOUND WORDS

When we join two nouns together to form a compound noun, no hyphen (-) is usually required, e.g. *paperclip*. You may see a hyphen used for some activities, such as *bird-watching* or *train-spotting*.

When we form a compound adjective, we often need to insert a hyphen between the words we are joining, especially when the two words are different types (noun + verb), e.g. *radio-controlled*.

We often create compound adjectives in order to say what we want more briefly, e.g. *design that is done with the help of a computer = computer-aided design*.

2 Match the compound adjectives in the box with the definitions (1–5).

all-purpose   computer-controlled   everyday
stand-in   time-wasting

1 that is used regularly in our daily lives
2 that is operated through a machine
3 that can be used in many ways
4 that takes up time unnecessarily
5 that is used as a replacement for something

3 Complete the sentences with compound words from exercises 1 and 2.

1 After leaving the building, the thief left muddy _____ on the driveway, which helped the police to find him.
2 Julia Roberts is ill, so we'll have to use a _____ actress for today's rehearsal.
3 The Swiss Army knife is a useful, _____ tool, which is indispensable on camping trips.
4 Attach these papers together with a _____ .
5 I broke my _____ trying to get the lid off the jar.
6 The cat climbed to the top of the building, and leapt across the _____ to escape from the dog.

evaluative adjectives and adverbs

4 These adjectives were used in the texts on page 87. Are they used to express a positive evaluation, a negative evaluation, or are they neutral?

Text A: *tedious, misplaced, alluring*
Text B: *intricate, astounding, extensive, dull, appealing*
Text C: *shallow, shiny, monotonous, frustrating, reflective*
Text D: *compelling, understated, crumpled, rich, alluring*

KEY WORD *pay*

5 Choose the most suitable word or phrase to complete the sentences.

1 In his speech, the headmaster paid _____ to the hard work of the students who had participated in the school play.
   a homage
   b attention
   c tribute

2 All I did was pay _____ about how attractive you look today, and you slap my face!
   a you respect
   b you a compliment
   c my respects to you

3 Look, if you can just take me with you to Paris, I promise I'll pay _____ the trip.
   a the penalty for
   b my way on
   c through the nose for

6 **Explain the meaning of the phrases in italics in these sentences.**

Hi, Tanya! I thought I'd *pay you a visit* on my way back from Moscow. Will you be home?

Solar heating is quite expensive to install, but after the first three years, it starts to *pay for itself*.

LISTENING interview about an artist

7 **Discuss. How do you feel about the kind of art shown in the photos? What do you like or dislike about it?**

8 🔊 **31** **Listen to two people discussing one of the pieces shown in the photos above. Which photo are they talking about?**

UNDERSTANDING STATED OPINION

In Listening, Part 3, some questions may require an understanding of the speaker's opinion of the subject they are talking about. You need to listen carefully and decide whether the speaker is criticising something or praising it.

9 **From what the speakers say, we understand that**

a they both like the powerful use of materials in the piece.

b Joe doesn't think the colours in the piece are garish.

c Clare thinks the piece is bulky.

d Joe is impressed by the symbolism in the piece.

10 🔊 **32** **Listening, Part 3**

Listen to an interview about Vasilis Kapodistrias, the artist whose work is shown in the photographs. For questions 1–6, choose the answer (A, B, C or D) which fits best according to what you hear.

1 George describes Kapodistrias's art as
   A a way of making sculpture popular.
   B influencing another artist.
   C appealing to more than one of the senses.
   D a reflection of the artist's mood.

2 When did Kapodistrias become interested in three-dimensional art?
   A while he was studying photography at university
   B after he became tired of painting landscapes
   C as a boy, while watching his father painting
   D after using a range of techniques

3 One reason for Kapodistrias's present choice of materials is
   A the fact that they are long-lasting.
   B a desire to increase awareness of their different uses.
   C his use of them in his work as a dentist.
   D a sense of responsibility towards the environment.

4 What does George say about how Kapodistrias approaches painting?
   A He is influenced by techniques he has studied in art courses.
   B He aims to evoke particular responses in other people to his work.
   C He is inspired by the shape of the materials that are available.
   D He starts work without having a particular outcome in mind.

5 According to George, one reason why Kapodistrias has not held an exhibition is that
   A he is concerned about how other people might react.
   B he thinks the publicity would distract him.
   C he would be embarrassed if his work doesn't sell.
   D he feels his work is too personal to be shared with other people.

6 What is George's opinion of Kapodistrias's work?
   A He believes it requires too much effort from the viewer.
   B He does not share the general attitude towards it.
   C He thinks Kapodistrias will soon be recognised as a major artist.
   D He does not like certain aspects of it.

GRAMMAR changing sentence structure: change in emphasis, or different meaning?

1 **Compare the sentence below with the two sentences that follow it. Which one has a different meaning?**

The paperclip has yet to be superseded by some modish, bleeping computer-controlled device.

1 Yet another modish, bleeping, computer-controlled device has superseded the paperclip.

2 A modish, bleeping, computer-controlled device has not superseded the paperclip yet.

2 **Compare the pairs of sentences. How do changes in structure or punctuation affect meaning?**

1 a As I thought, this poem wasn't written by W.H. Auden.
   b This poem wasn't written by W.H. Auden as I'd thought.

2 a Karl started learning to drive two years ago.
   b Karl has been driving for two years.

3 a It was Sally that borrowed my Shakira CD.
   b It was my Shakira CD that Sally borrowed.

4 a Paul bought the painting which had belonged to an Italian nobleman.
   b Paul bought the painting, which had belonged to an Italian nobleman.

5 a She'd paint flowers and trees unlike the others in her class.
   b She'd painted flowers and trees, unlike the others in her class.

3 **◉ 33** **Listen to the pairs of sentences. In each case, what is the effect of the changes?**

1 a I don't know where she finds the time to do all those activities.
   b Where she finds the time to do all those activities, I don't know.

2 a Although this exercise may seem boring, it is useful.
   b Boring though this exercise may seem, it is useful.

3 a You need a complete break from the office.
   b What you need is a complete break from the office.

4 a They are creating unnecessary waste.
   b What they are doing is creating unnecessary waste.

5 a Don't get upset. You just need to go and talk to your teacher about the problem.
   b Don't get upset. All you need to do is talk to your teacher about the problem.

4 **◉ 34** **Listen to this sentence read with varying intonation. How does the meaning of each sentence differ?**

Vincent Van Gogh cut off his ear after a quarrel with his good friend Gauguin.

5 **Write the question that might have been asked to obtain each sentence as an answer.**

▶ GRAMMAR REFERENCE (SECTION 9) **PAGE 215**

USE OF ENGLISH key word transformation

Reading and Use of English, Part 4 Key word transformation

In this part of the Reading and Use of English paper you are sometimes asked to transform a sentence in a way which makes it more emphatic. It is important to make sure that the changes you make do not alter the meaning of the sentence.

6 **Transform the sentences. Make sure that the second sentence has the same meaning as the first one.**

1 Mary said Pete crashed her car last night.
   WHO
   According to _____ crashed her car last night.

2 Although it's cold, we're still going rowing.
   MAY
   Cold _____ still going rowing.

7 **Reading and Use of English, Part 4**

For questions 1–6, complete the second sentence so that it has a similar meaning to the first sentence, using the word given. Do not change the word given. You must use between three and six words, including the word given.

1 I like going on holiday, but not the journey.
   WHAT
   I like going on holiday, _____ is the journey.

2 'Paul didn't break the window, John did', said Claire.
   TO
   According _____ who broke the window.

3 She has so many commitments that I can't understand how she manages to stay calm.
   HOW
   With all her commitments, _____ is a mystery to me.

4 Susan's music is bothering the neighbours, not me.
   BUT
   It's _____ Susan is bothering with her music.

5 Even if it rains, we won't cancel the match.
   MAY
   Rain _____ won't be cancelled.

6 Some children in Class 3 painted pictures of the sea and won an award.
   WHOSE
   The children in Class 3 _____ won an award.

SPEAKING suggesting solutions, justifying ideas

8 Discuss. Colours symbolise different things in different cultures. What do you associate black and white with in your culture?

9 Match the colours in the box with the emotional associations (1–10) that are suitable for you.

black	blue	green	grey	lavender
navy blue	orange	purple	red	yellow

1 is cool and calm, and is associated with making time pass more quickly
2 is known for raising blood pressure, and is associated with excitement and danger
3 is associated with sophistication and rebelliousness
4 is associated with happiness, but also cowardice and deceit
5 is warm and encouraging, and is often associated with transition
6 is calm and gentle, and is associated with women and nostalgia
7 is a balance between cool and warm colours, and is associated with being unique and mysterious
8 is cool and calm, and is associated with balance, harmony and stability
9 is a neutral colour, and seldom evokes strong emotion
10 is a strong, dominant colour, associated with importance and confidence

10 Work in pairs. Which colour would you choose to decorate these rooms?
- a bedroom
- a living room
- a kitchen
- a classroom

Speaking, Part 3

11 Work in pairs. Here are some proposals for the front cover of a book on contemporary house design. Discuss how suitable these proposals might be for the cover. Use the In Other Words box to try and persuade your partner to agree with you. Talk together for two minutes.

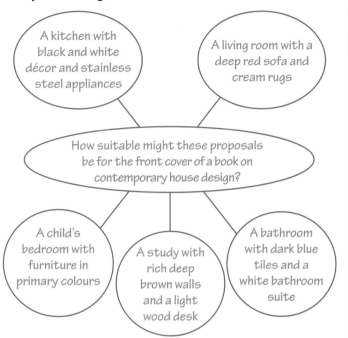

A kitchen with black and white décor and stainless steel appliances

A living room with a deep red sofa and cream rugs

How suitable might these proposals be for the front cover of a book on contemporary house design?

A child's bedroom with furniture in primary colours

A study with rich deep brown walls and a light wood desk

A bathroom with dark blue tiles and a white bathroom suite

Now you have a minute to decide which proposal you think is the most suitable for the front cover.

IN OTHER WORDS

EMPHATIC PHRASES

Emphatic phrases can be persuasive. Compare the following sentences:
An effective front cover is needed to make people want to read the book.
What's needed is an effective front cover to make people want to read the book.
What's needed here is X.
It's X that will attract …

12 Use the phrases in the In Other Words box to make the sentences more emphatic.
1 A bright child's bedroom is something that will attract people's attention.
2 Strong colours create an impression of dynamic creativity.
3 A cool, calm bathroom is what appeals to most people.
4 A photo of a kitchen in contrasting colours is needed.
5 I think it should be kept simple.
6 One bold design on a neutral background will make people curious.
7 Let's choose colours which reflect sophistication and originality.
8 Warm, inviting colours will stimulate interest.

WRITING supporting your ideas in an essay

1 Discuss. Art is considered by many people to be an important part of life. Do you agree? Explain why.

2 Read the exam question.

Writing, Part 1

Your seminar group has had a discussion on the value of different art forms to society. You have made the notes below:

> **Art forms**
> - photography
> - music
> - painting
>
> **Some views expressed during the discussion:**
> 'Photographs provide us with lasting images to remind us of events.'
> 'Music is an important form of self-expression.'
> 'Some famous paintings are invaluable.'

> Write an essay for your tutor discussing two of the art forms in your notes. You should explain which art form you think has most value for society and provide reasons to support your opinion.
> You may, if you wish, refer to the views expressed during the discussion, but you should use your own words as far as possible.

3 Look at this table showing the ideas for a paragraph on the value of photography. Add some of your own ideas to the plan.

	Reasons for importance	Examples
Photography	shots of key events	sporting triumphs
	instant emotions	people's faces

4 Read the paragraph and underline the words / phrases that the writer uses to incorporate supporting points.

Since the invention of photography, we have valued people who are skilled at this art. The main reason for this is that a good photograph can capture a key moment in a story or event in a way that other art forms cannot. Take the Olympic Games, for instance. Newspapers around the world were full of photographs showing the moments of victory that occurred. At the same time, we experienced the feelings of joy, despair and exhaustion that the competitors went through by looking at photographs of their facial expressions. In many areas of life, photographers provide us with split-second impressions of emotion and behaviour that we can keep for all time.

5 What is the purpose of the last sentence in the paragraph in exercise 4?

IN OTHER WORDS

USEFUL LANGUAGE FOR INTRODUCING REASONS AND EXAMPLES

The main reason for this is …
This is because …
One of the main reasons why …
Another reason why …
For this reason, …

Take for example … / Take … for example.
One example of this is …
For example, … / For instance, …
such as …

6 Complete the paragraph about painting with expressions from the In Other Words box.

Painting differs from photography in that the artist has to produce the content so, (1) _____ , I would argue that painting is a more challenging skill. (2) _____ , not everyone can produce the sort of painting that they would like to hang in their home or workplace, but we do sometimes frame our own photographs and display them. (3) _____ painting is important is that it has such a rich history as an art form. The museums of the world are full of ancient paintings and they can be worth huge sums of money. In fact, paintings (4) _____ the Mona Lisa are global treasures and almost beyond monetary value.

7 Write the notes for the painting paragraph.

8 Write an introduction and a conclusion for the essay.

9 Writing, Part 1

Your class has attended a lecture on art-based activities for children. You have made the notes below:

Activities
- learning poems
- drawing pictures
- visiting art museums

Some points raised during the lecture:
'Many people remember the poems they learnt as children.'
'Children need the creative outlet of drawing.'
'Museums can help children appreciate good art.'

Write an essay for your tutor discussing two of the activities in your notes. You should explain which activity you think has most to offer young children and provide reasons to support your opinion.
You may, if you wish, refer to the points raised during the lecture, but you should use your own words as far as possible.

Read the exam question above. Choose two of the activities and brainstorm some ideas. Then write your answer using the In Other Words box to help you support your opinions.

VIDEO Aboriginal rock art

1 Describe what you can see in the photo. Who do you think made this artwork?

2 Work in pairs. Student A, read paragraph A and answer question 1. Student B, read paragraph B and answer question 2. Then tell your partner the answers to your question, giving information from the paragraphs to support your answer.

1 Why is art relevant to Australian Aborigines?
2 Where do you think the rock art shown in the photo is from?

A

The Aboriginal people settled in Australia about 55,000 years ago and their cultural history stretches back further than any other group of people. Aboriginal society has a long tradition of passing on knowledge, cultural values and beliefs through a combination of drawing, oral story-telling, song and dance.

B

Aboriginal rock paintings are found across Australia but can be divided into three main styles, according to geographical regions. In Queensland the typical rock art shows human and animal forms, whereas in Central Australia circles and dots are more characteristic. In Arnhem Land, in the north of the country, the rock paintings show complex and detailed figures.

3 Watch the video and answer the questions.

1 What are the men looking for as they fly over Arnhem Land?
2 How old is Aboriginal rock art?
3 What does the anthropologist say about the quality of the art they look at?
4 What do the drawings represent?
5 What is the relevance of the Rainbow Serpent?
6 How are the paintings connected to Aboriginal stories?

4 Watch the video again. Check and expand your answers to the questions in exercise 3.

5 Complete the paragraph with five of the expressions in the box.

> more and more   one of the most important
> particularly   there are fewer and fewer
> there are hundreds of   there is a danger that

(1) _____ sites in Arnhem Land with rock paintings depicting different aspects of the Dreaming – rivers and mountains, humans and social order. (2) _____ Dreaming stories is that of the Rainbow Serpent, who was regarded as the creator of all things and is (3) _____ connected with water. These days, as (4) _____ tribal elders who can speak the original languages, (5) _____ some of the Dreaming may be lost to future generations.

6 Work in pairs. Compare the way your society or community passes on knowledge and beliefs with what you have learnt about Aborigines. What are the most important means of communication in your case?

SPEAKING Part 3 collaborative task

IDEAS GENERATOR

MAKING A DECISION

In Part 3 of the Speaking test you need to negotiate with your partner to try and reach a decision. This is similar to the task you did in exercise 6. To develop the discussion in Part 3, you also need to talk about how your ideas relate to each other in order to choose the most important, popular, successful etc. You can prepare for this by comparing things. For example, look at the three ideas for a wedding present (1–3) and decide which adjectives (a–f) describe them.

1 a cartoon-style drawing of the couple
2 a 3-D photo of the couple
3 a ceramic model of the couple

a artistic
b fun
c personal
d realistic
e stylish
f valuable

Look at the Useful Expressions box and complete the first five comments with ideas about the wedding presents.

7 Work in pairs. Discuss the wedding present ideas and decide which is the best present, in your opinion. Use all of the expressions in the Useful Expressions box.

USEFUL EXPRESSIONS

NEGOTIATING

One thing I think is important / useful / worth considering is …
Perhaps X is more … than Y.
I don't think that X is as … as Y.
Would you agree that … ?
What do you feel is … ?
Is there anything else you can think of?

8 Work in groups of four. Choose one of the tasks, A or B.

A
You work in a shop in Australia that sells souvenirs to tourists. Look at the list of products and add three more. Then decide which products to promote in the window display of the shop. Consider quality, price, design, the shop's target market and any other aspect you think relevant.

- bottle openers
- calendars
- key rings
- mini boomerangs
- mugs
- socks
- T shirts
-
-
-

B
Your school is organising an arts and crafts weekend for unemployed teenagers. Look at the list of activities and add one more. Then decide which four activities to offer. Consider the appeal to young people, skills needed, costs involved and any other aspect you think relevant.

- dress design
- photography
- portrait painting
- pottery
- toy making
- T-shirt printing
- web page design
-
-
-

9 Work in pairs. Do the other task in exercise 8. Compare your decision with the other pair from your group.

VIDEOSCRIPT 9 is on page 255.

10 THE GOOD LIFE

GETTING STARTED

1 What do you understand by ethical living? Do you live ethically? What factors do you think contribute to an ethical lifestyle?

READING gapped text

2 Discuss. 'Quality of life' versus 'quality time'. How much should spouses or parents be willing to sacrifice in order to provide a comfortable and secure lifestyle for their families?

EXAM SPOTLIGHT

Reading and Use of English, Part 7
Text structure, paragraph cohesion and coherence

Part 7 of the Reading and Use of English paper is designed specifically to test a student's understanding of the way a text is structured. It's therefore important to be aware of the way that paragraphs are joined together (cohesion) in such a way that they make sense (coherence).

3 The article that follows can be divided into three clear sections, each section talking about a different family. Skim read the text and the missing paragraphs on page 97 to complete the information below.

Last name of family
1 *Chitnis*   2   3
Names of the couple
1   2   3
Information about the children
1   2   3

4 What effect has long-distance separation had on each family?

PARAGRAPH COHESION

Writers use a variety of techniques to join their paragraphs together in a coherent manner. These techniques include:

*   reference devices: *this, that, one of these …*
*   names of people, places, organisations, or pronouns: *Jane, Moscow, the hospital, he …*
*   time indications: *Two years later, After that …*
*   continuity of theme: *It was for this reason that …*
*   linking words: *furthermore, therefore …*

5 Read missing paragraph A. Underline any key words that may help reveal where in the original text it belongs. Who does *he* refer to? Does this help you find where the paragraph belongs?

6 Look back at the main article and underline any key words or reference devices at the beginning and end of paragraphs.

EXAM SPOTLIGHT

Reading and Use of English, Part 7
Odd paragraphs

Remember that there will be one extra paragraph that does not fit in anywhere. You need to be careful because there will be words or themes similar to the main text that might confuse you.

7 Read missing paragraph B. Underline any key words or phrases. Which of the three families is it referring to? Does it refer to anything mentioned in the main text?

8 Read missing paragraph C. Who is mentioned here? Is this person mentioned anywhere in the main text or in any other paragraph? What kind of information is given here?

LONG DISTANCE FAMILIES

You want the kids to grow up in the country and live in a nice house, but you could never afford it without your metropolitan salary.

Anthony Chitnis is one of a growing UK tribe of long-distance dads: fathers (and it almost always is fathers) who live apart from their family for all or part of the week because their job is based hundreds of miles away. So for Anthony, Tuesday is the day when he kisses his wife and three children goodbye for three days: and he doesn't like what that means for any of them.

1 […]

Leaving Jane and the children behind for half of every week hasn't, Anthony admits, got any easier. 'The truth is that I just miss them all an awful lot. I'm lucky – I've got a small flat in London. But it's not home. You phone a lot, but it's hard.'

2 […]

The Chitnises are both extremely supportive of the other's point of view: what's more, Jane's parents live next door, so she has plenty of practical back-up when Anthony is away. But even they are finding long-distance family life tough going, and they're certainly not alone.

3 […]

These considerations played a major role for the Yardley family when Jonathan, a marketing director, arrived home and said he'd been offered an exciting new job – in Germany. 'It was a good career move for him,' says Jean. 'But we knew uprooting our four children would be impossible. We thought it would work: he'd be home every weekend.' And at first it was fine. 'We really trusted one another. And though the children missed him, we worked hard to make the weekends special.'

4 […]

Two years ago, Jonathan took a new job in Tokyo, returning only every other month or so. Jean knew it was the beginning of the end, and the couple divorced earlier this year. When she looks back, says Jean, she can see that what undermined their marriage was the lack of everyday sharing. 'That's what binds a marriage together. I honestly think if Jonathan had stayed here, though we might have had some tough times, we'd have rocked on together somehow.'

5 […]

'We talk on the phone several times a day, and he tries to speak to our two girls every day. The downside is that you don't enjoy one another the way you used to: when he's home there's a danger of not having time to appreciate the good things about one another.'

6 […]

The bottom line is that family life is all about being together: taking one key player out of the equation can add up to an intolerable strain that ends up with the family splitting permanently. Which is ironic given that in most cases the prime motivating factor was the children's quality of life.

9 **Reading and Use of English, Part 7**

You are going to read an extract from a magazine article. Six paragraphs have been removed from the extract. Choose from the paragraphs A–G the one which best fits each gap (1–6). There is one extra paragraph which you do not need to use.

A 'But the years went by, and somehow it all went wrong. He found it hard to switch from his weekday bachelor existence in Germany into this frenetic, four-kid household at weekends. And I started to feel I couldn't share stuff with him because I didn't want to upset him.'

B There are plenty of reasons why families live like this: job insecurity, technological change, cheap flights. It's no longer unthinkable for a parent to say yes to a job that's many miles from home.

C Anne Green, who has studied long-distance commuting and its effect on family life, says that more and more families are dual-career. But 'one partner getting a new job in another part of the country doesn't necessarily mean the other one's career can automatically be grafted there too,' she says.

D 'We left London for Lancashire because we wanted the children to go to school here, and Jane's family were here,' he says. 'And we're very happy. But to make the money I need to support them, I needed a metropolitan income: I can work in my company's Leeds office on Mondays and Fridays, but from Tuesday to Thursday I'm in London.'

E One of the biggest dangers, says Laurie, is that it's easy to get tough and hardened. 'I think we've survived it and we'll be OK, but it takes its toll: I think things will be a lot easier when we're back together.'

F For Jane, the days when Anthony is away are always unsettling. 'It's in the back of my mind that things aren't quite right, that we're not all together.'

G For Laurie Veninger, whose husband, Jim, works in Holland from Monday to Friday, the alarm bells have started to sound. As a result, he is returning to a new job in the UK. 'I think Jim taking a job abroad was right at the time, but the girls have never got entirely used to it. And it's been hardest on Jim himself. The stress of all this commuting and of being away from us is visible.'

LANGUAGE DEVELOPMENT fixed phrases

1 Match the fixed phrases (1–8) with the definitions (a–h).

1 alarm bells started to sound
2 nitty gritty
3 rock the boat
4 stresses and strains
5 take [its] toll on
6 the bottom line
7 tough going
8 up sticks

a the most important, interesting or unpleasant facts of a situation
b the most basic or most important factor that you have to consider about a situation, often related to money
c to upset a calm or stable situation by causing trouble
d to have a bad effect or cause a lot of suffering
e something that makes people feel worried or concerned about something
f to get up and leave a place to go somewhere else
g a situation that is difficult or problematic may be described as this
h the various problems and pressures that are a part of a situation

KEY WORD pull

2 *… whatever deals he does or doesn't manage to pull off in his City office.*

What does *pull off* mean here?

3 Complete the sentences with a phrasal verb made from *pull* and a particle from the box.

> back   down   off   out of   over   through
> together   up

1 Armed forces were _____ from the front, but kept in position in case there was an escalation of the conflict.
2 It's about time they _____ that old building – it's about to fall down anyway.
3 Oh come on, Amanda – _____ yourself _____ and stop crying about this boy.
4 A leg injury forced the athlete to _____ the next race.
5 The police car flashed its sirens in order to tell the driver to _____ to the side of the road.
6 He was so ill we weren't sure if he was going to _____ or not.
7 James, why don't you _____ a chair and come and join us?
8 Everyone clapped when he managed to _____ a double backwards somersault in mid-air.

4 Complete the sentences with one of the phrases from the box in its correct form.

> pull a face   pull a fast one on someone
> pull a muscle   pull out the stops
> pull someone's leg   pull strings   pull your weight
> pull yourself together

1 He didn't warm up properly before the race, so it's not surprising he _____ .

2 If you want to win this match, you're going to have to _____ .

3 The little girl _____ as soon as her teacher's back was turned.

4 Kelvin told me he'd won the lottery, but I think he must have been _____ again.

5 If you don't _____ Annie, I'm going to have to slap you!

6 She only got the part in the play because her uncle was able to _____ with the theatre manager.

7 If you don't start _____ around here, you'll have to find somewhere else to live!

8 Jimmy is a bit of a prankster. He tried to _____ the new teacher by changing the signs on the staff toilet doors!

LISTENING (1) identifying feelings

5 Discuss. What do you think the term 'sustainable living' means? What aspects of your life would you have to change if you wanted to be totally self-sustaining?

EXAM SPOTLIGHT

Listening, Part 4 Focus on questions

In this part of the Listening paper, you hear five people talking about different things, and one task might be to identify how they feel. You also have two tasks to do and will need to listen out for at least two different things that each speaker says. In order to help you focus on the subject matter, as well as underlining the key words in the question, underline the key words in the options given.

Example: *surprised at how easy it is*
Think about words and phrases that might express surprise, e.g. *taken aback, amazed, astonished, didn't expect, unexpected, unforeseen*, etc.

6 Read the list of options (A–H) in tasks one and two below, and underline the key words. Then brainstorm a list of words that could be associated with those key words.

7 ◉ 35 **Listening, Part 4**

You will hear five short extracts in which people are talking about efforts to protect the environment.

8 Discuss. Which of the ways of protecting the environment that are mentioned do you find useful? Have you adopted them? Would you like to adopt any of them?

TASK ONE
For questions 1–5, choose from the list (A–H) how each speaker feels about their current efforts to protect the environment.

TASK TWO
For questions 6–10, choose from the list (A–H) a childhood memory that each speaker mentions.

While you listen you must complete both tasks.

A frustrated at not having more of their waste recycled

B concerned their actions may limit other people's activities

C surprised at how easy it is to recycle waste

D relieved they have reached their personal target

E sceptical about the benefits of their efforts

F sorry not to have persuaded others to follow their example

G embarrassed by other people's attitude towards them

H disappointed not to know how their waste is used

Speaker 1 □
Speaker 2 □
Speaker 3 □
Speaker 4 □
Speaker 5 □

A excitement caused by parents' innovations

B using food waste in the garden

C discomfort caused by a parent's efforts to save money

D parents reorganising household chores

E getting into trouble for forgetting to do something

F a suggestion to find alternatives to commercial products

G realising that an attempt at recycling was misguided

H parents avoiding waste of a natural resource

Speaker 1 □
Speaker 2 □
Speaker 3 □
Speaker 4 □
Speaker 5 □

GRAMMAR direct and reported speech

1 In order to make their articles more engaging and lively, journalists frequently use direct speech. Look back at the article on page 97 and underline the direct speech. What effect does this have?

DIRECT SPEECH TO REPORTED SPEECH

In the Reading text we saw the following sentence: *I can work in my company's Leeds office on Mondays and Fridays, but from Tuesday to Thursday I'm in London.*

In a more formal or literary text, this could have been rewritten as *Anthony said he could work in his company's Leeds office on Mondays and Fridays, but from Tuesday to Thursday he was in London.*

2 Underline the changes that have been made to the first sentence in the tip box. What rules can you identify?

▶ GRAMMAR REFERENCE (SECTION 10.1) **PAGE 216**

3 Rewrite the sentences using reported speech.

1 Anthony: 'I've got a small flat in London. But it's not home.'
2 Jean: 'It was a good career move for him, but we knew uprooting our four children would be impossible.'
3 Laurie: 'I think Jim taking a job abroad was right at the time, but the girls have never got entirely used to it.'

REPORTED SPEECH TO DIRECT SPEECH

Using direct speech in a piece of writing can make an article, informal letter, narrative or descriptive account more lively and interesting. The sentence *Jonathan, a marketing director, arrived home and announced he'd been offered an exciting new job – in Germany* could also be rewritten as *Jonathan, a marketing director, arrived back at the family home and said, 'Jean, I've been offered an exciting new job – in Germany!'*

4 What changes have been made to the first sentence in the tip box?

5 Rewrite the reported statements as direct speech.

1 Paul told me that he'd had a good time in Spain and couldn't wait to go back the following summer.
   '_____ !' said Paul.
2 Liam said he had been to the concert the night before and was feeling rather tired.
   '_____,' Liam told me.
3 Amelia refused to come with us because she said she hated the theatre.
   '_____.' Amelia said.

6 When reporting direct speech, avoid using *said* and *told* too often. To enrich your sentences, use a variety of reporting verbs. Choose the correct option in italics to complete the sentences.

1 She *admitted / complained / doubted* that she had not been listening to a word I said.
2 I *deny / report / propose* that we all listen to what Georgina has to say.
3 He *believed / demanded / repeated* that he be released from custody.
4 She *announced / considered / swore* to leave if he ever did it again.
5 He *begged / mentioned / insisted* her not to break off their relationship.
6 She *decided / objected / suggested* going for a walk.

▶ GRAMMAR REFERENCE (SECTION 10.2) **PAGE 216**

7 Reading and Use of English, Part 4

For questions 1–6, complete the second sentence so that it has a similar meaning to the first sentence, using the word given. Do not change the word given. You must use between three and six words, including the word given.

1 'I had nothing to do with the robbery!' said Adrian.
   DENIED
   Adrian _____ the robbery.
2 'You are coming home for some lunch and I won't take no for an answer!' Tom said to me.
   INSISTED
   Tom _____ home for lunch.
3 'It's going to snow this week – I can tell,' William announced.
   PREDICTED
   William _____ that week.
4 'I'm sorry for what I said yesterday,' said Andrew.
   FOR
   Andrew _____ the day before.
5 'You really should try our local Thai restaurant – it has fantastic food,' said Lewis.
   RECOMMENDED
   Lewis _____ our local Thai restaurant because it has fantastic food.
6 'I really don't want you to get a tattoo!' Mum said.
   OBJECTED
   Mum _____ tattoo.

SPEAKING organising a larger unit of discourse

EXAM SPOTLIGHT

Speaking, Part 2 Organising a larger unit of discourse

Part 2 of the Speaking test consists of an individual 'long turn' for each candidate. You will be given three pictures and expected to talk about two of them for one minute. It's not enough at this level simply to describe what the pictures show. The focus is on organising a larger unit of discourse – by comparing, describing, expressing opinions, explaining and speculating.

8 **Look at the pictures at the top of page 235 and decide which two are the most interesting, or which you can talk most about. If they are very different, there will be more things to contrast. In order to organise your one-minute discourse, think about:**

1 what the pictures show (describing) or might be showing (speculating).

2 how the pictures are similar or what common themes they share (comparing).

3 how they differ or show different points (contrasting).

4 how you can best answer the question you have been asked based on the pictures (expressing your opinion, explaining).

Speaking, Part 2

9 **Work in pairs.**

Student A: Look at the three pictures at the top of page 235. They show three different methods of food production. I'd like you to compare two of the pictures and say how these methods of food production might affect people's health and the environment.

Student B: Which do you think is the most environmentally-friendly method of food production?

Student B: Look at the three pictures at the bottom of page 235. They show different methods of energy production. Compare two of the pictures and say how these methods of energy production might affect people's health and the environment.

Student A: Which do you think is the cleanest method of energy production?

USE OF ENGLISH multiple-choice cloze

10 **For each sentence, decide which answer (A, B, C or D) best fits each gap.**

1 Bob doesn't care what people say about him – he's got a very _____ skin.
   A hard   B thick   C solid   D heavy

2 Martin infuriated me to such a _____ that I walked out and went home.
   A degree   B lot   C depth   D length

3 It's no _____ saying you don't like mushrooms now – I've already made dinner.
   A worth   B value   C benefit   D good

4 Ulrich speaks English with a _____ German accent.
   A hard   B thick   C solid   D stiff

5 £50 was a small _____ when I was your age!
   A fortune   B wealth   C treasure   D packet

11 **Reading and Use of English, Part 1**

For questions 1–8, read the text below and decide which answer (A, B, C or D) best fits each gap.

Copthorne Wood under threat

Copthorne Wood is an ancient woodland. Records show that it was already well-established in the 11th century, when deer and numerous other animals (1) _____ freely in it. For the past 50 years it has been fully open to the public, (2) _____ one small section that is a site of special scientific interest. The wood provides an excellent (3) _____ for many species of insects, including some butterflies that are found in very few other (4) _____ . The government has recently (5) _____ plans to construct a motorway through the wood. This would involve cutting (6) _____ almost all the trees. Not only would this have a disastrous effect on wildlife, but it would also destroy the only woodland that the people of this area can enjoy. A protest group has been formed to (7) _____ these plans and persuade the government to (8) _____ its decision. If you care about the environment, contact us today. The more people protest against this plan, the greater our chance of success.

1 A strolled   B rambled   C roamed   D drifted

2 A apart from   B besides   C alongside   D irrespective of

3 A residence   B house   C dwelling   D habitat

4 A positions   B locations   C conditions   D situations

5 A announced   B proclaimed   C spread   D notified

6 A down   B away   C up   D off

7 A contrast   B oppose   C contradict   D object

8 A retrace   B backtrack   C reverse   D undo

LISTENING (2) note-taking

1 Discuss. Have you heard of 'freecycling'? If not, what do you think the term means?

2 ⊙ 36 Listen to Dave, Julia and Anna talking about what freecycling means to them. Note down the things that each person has acquired and given away and what other items freecycle members might offer.

	Dave	Julia	Anna
Acquired	bathroom cabinet		
Given away			
Other items			

3 What are the main advantages of freecycling according to what you heard?

WRITING a proposal

> **EXAM SPOTLIGHT**
>
> **Writing, Part 2** A proposal
>
> When you write a proposal, you need to think carefully about who it is for and why you are writing it. The exam question will give you this information. You should use this to help you decide what to include in your proposal and how to organise the information so that it is clear and effective.

4 Read the exam question below and write down some possible headings for paragraphs within your proposal.

> You have read this short article in your local newspaper.
>
> > Our readers have been writing in to us complaining about the number of items they see that have been thrown away at rubbish tips, despite appearing to be in reasonable condition.
> >
> > The Editor is inviting readers to send in a proposal outlining the reasons for this problem and suggesting how we could repair or re-distribute unwanted items and avoid unnecessary waste. The newspaper will print the best proposal.
>
> Write your **proposal** in 220–260 words in an appropriate style.

5 Read the proposal and complete the gaps with appropriate headings.

> **1** _____
>
> This is a proposal to suggest ways in which we can reduce the amount of waste we produce in our city. As consumers, we have grown accustomed to thinking that the products we buy will only last a short time. Once they break down, we tend to throw them away without a second thought. In my view, we need to train ourselves to think again.
>
> **2** _____
>
> In the past, our grandparents used to fix broken machinery and repair clothes. Nowadays, we think it's easier not to bother. We argue that we don't have enough time or we lack the equipment needed to do it ourselves. My solution to this would be to advertise local 'repair agents' who can do this work for us. If the newspaper provided a list of people, with contact numbers, to fix things for us, this would provide much-needed employment for people in our city and help cut down on waste.
>
> **3** _____
>
> Another great solution is to put a shop next to the rubbish tip where we chuck away things we don't need, like furniture. Why doesn't the paper go to the local council and ask them to do this? Then, we wouldn't just throw things away or recycle them – some could be sold on to people who need them. So anyone who's too hard up to buy new items may be able to have second-hand ones that only need a quick fix!
>
> **4** _____
>
> Overall, I believe that these two ideas would help change our attitudes and prevent us from being so wasteful.

6 In a proposal, you will need to demonstrate appropriate use of a range of functions. Which functions below is the writer being asked to fulfil in this task? Underline examples of these in the answer above. What other functions might you use in a proposal?

> comparing   complaining   describing
> evaluating   explaining   expressing opinion
> giving advice   hypothesising   judging priorities
> justifying   narrating   outlining   persuading
> recommending   suggesting

USING REGISTER

One of the things you will be expected to demonstrate in the Writing paper is correct use of register – that is, the language, tone and formality that are appropriate in different types of writing.

7 Look at the proposal again. What register is used? Is it formal, informal or neutral? Is it consistent? Think about the purpose of the proposal. Who is the intended audience? Underline the sentences that make this clear.

8 Decide which of the sentences are formal, informal and neutral.

1
a   The purpose of this proposal is to put forward a number of suggestions as to how we could change the situation.
b   By writing this proposal, I hope to offer you an insight into what we could do to change things.
c   Read this proposal and find out what I'm planning to do – with or without you!

2
a   My solution to this would be to …
b   I've got a fantastic solution for this.
c   A number of solutions can be proposed that might alleviate the situation.

3
a   It's hopeless – we can't put up with this attitude any longer.
b   Only by changing people's attitudes can the situation be improved.
c   If we change people's attitudes, the situation will improve.

9 Work in pairs. Discuss the sentences in exercise 8. Which sentences tend to be longer / use the passive / use slang or colloquial language more often? Which style is generally unsuitable for a proposal?

10 Rewrite the third paragraph of the proposal in a more appropriate tone. Use language from the In Other Words box.

IN OTHER WORDS

USING REGISTER

approaches
cannot afford
discard
handle
in this way
minor repairs
propose
rather than
respond to
set up
such as
unwanted items

Writing, Part 2

11 Read the exam question. Follow the steps to prepare your proposal.

> You are studying at a college and living away from home. You have received the following leaflet from your student union.
>
> > All students need to consider how they can help conserve resources such as water and electricity. Remember, using less means paying less too.
> >
> > The Students' Union is inviting students to send in a proposal outlining the reasons why we may be wasteful of water and electricity and suggesting steps they can take to avoid this.

1   Write down possible headings for each paragraph.
2   For each paragraph heading brainstorm ideas about what information that paragraph might include. You can make up the ideas.
3   Think about who your intended audience is and decide what register is required: formal, neutral or informal.
4   Look at your plan and check that you have covered at least two of the functions you selected in exercise 6.

12 Write your proposal in 220–260 words in an appropriate style.

GETTING STARTED

1 Which of these views do you agree with? Why?

1 'There is joy in work. There is no happiness except in the realisation that we have accomplished something.' Henry Ford
2 'Working gets in the way of living.' Omar Sharif
3 'The reward for work well done is the opportunity to do more.' Jonas Salk
4 'All I ever wanted was an honest week's pay for an honest day's work.' Steve Martin

READING interpreting literature

2 Discuss. What do you think the difficulties would be in finding work and living in another country?

3 Read the extract on the opposite page. Chanu and Nazneen are husband and wife, and their daughters are called Shahana and Bibi. Decide whether the following statements are true (T) or false (F). Underline the parts of the text which give you the answers.

1	The family seems wealthy.	T / F
2	Nazneen is self-opinionated.	T / F
3	Chanu has been unable to find work.	T / F
4	Shahana is satisfied with the family circumstances.	T / F
5	Chanu associates work with self-respect.	T / F

4 Reading and Use of English, Part 5

Read the extract again. For questions 1–6, choose the answer (A, B, C or D) which you think fits best according to the text.

1 According to the second paragraph, how does Shahana appear to feel about her family's behaviour?
  A unimpressed   C delighted
  B angry   D concerned
2 What do we learn about Chanu from the way he goes about helping Nazneen?
  A He is an astute businessman.
  B He needs to feel a sense of purpose.
  C He doesn't trust Nazneen to work on her own.
  D He is an official in a clothing factory.
3 Why does Nazneen pick up one of Chanu's books?
  A She would like him to read to her.
  B She wishes he would start reading again.
  C She feels he's working too hard.
  D She hopes he'll do some tidying up.
4 Why is Nazneen happy when Chanu goes out all day?
  A She's relieved he's stopped working.
  B It means he trusts her to work on her own.
  C He seems happier when he returns.
  D She likes to see him wearing a suit.
5 Why does Chanu show his driving licence?
  A He's fiercely proud of having it.
  B He's just passed his driving test.
  C Its frame has broken.
  D It is proof of his qualifications.
6 From the passage as a whole, what impression do we gain of Chanu's character?
  A He wants to be respected.
  B He is arrogant.
  C He is mean with money.
  D He is pessimistic.

5 Discuss. What's going to happen in the story?

The Middleman

Nazneen wanted to begin at once but Chanu insisted on calling the girls. 'When I married her, I said she is a good worker. Girl from the village. Unspoilt. All the clever-clever girls – ' He broke off and looked at Shahana. 'All the clever-clever girls are not worth one hair on her head.'

Bibi opened and closed her mouth. Her white lacy socks had fallen around her ankles and her shins looked dry and dusty. Shahana had begun to use moisturiser. Yesterday she had refused to wash her hair with Fairy Liquid. She wanted shampoo now.

Nazneen held on to the casing of the sewing machine. Chanu waggled his head and beamed at her. She fixed the thread and began. One trouser leg, then the other. When she had finished, they clapped and Bibi became sufficiently carried away to venture a small cheer, and Chanu's applause was emphatic, and Shahana smiled fleetingly and marched back to the bedroom.

Chanu brought home holdalls of buttonless shirts, carrier bags of unlined dresses, a washing-up tub full of catchless bras. He counted them out and he counted them back in. Every couple of days he went for new loads. He performed a kind of rudimentary quality control, tugging at zips and twiddling collars while probing his cheeks with his tongue. Chanu totted up the earnings and collected them. He was the middleman, a role which he viewed as Official and in which he exerted himself. For a couple of weeks he puzzled feverishly over calculations, trying to work out the most profitable type of garment assignment, the highest-margin operation. But he had to take what was going and the calculations themselves were a low-margin endeavour. Then he had time to supervise in earnest and he made himself available at her elbow, handing thread, passing scissors, dispensing advice, making tea, folding garments.

'All you have to do,' he said, 'is sit there.'

She got up to stretch her legs. She picked up one of his books and blew off some lint, hoping something in him would respond to the call of neglected type.

'We're making good money this week.' He pulled at his lower lip, working it out. 'Don't worry. I'll take care of everything.' For two whole months she did not even know how much she had earned. It was a relief when, for the first time since the piecework began, Chanu retired to the bedroom one evening and called for a page-turner. The next day, a

Saturday, he made a kind of fortress of books around him on the sitting-room floor and delivered a pungent oration on the ancient history of Bengal. On Sunday he shaved with extra care and limbered up in front of the mirror in a suit, but did not go out. The next day he went out all day and came back singing fragments of Tagore.

It was a good sign.

Tuesday and Wednesday passed in the same pattern and Nazneen completed the linings of 37 mini-skirts. She had no more sewing to do.

Chanu gathered his family together and exorcised some troublesome blockages in his throat. 'As you are all aware.' He noticed Shahana's dress. She had hitched up her uniform at school so that it bloused over the belt and rode up towards her thigh. Without changing her expression she began to inch it slowly downwards.

'As you are all aware, we have decided – as a family – to return home. Your mother is doing everything possible to facilitate our dream through the old and honourable craft of tailoring. And don't forget it was we who invented all these weaves of cloths – muslin and damask and every damn thing.' He seemed uncertain. He looked at his daughters as if he had forgotten who they were. Only when his darting gaze fixed on Nazneen did he remember himself.

'Ahem. So. We are going home. I have today become an employee at Kempton Kars, driver number one-six-one-nine, and the Home Fund will prosper. That is all I have to say.'

Nazneen and Bibi clapped their hands. It came as a surprise that Chanu could drive a car.

As if to dispel their silent doubts he took a tattered piece of paper from his pocket. 'Driving licence,' he said in English. He inspected the document. '1976. Never had it framed.'

So Chanu became a taxi man and ceased to be a middleman. And on the first hot day of the year, when the windows were closed against the ripening of waste bins and the flat hummed to the tune of its pipes, and Nazneen had mopped up the overflow from the blocked toilet and washed her hands and sighed into the mirror, a new middleman appeared. Karim, with a bale of jeans over his broad shoulder.

This was how he came into her life.

LANGUAGE DEVELOPMENT idiomatic phrases with *out*

1 **Look at the sentences from the text on page 105. Explain what the underlined phrasal verbs mean.**

1 *For a couple of weeks he puzzled feverishly over calculations, trying to <u>work out</u> the most profitable type of garment assignment …*
2 *He <u>counted</u> them <u>out</u> and he counted them back in.*

2 **Complete the sentences with the phrases in the box.**

> out of it   out of luck   out of order
> out of respect   out of the blue
> out of the question   out of this world
> out of your mind

1 'You can't go to the cinema on a school night, when you've got school tomorrow,' said Jane's mum. 'It's _____!'
2 I hadn't seen her for months, and she just turned up _____ !
3 You must be _____ to spend €150 on a ticket for the U2 concert! It's far too expensive!
4 You should go to the farewell dinner _____ for your boss. He's been good to you over the years.
5 The view from the top of the London Eye is _____ ! On a clear day, you can see for miles.
6 I didn't enjoy the party yesterday. All my younger brother's friends were there, so I felt a bit _____ .
7 You can't use this machine; it's _____ , I'm afraid.
8 Have you got change for a £20 note? Sorry, but you're _____ . I've only got a 50.

KEY WORD *money*

3 **Which of these verbs can be followed by *money*?**

> borrow   charge   clean   drive   earn
> heighten   hire   inherit   launder   lend   lose
> lower   make   owe   pay   raise   refund
> save   spend   trade   waste

4 **Choose the correct meaning of the phrases in italics.**

1 Why don't you offer him a fiver to take her a message? Everybody knows *money talks*!
   a you get things if you pay for them
   b you can communicate with money
2 Dallas knew he couldn't beat Karen at chess, but he was determined to *give her a good run for her money*.
   a not let her win easily
   b to cheat
3 You can't hope to win Molly's love by *throwing money at her*!
   a repeatedly telling her how rich you are
   b spending lots of money on her

5 **Match the money phrases (1–6) with the definitions (a–f).**

1 pump money into something
2 not be made of money
3 have money to burn
4 get your money's worth
5 put your money on something
6 put your money where your mouth is

a bet money on the result of a race or competition
b get something that is worth the money you paid for it
c show by your actions that you really believe what you say
d give money to a company or business to help it become successful
e not be able to afford everything
f have enough money to be able to buy a lot of unnecessary things

6 **Reading and Use of English, Part 3**

For questions 1–8, read the text below. Use the word given in capitals at the end of some of the lines to form a word that fits in the gap in the same line.

> ### Just for the fun of it!
>
> People do all sorts of things to deal with a lack of money. A (1) _____ law student found a novel way to free himself from (2) _____ difficulty. Using his computer, he embarked on a number of (3) _____ activities which involved obtaining credit card and bank details from (4) _____ websites. He then used them in (5) _____ to acquire cars, clothes and cash, equivalent in total to the grand sum of £250,000. 'It felt like a bit of fun,' he said, when questioned, 'and a pastime which developed into an easy way of making money.' He even sent one of his victims a bouquet of flowers, paid for by using their stolen bank details! He admits he became too confident. 'I thought it would be impossible to get caught, and just got carried away!' His (6) _____ ways soon aroused the (7) _____ of the fraud prevention service, eventually leading to his arrest. He was charged with (8) _____ to defraud, and served a three and a half year prison sentence.
>
> PENNY
>
> FINANCE
>
> FRAUD
>
> SECURE
> TRANSACT
>
> CARE
> SUSPECT
>
> CONSPIRE

LISTENING sentence completion

7 Discuss. Which of the following views on the use of credit cards do you agree with? Why?

1 It's so much easier than carrying a load of cash around, ready for someone to steal!
2 The problem with cards is, you don't know how much money you're spending!
3 It's easy to run up a lot of debts!
4 Credit cards aren't very secure any more. It's easy for someone to steal your number, without you realising it.
5 I'm less likely to buy silly little things if I don't carry cash. I feel more in control of my spending with a card.

EXAM SPOTLIGHT

Listening, Part 2 Dates, statistics and figures

In Listening, Part 2, you may hear some dates or pieces of statistical information. They may be the answers you need to complete sentences, or they may help you to find the missing words or phrases. Try to predict what type of information is required in a gap, for instance a date or number. If a figure is given in the task, think about how it will sound – particularly when it can be said in different ways; for example, *2011* may be said as *twenty eleven* or as *two thousand and eleven*, and approximate figures could be introduced by words and phrases such as *almost*, *an average of*, *nearly*, *getting on for*, *just over*, *approximately*, *about* and *around*.

8 Read the sentences and decide what kind of information you should listen for.

1 In 2011, British families spent an average of _____ a week.
2 Average weekly expenditure in _____ was £455.
3 Families spent £65.70 a week on _____ in 2011.
4 _____ accounted for almost £64 a week.

9 ⊙ 37 Listen to an economics lecturer talking about weekly family spending in the UK in 2011, and complete the sentences in exercise 8. Were your predictions correct?

10 Read the text for the sentence completion task in exercise 11, and try to predict the kind of words you need to fill the gaps.

11 ⊙ 38 Listening, Part 2

You will hear part of a talk about significant stages in the early history of credit. For questions 1–8, complete the sentences with a word or short phrase.

It is now believed that the earliest agricultural communities operated a
(1) _____ .

The Babylonians and Assyrians seem to have used credit since about
(2) _____ .

There are records of the ancient Egyptians buying (3) _____ on credit.

Towards the end of the Roman Empire, credit was used as a way of
(4) _____ , which had become difficult.

In the Middle Ages, trade in the rich
(5) _____ of Italy depended on credit bills.

In Italy, money could be invested in a
(6) _____ undertaken for trading purposes.

In the Middle Ages, letters promising to pay at a later date were accepted at
(7) _____ .

The (8) _____ to organise funding for the first English settlers in North America lasted three years.

GRAMMAR modal auxiliaries (2)

1 Match the sentences (1–5) with the functions of the modal verbs (a–e).

1 What were you doing? You might have had an accident!
2 It would be easy. She'd tell her teacher she'd had her rucksack stolen on the bus.
3 As it's raining, we might as well go home.
4 Oh no! There would be a traffic jam when I've got an important meeting!
5 It's 11 o'clock, so the headmaster will be in his office now.

a Modal for criticism
b Modal for prediction
c Modal for resignation
d Modal for a plan
e Modal for annoyance

MAKING PLANS

For making decisions about future plans, *will* and *would* can be used:
I think I'll go to see Maria this afternoon.
That was it! She would give her mum a surprise birthday party.

MAKING PREDICTIONS

Will and *would* can also be used to make predictions:
It won't be easy to park in town today, because of the carnival.
He sighed and thought it would be difficult to avoid going to the party.

CRITICISM

To express criticism or annoyance, *might* and *could* can be used:
Drive more carefully! You might have killed that little boy!
You could at least apologise to her!

ANNOYANCE

Will and *would* can also be used to express annoyance:
She will keep practising on the violin while I'm trying to study!
There would be a power cut now, just when I want to watch a film!

RESIGNATION

To express acceptance of a situation when there is no better alternative, *may as well* and *might as well* can be used:
You're never going to be good at gymnastics, so you may as well stop.
I don't think Penny's coming, so we might as well leave.

2 Complete the dialogues with a suitable modal.

1 A: I think I _____ go shopping this afternoon.
  B: Remember there's a demonstration going on against the building of a new shopping centre. Some of the roads _____ be closed.
  A: Oh, yes! I'd forgotten! I _____ stay home and do some homework, then!

2 C: I wish you _____ stop making so much noise! I'm trying to work!
  D: Well, you _____ give up and go out for a walk, because I'm putting these shelves up, and I _____ have time later.
  C: You _____ told me about this earlier!

3 E: Peter's called to say he _____ be coming to the concert tomorrow.
  F: Typical! He _____ cancel at the last minute! Now what am I going to do with the extra ticket?
  E: We _____ try and sell it outside the hall. Someone _____ want it!

▶ GRAMMAR REFERENCE (SECTION 11) **PAGE 217**

3 Reading and Use of English, Part 4

For questions 1–6, complete the second sentence so that it has a similar meaning to the first sentence, using the word given. Do not change the word given. You must use between three and six words, including the word given.

1 I don't know why you bother going to that German class, since you never do your homework!
  WELL
  You never do your homework for German, so _____ give it up!

2 Sally decided then and there to go to France as a nanny for a year.
  BECOME
  'I know! I _____ go to France for a year!' said Sally.

3 Why didn't you offer to pay for the damage to that woman's car, seeing as the accident was your fault?
  OFFERED
  You _____ for the damage to that woman's car, since the accident was your fault!

4 'Kathy doesn't like David very much, so she's not going to be easily persuaded to go to his party,' said John to himself.
  PERSUADE
  John realised that _____ Kathy to go to David's party, as she didn't really like him.

5 Those kids next door keep playing basketball against my living room wall!
  STOP
  I wish those kids _____ against my living room wall!

6 You haven't done anything – not even the dishes.
  COULD
  You _____ the dishes.

USE OF ENGLISH multiple-choice cloze

In Reading and Use of English, Part 1, it may be necessary to look at more than the target sentence in order to see the development of an argument. Then you can decide which word or phrase is correct.

4 Choose the correct phrase to complete the sentences.
1 Al hated crowds. So, he _____ go to a football stadium.
   a would often   c would never
   b might not   d would prefer to
2 I've been studying in my room all week! Can we do something _____ staying indoors today?
   a as well as   c except for
   b but for   d other than

5 **Reading and Use of English, Part 1**

For questions 1–8, read the text below and decide which answer (A, B, C or D) best fits each gap.

After my multilingual English class talked excitedly about the board game Monopoly recently, I searched on the Internet. To my surprise, I found several sites (1) _____ the use of Monopoly in the classroom, to teach accounting, economics and even sociology! And therein (2) _____ the secret of the game's success, according to some teaching experts. There are important lessons to be learnt from it. (3) _____ changes in the game over the years, its guiding (4) _____ remains the same – to become the richest player through buying, selling and renting property. However, it doesn't embrace the 'get-rich-quick' philosophy; (5) _____ it. The experts say it teaches us how to stay rich, by investing (6) _____. And that idea appeals to people the world over, (7) _____ of nationality, age or gender. Monopoly makes players think about how to make money work for them. So, if you're wondering how to teach your children about finance, you could do a lot (8) _____ than introduce them to this game.

1 A arguing B sponsoring C counselling
   D advocating
2 A falls B stays C lies D puts
3 A Although B However C Despite
   D Nevertheless
4 A perception B thought C notion
   D principle
5 A in spite of B far from C instead of
   D nothing but
6 A prudently B watchfully C gingerly
   D warily
7 A notwithstanding B regardless
   C thoughtless D dismissive
8 A better B more C worse D less

6 **Discuss.** Do you think the way you play a game like Monopoly can tell you something about what kind of career you will follow in the future?

SPEAKING disagreeing with someone else's opinion

7 ⊙ 39 **Listen to two candidates, Fernando and Katrina, answering the following question:**
Some people say that having any job is better than no job at all. What do you think?

Tick any of the phrases in the In Other Words box that they use to respond to each other's comments.

IN OTHER WORDS	**DISAGREEING**
	I think it depends on … ☐
	Perhaps, but don't you think … ☐
	Yes, but if … , what then? ☐
	I'm afraid I don't agree with you. ☐
	For me, doing such a thing would be … ☐
	That becomes a problem if … ☐
	I cannot say the same for me … ☐

8 **Work in pairs. Answer the following question in a similar way. Use phrases from the In Other Words box where appropriate.**

Some people believe that money is the most important thing in life. Do you agree?

WRITING   a report – being concise

1 **Discuss. Which of the two places in the photographs would you prefer to shop in? Give reasons for your choice.**

Writing, Part 2

2 **Read the exam question. What is it asking you to do?**

> You are the marketing manager of a large department store chain. The managing director has asked you to investigate a recent fall in sales. You asked the shop's customers their views on the various departments in the store.
>
> Read some customers' comments below, and write a **report,** briefly outlining the situation, and making recommendations for improvements.
>
> *'There's hardly anything for boys in children's clothing, and what is available is too pricey!'*
> *'The stationery department is well laid out, making it easy to find what you need.'*
> *'Well, I don't think much of the furniture in the store. Choice is limited, and rather old-fashioned in style. Not worth travelling all the way to the fifth floor for!'*
> *'My husband and I buy all our clothes here. There's plenty of choice, and the changing rooms are spacious too!'*

3 **Read the following report. How could it be improved?**

Reason for writing

The aim of this report is to examine the reasons behind the recent fall in sales in the store. The report aims to provide an overall view of the current situation, and is based on points raised by the store's customers with regard to the various departments in the store. We asked customers to tell us which departments they visited most frequently, and which departments they hardly ever visited, and why.

Departments visited most frequently

Many customers told us they were more than satisfied with both the ladies' and the men's clothing departments. Some people even went so far as to say that they bought all their clothes there. They expressed the view that there was plenty of choice, and also said that the changing rooms were spacious. Another very popular department was the stationery department. Here, customers commented particularly on the successful layout, which helps the customer find what he or she needs very quickly and easily.

Departments that customers are dissatisfied with

By far the least popular department in the store is the furniture department, with many customers complaining that there is little choice, and what is available is rather old-fashioned in style. Some said it just wasn't worth travelling all the way to the fifth floor to visit this department. Besides this department, complaints were also made about the children's clothing department. Several customers complained about the lack of items in stock for boys, and also suggested that prices were too high.

Conclusion

It is clear from the comments customers made that improvements should be centred around the furniture and children's clothing departments. The buyers for these departments need to alter their approach, and search for more varied and modern products. Considerable investment should perhaps be made in expanding the furniture department, while the buyer for children's clothing should search for new brands, and concentrate more on striking a balance between girls' and boys' clothing. If all this can be achieved, then sales will almost certainly improve in these departments, and the store in general will surely benefit.

Writing, Part 2 Keeping to the word limit

In Part 2 of the Writing paper you are expected to write 220–260 words. It is necessary to be concise when expressing your points, and to avoid repetition.

One way you can make sure you keep within the required word limit is to keep your opening paragraph in particular as brief as possible.

Work in pairs. Reduce the opening paragraph of the report opposite to one sentence.

Discuss. What's good about the report? Note down the most important points you need to keep when reducing its length.

Make the rest of the report more concise using the box below to help you.

MAKING YOUR WRITING CONCISE

Join points together in one sentence by using a variety of language.

- Improve the opening paragraph, by using some of the following phrases.

This report aims to provide an overall view of the current situation … , based on … , and to make suggestions for …

- Do the same for the main paragraphs.

The ladies' and men's clothing department is experiencing a boom in sales …

This can be attributed to …

Similarly, …

In contrast, sales in the furniture and children's clothing departments have dropped considerably …

Complaints have been made that …

In the children's clothing department, concern was expressed over … and prices were thought …

- Reduce the length of the concluding paragraph to one or two sentences.

It is clear from the comments that considerable investment should be put into expanding and modernising … , while a wider range of … at more reasonable prices.

7 Writing, Part 2

Read the exam question and write your report in 220–260 words.

You are the assistant manager of a large theme park. The manager has asked you to investigate the recent decrease in the number of visitors to the park. You asked visitors to fill in a questionnaire about the rides.

Read some of the comments customers made about particular rides below. Then write a **report,** summarising the findings and making recommendations for improvements.

'Captain Hook's Ship is brilliant!'
'While my ten-year-old son can go on everything, there's nothing for my three-year-old daughter, so she gets fed up quickly.'
'You can't buy much to eat, apart from cakes and biscuits.'
'Boone's Park down the road has got more rides to choose from, and you pay one entrance fee, instead of paying for individual rides.'

VIDEO rainy day flea market

1 **Look at the photo of a flea market and choose the correct description.**

   1 an outdoor antiques market where dealers offer hard-to-sell objects for sale
   2 an open-air market selling cheap and often second-hand goods
   3 a seasonal market selling designer goods that are no longer in fashion

2 **Have you ever bought anything at a flea market? Did it have a fixed price? What kind of items might you find at a flea market? Use some of these words.**

   | brand new goods | cast-offs | curios | junk |
   | ornaments | unwanted items | vintage goods | |

3 **Watch a video about a flea market in which Jimmy, an experienced dealer, tries to help novice sellers Natalia and Jill. Answer the questions.**

   1 What effect does the weather have on the dealers and the buyers?
   2 How would you describe Jimmy's feelings about Natalia's decisions?
   3 How would you describe Jill's attitude?
   4 Who made more money, Natalia or Jill?

4 **Watch the video again. Who says these things – Jill, Jimmy or Natalia?**

   1 I'm getting tired.
   2 I wasn't ready to let them go.
   3 Even if she didn't want to sell them, they bring people into the booth.
   4 She should've listened. Big mistake.
   5 So far we just made money for my mom to take a cab.
   6 It's just my luck.
   7 I could not care less about the rain.
   8 I'm asking $100.
   9 Sometimes it's best to let somebody educate you.
   10 It's raining money.

5 **Work in pairs. Answer the questions.**

   1 What was Natalia's point of view about the folding chairs?
   2 What was Jimmy's point of view?
   3 Who do you agree with? Why?

6 **Work in pairs. You are Natalia and Jill. You meet up at the end of the day. Discuss your experiences, how you feel the day went and what you have learnt.**

   Natalia: make sure you tell Jill about the chairs.
   Jill: make sure you tell Natalia about the Art Deco print.

SPEAKING Part 2 discussion

IDEAS GENERATOR

ALTERNATIVE VIEWPOINTS

In Part 4 of the Speaking test you need to express opinions, whether they are in agreement or not with your partner. There is always more than one way of looking at a situation, as you saw in exercise 5. It doesn't matter which point of view is 'right' or 'wrong'.

You can prepare for the discussion part of the Speaking test by thinking about the 'pros and cons' of a statement or position. After stating your opinion and your reasons, you can invite your partner to respond.

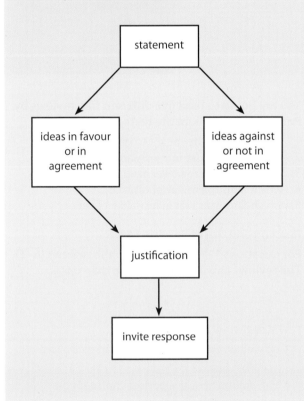

7 **Read the statement and decide which of the comments (1–6) agree with that position. Think of a justification or example for each comment.**

> *Credit cards are a good solution if you haven't got enough money to buy something.*

1 It's better than borrowing from family or friends.
2 There's a risk of not being able to pay off your debt.
3 You can take advantage of special offers or good prices.
4 You don't have to wait until you've saved up money.
5 You end up paying more than the original price.
6 Your spending can get out of control.

8 **Work in pairs. Discuss the statement in exercise 7. Use the diagram in the Ideas Generator to structure your discussion.**

9 **Work with a new partner. Review the useful phrases for disagreeing on page 109. Then repeat the discussion in exercise 8.**

10 **Think of two 'pros' and two 'cons' for each statement. Then work in pairs and discuss two of the statements.**
   Student A: agree with the statements.
   Student B: disagree with the statements.
   Then swap roles and discuss the other two statements.

   1 Borrowing money from a friend is never a good idea.
   2 Money makes the world go around.
   3 Children should get a weekly allowance from their parents.
   4 Having too much money makes you unhappy.

11 **What did you find most difficult about the task in exercise 10? How can you improve your performance?**

VIDEOSCRIPT 11 is on page 255.

12 BEHIND THE SILVER SCREEN

GETTING STARTED

1 How much do you know about cinema?

1 What do we call a film which is full of suspense and mystery?
2 What do we call a film or TV programme that tells us something about real life?
3 What is the group name for all the people who act in a film or on stage?
4 What's another word for the music in a film?
5 What kind of film tells a story with music and songs?
6 What kind of special effects are used in many modern films?

2 Which of the following do you consider the most important elements in a film? Put them in order.

> acting   cast   cinematography   costumes
> direction   music / score   script / screenplay
> setting   special effects   story / plot

READING understanding humour, irony and sarcasm

UNDERSTANDING HUMOUR, IRONY AND SARCASM

In the Reading parts of the Reading and Use of English paper you may be presented with a text that contains elements of humour, including irony or sarcasm. Every culture and nation has its own type of humour that may not always be shared with other cultures. One of the hardest things to 'understand' in a foreign language is humour. While you will not be expected to 'appreciate' humour in the *Cambridge English: Advanced* exam, it is important to recognise when the writer is being sarcastic, or using irony, to get their message across.

3 You are going to read five different film reviews by Peter Bradshaw. Skim the texts and decide:

1 which reviews are meant to be humorous.
2 which reviews use irony or sarcasm.
3 which films the reviewer liked.
4 which films the reviewer disliked.
5 which films you would most like to see.

4 Reading and Use of English, Part 8

For questions 1–10, choose from the reviews (A–E). The reviews may be chosen more than once.

> **Which review mentions**
>
> 1 a well-written script that is smart as well as funny? _____
> 2 an actor who is the perfect choice for the role he plays?
> 3 a film that's so bad it should get a prize ? _____
> 4 a film set during a period of historical conflict? _____
> 5 a storyline scenario that the reviewer finds hard to believe? _____
> 6 a character who channels negative energies into positive action? _____
> 7 a film with a theme that the reviewer thinks has been overdone? _____
> 8 a character that makes a fool of himself? _____
> 9 a film that is better for having fewer jokes than others like it? _____
> 10 a film that could have been longer? _____

5 In Review B, the writer describes the romcom as *wooden and deathly*. What does he mean?

6 Look back at the reviews and find the adjectives the writer uses to describe these aspects in the films. Explain what he means in each case.

1 _____ film-making (text A)
2 _____ dialogue (text A)
3 _____ leading man (text A)
4 _____ moment (text A)
5 _____ music (text C)
6 _____ gags (text D)
7 _____ casting (text E)
8 _____ role (text E)

A CASABLANCA

Michael Curtiz's rereleased 1942 classic is irresistible, big-hearted film-making – a unique kind of romantic noir – with cracking dialogue and a thrilling leading man in Humphrey Bogart as bar owner Rick: a stateless, cynical American in second world war Casablanca, where desperate refugees plead for transit papers. Rick is coolly at the centre, apparently needing nothing and wanting nothing, but nursing a broken heart after an affair with Ingrid Bergman, who is married to legendary Resistance fighter Paul Henreid. Rick comes to transform his emotional pain into a gallant and passionate support for his love rival's battle against the Nazis. There are too many spine-tingling moments to list.

B THE TRUTH ABOUT LOVE

The Worst Film of the Year awards race has now been called off. It has been rendered redundant by this wooden and deathly romcom* that was made three years ago, and is now being dragged out of the freezer. Jennifer Love Hewitt is a doctor living in Bristol. Jimi Mistry plays her love-rat husband. Most worryingly of all, poor Dougray Scott has to play the decent guy who is tragically, secretly enamoured of Hewitt. You can tell how adorably macho yet sensitive he is by the way he is seen caulking his boat in the harbour. Maybe the worst moment comes at the beginning when Scott, allegedly moonstruck with love for Hewitt and walking home alone, has to go into a goofy and horrifically embarrassing sort of hopscotch. Not one for the showreel.
* romantic comedy

C ROCKY BALBOA

Euphorically running up those Philadelphia steps to the pounding music must take a little longer for Rocky these days, you'd think, but he's back for one last wildly implausible shot at heavyweight boxing glory – in a movie called *Rocky Balboa*. Just that. Not *Rocky 10* or *Rocky 18*, but *Rocky Balboa*, which is evidently supposed to have a dignified, end-stopped ring to it: simply his full name, a man movingly rendering up a final account of himself. Incidentally, Sylvester Stallone is 60. It could be that Rocky the Italian Stallion, the legendary boxer he first created in 1976, is supposed to be younger than that, but no one in this film ever has the bad taste to mention his precise age. At any rate, Rocky is now a melancholy widower running an Italian restaurant. Then he gets a chance to prove himself in the ring. Again.

D THE SIMPSONS MOVIE

The Simpsons are finally, triumphantly, here, after much whingeing and whispering that we've all got Simpsons fatigue and that the movie was only going to be a feature-length version of the TV show. To which I can only say 'only'? It's only going to be superbly funny and well-written all the way through? With a creative IQ that easily outpaces 99% of everything else Hollywood churns out? And as for Simpsons fatigue, I was too busy laughing to notice any. The gags are razor-sharp and lightning-swift; they keep coming, and the writing just puts everything else to shame, in the cinema just as on television. So many movies promise what they could never deliver in a million years. *The Simpsons Movie* gives you everything you could possibly want, and maybe it's a victim of its own gargantuan accomplishment. 85 minutes is not long enough to do justice to 17 years of comedy genius. It's still great stuff.

E CASINO ROYALE

Daniel Craig has taken on the mantle of 007, and the result is a death-defying, sportscar-driving, cocktail-recipe-specifying triumph. Daniel Craig is a fantastic Bond, and all those whingers out there who think otherwise should hang their heads in shame. Craig was inspired casting. He has effortless presence and lethal danger; he brings a serious actor's ability to a fundamentally unserious part; he brings out the playfulness and the absurdity, yet never sends it up. He's easily the best Bond since Sean Connery, and perhaps, even … well, let's not get carried away. It is all ridiculously enjoyable, because the smirking and the quips and the gadgets have been cut back. Mr Craig brings off cinema's most preposterous role with insouciant grit: I hope he doesn't quit too soon. For the first time in ages, I am actually looking forward to the next James Bond movie.

LANGUAGE DEVELOPMENT modifying and intensifying adjectives

1 **In the film reviews, the writer uses certain adverbs to intensify or modify the meaning of the descriptive adjectives. Look back at the reviews and underline the phrases below. What are they describing?**

1 horrifically embarrassing (review B)
2 wildly implausible (review C)
3 superbly funny (review D)
4 ridiculously enjoyable (review E)

EMPHASISING ADJECTIVES

In addition to the standard quantifying adverbs (such as *extremely, very, incredibly, terribly, really* etc), you can often emphasise what you want to say by forming an adverb from an adjective with a similar meaning to the adjective you want to use.
For example: *hilarious + funny = hilariously funny*.

2 **Form adverbs from the words in the box to complete the sentences. In some cases more than one answer may be possible.**

back-aching   delightful   genuine   ridiculous
strange   tedious

1 I didn't like the music but the children's dance was _____ entertaining.
2 That was one of the most _____ boring films I've ever had to endure.
3 The plot was _____ silly, but I watched it anyway.
4 Although it was a bit weird, the programme was still _____ fascinating.
5 The documentary was _____ interesting despite being far too long.
6 I enjoyed the opera, despite having to sit in _____ uncomfortable seats.

3 **What is wrong with these sentences?**

1 Angelina Jolie is very brilliant. She's my favourite star.
2 It was an absolutely good film. You really should go and see it.

4 **Which of the adjectives in the box are gradable and can therefore be preceded by *very* and other intensifying adverbs?**

annoying   delightful   disastrous   dull
exciting   fascinating   funny   good   hilarious
interesting   original   perfect   ridiculous   scary
unbelievable

5 **Which of the intensifying adverbs in the box can be used with non-gradable adjectives, such as *brilliant*? Can any also be used with both gradable and non-gradable adjectives?**

absolutely   awfully   completely   extremely
fairly   incredibly   pretty   quite   rather   really
totally   very

6 **Some adverbs and adjectives form collocations. Choose the option that would NOT normally follow the word in bold.**

1 **highly**   *unlikely / amused / angered / qualified*
2 **bitterly**   *embarrassed / cold / disappointed / resentful*
3 **deeply**   *hurt / ill / offended / moved*
4 **greatly**   *confused / mistaken / changed / different*
5 **seriously**   *injured / ill / wounded / kidnapped*
6 **fully**   *aware / insured / amused / conscious*
7 **perfectly**   *simple / cold / fair / reasonable*
8 **most**   *kind / generous / helpful / nice*

7 **Work in pairs. Discuss the questions. Use adjectives and intensifying adverbs. What do you think of these types of film?**

1 musicals
2 old classic black and white films
3 Hollywood films with happy endings
4 Chinese martial arts films
5 romantic films
6 horror films

KEY WORD *quite*

QUITE CAN BE USED:

1 to indicate that something is true to a fairly great extent, but is less emphatic than *very* or *extremely*.
2 with non-gradable adjectives to mean *absolutely*.
3 to emphasise what you are saying.
4 after a negative to make what you are saying less definite or weaker.
5 in front of a noun group to emphasise that a person or thing is very impressive or unusual.
6 to express your agreement with someone.

8 **○ 40** **Listen to sentences a–f. Which of the points above (1–6) do they demonstrate?**

a 'I think it's time Roger retired.' 'Yes, well, quite!'
b Gillian is quite a little trouble maker, isn't she!
c I think it's quite a good idea to take her advice.
d It's quite clear to me that you were not listening.
e After the accident, he was never quite the same.
f I thought the script was quite ridiculous.

LISTENING understanding purpose and function

9 **Work in pairs. Discuss the following points.**

1 Films adapted from books can never be as good as the book.
2 Arty films are better than mainstream films.
3 There should be more women film directors.

UNDERSTANDING PURPOSE AND FUNCTION

Understanding the purpose and function of what you're listening to can help you answer questions correctly. By reading the questions carefully before listening, you may be able to work out the purpose or function of each extract.

---

10 **Read questions 1–6 in exercise 11. Which extract attempts to:**

a establish a socio-political message?
b inform us of how someone got started on their career?
c highlight the differences of opinion between two speakers?

11 ⊙ 41 **Listening, Part 1**

You will hear three different extracts. For questions 1–6, choose the answer (A, B, or C) which fits best according to what you hear. There are two questions for each extract.

Extract One
You hear part of an interview with a filmmaker called Richard Morrison.
1 Richard's style of filmmaking was strongly influenced by
A seeing films about family life.
B having access to his father's camera.
C films that diverged from mainstream cinema.

2 Why does Richard claim he is not interested in making 'arty' films?
A He doesn't think they are popular enough.
B He wants to express his message in a different way.
C He thinks they tend to be too short.

Extract Two
You hear two people talking about adaptations of children's books into films.
3 The woman suggests that film adaptations of children's books
A tend to correspond with childhood memories of the books.
B can renew an interest in the original literature.
C can put people off ever reading the books again.

4 What does the man think about film adaptations of children's books?
A He wonders why the films are made.
B He thinks people who love the books shouldn't see the films.
C He doesn't want his own interpretation of the books to be affected.

Extract Three
You hear part of a radio programme in which two women are discussing female film directors.
5 The first woman's main point is that
A there should be more female directors.
B women should make films that are more commercial.
C attitudes towards women in the film industry are too hostile.

6 According to the second woman, the main reason why it is difficult for women to become film directors is that
A there are too few opportunities in the film industry for new directors.
B men are more likely to be creative.
C woman may not be so skilled at financing films.

12 **Discuss. Besides Hollywood movies, what other kinds of films are there?**

GRAMMAR participle clauses

1 **Match the sentences (1–3) with the options (a–c).**

1 Climbing out of the pool, he reached for his towel.
2 Carrying a heavy tray, she walked into the bar.
3 Emptying the bag, he dropped the coins on the floor.
a two actions occurring simultaneously
b the second action is caused by, or is a result of the first action
c one action is immediately followed by another

PARTICIPLE CLAUSES

Participle clauses are often used to join separate sentences or clauses together and they can make a sentence more descriptive or interesting. They tend to be used more often in formal or written English than spoken English. They are formed with the present or past participle form of the verb and often replace a noun, pronoun, relative pronoun or conjunction.

2 **Read the sentences and note the changes that have been made.**

Present participle clauses

1 Joe walked into the room. He was humming a tune.
   *Joe walked into the room **humming** a tune.*
2 It was a sunny day so we decided to go for a walk.
   *The day **being** sunny, we decided to go for a walk.*
3 He didn't know if his parents would agree, so he decided to ask them.
   *Not **knowing** if his parents would agree, he decided to ask them.*

Past participle clauses

4 She opened the door and looked down the road.
   ***Having opened** the door, she looked down the road.*
5 As / Since / Because she had passed with top marks, she got into Oxford.
   ***Having passed** with top marks, she got into Oxford.*
6 As / Since / Because the house was designed by a top architect, it should be impressive.
   ***(Having been) Designed** by a top architect, the house should be impressive.*

▶ GRAMMAR REFERENCE (SECTION 12) **PAGE 217**

3 **Replace the underlined words in the sentences using a participle clause. Make any other changes that are necessary.**

1 <u>Because</u> I didn't know what else to do, I called Mum.
2 The sea <u>was</u> so warm that they decided to go for a swim.
3 <u>Since</u> we had been told off, we stopped talking.
4 <u>As</u> I had told Annette my secret, I wasn't surprised that everyone knew about it.
5 Jackson was looking for a film to watch. <u>He</u> switched on the TV.
6 <u>Seeing as</u> she had fallen in love with him, she decided to write him a poem.

4 **Replace the underlined parts of the film review with a participle or participle clause. Put brackets around words that could be left out.**

LARA CROFT TOMB RAIDER
THE CRADLE OF LIFE

In the second Tomb Raider film, *The Cradle of Life*, Academy Award Winner Angelina Jolie once again brings glamour and strength to her role as Lara Croft, <u>who has been recognised as one of the world's most dynamic action heroines</u> ever to hit the big screen. <u>As she faces</u> her greatest challenges yet, the intrepid tomb raider must travel the world on a spectacular adventure. <u>She demonstrates her physical prowess and reveals her courage as never before, and Lara proves</u> that nothing can prevent her from searching to find the mysterious whereabouts of a hidden site known as The Cradle of Life. <u>She knows that Pandora's box is concealed there, and that she must protect the secret</u> of its location in order to save the world from <u>the most unspeakable evil that anyone has ever known</u>.

PARTICIPLES AS ADJECTIVES

Participles can be used as adjectives before nouns when the meaning is to describe a general quality, not a current event.

5 **In which sentence is the present participle used as an adjective?**

1 Gillian was an annoying child.
2 Gillian was annoying the grown-ups.

6 **Sometimes the past participle adjective has to be used after the noun, not before it. Which of the sentences is correct?**

1 Any discussed questions at the meeting …
2 Any questions discussed at the meeting …

PARTICIPLES WITH OBJECTS

When a participle has an object the whole expression can sometimes be used as an adjective before a noun. For example, a *triumph that defies death, drives a sports car and specifies cocktail recipes* could be written as *a death-defying, sportscar-driving, cocktail-recipe-specifying triumph*.

7 **Rewrite the sentence.**

The vegetables were grown organically.
They _____ .

8 Rewrite the sentences using a participle phrase.

1 We felt tired after the journey.
It was a _____ .

2 The people this concerns should come to the meeting.
The people _____ .

3 They are Swiss but they speak French.
They _____ .

4 The colours on the curtains had faded.
The curtains had _____ .

5 The dogs that were barking were getting on my nerves.
The _____ .

6 The teacher had retired.
He was a _____ .

7 The only seats that were left were in the balcony.
Only _____ .

8 Her children have grown up.
She has _____ .

SPEAKING exchanging ideas (parts 3 and 4)

EXCHANGING IDEAS

In Speaking, Part 3, you and your partner will be asked to talk together for a total of three minutes. Sometimes you may be in groups of three, but then you will need to talk for about five minutes in total. The interlocutor and assessor will be assessing each of you separately. In Part 3 they will be listening in particular for how you interact with your partner(s) and exchange ideas. Of course, you are being assessed for your grammar and vocabulary, discourse management and pronunciation and interactive communication throughout the whole Speaking test.

Speaking, Parts 3 and 4

9 Work in pairs or groups of three. Turn to page 236 and look at the task.

10 Work in pairs. Discuss the questions on page 236.

USE OF ENGLISH open cloze

EXAM SPOTLIGHT

Reading and Use of English, Part 2
Identifying parts of speech

As we have seen, in Reading and Use of English, Part 2, it's advisable to read the whole text carefully in order to understand the gist and to look out for negative meaning, inverted structures, conjunctions and so on. Make sure you know what part of speech should go in each gap as this will make it easier to guess the missing word if you do not know it.

11 Read the sentences. Match the underlined words with the parts of speech in the box.

> adjective adverb article auxiliary conjunction
> modal noun particle preposition pronoun
> quantifier relative pronoun verb

1 It was, <u>without</u> doubt, one of the best evenings I've ever had.
2 You have to be <u>absolutely</u> certain that you want to go into the business.
3 If you don't hurry <u>up</u>, you're going to miss the show.
4 Why don't you <u>make</u> an effort with Steve?
5 You really <u>should / must</u> try harder!
6 Amy, <u>who</u> knew nothing about the film industry, enjoyed herself enormously.
7 Very <u>little</u> is known about his childhood.
8 She ordered the pizza <u>although</u> she knew she wouldn't eat it.
9 <u>Anyone</u> who has been to Greece will know that the light is different there.
10 Given <u>the</u> lack of knowledge we have, it's amazing that we don't do more research.

12 Reading and Use of English, Part 2

For questions 1–8, read the text below and think of the word which best fits each gap. Use only one word in each gap.

Writing a great screenplay

When talking about a film we may comment on the acting, the directing and the plot, but only very rarely (1) _____ we think about the scriptwriting. Scriptwriters (2) _____ general are denied most of the glory, and (3) _____ from two Academy Awards given out for writing each year, even the most talented screenwriters tend to remain more or less anonymous. And this is (4) _____ the fact that the script is the fundamental tool of the film; (5) _____ it, there would be no film to speak of.
Even if the script is (6) _____ of the few to be taken up by a director, the writing process doesn't end there. Everyone on the set may have a go (7) _____ embellishing and tweaking it. Difficult though it is to reach the top, there is a demand for good scripts. Even in Hollywood, where thousands of scripts are read weekly, there is a desperate shortage (8) _____ material that is fresh in voice and vision.

WRITING a film review

1 **⊙ 42 Listen to some people describing their favourite films. Can you guess which films they are describing? Have you seen these films?**

Writing, Part 2

2 **Read the exam question below and underline the key words.**

> Your college magazine has invited its readers to send in a review of a film they've recently seen, briefly outlining the plot, and giving their opinions on the acting, directing and any other elements of the film that stood out. You recently saw a film at the local cinema and have decided to write a review.

3 **Before you start writing your film review, think carefully about how you are going to plan it. Make notes about these points.**

1 Choose a film: write down the names of three films you know you could write about (one you loved, one you hated and one that failed to move you either way).

2 Write a brief summary of one of the films you chose above, using no more than 100 words. Be succinct. Don't waffle.

3 Do you know the names of any of the cast, the director, the writer, etc? If not, it doesn't matter, just use the character names when you talk about the story. If you can, fill in the names of the people involved in the film you summarised above.

4 Talk about the elements of the film that really impressed you or failed to achieve a positive effect. Write a word or short phrase about the following elements in the film that you chose above: acting, setting, costumes, plot, script, directing, etc.

TIP:
Your favourite film is not necessarily the best one to describe. The best one might be a film you hated, or were indifferent to. Try to think of a film that is clear in your mind and you know a few things about (i.e. who was in it, or who directed it).

TIP:
Try to keep your words down here. You don't need to tell the whole story in detail – only the main idea. Don't give away the ending or destroy any moments of suspense for your reader. Sometimes you only need to describe the scenario at the film's opening.

TIP:
If you do know the names of the main characters, then either put them in brackets after the character's name or say: [Actor's name] who plays [character's name]… If you don't know the character names, use generic terms like: the hero, the heroine, the protagonist, the villain, etc.

TIP:
If possible, avoid saying I loved … or I hated … too often. Use the passive or describe the effects or results of the film on the audience.

DESCRIPTIVE LANGUAGE

Think about the words you can use to describe elements of the film. Try to use descriptive adjectives with modifying or intensifying adverbs – and try to avoid saying *very*, *really*, *good* or *bad* too often. Some noun and adjective groups often form collocations. For example: *wooden acting*, *two-dimensional characters*, *a moving story*, *a complicated plot*. Read film reviews as often as you can, and make a note of any collocations you come across.

4 **Rewrite the sentences so that they do not use the first person (*I*).**

I really loved the music because it was so powerful and it added emotion to the film.
The powerful music added emotion to the film.

1 I didn't like the script because it was dull and failed to bring life to the story.
2 I wasn't impressed by the wooden actors and their performances didn't convince me.
3 I thought the story was quite interesting but I think it could have been developed further.

5 **Rewrite the underlined words in your own words.**

1 The scenery was <u>very nice</u>.
2 The actor who played the main role was <u>really good</u>.
3 The script was <u>very boring</u>.
4 The directing was <u>not very good</u>.

6 **Read the review opposite and tick the elements in the box that have been mentioned.**

> acting   cinematography (filming)   costumes
> directing   editing   genre   music   plot   script
> sets   special effects   the reviewer's opinion

The Illusionist

(2006, USA, Thriller/Period/Romance, cert PG, 109 mins)

Set in Vienna at the turn of the century, the film centres around an enigmatic showman, Edward Abramovitz, <u>who is charismatically played</u> by Edward Norton. <u>He discovers that he has a talent for magic, and</u> he soon charms a beautiful young duchess called Sophie with his tricks. Unfortunately, <u>because he is</u> the son of a low-born cabinet-maker, he knows they are not destined to be together. She begs him to use his magic so she can disappear with him but the pair are soon tragically parted and forced to go their separate ways.

Years go by and Abramovitz is now appearing on stage in the capital, staggering the audience with his tricks. <u>He has changed his name, and he is known as</u> Eisenheim the Illusionist: clearly a brilliant magician and a phenomenal success. <u>In need of</u> an assistant one night, fate brings him face to face with the beautiful fiancée of the Crown Prince Leopold, <u>who is played</u> very convincingly by Rufus Sewell. The supercilious prince allows his intended bride (Jessica Biel) to descend from the royal box and assist Eisenheim with a trick. As he looks into her eyes, in front of hundreds, the young magician recognises her as his beloved Sophie and fate begins to take its course once again.

Adapted from a 1997 short story <u>which was written</u> by Pulitzer prize-winner Steven Millhauser, director Neil Burger has created a slick and subtle piece of work. The film skilfully sketches in the background historical detail, and makes it the setting for an elegant 19th century tale.

7 **Rewrite the underlined parts of the text using a participle clause and deleting any unnecessary words.**

> **EXAM SPOTLIGHT**
>
> **Writing, Part 2** Writing reviews
>
> In the Writing paper you may be asked to write a review. This could be a review of a film, a book, a musical concert, a theatrical performance, an art exhibition or something similar. You may have to use your own imagination or experiences and adapt these to suit the review topic.

8 **Think of a subject for each of the review types mentioned below so that you will be prepared if you are asked to write about any of them in the exam.**

a book   a musical concert
a theatrical performance   an art exhibition

9 **Write one of the following.**

1 Write a review of one of the films you've outlined in exercise 3.

2

> A bookshop website has invited its readers to send in a review of a film they've seen that's been adapted from a book. You have just seen the film version of a book that you've also read and you decide to write a review, commenting on how successful you think the adaptation to screen has been. Say whether you would recommend it to other readers and why.

REVIEW 3

1 Match the adjectives in A with the intensifiers or modifiers in B to complete the sentences.

A

bitterly
deeply
deliciously
fully
greatly
most
perfectly
ridiculously
tediously
thoroughly

B

annoying
aware
disappointed
dull
kind
mistaken
mouthwatering
offended
reasonable
small

1 The film was _____ , and we left half way through it.
2 Her handwriting is so _____ that you can hardly read it!
3 I was _____ by your unkind words, and expect an apology!
4 It's _____ of you to give me flowers, Mr Jones! Thank you!
5 Sally was _____ not to be chosen for a part in the school play, and cried all the way home.
6 I am _____ of all the hard work you've put in, but I'm afraid your essay is irrelevant.
7 Ron has a(n) _____ habit of repeating you when you're talking to him.
8 You are _____ if you think I'm going to the party with you dressed like that!
9 The food in that restaurant was good, but the _____ desserts were the best part!
10 Your reaction to the news is _____ , and I understand how you feel, so don't apologise.

2 Complete the sentences with the phrases in the box. Make any necessary changes.

bottom line   nitty gritty   out of luck
out of order   out of the blue   out of the question
out of your mind   rock the boat   take its toll
tough going

1 That last part of the race was _____ , as it was mainly uphill and our legs were tired.
2 Sorry, but you're _____ ! We sold the last one this morning.
3 The long wait for news of her whereabouts had _____ on Jane's parents, and they looked tired and drawn.
4 Right, team! Let's get down to the _____ ! Who's going to be responsible for feeding the pigs?
5 Don't use the toilet on the third floor! It's _____ .
6 It's _____ for a seven-year-old to go skydiving, Milton! You're too young!
7 I know things have been going well between you and Fred lately, and I don't want to _____ , but I'm afraid I have something to tell you.
8 I know packaging is important, but the _____ is this: will the product sell?
9 You must be _____ to want to take four six-year-olds camping!
10 I hadn't heard from Claire for years, and then, _____ she phones me!

3 Reading and Use of English, Part 3

For questions 1–8, read the text below. Use the word given in capitals at the end of some of the lines to form a word that fits in the gap in the same line.

Second-hand clothes, anyone?

The last few years have seen a revival of interest in recycling old clothes and textiles. There is a growing (1) _____ of the negative impact the clothing industry has on the environment, and anti-consumerism (2) _____ are vociferous in their criticism of the (3) _____ nature of the fashion industry. As a result, buying brand new clothes from a retail store is now seen by many as (4) _____ . A growing number of websites market clothes which have been manufactured using (5) _____ practices, and several offer tips on how to revamp your wardrobe at very little cost. No longer is it (6) _____ to buy your clothes from second-hand outlets or charity shops, and (7) _____ university students are now being joined by professional women in doing so!

AWARE

ACTIVE
MATERIAL

ETHIC
SUSTAIN

FASHION
PENNY

A new craze has taken things a step further: clothes swapping events, to which you take your (8) _____ clothes along, and using a points system, you 'buy' other items on offer. Second-hand clothes have never been so sought after!

WANT

4 Make the following sentences more emphatic.

1 You should go out and meet people more.
   What _____ .
2 Because I didn't want to disturb them, I left without saying goodbye.
   Not _____ .
3 I don't understand how he managed to work it out that way.
   How _____ .
4 Calm down! You just need a break from working on the computer.
   All _____ .
5 The weather was so cold that they decided to light a fire.
   So cold _____ .
6 Since she had dreamed of going to Alaska all her life, Grace was extremely excited.
   Having _____ .
7 I don't know where he gets his bad temper from!
   Where _____ .
8 Because she hoped to become an Olympic swimmer, Hannah trained very hard.
   Hoping _____ .
9 As I hadn't seen Mike and Helen for several years, we had a lot to talk about.
   Not _____ .
10 Although this car is old, it is reliable.
   Old _____ .

5 Complete the dialogue with a suitable modal auxiliary phrase and the verbs in brackets.

Andy: Neville's late. It's not like him.
Sharon: I suppose he (1) _____ (get) lost.
Andy: He (2) _____ (not get) lost! My instructions were pretty clear! Anyway, he (3) _____ (phone) if he was stuck.
Sharon: Knowing Neville, he (4) _____ (not have) a mobile phone. He hates them! It's annoying, though. He (5) _____ (be) late when we want to go to the cinema!
Andy: Well, seeing as he hasn't come, we (6) _____ (go).
Sharon: What if he turns up and we're not here?
Andy: That (7) _____ (be) his fault for being …
Neville: Hi, guys! Sorry, I'm late. I missed the bus!
Sharon: Well, you (8) _____ (call) us!
Neville: I (9) _____ (do), but my mobile wasn't working.
Andy: Anyway, we're too late for the cinema now, so what shall do? We (10) _____ (order) a pizza and watch a DVD.
Sharon: Yeah, why not!

6 Replace the underlined words in the sentences with a suitable reporting verb. Make any other necessary changes.

1 He said he was sorry he had missed her party.
2 Tommy said he hadn't put worms in the teacher's bag.
3 She said she would kill herself if he left her.
4 He said she had lied to him.
5 We told him that the Indian restaurant on the corner was good.
6 Clare said she had taken the money.
7 Julie said she thought it would be a beautiful wedding.
8 They told us it was dangerous to go near the railway tracks.

7 Reading and Use of English, Part 4

For questions 1–6, complete the second sentence so that it has a similar meaning to the first sentence, using the word given. Do not change the word given. You must use between three and six words, including the word given.

1 I think it's terrible that you didn't apologise to her for breaking that vase!
   MIGHT
   You _____ breaking that vase!
2 'I demand to see the manager at once!' said the angry customer.
   INSISTED
   The angry customer _____ immediately.
3 We went for a coffee because the train was delayed.
   BEEN
   The train _____ , we went for a coffee.
4 We'd thought Dale would cancel dinner, but he didn't.
   AS
   Dale _____ we'd expected.
5 Although she had no idea where she was going, she packed her bags and left.
   KNOWING
   She packed her bags and left, _____ she was going.
6 My poor head! Someone please tell Nick to stop practising on his drums!
   WOULD
   I wish _____ stop practising on his drums! I've got a headache!

13 GETTING THE MESSAGE ACROSS

GETTING STARTED

1 **Work in pairs. Put the communication verbs in the box into the categories below.**

> broadcast clarify convey exchange explain
> impart instil publicise publish reveal send
> share transmit

Ideas Information Messages Knowledge

2 **Complete the sentences with one of the verbs from exercise 1. Note that more than one answer may be possible.**

1 I'm not sure I understood you there, Dan. Could you give me an example to _____ your idea?

2 The soldier struggled to get the radio to work so that he could _____ a message to headquarters and warn them that the enemy was advancing.

3 The artist uses powerful images to _____ his ideas about life and death.

4 As a teacher, Jack endeavoured to _____ not only knowledge but also wisdom to his students.

5 The sales manager tried to _____ determination into his sales team.

6 Social media sites are great places to _____ interesting articles and fun pictures.

7 _____ your own online book is very quick, simple and cheap these days.

8 The news was _____ on every TV channel when the president resigned.

READING understanding text structure

3 **Decide which structure (a or b) the texts (1 and 2) will usually have.**

1 an examination of the historical development of the car

2 an analysis of conflicting scientific opinion

a comparison of lines of argument, supported by examples

b a straightforward chronological pattern

4 **Read the title of the extract opposite. What do you think the article is going to be about?**

5 **Reading and Use of English, Part 7**

You are going to read an extract from an article. Six paragraphs have been removed from the extract. Choose from the paragraphs (A–G) the one which fits each gap (1–6). There is one extra paragraph which you do not need to use.

Hello,
is there anybody out there?

In 1974, the world was still in the grips of the space race, with manned missions to the moon and space probes being launched to far-off planets. The possibilities for space exploration seemed limitless and what, or who, we might find out there no longer just the stuff of science fiction. At an observatory in Puerto Rico, astronomer Frank Drake transmitted a message out into space using a powerful radio telescope, the first deliberate attempt to communicate with extra-terrestrial life.
1 […]

Drake went on to be involved with fellow members of the SETI Institute, set up to investigate extra-terrestrial intelligence, in the first physical messages to be sent into space. Together with Carl Sagan, he put together the Voyager Golden Records which were placed aboard two Voyager spacecraft that were launched by NASA in 1977. These contained images and sounds from Earth, together with recordings of spoken messages in 55 different languages. By August 2012, the Voyager 1 probe had reached the outer limits of our solar system and just entered interstellar space.
2 […]

However the means may vary though, in terms of sophistication and potential reach, the question remains about what any message aimed at life beyond our planet should contain. In his Arecibo message, Drake opted for a mix of scientific and physical information about us and our planet together with the appeal of mathematical principles. The binary code of Drake's message, for example, was arranged into 73 lines of 23 characters per line, both prime numbers which it was believed may help aliens decode the message.
3 […]

This mathematical approach has its critics though. As Seth Shostak, senior astronomer at SETI, points out, it'd be pretty disappointing if the first message received from beyond our planet was something as basic as the value of Pi, which after all, we all learnt in high school. He suggests that in fact, it's not worth worrying too much about a deliberate message, because we're broadcasting all the time via the radio and TV signals being transmitted constantly around the world. If aliens are tuning into anything, it'll be the BBC or NBC or the latest reality TV show.
4 […]

Communication is, of course, two way and there's interest in not just the messages we send out, but the ones that we might receive too. Much of SETI's research in recent decades has been focused on trying to detect possible incoming signals from outer space. The Optical SETI project, under the direction of Frank Drake, uses the Lick Observatory's 40-inch Nickel Telescope to detect pulses of laser light deliberately sent out from civilisations many light years away.
5 […]

Another problem is that aliens may not even know we're here and so may not be targeting us directly. From a point of view thousands of light years away, they may only have the haziest information about our planet and have little to tell them that it supports sentient life any more than, say, Mars or any of our other near neighbours.
6 […]

Arguments over practical and technical considerations aside though, many astronomers are confident that they'll detect some form of extra-terrestrial intelligence in the next few decades. However, for the moment, one thing seems clear, the answer to the question 'Have we found aliens?' is from most experts 'No, not yet'. So we still have time to decide how we'll respond when the call does finally come in.

A Of course, debate about how to contact alien life beyond our planet is not new. Back in the 19th century, Austrian astronomer Joseph von Littrow was associated with a project to dig huge circular trenches in the Sahara Desert which would be filled with kerosene and set ablaze so as to be visible from space.

B Some researchers believe that the best way to find a common language with extra-terrestrials is through the universal truths of mathematics. Paul Horowitz, a professor of physics at Harvard University, argues that mathematical patterns such as prime numbers or the value of Pi are maybe the most fundamental way to initiate a message.

C Researchers admit though that there are areas where such searches are weak. Shostak concedes that we don't as yet have the capability to be searching for signals on all frequencies, all of the time, from anywhere in the universe. He predicts however that with increases in computing power, it's only a matter of time before such a level of monitoring may be possible.

D What are the chances of us picking up such a message sent out somewhere in our general direction? How will we recognise it when it arrives and how will we make any sense of it? Taking all the mind-blowingly enormous parameters of space, time and probability into account, to the layman, the prospect of actually exchanging any kind of messages with extra-terrestrials seems very remote indeed.

E The Arecibo message, as it came to be known, was in binary code, a sequence of 1,679 ones and zeroes broadcast as radio waves and aimed at the globular star cluster M13, roughly 21,000 light years away on the edge of the Milky Way. The message took less than three minutes to send and if correctly decoded would reveal a bitmap image containing, among other things, a human figure and a graphic of the double helix structure of DNA. Of course, any response to this message would take hundreds, if not thousands of years to get back to us.

F The Drake Equation, first formulated by Drake in 1961, sets out specific factors thought to play a role in the development of extra-terrestrial civilisations advanced enough technologically to be potential targets for interstellar communication. The equation has no unique solution but is intended as a tool to prompt debate and research into the possibility of communicating with life on other planets.

G Other commentators suggest that any advanced life-form would simply tap straight into the vast array of data out there in cyberspace. Surely the Internet would provide an overview of life on Earth in all its infinite variety and complexity that no single message could possibly convey? Whether that's the picture we would like to present to the rest of the universe, however, is open to question.

LANGUAGE DEVELOPMENT nouns followed by particles

1 Complete the sentences taken from the text on page 125 with the correct particle.

1 By August 2012, the Voyager 1 probe had reached the outer limits _____ our solar system.

2 Of course, debate _____ how to contact alien life beyond our planet is not new.

3 He predicts that with increases _____ computing power, it's only a matter of time.

4 Any response _____ this message would take hundreds, if not thousands of years to get back to us.

2 Choose the correct particle to complete the sentences.

1 Scientists are in dispute _____ what kind of message should be sent into space.
   a for   b with   c on   d over

2 Kathleen is an authority _____ communication in dolphins.
   a on   b over   c for   d about

3 For years, the SETI Institute has been trying to set up a channel _____ communication between humans and extra-terrestrial intelligence.
   a in   b of   c over   d with

4 Few people have been privileged enough to have had contact _____ dolphins or whales in the wild.
   a over   b to   c with   d between

5 I've been in communication _____ an expert in New York, and he is going to send me some information.
   a to   b on   c for   d with

6 The Internet allows us access _____ more information than ever before.
   a on   b in   c to   d for

7 There has been a breakdown in communication _____ the workers and the management.
   a from   b with   c between   d for

8 The Moon alphabet was developed as an alternative _____ Braille.
   a for   b to   c of   d over

KEY WORD *set*

To *set something ablaze*, *set something alight* and *set fire to something* all mean to start a fire. Many other phrases with *set* mean *start* or *establish* something.

3 Which of the words in the box can follow *set*?

> a desire   a goal   a pattern   a point
> a precedent   a standard   a trend   an example
> in motion   money

4 Match the actions (1–10) with the person who does them (a–j).

1	set sail	a	surgeon
2	set a record	b	a happy couple
3	set a date	c	a teacher
4	set up a business	d	an athlete
5	(try to) set the world to rights	e	a hunter
6	set a test	f	a waiter
7	set a table	g	a writer
8	set a bone	h	an idealist
9	set pen to paper	i	an explorer
10	set a trap	j	an entrepreneur

5 Reading and Use of English, Part 4

For questions 1–6, complete the second sentence so that it has a similar meaning to the first sentence, using the word given. Do not change the word given. You must use between three and six words, including the word given.

1 There is a lot of disagreement among politicians about government spending on space travel.
   DISPUTE
   Politicians are _____ government spending on space travel.

2 An impression of what life was like thousands of years ago can be gained from the cave paintings.
   CONVEY
   The cave paintings _____ what life was like thousands of years ago.

3 Don't bother trying to stop Steven – he's determined to go.
   SET
   Steven _____ , so don't bother trying to stop him.

4 Scientific information is available to the general public via the university website.
   ACCESS
   The university website allows _____ scientific information.

5 Darren used examples of local businesses to illustrate his idea.
   CLARIFIED
   Darren _____ putting forward examples of local businesses.

6 Just as we were leaving to go on holiday, my boss called me to say there was an emergency meeting!
   SET
   We _____ holiday, when my boss called me to an emergency meeting!

GRAMMAR (1) text references (*this, that, it, such, these, those*)

REFERENCE WORDS

Every written text contains several features which enable the reader to understand how it is organised. Reference words are used to refer to something that has already been mentioned, or they may point forward to an example, or the next point. *This, that, it, these, those* and *they* are reference words.

6 The following sentences all appear in *Hello, is there anybody out there?* on page 125. What does each of the words in italics refer to?

1 *These* contained images and sounds from Earth, together with recordings of spoken messages in 55 different languages. (line 15)
2 *This* mathematical approach has its critics though. (line 29)
3 Whether *that's* the picture we would like to present to the rest of the universe, however, is open to question. (paragraph G)
4 *They* may only have the haziest information about our planet and have little to tell *them* that it supports sentient life. (line 49)

7 *Such* is also a reference word. What does it refer to in this paragraph?

Many scientists believe that studying communication in animals like dolphins and chimpanzees can help us to come closer to understanding the reasons for our own ability to speak. Such ideas have given rise to a number of research projects around the world.

8 Complete the text with suitable reference words.

Dolphin chatter

Dolphins are social creatures. Like humans, they form attachments to each other and live in 'families'. Following a 'safety in numbers' policy rather like our own, dolphins hunt for food in numbers and defend themselves more effectively in numbers. A mother needing to look for food will leave her offspring in the care of another adult female in the group. They also play together. (1) _____ behaviour would not be possible without good communication.

They achieve (2) _____ by producing whistles and other sounds. Since it is difficult to see underwater, dolphins send out high-pitched signals to find food, or detect danger. (3) _____ signals bounce back from whatever they hit and the dolphins are able to interpret what (4) _____ are. (5) _____ process is known as 'echolocation'. The human ear is unable to hear the dolphins' signals, but we have managed to develop machinery which can pick (6) _____ up. After years of careful study, scientists have ascertained that they use (7) _____ system to call each other when they find food, and to ask for help or warn each other of danger. Dolphins also appear to 'chat' rather like we do, and while scientists are still far from being able to decipher exactly what they say, they are able to recognise certain sounds, along with the dolphins' use of body language. For instance, when they rub fins after being apart for a while it signifies a form of greeting. They clap their jaws together when there is a fight, and (8) _____ seems to mean 'back off'.

Another area of study which scientists are particularly interested in is (9) _____ of communication between mother dolphins and their offspring. In one experiment, a mother and her calf were placed in separate tanks which were connected by an audio link. They proceeded to chatter by squawking and chirping to each other, and appeared to know who they were talking to.

The question is, will we ever be able to communicate with dolphins? Now (10) _____ would really be something worth talking about!

▶ GRAMMAR REFERENCE (SECTION 13) **PAGE 218**

9 Discuss. Why might it be useful to be able to communicate with animals such as dolphins and chimpanzees? What, if anything, could we learn from them?

USE OF ENGLISH word formation (1)

SUFFIXES

A suffix is a letter or group of letters that is added to the end of a word in order to form a different word. There are many different kinds of suffix in the English language, which form adjectives, nouns or verbs.

EXAM SPOTLIGHT

Reading and Use of English , Part 3 Word formation

Adjectives ending with the suffixes *-able* and *-ible*
If in doubt, use *-able*, as this is far more common than *-ible*.

a   *-ible* is normally used when the adjective is related to a noun that adds *-ion* (not *-ation* or *-ition*, just *-ion*) to a verb or adjective.

corrupt – corruption – corruptible

b   If the part of the word before the suffix is not a complete word in itself, the suffix is usually *-ible*.

horror – horrible (there is no word *horr*)

c   If the word that the adjective relates to ends in a single *-e*, this is usually dropped before the suffix is added.

advise – advisable

d   If the part of the word before the suffix ends in *-ce* or *-ge*, the *-e* often remains, in order to preserve the pronunciation of the *c* or *g*.

replace – (ir)replaceable

e   A final *-y* becomes *-i* before *-able* (*-ible* never occurs after *-i*).

envy – enviable

f   If the final consonant of a verb is doubled in the present participle, it is also doubled before *-able*.

forget – forgetting – (un)forgettable

g   However, if the verb ends in *-fer*, the *r* is not doubled before *-able*.

prefer – preferring – preferable

h   In most other cases, the adjective is formed with *-able*.

1   Write the positive and negative adjectives ending in *-able* or *-ible* formed from the words in the box.

answer   change   conceive   dispense   exhaust
notice   pronounce   regret   rely   repress   stop
terror   transfer   vary   vision

2   Some words require further changes in addition to the suffix. Write the positive and negative adjectives with *-able* or *-ible* for these words, using a dictionary if necessary.

comprehend   destroy   divide   negotiate
perceive   repair

SPEAKING sustaining interaction

3   ⊙ 43   **Listen to two candidates starting to discuss the task on page 237. How successful are they at interacting?**

SUSTAINING INTERACTION

Sometimes your Speaking test partner may not have much to say, perhaps because they're nervous. However, in Speaking, Part 3, it's necessary to keep the conversation flowing between you. Make sure you give your partner time to express a view, perhaps by asking them a direct question about one of the ideas in the prompts, before you comment on it yourself. Remember, this will gain you marks, for attempting to interact, while at the same time giving your partner the chance to speak!

4   Look at the audioscript on page 250, and suggest ways Carlos might encourage Magda to respond in a more convincing way.

5   Work in pairs. Look at page 237 and talk about how effective these advertising methods might be for a new language school. You have about two minutes.

Now you have a minute to decide which method of advertising would be the most effective for a new language school. Remember to interact naturally.

LISTENING communicating with a purpose

EXAM SPOTLIGHT

Listening, Part 4 Purpose

In Listening, Part 4, you may be asked about the speaker's purpose, that is, what they are trying to achieve by speaking. The way speakers express themselves can help you to identify their purpose.

6 **Match the sentences (1–8) with their purposes (a–h).**

1 Could you tell me how much you charge for one of your workshops, please?
2 On the other hand, you could always pick up the phone and talk to him.
3 I'm afraid I really don't have time to help you with your presentation today.
4 I'm not so sure. That doesn't look to me like George's handwriting.
5 Let Jill finish explaining before you start talking.
6 Would you like me to check your report before you submit it?
7 The presentation starts at 3 o'clock and should finish about 4.30.
8 Do you think you could have a look at this email before I send it?

a disagreeing about something
b asking for information
c giving an order
d giving information
e offering to do something
f refusing to do something
g requesting some assistance
h suggesting an alternative

7 **Listening, Part 4**

🔘 44 **You will hear five short extracts in which people are talking about communicating.**

8 **A number of communication issues were raised by the speakers in exercise 7. Work in groups. Discuss one of the following points of view.**

1 Modern technology has increased the amount of communication that takes place, but encourages us to write and speak carelessly.
2 We spend too long talking about what needs to be done and not enough time doing it.
3 In a multicultural society, the problem of communication within public services needs to be addressed.
4 Communication skills should be taught in schools.

TASK ONE
For questions 1–5, choose from the list (A–H) what each person says about communication.

TASK TWO
For questions 6–10, choose from the list (A–H) what each speaker is trying to achieve by talking.

While you listen you must complete both tasks.

A They have gained confidence in their own ability.
B They admire the ability to communicate very precisely.
C They have witnessed how communication can resolve conflict.
D They believe that people's writing skills are getting worse.
E They are concerned about the messages presented in the media.
F They consider inaccurate writing unacceptable.
G They believe good communication skills should be rewarded.
H They think the language of the media should be simplified.

Speaker 1 ☐
Speaker 2 ☐
Speaker 3 ☐
Speaker 4 ☐
Speaker 5 ☐

A to raise funding
B to give reasons for starting a business
C to encourage active participation
D to reject criticism
E to resolve doubts
F to support a proposal
G to present their personal plan of action
H to justify a refusal

Speaker 1 ☐
Speaker 2 ☐
Speaker 3 ☐
Speaker 4 ☐
Speaker 5 ☐

GRAMMAR (2) *it / there* as introductory pronouns

1 Work in pairs. What is the difference between the pairs of sentences?

1 a It's very windy.
  b There's a lot of wind.
2 a It's a long way to Glasgow.
  b There's a long way still to go before we reach Glasgow.
3 a It's time to do your homework.
  b There's time to do your homework and go to the cinema, if you start now.

INTRODUCTORY *IT*

We usually introduce the sentence with *it* when …
1 an infinitive is the subject of a sentence.
2 we're beginning a sentence with a comment.

We also use *it* before …
3 impersonal verbs followed by *that*.
4 some verbs which require *it* before them.

INTRODUCTORY *THERE*

We use *there + be* when …
5 the subject of a sentence is an indefinite noun.
6 asking a general question.
7 introducing a noun followed by a relative clause.
8 *there* can be followed by another auxiliary + *be*.

2 Match the sentences (a–h) with the rules (1–8) in the box above.

a It appears that he isn't coming after all.
b It's odd you don't like this painting.
c There's something I have to do in town.
d It struck me how like her father she was.
e There may be something stuck behind the door.
f It's better to check what you write.
g There's a man on the phone for you.
h Is there anything I can do?

3 Complete the sentences with *it* or *there*.

1 'How far is _____ to Brighton?' '150 kilometres.'
2 _____ is no time to go home and get changed. We have to leave now.
3 _____'s a book on the table. Whose is _____ ?
4 Mum, _____'s nothing to do here. _____'s boring!
5 _____'s too cold to go out today. Is _____ anything on TV?
6 _____ may be some sense in going that way, but _____ is advisable to check the traffic news first.

WRITING a proposal

4 Writing, Part 2

You have read this advertisement on the website of a local charity that provides equipment and support for children in hospital:

Well Children – Charity Appeal

We are grateful for all the donations we receive from the local community. However, we still need more fundraising ideas.

We are inviting supporters of our charity to send in a proposal outlining an activity that might help us raise more money and explaining why you think your activity would be successful.

Write your **proposal**.

---

5 Discuss. Should your answer to the writing task above be formal, neutral or informal?

6 Which of these points could you include in your answer?

1 A description of what the charity, Well Children, does
2 A brief introduction to yourself
3 A neutral or formal tone throughout
4 Reasons for your choice of activity
5 An appeal to readers to support the charity
6 Your reasons for supporting the charity
7 A description of your proposed activity
8 Other activities that might help raise money
9 A summary of your ideas

7 Read the proposal opposite. Which of the points in exercise 6 does it include?

8 The proposal opposite includes some useful expressions. How does the writer say the following?

1 I am writing in reply to …
2 I would like to propose …
3 I think …
4 … in different ways
5 I'm sure …

Introduction

Being a strong supporter of 'Well Children', I know what a **fundamental** role the charity <u>has</u> in children's lives. In response to your **appeal**, I am proposing an activity that I think will help raise money and pass the word.

Fundraising Activity

I would like to put forward the idea that the charity <u>has</u> a Dragon Boat Race and <u>invites</u> local companies to <u>join</u>. Basically, Dragon Boat Racing needs a team of about 20 people and a boat that <u>is</u> a long canoe with paddles. Each team decorates its boat, with a dragon head at the front, and the members can wear outfits in **vibrant** colours that identify them. During the race, **one** team member <u>hits</u> a drum at the front of the boat, while the others paddle as fast as they can. The first team to complete the race wins.

Why a success?

In my view, this activity would be successful on two levels. Firstly, team members would have an incentive to advertise the event to everyone they know, so that the news <u>gets to</u> a lot of people and <u>makes</u> a lot of **sponsorship**. This would give funds a much-needed boost. Also, the event itself would appeal to a very wide range of spectators because it would be fun to watch. In this way, many people would <u>know</u> about 'Well Children' and all the incredibly valuable work it does.

Conclusion

There are numerous activities that can help **raise awareness**, but I feel certain that a Dragon Boat Race would be a **spectacular** way of <u>pushing</u> the charity and increasing public donations.

9 Some of the verbs in the model answer are incorrect or imprecise. Use the verbs in the In Other Words box to replace the underlined verbs and make the meaning more accurate. You may need to change the form of the verb.

IN OTHER WORDS

BEING PRECISE

beat   boost   get to hear   hold   involve
participate   play   produce   publicise   resemble
reach   spread

Writing, Part 2

10 Read the exam question. Brainstorm ideas about the aim of the proposal, the different methods you could suggest, the headings and the kind of language you should use in your answer.

> You recently enjoyed a meal at a local college restaurant run by the catering department and its students. After the meal, the principal handed out this notice.
>
> 'If you enjoyed your meal with us, please help raise awareness of our restaurant among the local community.
>
> We welcome proposals that suggest two methods we can use to advertise the college restaurant and that explain why these methods would produce more custom.'

11 Write your proposal in 220–260 words.

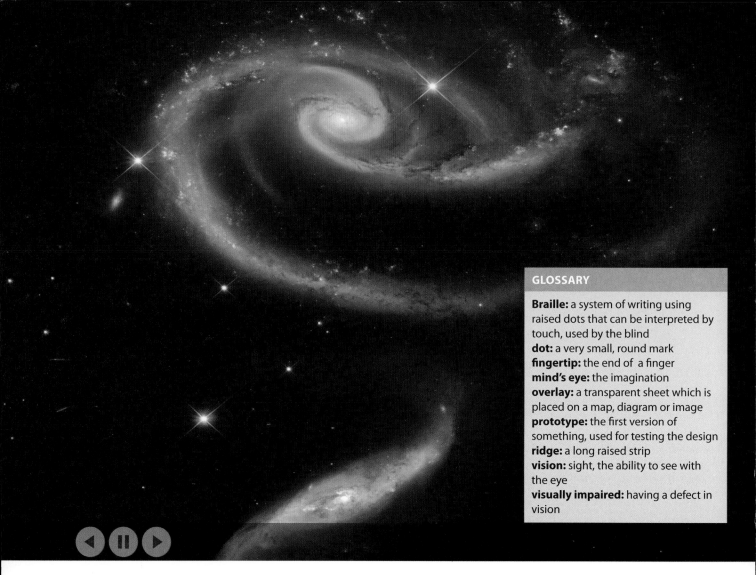

VIDEO the Braille Hubble

1 **Read about the Hubble Space Telescope. Replace the words in bold with the words in the box.**

> data   extremely   images
> orbits   spectacular
> the general public

The Hubble Space Telescope
(1) **goes around** the Earth just outside the Earth's atmosphere, and this means it can take
(2) **very** detailed, high-resolution
(3) **pictures** of space. As well as providing important
(4) **information** to astrophysicists, these photos have become popular with
(5) **people** because of their
(6) **amazing** beauty.

2 **You will watch a video set in a school for deaf and blind children. Before you watch, add your ideas to this mind map.**

problems — communication for deaf and blind people — solutions

3 **Work in pairs. How might you teach visually or hearing impaired children about space?**

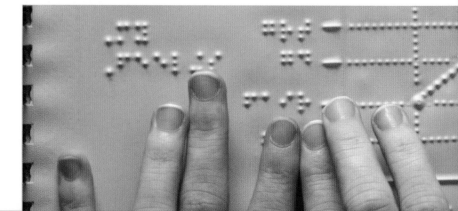

Watch the video. Choose the correct option (a or b) to complete the sentences.

1 Students at the Colorado School for the Deaf and Blind are using the book *Touch the Universe*
   a to learn about space and astronomy.
   b to help the author improve the book.

2 An unusual feature of the book is
   a Braille interpretations of the images.
   b Braille text describing the images.

Did anything you saw in the video surprise you? What? Why?

Watch the video again. Make notes to answer the questions.

1 What kind of thing can the students 'see' in the images?
2 What is the plastic sheet for?
3 Why are the students' opinions important?
4 What was the problem with the book's early version?

PEAKING Part 3 collaborative task

 IDEAS GENERATOR

MAKING YOUR RESPONSES RELEVANT TO THE DISCUSSION

In Part 3 of the Speaking test you need to keep the discussion going and try to develop it. To do this you need to express your own ideas clearly but you also need to listen carefully to what the other candidate says and take that into account. Read part of a discussion answering exercise 6, question 3. Read A's comment and the three possible responses from B. Which do you think would the best response in the Speaking test? Why?

Q: Why are the students' opinions important?

A: Well, I guess because the author is actually going to listen to their feedback and make changes to the book.

B1: Yes, the book will be improved after the students' comments.

B2: Yes, the students are able to say what the problems are when they read the Braille pages.

B3: Yes, I think that's it. And clearly these students are really motivated to be involved in this.

Work in pairs. Exchange your ideas from exercise 6. Listen to your partner, comment and respond.

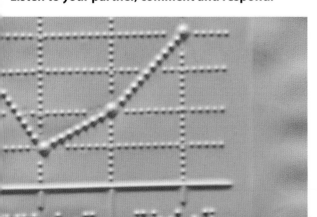

8 **You can use the phrases in the Useful Expressions box to signal that you have listened to your partner. Do the expressions suggest agreement or disagreement with what your partner has said?**

USEFUL EXPRESSIONS

LISTENING AND MOVING ON
Yes, I think that's right. And / But … *That's a good point, and also …* *As you say, …* *Yes, in other words …* *You're right. On the other hand …* *I see what you mean. And / But …*

9 **Work in pairs. Read A's comment in answer to the question. Take turns to respond as B, using all the expressions in the Useful Expressions box.**

Q: What was the problem with the book's early version?

A: There was something wrong with the plastic sheets.

B: …

10 **Work in pairs. Take turns as A and B. A gives an answer to the questions (1–6). B responds and develops the discussion. Try to use the expressions from the Useful Expressions box.**

1 Which news media has more impact: TV, newspapers or websites?
2 What's the best way to send a message to possible alien life forms: music, images or text?
3 Which is the best place to advertise a bicycle you want to sell: a local paper, eBay or a local shop window?
4 What's the most effective way of applying for a job: sending a CV, writing a letter or filling in a form?
5 What's the best way to raise money for charity: text messages, street collections or selling special products?
6 Which revision method leads to the best exam results: studying alone, revising with friends or relaxing and forgetting about it?

11 **Think about your performance in exercise 10. Which area do you need to improve in: ideas for things to say or ways of saying things in English? What can you do to improve?**

VIDEOSCRIPT 13 is on page 256.

14 GAIA'S LEGACY

GETTING STARTED

1 🔘 **45 Listen to a palaeontologist talking about the appearance of life on Earth and complete the table.**

Event	Time (millions of years ago)
1 The first multi-celled animals (sponges) appear	700
2 Animals without backbones (invertebrates) appear (jellyfish)	
3 The first animals with backbones (vertebrates) appear (fish)	
4 Plants appear on land	
5 Insects appear on land	
6 Fish develop lungs and leave the sea (amphibians)	
7 Reptiles (snakes, lizards) appear	
8 Dinosaurs start to dominate	
9 Mammals appear	
10 Birds appear	
11 Primates (monkeys, apes) appear	
12 Apes that use their hands to make tools appear	
13 Apes that walk on two legs appear	
14 Modern humans appear	

READING multiple-choice questions

2 Discuss. Have you heard of *Gaia* before? Who or what is it?

3 Skim read the text and answer exercise 2 in your own words.

MATCHING GIST TO DETAIL

Very often multiple-choice questions will ask you to match detailed information in the text to more generalised question stems.

4 Read the paragraph and decide which of the options (A, B, C or D) is the most accurate summary. Underline the parts of the paragraph that provide the answer.

In other words, he knew that when looking at the Earth in this way, what he was seeing was not so much a planet that just happened to be suitable for sustaining life, but a self-evolving and self-regulating living system, that could adjust itself to support life. This seemed to qualify the Earth as a living entity in her own right.

He realised that he was looking at a system
A that had multiple life-support systems.
B that was suitable for sustaining evolved life.
C that qualified as a living being in order to sustain life.
D that had the means to adapt conditions for life to exist.

5 Turn to Information File 4, page 241, and answer the questions.

PLANET EARTH – THE GAIA HYPOTHESIS

According to accounts, when the first astronauts in space looked down and saw the Earth floating in the vast black void, they had what can only be described as a profound spiritual experience; in an instant they had attained a 'global consciousness' in which all national and international boundaries disappeared, and they were left with the awesome realisation that they were mere 'planetary citizens'. To the astronauts, the planet looked as if it were some huge, single, living system. The photographs they brought back touched us all in some way, and the blue sphere in space came to symbolise the oneness of all humanity and life on Earth. The idea that the planet might be alive, strange though it sounds, was soon to gain credence, even among the scientific community.

Not long afterwards, in the 1970s, the hypothesis that the Earth's biosphere actually functions as a single living system was put forward by Dr James Lovelock, a British scientist and inventor who had been commissioned by NASA to help determine whether or not there was life on Mars. By comparing the atmospheres of both planets, he soon realised that, while Mars had a stable, unchanging, 'dead' atmosphere, Earth had no such equilibrium, and that there were some complex processes going on. It was this imbalance that made the planet suitable for sustaining life. He postulated that: 'the physical and chemical condition of the surface of the Earth, of the atmosphere and of the oceans has been, and is, actively made fit and comfortable by the presence of life itself ... in contrast to the conventional wisdom which held that life adapted to the planetary conditions as it, and they, evolved their separate ways.'

Lovelock knew that when looking at the Earth in this way, what he was seeing was not so much a planet that just happened to be suitable for sustaining life, but a self-evolving and self-regulating system that adjusted itself to support life. This seemed to qualify the Earth as a living entity in her own right, so he named her 'Gaia'.

Lovelock first published his idea in 1979, although the science behind the hypothesis was still imprecise. The ideas in the book provoked a storm of criticism, but also generated a lot of research, which has since led to profound new insights about life on Earth. For instance, Lovelock knew that the heat of the sun had increased by 25% since life began on Earth, yet he did not understand by which process the temperature on the surface had been kept at the optimum conditions suitable for sustaining life. Since that time, many of the mechanisms by which Gaia regulates her systems have been identified. For example, it has been shown that cloud formation over the open ocean is almost entirely a function of the metabolism of oceanic algae. Previously, it was thought that this cloud formation was a purely chemical phenomenon. Further research suggested that Gaia has automatically been controlling global temperature, atmospheric content, ocean salinity, and other factors in order to 'maintain the conditions suitable for its own survival', in much the same way that any individual organism regulates its body temperature, blood salinity, etc.

Similarly, all the life forms on the planet are a part of Gaia, in a way analogous to the different organs in a body, each with its own function. The oceans and atmosphere act as the planet's circulatory and temperature control systems, while the tropical rainforests could be compared to the liver, cleansing the body of toxins. In their diversity, the myriad life forms of earth co-evolve and contribute interactively to produce and sustain the system as a whole.

The Gaia theory has already had a huge impact on science and has inspired many leading figures, who have written and spoken eloquently about how we can model human activities that are beneficial to the living systems of our planet. By making us more aware of the damage we are doing to the ecosystem, Gaia theory may also help us to survive. We are just one part of a larger system, and are reliant on that system for our continued existence. As Lovelock said: 'if we see the world as a superorganism of which we are a part – not the owner, nor the tenant, not even a passenger – we could have a long time ahead of us and our species might survive for its "allotted span". It all depends on you and me.'

LANGUAGE DEVELOPMENT idioms from nature

1 Choose the best option, a or b, to complete the sentences.

1 The *tip of the iceberg* refers to
   a a very small part of a much larger problem.
   b a very cold and uncomfortable place.

2 If we say that someone has *come up in the world* we mean
   a they have reappeared after a very long absence.
   b they have more money and/or a better social position that they had before.

3 If we say that two people or situations are *worlds apart* we mean
   a they are very different.
   b they are far away from each other.

4 If you are *in deep water* you are
   a potentially in a lot of trouble.
   b stranded far from home.

5 If you *get bogged down* in something you are
   a stuck in an uncomfortable situation.
   b prevented from making progress or getting a job done.

6 You may say that you're *not yet out of the woods* if you are
   a still having difficulties or problems.
   b lost.

7 If you *get wind of something* you
   a are suspicious of someone's activities.
   b hear of something that you weren't supposed to hear about.

8 If you decide to *clear the air* you probably need to
   a resolve a problem or disagreement with someone.
   b tell someone you lied to them.

ADJECTIVES FOLLOWED BY PARTICLES

Certain adjectives are usually followed by a particular particle, so you should learn them as phrases.

2 Complete the sentences with the particles in the box.

about	at	by	for	from	in	of	on	to
with								

1 Miranda was ashamed _____ her past and refused to talk about it.

2 If you are serious _____ becoming a quantum physicist, you'd better start doing your homework.

3 Julian was becoming obsessed _____ his butterfly collection.

4 Unfortunately, I was never much good _____ maths, but I've always loved biology.

5 I had measles when I was younger, so I'm immune _____ the disease now.

6 The group was very distressed _____ the news that the river dolphin is now presumed to be extinct.

7 The species is now endangered and eligible _____ government legislation to protect it.

8 People who don't eat enough fresh fruit or vegetables may become deficient _____ essential enzymes.

9 The word *geology* is derived _____ the Greek words for *earth* and *study*.

10 Lizzie has never really been keen _____ insects, so I'm surprised she has joined an entomology study group.

KEY WORD *earth*

3 Match the words (1–10) with the definitions (a–j).

1 Earth / the Earth
2 earth
3 come back down to Earth
4 where / what / who on Earth …?
5 a down-to-earth person
6 cost the Earth or paid the Earth
7 hell on Earth
8 earthbound
9 earthly
10 earth-shattering

a very surprising or shocking
b face reality again after a period of great excitement
c something that is unable to fly or is on the ground, not in the air
d the planet where we live
e used for emphasis
f someone who is practical-minded
g ground, soil, sand, mud
h when something is very expensive
i a very bad or unpleasant experience
j of the material, physical plane (not the spiritual or metaphysical plane)

GRAMMAR unreal tenses

4 *To the astronauts, the planet looked as if it were some huge, single, living system.*

Which of the following statements was true at the time the astronauts looked at the Earth?

a The planet appeared to have been a *single living system*.

b The planet appeared to be a *single living system*.

UNREAL PAST

We sometimes use past tenses to describe things in the present or future that are imagined or unreal.

---

5 **Underline the verbs in the sentences below. What time is being talked about in each case?**

1 If only I were rich enough to save the world's trees!

2 Suppose you had the chance to do one selfless act. What would it be?

3 I'd rather you didn't smoke in here.

4 You wouldn't have been fined if you hadn't dropped that litter.

5 It looked as if it was going to be a beautiful day.

6 Were I able to go back in time, I would probably visit the Jurassic era.

7 It's time we did something about global warming.

8 If only I hadn't had that extra burger!

▶ GRAMMAR REFERENCE (SECTION 14) **PAGE 218**

6 **Match the sentences in exercise 5 with functions a–h.**

a comparison or prediction

b hypothetical past situation

c wishes

d regrets

e advice or suggestions

f preferences

g imagining

h hypothetical or impossible present situation

7 **Complete the sentences with the correct form of the verbs in brackets.**

1 I wish I _____ (be) able to travel all over the world.

2 It looked as if it _____ (be) about to start raining.

3 If only we _____ (not / make) such a mess of Earth.

4 It's about time we _____ (take) some responsibility for our actions.

5 I'd rather you _____ (take) the bus every day instead of driving.

6 _____ (be) I rich, I would buy a ticket to space.

7 Lilla wishes Richard _____ (not / buy) that expensive motorbike.

8 I'd sooner he _____ (not / tell) me about his stomach problem – I feel sick now.

9 If the house _____ (be) demolished, I wouldn't want to know about it.

10 Russ looked as if he _____ (see) a ghost.

8 **Complete the text with suitable words.**

From time to time I find myself wishing that things could be different. If (1) _____ we lived in a world where everyone (2) _____ at one with their environment, and respected the Earth and all the creatures that dwell on her. We mostly act (3) _____ if we were the most superior beings on the planet. Imagine if we (4) _____ in fact merely the guardians instead! If we (5) _____ not believed the Earth belonged to us in the first place, we would never (6) _____ hurt her in the way we have. I would much (7) _____ contribute something to the Earth (8) _____ be constantly taking from her. I (9) _____ we could all stop thinking about what we want for ourselves and think about what the planet needs instead. Isn't it about (10) _____ we ended the destruction? I'd sooner we (11) _____ in a world full of natural wonders than a world we had trashed for our pleasure! It's almost as (12) _____ we had no imagination!

9 **Reading and Use of English, Part 4**

For questions 1–6, complete the second sentence so that it has a similar meaning to the first sentence, using the word given. Do not change the word given. You must use between three and six words, including the word given.

1 Why don't you turn off the television and get some fresh air!

HIGH

It's _____ the television and got some fresh air!

2 Instead of colonising another planet I think we should try to save this one.

RATHER

I _____ this planet than colonise another.

3 It's a pity I was so careless and ignorant in my youth.

WISH

I _____ so careless and ignorant in my youth.

4 It will be amazing if you see a blue whale!

IF

Imagine _____ a blue whale!

5 The Yangtze River dolphin became extinct because the river was so polluted.

BEEN

If the river _____ , the Yangtze River dolphin would not have become extinct.

6 Miriam doesn't know everything but sometimes she behaves like she does.

IF

Sometimes Miriam behaves _____ she doesn't.

LISTENING sentence completion

1 **Discuss. Despite overwhelming odds, life exists on Earth. What are some of the things that make life on Earth possible, although we tend to take them for granted on a daily basis?**

> **EXAM SPOTLIGHT**
>
> **Listening, Part 2** Focused listening
>
> In this part of the Listening paper, it's essential that you know what to listen for. The only way to do this well is to study the questions you have been given. You will hear all the words you need to write down but the sentences will not be exactly the same as the ones that are written.
>
> For example, you may be given this sentence to complete:
>
> *The circumstances leading up to the (1) _____ of the dinosaurs are not often questioned.*
>
> The sentence you hear may be:
>
> *There are many theories as to what caused the extinction of the dinosaurs 65 million years ago but few people ever wonder about what led to the appearance of the dinosaurs in the first place, and the circumstances which enabled them to survive as the dominant species on Earth for 160 million years.*

2 **Answer the questions.**

1 Which words or phrases in the sentence above also appeared on the audio?
2 Which words or phrases in the sentence are a paraphrase of those on the audio?
3 Are there any words on the audio that may appear to fit in the sentence above, but which would be wrong in meaning?

3 **Read the sentences and underline any key words to listen out for.**

There have been animals living on land for approximately (1) _____ years.
Today's atmosphere consists of approximately (2) _____ % oxygen, in relation to other gases.
With an abundance of oxygen, many animals were free to leave the water and (3) _____ the land.
When oxygen levels were greater, many animals underwent a much faster stage of (4) _____ .
Around 400 million years ago, many species of animal became (5) _____ when oxygen levels fell sharply.
Around 300 million years ago higher oxygen levels enabled (6) _____ to flourish.
Many animals (7) _____ and died because they could not adapt quickly enough to periods of low oxygen levels.
Birds can fly at (8) _____ with a shortage of oxygen, due to the air sacs near their lungs.

4 **Discuss. Which words would you expect to hear in each of the gaps? What part of speech and what possible meaning could they have?**

Listening, Part 2

5 ⊙ 46 **You will hear a palaeontologist talking about atmospheric conditions in the Earth's past. Complete sentences 1–8 in exercise 3.**

SPEAKING evaluating

6 **Discuss. How serious might the threats in the box be to the ecology of our planet?**

> a reduction in wildlife habitats
> climate change   deforestation   pollution
> the loss of certain species

> **EXAM SPOTLIGHT**
>
> **Speaking, Part 3** Making decisions
>
> In this part of the Speaking test, you and your partner will discuss a task for two minutes and then you will be asked to make a decision related to the task. The important thing is not the decision you make, but the process by which you make it – the negotiation. For this kind of task you have to learn to 'think out loud' and articulate the ideas that are going through your head.

7 ⊙ 47 **Listen to the discussion between two students who have been asked to make a decision about the task in exercise 6. Note down the main ideas they mention.**

Elisabeth mentions: _____
Giovanni mentions: _____

8 **What do Elisabeth and Giovanni decide is the most serious threat?**

9 **Work in pairs. Turn to page 238, where you will see photos of some critically endangered animal species in the world today. Decide which species you would prefer to protect and explain your reasons.**

USE OF ENGLISH word formation (2)

10 Look at these words and underline the suffixes (look back at the definition of suffixes on page 128 to help you).

globe → global, globalise, globalisation, globally

Which suffix is used for

1 a noun?   2 a verb?   3 an adverb?

11 Add the correct suffix to the stems.

1 affection (n) → _____ (adj)
2 evolve (v)   → _____ (n)
3 active (adj)   → _____ (v)
4 history (n)   → _____ (adj)
5 diverse (adj) → _____ (n)
6 develop (v)   → _____ (n)
7 modern (adj)   → _____ (v)
8 child (n)   → _____ (adj)

12 **Reading and Use of English, Part 3**

For questions 1–8, read the text below. Use the word given in capitals at the end of some of the lines to form a word that fits in the gap in the same line.

Humanity's place in biodiversity

Some experts estimate that there are somewhere between ten and 100 million species on Earth, although no one can say with (1) _____ which figure   CONFIDENT
is closer. Fewer than one in ten of all the species that have been given
(2) _____ names have been   SCIENCE
closely studied.
We have to (3) _____ our goals   BROAD
in studying species because the study of biodiversity has a time limit. Species are rapidly disappearing as a consequence of human activities, primarily the
(4) _____ of natural habitats.   DESTROY
20% or more of the species of plants and animals could suffer (5) _____ in   EXTINCT
the next few years unless we do something drastic to save them. The loss of many species will mean that new sources of scientific information and incalculable
potential (6) _____ wealth will be   BIOLOGY
destroyed. Ecosystems are also essential for humanity. Human beings co-evolved with the rest of life on Earth. It would be
(7) _____ to suppose that we   MAD
can continue to diminish biodiversity
(8) _____ without threatening our   DEFINITE
own existence.

WRITING an essay (discussing issues that surround a topic)

1 Read the exam question.

Write an essay for your tutor, discussing two of the issues in your notes. You should explain which issues you think are the most serious ones facing the world today and provide reasons to support your opinions.

2 One way to organise your ideas is to put them into categories. Look at the notes below and add the ideas to the spidergram in the most appropriate place.

- claims on territory / land
- poverty and famine
- species extinction / loss of biodiversity
- illness and disease
- depletion of Earth's resources

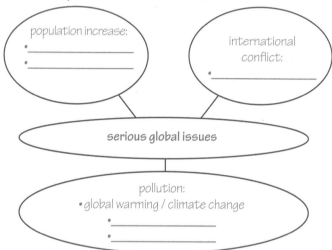

population increase:
- _____
- _____

international conflict:
- _____

serious global issues

pollution:
- global warming / climate change
- _____
- _____

3 In order to answer the question, you need to identify the two issues that stand out as being the most serious. Look at the essay below written by a student. Which issue does the writer think is the most serious one facing the world today and what reasons does she give?

The two most serious issues facing the world today

I think that the most important issue facing the world today is in fact the increase in human population on the Earth. That's because it is actually the main cause of all the other problems which the world is facing today and it makes them worse. Because the number of people on Earth is increasing very fast, the human population on Earth is responsible for using up the Earth's resources. Also, because there are so many people there is more and more pollution and this causes climate change which is causing species extinction and bringing about the loss of different species. In the end this affects us all because with all the animals and plants gone we would not be able to survive anyway.

4 Discuss. What do you think about the essay in exercise 3? How can it be improved?

5 Use a dictionary to find the meaning of the words (1–4). Which words or phrases in the sample essay could they be used to replace?

1 exacerbate (v)
2 exponentially (adv)
3 deplete (v)
4 biodiversity (n)

EXAM SPOTLIGHT

Discussing issues that surround a topic

As we learnt in Unit 6, an essay should be organised clearly. It begins with an introduction, and then develops the argument, and concludes with an appropriate ending. In Writing, Part 1 you have to discuss two issues and decide which is the most important / serious, etc.

6 Look at the more detailed spidergram. The central issue is the population increase. Read the issues that surround it and complete the spidergram with the global problems listed in exercise 2.

Global issues caused by the human population

1 _____:
the Earth's human population has to be fed, clothed and accommodated. This means we have to use the Earth's resources which are fast running out.

2 _____:
7 billion people on Earth using fossil fuels for energy releases carbon dioxide into the atmosphere, which heats the Earth, thereby affecting the global climate.

3 _____:
the vast number of people on Earth means there is not enough space for other species to exist in harmony.

**Human Population
7 billion people and counting …**
The total world human population, now at 7 billion, is projected to rise exponentially to 9 billion by 2050.

4 _____:
nobody knows how many people the Earth can support but at the moment millions of people are living below the breadline.

5 _____:
there are so many human beings on the planet that if a particularly contagious viral outbreak were to occur, it would spread very quickly.

6 _____:
because we have conquered every last scrap of land and sea, wars based on the claim for territory are increasing as the population increases.

7 Using the spidergram above, write your own paragraph plan for the task. Decide which points you would keep, and which you would leave out. Write a suitable introduction and conclusion.

Writing, Part 1

8 Read the exam question. Brainstorm your ideas, drawing a spidergram with your main cause at the centre and reasons for reaching your conclusion pointing to it.

Your class has been discussing the causes of crime and you have made the notes below:

Causes of crime
- poverty
- addiction
- living environment

Some issues raised in the discussion:
'People steal to feed their families.'
'Drug addiction leads straight to crime.'
'Councils should clean up areas that have a high crime rate.'

Write an essay for your tutor, discussing two of the causes of crime in your notes. You should explain which cause you think is the most significant and provide reasons to support your opinions.

9 Write your essay in 220–260 words in an appropriate style

15 OUR GLOBAL VILLAGE

GETTING STARTED

1 **Do you recognise the custom shown in the picture? Which country do you associate it with?**

2 **Describe a special or unique custom or tradition from your country or culture.**

READING cross-text multiple matching

CROSS-TEXT MULTIPLE MATCHING

Part 6 of the Reading and Use of English paper consists of four short texts on a common theme. They usually come from academic sources and express the writers' opinions in relation to the topic. There are four questions, which require you to compare the opinions expressed by all the writers.

3 **Read texts A–D and mark the statements yes or no.**

Text A

1 The writer believes that progress only occurs when we ignore the traditions of the past.
2 The writer thinks that our role is to decide which traditions suit our modern way of life.

Text B

3 The writer believes that people who don't like change will find it difficult to improve their lives.
4 The writer is of the opinion that tradition serves as a foundation from which to explore relevant solutions to the issues of modern life.

Text C

5 The writer thinks that individuals and institutions follow traditions without considering whether they are the best thing to do in a given situation.
6 The writer's attitude towards tradition is that it limits our ability to move ahead.

Text D

7 The writer expresses the view that we are held back by tradition.
8 The writer thinks that to keep making adjustments to traditions has a negative impact on society.

Is tradition an obstacle to progress?

A Tradition isn't an obstacle to progress but rather a catalyst for progress. We needn't concern ourselves with mundane aspects of everyday life because as individuals we simply follow the customs that have been ingrained in us for a lifetime. Certain aspects of tradition guide our lives and save us from its potential pitfalls. The final outcome is assured: there's no need to experiment. This provides emotional peace, enabling us to focus our energy on advancement and progress in other areas – both of ourselves and of society at large. However, there remains a need for weeding out those traditions that are detrimental to certain groups in modern society and which hold no place there. We're enlightened beings; we can differentiate between good and bad, and it should be our endeavour to promote the positive and eliminate the negative in keeping with our times.

B A determination to cling to tradition can undoubtedly get in the way of change: 'If it was good enough for previous generations, it's good enough for me!' some insist. While it's true it would be foolish to throw away tried and tested methods, we must realise it is only through change that we can achieve our full potential. Those who remain stuck in their ways will never reach that goal. What's wrong with advancement? Traditions containing the best ideas of the past are not necessarily the way forward. Their biggest value is in offering non-controversial starting points from which to solve the problems of today. We cannot disregard traditions – it's only in understanding how they came to exist that we get to grips with the past and figure out the future. Progressive minds are the way for change. Thoughtful people critically evaluate traditions; we must not follow them blindly.

C Most of what we do in our daily lives follows procedures that come from the past. They are habits and customs created throughout the centuries, and they have a profound relation to the unchanging natural order of things. When people or institutions adopt a custom it is because its efficiency had already been tested and approved for generations as the best way to act. Therefore, people and institutions have a large stock of these wise customs and a natural tendency to continue them. They confer stability. Things become fixed in tradition because they work well that way: they aren't seen as a straitjacket, limiting movement. One may adjust the custom, but only to improve it, not destroy it. Of course, if one was to call every practice 'tradition' and refuse to change anything for its sake, society wouldn't move forwards at all.

D Some object that tradition produces stagnation because nothing changes. This is a rash judgement. Traditions don't become mouldy; they constitute an inheritance of wise practices and customs that prevent us from having to waste time figuring out what our ancestors have already figured out – where's the point in trying to re-invent the wheel? It is constantly starting again that produces stagnation. Leave well enough alone. When one accepts established solutions for problems, one is free to accomplish creative additions in other unexplored fields. This is the way societies progress and rise to a higher level of civilisation. To constantly change everything is to condemn society to instability, perpetually remaining at the same level of civilisation, or even falling into decay. Important traditions which are held sacred don't interfere with progress: they give us a sense of belonging. When we belong, we care enough to think about how we can improve our own lives and the lives of those around us.

4 Reading and Use of English, Part 2

You are going to read four extracts in which the writers consider whether maintaining traditions is an obstacle to progress. For questions 1–4, choose from the extracts A–D. The extracts may be chosen more than once.

Which writer

1 has a similar view to A about whether tradition can enable us to advance as a society?

2 has a less positive opinion than the others about the importance that some people attach to tradition?

3 has a different opinion from the others with regard to the role that tradition plays in promoting a feeling of security in life?

4 shares an opinion with B about whether we should select which traditions to follow?

5 Discuss. Which of the above texts is closest to your own opinions?

LANGUAGE DEVELOPMENT phrasal verbs and phrases with *pass*

1 **Complete the phrasal verbs with a particle from the box.**

> as   away   by   off   on   out   over   up

1 Arnold's been passed _____ for promotion again – it's no wonder he's upset!
2 Could you pass the message _____ to Roger when you see him?
3 Do you really think I would pass _____ the chance of a free holiday to Florida?
4 She tried to pass him _____ as her brother but I know she doesn't have a brother.
5 Unfortunately, his father passed _____ last week after a long battle with cancer.
6 He has olive skin and could easily pass _____ someone from a Mediterranean country.
7 Emily passed _____ at the sight of the cut on my finger.
8 If you pass _____ the supermarket on your way home, could you get some milk?

2 **Choose the best option to complete the sentences.**

1 Julian passed his exam with flying _____ .
   a clouds   b colours   c balloons
2 What can I do to pass the _____ until the party starts?
   a hour   b day   c time
3 Parliament recently passed a(n) _____ to abolish blood sports.
   a Act   b check   c tab
4 You know whether you were right or wrong. It's not up to me to pass _____ .
   a verdict   b sentence   c judgement
5 Michelle was angry about the broken vase but she decided to _____ it pass.
   a let   b make   c give
6 Never fear! Not a word of what I saw here tonight shall ever pass my _____ .
   a mouth   b tongue   c lips
7 And so, after many years spent locked in the tower, it _____ to pass that the princess escaped on the back of a dragon.
   a ran   b came   c flew
8 It's time William took responsibility for his actions instead of always trying to pass the _____ to someone else.
   a buck   b dollar   c bill

KEY WORD *pass*

3 **Which of the following sentences is incorrect? Why?**

1 Julian passed me in the street.
2 Julian walked right passed me in the street.

4 *Morris dancing is a traditional English form of folk dancing. It is distinctive for its fast, elegant weaving movements created by the dancers passing over and under sticks or swords whilst remaining linked.*

Match one of the definitions (1–4) with the meaning of *pass* in this sentence.

1 To go past someone or something without stopping.
2 To go in a particular direction.
3 If you pass something through, round, over or under something, you move it or push it that way.
4 If you pass something to someone, you give it to them.

5 **Work in pairs. Write example sentences for five of the definitions of *pass* below, then swap with your partner and match their sentences with the definitions 1–9.**

1 If something passes to someone, it means they inherit it.
2 If you pass information to someone, it means you give them information.
3 If you pass a ball to someone in a game or match, it means you throw, kick or hit it to them.
4 When a period of time passes, it has finished.
5 If you pass a period of time in a particular way, you spend it that way.
6 If you pass through a stage or phase, you experience it.
7 If something passes a level or amount, it goes above it.
8 If you pass a test, it means you have reached the required standard.
9 If a government passes a law, they agree to it.

LISTENING (1) multiple speakers

The speakers in Part 3 of the Listening paper may express conflicting attitudes or opinions about a topic, so it's important to pay attention to what each speaker says and to make notes about their opinions.

6 ⊙ 48 **You are going to hear part of a radio interview in which the function and origin of kissing is being discussed. As you listen, decide which speaker, A or B, gives us the following information.**

A Professor Rosemary O'Bryan
B Dr Andrew Peters

1 A mother may kiss her child to cement the bond between them.
2 The biological function of kissing allows an individual to choose the right mate.
3 Chimpanzees kiss to make up after fights.
4 The first romantic kiss happened in France in the sixth century.
5 In the first half of the 20th century, romantic kissing was largely a western habit.
6 In Polynesia and Lapland people rub noses to show affection.
7 Bonobo monkeys will kiss for just about any reason.

7 **Listening, Part 3**

Now listen again. For questions 1–6, choose the answer (A, B, C or D) which fits best according to what you hear.

SPEAKING talking about your country, culture and background

8 **Work in pairs. Take turns talking about your country, culture, customs, traditions and taboos. Ask each other questions and try to find out as much as possible.**

Speaking, Part 1

9 **Answer the questions.**

1 Are there any traditions or customs in your country which are unique to your culture or are particularly meaningful to you? Why?
2 Which international traditions, festivals or ceremonies are celebrated differently in your country? What are the differences?
3 Many of the world's more ethnic traditions are dying out. Are there any customs or traditions that you think will never disappear from your culture? Why?

USEFUL LANGUAGE

TALKING ABOUT YOUR BACKGROUND

In [country] the people are …
We have many unique cultural traditions, for example …
In my country it is customary to …
A tradition which I particularly value is …
I consider myself quite (un)traditional / (un)conventional …
It would be a great pity if …

---

1 According to Rosemary O'Bryan, kissing may originally have developed from a mother
   A using her mouth to clean and educate her child.
   B touching her child to show she is about to feed him or her.
   C chewing solid food for her child to eat more easily.
   D teaching her child to show respect to others.

2 According to Andrew Peters, the main reason women kiss prospective mates is to
   A decide who has the most attractive smell.
   B groom and bond with their partners.
   C choose the best providers for their children.
   D increase the survival chances of their offspring.

3 According to Andrew Peters, kissing is also a means of
   A social bonding in chimpanzees.
   B chemical pairing in mammals.
   C avoiding fights by primates.
   D establishing social order in ape societies.

4 In ancient times a kiss was
   A not necessarily a sign of affection.
   B never given on the lips.
   C only bestowed by a husband.
   D not considered polite.

5 According to Rosemary O'Bryan, by the middle of the 20th century, romantic kissing
   A had only just become common.
   B had spread to non-western cultures through films.
   C was assumed in the west to be universal.
   D was regarded as strange in some Asian countries.

6 Andrew and Rosemary disagree about whether
   A rubbing noses constitutes a form of affection.
   B kissing is becoming more common.
   C kissing is instinctive behaviour in all mammals.
   D kissing exists in all cultures.

GRAMMAR adverbial clauses

1 **Read the extract from track 48. What do the words in bold tell us?**

> Correct, and **thus** we get more information about our biological compatibility. Women are more attracted to men who are more genetically compatible to them, and a woman picks this up **by** breathing in his pheromones. Any resulting offspring will have better resistance to a greater number of diseases, and will **consequently** have a better chance of survival. **That's why** we still like to kiss – to maximise our chances of sampling each other's aroma.

CLAUSES OF TIME, PURPOSE, REASON, CONCESSION AND RESULT

Adverbial clauses give information about the circumstances of the event described by the verb in the main clause. They can tell us about when or where an event happened, the manner or place in which it happened, the reason why it happened, or the purpose for which it was intended. Or they can tell us about the result of an event, or indicate comparison or contrast (concession) with other events or circumstances. Adverbial clauses are usually preceded by a word or phrase which gives this information.

2 **Add the sentences to the table below.**

1 It got **so** hot **that** I couldn't concentrate.
2 It was as bad **as** I'd feared.
3 I walked fast **because** it was late.
4 She wanted to know **where** I'd been.
5 He asked me **how** I had done it.
6 She smiled **so that** I'd feel welcome.
7 **If** I'd known you'd be late, I'd have started without you.

Time	*I'll meet you **when** I've finished.*
Place	
Manner	
Comparison	
Cause / reason	
Purpose	
Result	
Condition	
Concession	*She won the game **although** she'd never played before.*

▶ GRAMMAR REFERENCE (SECTION 15) **PAGE 219**

3 **Choose the correct options in italics to complete the sentences.**

1 *As a result / Due to / Consequently* the fire, many birds lost their nests.
2 I wrote the book *so that / in order that / in order to* highlight the social problems.
3 I want you to call me *the minute / as soon / until* you get home.
4 Gillian has never played tennis before. *Nevertheless / Although / Despite* she is determined to have a go.
5 *Notwithstanding / No matter how / So much* tired he is, he won't stop till he's finished.
6 *Seeing as / Therefore / In case* it hadn't rained all week, I watered the garden.

4 **Reading and Use of English, Part 4**

For questions 1–6, complete the second sentence so that it has a similar meaning to the first sentence, using the word given. Do not change the word given. You must use between three and six words, including the word given.

1 I got wet because I forgot to take an umbrella with me.
CONSEQUENTLY
I forgot to take an umbrella with me _____ wet.

2 To ensure he'd get the job, John researched the background of the company.
ORDER
John researched the background of the company _____ sure he'd get the job.

3 It's such a beautiful afternoon, so why don't we go out?
SEEING
Let's go out, _____ a beautiful afternoon.

4 I was the only person with any money, so I paid for everyone.
BEING
I paid for everyone, _____ with any money.

5 Even though he hated thrillers, he decided to go to see the film.
SPITE
He decided to go to see the film, _____ he hated thrillers.

6 I wanted to get fit, so I took up cycling.
WHY
The _____ cycling was that I wanted to get fit.

USE OF ENGLISH open cloze text

5 Reading and Use of English, Part 2

For questions 1–8, read the text below and think of the word which best fits each gap. Use only one word in each gap.

Body language and gestures

When travelling, it is important to take the time to learn about your host's customs (1) _____ that you do not seem ignorant or offensive. Often, something that we (2) _____ for granted as meaning one thing can mean something completely different elsewhere. For (3) _____ , the foot is the lowest part of the body and in Thailand it is held (4) _____ the lowest esteem; (5) _____ point a foot at a Thai is very insulting. Likewise, the head is the highest part of the body, and (6) _____ of this, it is never touched by others. A pat on the head in Thailand is an insult of the worst kind. Greetings in Asia usually take the form (7) _____ a bow. In Japan, your hands should be at your side. The inferior person will bow longer and lower. In Mediterranean countries on the (8) _____ hand, it is customary to greet a friend or family member with a kiss on each cheek.

6 Complete the sentences with words from the box. You can use the same word more than once.

leave pack party person return sight vision

1 Malcolm believes that if something is out of _____ , it's out of mind.

2 I wish you would go away and _____ me in peace!

3 The search _____ were very relieved when they found the missing child unharmed.

4 Thanks very much for your help. Just let me know when I can _____ the favour.

5 As they rounded the corner, the mountains came into _____ .

6 Not much work is done in this organisation in the middle of summer, when most people are on annual _____ .

7 This autobiography is strange; the author has written about himself in the third _____ .

8 The jury resolved to _____ a verdict of guilty.

9 The novel I've just read presents a depressing _____ of the future.

10 The police are searching for a _____ of wild dogs.

LISTENING (2) short extracts

7 Listening, Part 4

🔘 49 **You will hear five short extracts in which people of British origin talk about living abroad.**

TASK ONE
For questions 1–5 choose from the list (A–H) what each person says about living outside Britain.

TASK TWO
For questions 6–10 choose from the list (A–H) what each person says about their life.

While you listen you must complete both tasks.

A They have never lived in Britain.

B They wanted to move away from their family.

C They left Britain to study abroad.

D They never intend to go back to Britain.

E They feel equally at home in two countries.

F They moved abroad as a child.

G They went abroad to work.

H They left Britain to avoid social pressure.

Speaker 1 ☐

Speaker 2 ☐

Speaker 3 ☐

Speaker 4 ☐

Speaker 5 ☐

A They're pleased they're part of an extended family.

B They believe everyone should spend some time in different countries.

C In a cosmopolitan city they do not feel out of place.

D Their identity is who they are, not where they are.

E They don't want their English to deteriorate.

F They want their children to feel they belong in the country where they live.

G Being fluent in the language of the country is important to them.

H They don't expect their children to be interested in their heritage.

Speaker 1 ☐

Speaker 2 ☐

Speaker 3 ☐

Speaker 4 ☐

Speaker 5 ☐

LISTENING short extracts ▲ USE OF ENGLISH open cloze text ▲ GRAMMAR adverbial clauses ▲

15 OUR GLOBAL VILLAGE 147

WRITING a report

1 Discuss. Which of the following ceremonies have you witnessed or attended?

- baby shower or pre-natal baby party
- baptism or naming ceremony
- birthday celebration
- name day celebration
- coming of age ceremony
- engagement party
- wedding
- anniversary
- retirement party

Writing, Part 2

2 Look at the exam question. What do you need to include in your report?

> You are studying traditional culture as part of your university course. Your tutor has asked you to write a report on an important ceremony in your country.
> You should describe the ceremony and compare its popularity now with the past. You should also make recommendations regarding the future of the ceremony.

GENERATING IDEAS

It is important to ensure that you have enough to say in each paragraph of your report. As well as drafting your headings, you should jot down a few ideas that you can write about under each one. Sometimes it helps to write your headings or ideas as questions that you answer in your report.

3 Choose ideas from the box to go under each heading. Then add some of your own ideas under each heading.

Paragraph 1: The ceremony
Paragraph 2: What happens during the ceremony?
Paragraph 3: Has the ceremony changed?
Paragraph 4: Should the ceremony continue?

> Who attends?
> What do people do?
> Are there more or fewer ceremonies now?
> Do more or fewer people attend now?
> What's the purpose of the ceremony?
> Which ceremony is my report about?
> Do we need the ceremony?
> What should be changed?

4 **Read the report and underline the main ideas. What ideas does it cover in addition to the points in exercise 3? Which idea does the writer not cover? Why?**

Seijin Shiki

'Coming of age' is a young person's transition from childhood to adulthood, and countries celebrate this in various ways. In Japan, a person officially becomes an adult at the age of 20, and this is celebrated by a ceremony known as Seijin Shiki, which is held on the second Monday of January.

What happens during the ceremony?

On the day, all the young people participating in the ceremony go to a government building where they listen to a number of speakers. At the conclusion of the ceremony, presents and money are handed out to the new adults. Many women celebrate this day by wearing zori slippers and a furisode – a special traditional dress rather like the kimono – that has often been handed down through the family. Similarly, men wear traditional dress consisting of a dark kimono or hakama.

Has the ceremony changed?

Nowadays, fewer young people attend the ceremony compared to the past and this has raised some concerns among the older generation. In addition, some parents worry that the parties after the ceremony have become more important than the ceremony itself and, although women wear traditional clothes, some young men feel too uncomfortable in these and prefer to dress in dark suits.

Should the ceremony continue?

The Seijin Shiki marks an important milestone in the lives of young Japanese people and I believe we should continue to celebrate it. However, I would recommend that we relax some of the formal aspects of the ceremony, such as the clothing, to encourage more young people to attend.

NOT KNOWING THE RIGHT WORDS

Sometimes you may have to describe something that is unique to a particular language or culture. In these cases it is OK to use the word in its own language – put it in italics or between 'quotation marks' to identify it, and then give a short description or explanation of what it means.

5 **Find five Japanese words in the report and explain what they mean in your own words.**

6 **Plan a report in answer to the exam question below. Try to think of a custom that you know well, perhaps one that is unique to your culture. Make notes on the custom under the headings below, or make up your own headings.**

> You are studying traditional culture as part of your university course. Your tutor has asked you to write a report on an important custom in your country.
> You should describe the custom and compare its popularity now with the past. You should also make recommendations regarding the future of the custom.

1 The custom
2 What does the custom involve?
3 Has the custom changed?
4 Should the custom continue?
5

7 **Write your report in 220–260 words.**

GLOSSARY

bleak: offering very little hope for the future
harsh: severe, tough
hunter-gatherer: living by hunting animals and collecting plants
inventive: resourceful, able to invent ways of doing things
lush: with abundant vegetation
passage: a section of a text
verge: the edge or limit

VIDEO the Hadzabe tribe

1 **Have you ever done any of these things? Ask your classmates. If the answer is yes, ask a follow-up question to find out more using *When, Where, Why, How* or *What*.**

- use a bow and arrow
- collect berries to eat
- collect wild mushrooms
- make a fire from sticks
- plant your own vegetables
- use wild plants as medicine
- track wild animals
- make your own tools
- eat honey from a honeycomb
- make your own clothes

2 **Work in pairs. Answer the questions about the activities in exercise 1.**

1 Are any of them useful in your life today? Why / Why not?
2 Are any of them common in your culture? Who does them? When?

3 **Watch the video about the Hadzabe people in Tanzania. Which activities from exercise 1 do you see them doing?**

4 **Which aspect(s) of Hadzabe culture did the video focus on?**

1 their knowledge
2 their skills
3 their language

5 **Read the notes. Then watch the video again and complete the notes.**

Our links to the past
50% (1) _____ disappear by end of century
ancient traditions – increasingly kept alive for
(2) _____

The Hadzabe
one of last groups of (3) _____
Julius (Chief) reads (4) _____ like a book
one plant = (5) _____ berries + medicinal roots

The last Ice Age
Northern hemisphere > (6) _____
Africa > (7) _____ , people moved to find
(8) _____ + (9) _____
humans on the verge of (10) _____
ancestors of Hadzabe left (11) _____

6 **In the video the narrator said that some traditions only exist these days for tourists. Can you think of any examples of this? What about these traditions? Are they for local people, tourists or both?**

- bull fighting in Spain
- carnival in Rio de Janeiro
- changing the guard at Buckingham Palace, London
- Native American dances
- wearing traditional costumes

SPEAKING Part 1 interview

IDEAS GENERATOR

EXPLAINING FAMILIAR TOPICS

In Part 1 of the Speaking test you will talk about topics that are familiar to you but may not be familiar to other people, for example your country, its traditions and popular culture. To prepare for this you should make sure you have the vocabulary to describe and explain these things. For example, a typical activity for Hadzabe people is to exploit wild resources such as plants. How could you explain this to someone who had no experience of this? Which of these words would you use?

collect
expensive
identify
medicinal
nutritious
treat

In order to make your contribution in this part of the test as complete as possible, you can structure your answer as if you had been asked a series of *Wh-* follow-up questions. Think of five *Wh-* questions about one of the Hadzabe activities in exercise 1. Then tell your partner about the activity.

7 **Are there any traditions in your country in these categories? Write six words for each tradition you can think of.**

community events	historical events or people
clothing and costumes	homes
dance	important dates
education	music
family events	seasonal events
festivals	social interaction
food	sport

8 **Work in pairs. Take turns to ask and answer the questions. Use your notes from exercise 7.**

1 How popular are cultural traditions in your country?
2 Which cultural traditions would visitors or tourists find interesting?
3 Why are cultural traditions important to you?

9 **Think about your performance in exercise 8. Did you sound spontaneous? Work with a new partner. Repeat one of the question and answer exchanges and try to give the same information in a different way.**

VIDEOSCRIPT 15 is on page 256.

16 ENDINGS – AND NEW BEGINNINGS

GETTING STARTED

1 The verbs in box A all mean *to end*. Match them with items from box B to make collocations.

A

> abort   cease   complete   conclude   discontinue   end   extinguish   finalise   finish   settle   terminate

B

> a business deal   a contract   a course   a dispute   a fire   a form   a lawsuit   a meeting   a plan   a pregnancy   a questionnaire   a race   a rescue operation   a speech   an argument   an essay   differences   fire   hope   manufacturing a product   operations   production   school   trading

READING multiple matching

2 Read the five extracts opposite about something ending and making a new start, and find a person for whom:

1 the decision to change was upsetting.
2 the decision to change was a moral one.
3 the decision to change was made despite criticism from others.
4 the decision to change was made on health grounds.

3 Underline the information in each extract which helped you make your choice.

4 Reading and Use of English, Part 8

You are going to read five magazine extracts in which people talk about life-changing decisions. For questions 1–10, choose from the extracts (A–E). The extracts may be chosen more than once.

Which person/s

1 felt they were stuck in a rut before they made their change? _____

2 found the process of change surprisingly easy? _____

3 received valuable support when making their decision? _____

4 were forced by circumstances to make their decision? _____

5 were accused of being extreme in their treatment of the situation? _____

6 received unexpected benefits from making the change? _____

7 miss certain elements of their previous situation? _____

8 gave the matter a lot of thought before making their decision? _____

9 have learnt to take pleasure in small things? _____

10 initially chose to ignore an obvious fact about the way they lived? _____

Saying goodbye to ...

Have you ever made a decision to change your way of life? Hannah Wright talked to five people about some life-changing decisions they made ...

A

Homework was done as quickly as possible, to be finished in time for their favourite soap, and family conversation would be limited to comments on what was happening in *EastEnders*, or *Friends*.

The last straw, however, came when my son was diagnosed as obese. We decided drastic action was needed, so the TV was relegated to the back of the garage, and the children were signed up for swimming three times a week. Friends accused us of going too far, the kids blamed us for cutting them off from the rest of the world, but this was countered by the fact that my son lost ten pounds within a month, and my daughter suddenly found an interest in music that had so far been lying dormant. What's more, dinnertime conversation now centred on the children's real lives. So, saying goodbye to the 'box' was the best thing for our family, for in so doing, we learnt to concentrate on actually living.

B

I simply decided I'd had enough. I'd been on the treadmill for too long, and the daily battle of travelling to work each day had begun to wear me down. I realised I just wasn't enjoying life.

So, I left, and have never looked back. Making my home in a tiny village in rural France, I now wake up each morning to the sound of birds singing. My staple diet is salad grown mainly in my own garden, goat's cheese made by the lady down the lane, and eggs provided by another neighbour's hens. The pace of my life has slowed almost to a standstill, but nothing can compare to the peace in my mind. I may not have as much money, or a fast car, but I've now got far more time to appreciate the simple fact of living.

C

Saying goodbye to the place that had been our home for 35 years was a huge wrench. After we retired, however, we realised that managing such a large house was becoming too difficult. Then my wife fell and broke her hip, and that clinched it.

By far the hardest thing about downsizing was deciding what to part with. Heartbreaking though it was, we had to be ruthless, both with ourselves and each other. It was a very emotional time, and we didn't always see eye to eye, but we got through it. We told ourselves it wasn't the end of the world, merely the end of one phase of our life and the beginning of a new one. I won't say we don't miss the old place, and some of our things, but life is both a lot easier and less stressful than it was before we moved.

D

A professed animal lover, I nevertheless remained a confirmed meat eater, not allowing the glaring ethical dilemma to cloud my conscience. I blandly dismissed the arguments of morally superior friends who had already forsaken animal products for a life eating lettuce as exaggerated and extreme. Until, that is, a documentary about the horrors of battery farming and the slaughterhouse shocked me out of my ignorance. I made a vow that my consumption of animal products was a thing of the past.

I'd always thought it would be difficult to maintain a healthy diet without meat, but some well-chosen books on nutrition soon dispelled that myth. I'm really pleased I made that decision.

E

By the time of my daughter's fourth birthday, I was deep in the process of procrastination. Should I homeschool her or send her to kindergarten? I agonised over the decision, as I doubted my capacity to teach her. Then I asked my neighbour Peter, a dad who homeschooled his five children, for advice. He told me, 'You've made it through the sleepless nights of infancy and the tantrums of the two-year-old. You've taught your daughter to speak, feed herself, dress herself and behave correctly. Now you're finally dealing with a rational little human being! This is when the real fun of being a parent is about to begin ... but suddenly you think you're no longer qualified?'

My daughter never made it to kindergarten, and now, almost a decade later, I'm very glad I heeded Peter's advice.

LANGUAGE DEVELOPMENT word partners

1 **Choose the option which does NOT normally follow the words in bold.**

1 **It shocked me out of my** *ignorance / knowledge / complacency / daydream.*
2 **drastic** *action / measures / talk / changes*
3 **confirmed** *meat eater / bachelor / atheist / man*
4 **staple** *diet / gun / mind / ingredient*
5 **cloud my** *conscience / temper / mood / mind*
6 **dispel the** *myth / freedom / rumours / fears*
7 **be cut off from** *the rest of the world / civilisation / the road / society*
8 **emotional** *time / wreck / support / place*
9 **laid down the** *gauntlet / law / baby / deposit*

KEY WORD *end*

2 **Choose the correct phrase to complete the sentences.**

1 Ellen's lost interest in school. She stays out late, doesn't do her homework ... I'm at _____ ! I don't know what to do with her!
   a the end of the road
   b my wits' end
2 The first time I went babysitting, I was really thrown in at _____ , because I had to look after a nine-month-old baby and a two-year-old!
   a the deep end
   b the receiving end
3 Since he retired, George doesn't want to do anything. He sits in front of the television for hours _____ .
   a on end
   b no end
4 Our new neighbours are so noisy! Day and night, they're either moving furniture or arguing! I'm at _____ !
   a the end of my tether
   b the end of the world
5 I was at _____ last night, so I went to the cinema.
   a a loose end
   b a sticky end
6 Miles, I can't go on like this. We argue all the time. This is the _____ for us!
   a tail end
   b end of the road
7 I'd got the wrong _____ – Bob and Jenny are getting married, not splitting up!
   a end of the stick
   b end of the line

3 **Choose the correct word to complete the sentences. You can use a word more than once.**

| close   disposed   draw   end |

1 Organic waste can be _____ of by building a compost heap in your garden.
2 Now, everybody, I'd like to _____ your attention to the small child in the picture.
3 My sister and I are very _____ . We share all our problems.
4 The education minister seems to be favourably _____ towards making cuts in education.
5 Poor John was thrown in at the deep _____ on his first day at his new job.
6 Before you _____ any conclusions, why don't you get a second opinion from another doctor?

4 **Reading and Use of English, Part 4**

For questions 1–6, complete the second sentence so that it has a similar meaning to the first sentence, using the word given. Do not change the word given. You must use between three and six words, including the word given.

1 I'd become complacent, so losing the match to Michael Stephenson really taught me a lesson.
   SHOCKED
   Losing the match to Michael Stephenson _____ complacency.
2 Sorry! I misunderstood you. I thought you wanted me to lock the door.
   END
   Sorry! I got the _____ the stick! I thought you wanted me to lock the door.
3 Jake's announcement of his engagement surprised us, as we'd never expected him to get married.
   CONFIRMED
   We'd all believed Jake to be _____ until he announced he was getting married.
4 The new teacher has relaxed slightly now, but at first she was really strict!
   LAW
   The new teacher really laid _____ at first, but she's relaxed a little since then!
5 I'm not going to feel guilty that my parents are upset about my decision.
   CLOUD
   I'm not going to allow my parents' feelings to _____ about my decision.
6 The president called a press conference to reassure the public that the rumours of an alien invasion were not true.
   DISPEL
   The president called a press conference _____ an alien invasion.

GRAMMAR making and intensifying comparisons

5 **Underline the comparative forms in the sentences.**

1 They find life far more enjoyable than ever before.
2 Nothing compares to the joy of having your first child.
3 Petrol is significantly more expensive than it was six months ago.
4 The show wasn't as spectacular as we'd expected.
5 The more fruit and vegetables you eat, the healthier you will be.
6 This jam isn't nearly as tasty as the one my mother makes.

INTENSIFYING COMPARISONS

Mary is better than Alison at maths.
To intensify this comparison (make it stronger), we can make the following changes.
1 *Mary is **much** better than Alison at maths.*
2 *Mary is **significantly better** than Alison at maths.*
3 *Of the two girls, Mary is **by far the best** at maths.*

▶ GRAMMAR REFERENCE (SECTION 16) **PAGE 221**

---

6 **Intensify the comparisons in different ways.**

1 Brian is not as happy at this school as he was at his old one.
2 This is the best holiday I've ever had!
3 Shelley is not as calm as she used to be.
4 This film was more interesting than the last one he made.
5 Lyn works harder than Sue.
6 She's got more time for her family now that she's stopped working.
7 He goes to bed earlier, so he's got more energy during the day.
8 Renee takes longer to get ready in the morning than Shane.

7 **Complete the following sentences with the word in the box. More than one word may be possible.**

| a lot | both | by far | far | much | never | than |

1 I may not have as _____ money, or a fast car, but I've now got _____ more time to appreciate the simple fact of living.
2 _____ the hardest thing about downsizing was deciding what to part with.
3 Life is _____ a lot easier and less stressful _____ it was before we moved.

8 **Look at text A on page 153. Use suitable words and phrases to make comparisons about the family's lifestyle before and after they dispensed with the TV.**

9 ⊙ 50 **Listen to two friends comparing a new book with other novels by the same author. For questions 1–8, complete the sentences with a word or phrase of comparison.**

According to James, *The Last Will* was (1) _____ believable as the author's previous novels.

Sally feels that this book is (2) _____ the author's (3) _____ yet.

James thinks that the plot is rather unrealistic (4) _____ the author's first novel.

Sally particularly likes the fact that there is (5) _____ action in court in the latest novel.

James thinks the courtroom drama sections are (6) _____ ones in the book.

Sally believes that the protagonist is significantly (7) _____ richly drawn than in previous novels by the same author.

James feels the characters are (8) _____ well developed as they are in another book.

10 **Make comparisons between two books by the same author, or between a film and its sequel.**

USE OF ENGLISH multiple-choice cloze

1 Read the article about time travel. Do you agree with the writer's view?

Time travel possibilities

An object travelling at high speed ages slower than a (1) _____ object. So if you travelled into outer space and back at close to the speed of light, you could travel thousands of years into the Earth's future! Problems of time are not 'absolute', nor do they have a (2) _____ correct answer. Time is relative to the speed at which one is travelling. Einstein's relativity will eventually become part of a new science more (3) _____ in its description of our universe. Remember, the word 'relativity' (4) _____ from the fact that the world's appearance depends purely on our state of motion.

Humankind has succeeded in (5) _____ the cosmic curtains a crack, but questions raised by physicists remain among the most philosophical. Is time itself real? Does it (6) _____ in one direction only? Does it have a beginning or an end? What is eternity? Infinity? None of these questions can be answered to the physicists' (7) _____ . Yet the (8) _____ asking of these questions expands our minds.

2 Reading and Use of English, Part 1

For questions 1–8, read the text above and decide which answer (A, B, C or D) best fits each gap.

1	A stable	C	stationary
	B standing	D	standard
2	A lone	C	single
	B solitary	D	sole
3	A comprehensive	C	comprehending
	B compulsive	D	confounding
4	A ensues	C	affects
	B derives	D	evolves
5	A pulling to	C	pulling back
	B pulling out	D	pulling down
6	A happen	C	elapse
	B flow	D	shift
7	A pleasure	C	satisfaction
	B delight	D	happiness
8	A mere	C	only
	B just	D	slight

Reading and Use of English, Part 1
Consolidation of things to look for in this part

During this course you have learnt that when tackling Part 1 of the Reading and Use of English paper you need to look out for several things. This task tests your lexical knowledge, in terms of meaning and use. The options you are presented with in each question, therefore, may contain:

1 words which look similar, but have different meanings.
2 parts of collocations, fixed phrases and phrasal verbs.
3 words which have similar meanings, but are used in different contexts.
4 words which are followed by a different preposition, or have a different grammatical structure.

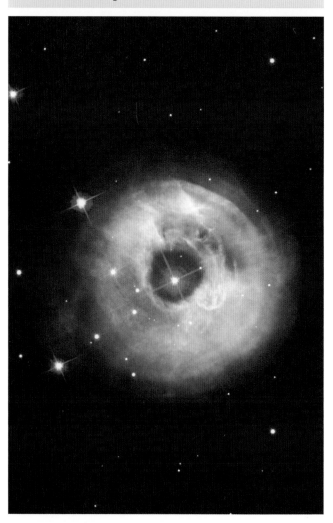

LISTENING three short extracts

RECOGNISING AGREEMENT AND DISAGREEMENT

In Listening, Part 1, you are sometimes required to recognise whether speakers agree or disagree.

3 🔘 51 **Listen to extract one and decide whether the statements below are true (T) or false (F).**

1 Neither speaker enjoys the peace and quiet. T / F
2 Both speakers miss their children. T / F

4 ⊙ 52 **Listening, Part 1**

You will hear three different extracts. For questions 1–6, choose the answer (A, B or C) which fits best according to what you hear. There are two questions for each extract.

Extract One
You hear two people discussing how they felt when their children left home.

1 Which word best sums up the woman's feelings towards her son leaving home?
A tension
B relief
C loneliness

2 The man and the woman agree that
A they sometimes feel lonely without the children at home.
B they sometimes dislike the responsibility of bringing up children.
C it is not fair to make demands on children once they leave.

Extract Two
You will hear part of an interview with a man talking about taking early retirement.

3 According to the speaker, one of the initial problems he faced when he retired was
A the fact that his wife expected him to do the shopping.
B the fact that his wife expected him to do everything with her.
C the difference between his wife's expectations and his own.

4 Which of the following does the speaker not think is important in order to enjoy one's retirement?
A having help from your children
B having sufficient funds
C having your own interests

Extract Three
You hear two people talking about working at home.

5 What does the woman say about starting her own business?
A She anticipated problems if she worked at home.
B She was mainly interested in the freedom of being self-employed.
C She struggled to maintain a balance between work and family.

6 Both speakers feel that
A it is easy to be distracted by domestic issues when you work at home.
B going to work in an office is preferable to working at home.
C making your own decisions is the main advantage of being self-employed.

SPEAKING individual long turn

5 Discuss. Have you ever dreamed of giving your bedroom a complete makeover? How would you change it?

COMPARING PICTURES

In Speaking, Part 2, you are presented with three pictures, and have to compare two of them. You are also asked a question about a particular aspect of the topic of the photos. Use as much variety of language as possible.

6 Work in pairs. Make a list of different comparative forms that could be used to express the following sentences.

a The second room is more cramped than the first one.
b The first room is much lighter than the second one.

▶ GRAMMAR REFERENCE (SECTION 16) **PAGE 221**

7 Work in pairs.
Student A, turn to page 239 and look at your pictures. They show different kinds of children's bedrooms. Compare them, and say what kind of child you think each one is suitable for, and why.

Student B, say which design you think would be most suitable for a girl aged four. Why?

Student B, turn to page 240, and look at your pictures. They show different designs for kitchens. Compare and contrast them, and say which one you would choose for your own house, and why.

Student A, say which design you like least. Why?

WRITING   letter of reference

1 **Read the exam question below, and underline the key points you would need to include in your answer.**

You are a teacher at an English language college in your home town. You have been asked to provide a letter of reference for a student of yours who has applied for a job as a nanny for an English family. The person appointed will be good at dealing with small children, and have knowledge of first aid.

You should include information about your student's character and personal qualities and skills, their previous relevant experience and reasons why they should be considered for this job.

Write your **letter**. You do not need to include postal addresses.

A LETTER OF REFERENCE

Providing a character reference for someone who has applied for a job or position of responsibility requires a fairly formal style.

It usually takes the form of a letter, but begins in a standard way, with the following phrases:

- *Dear Sir/Madam*, or *To whom it may concern*
  (for professional positions)
- *Dear Mr Green / Ms Smith*
  (if you are given a name)

You should always end formally. Use the following phrases:

- *Yours faithfully, …*
  (if the person's name is unknown)
- *Yours sincerely, …*
  (if the person's name is known)

When answering a question of this kind, read the instructions carefully, to make sure you include all the necessary information in your character reference. Remember, your letter should persuade the prospective employer that your student friend/former colleague is suitable for the job.

2 **Work in pairs. Complete the outline plan below for a letter of reference in answer to the question in exercise 1.**

Paragraph 1 (opening paragraph)

State the name of the person you are writing about, and your relationship with them, explaining why you feel qualified to discuss their suitability for the job.

Paragraph 2:

Paragraph 3:

EXAM SPOTLIGHT

Writing, Parts 1 and 2   Final reminder – check your work!

When you finish writing your answer in the Writing paper, it's very important to check your work.
You can use the following checklist when you write:
Relevance   Have you answered the question?
Register   Have you used the correct style of formal/informal language?
Use of language   Does it make sense, grammatically?
Range of vocabulary   Is it varied enough and appropriate?
Spelling and punctuation   Have you made any careless mistakes?
Organisation   Is the development of points organised, with an introductory paragraph, at least one paragraph developing the main points and a concluding paragraph?
Length   Is your answer long enough, or too long?
Remember, in both parts, you should write 220–260 words.

3 Read the letter of reference written in answer to exercise 1. Underline any mistakes you notice, and use the checklist on page 158 to consider its merits. What mark do you think it deserves?

Dear Sir/Madam,
I was asked to provide this reference for Maria Fernandez, who I know since 2004. As a teacher and the Director of Studies at the Top Grade English Language College in Cuenca, I teach Maria for the last five years. During this time, she had proved herself both a competent student, and a popular member of the school.
She rapidly progressed to Cambridge English: First level, achieving a B last December, and is presently studying for the Advanced examination. She is a warm, outgoing girl, who is great fun and popular with her fellow students. As the eldest of four, Maria has to take care her younger brother and sisters after school, since her parents both work. She likes telling stories, and often relates us funny tales of her five-year-old brother's antics.
A skilful musician, she took up the responsibility of preparing our youngest students to sing in the school play at the end of last term, and entertained a wonderful rapport with them overall. When one of the boys fell and cut his head, she remained serene and administrated to him efficiently, while maintaining control of the other children until one of the teachers arrived.
For these reasons, I am confident that Maria has the right qualities for this job, and have no hesitation in recommending you her.
Yours,
Amanda

Writing, Part 2

4 Prepare and write an answer to the following question. Use the checklist on page 158 to check your work.

> You have been asked to provide a letter of reference for a friend of yours who has applied for a job as a group leader in an English-speaking summer camp. The person appointed will be good at dealing with a range of young people and will display excellent leadership skills.
>
> You should include information about your friend's character and personal qualities and skills, their previous relevant experience and reasons why they should be considered for this job.
> Write your **letter**. You do not need to include postal addresses.

REVIEW 4

1 Complete the sentences with the words in the box.

annual   compatible   compulsive   conclude
conclusion   contagious   peace   returned
ruthless   terminated

1 His contract was _____ because he'd revealed company secrets.
2 If you want to cut this down to fewer than 200 words, you're going to have to be _____ .
3 Sally had to stay in her room for an extra day in case her measles were still _____ .
4 Helen didn't return the call so we drew the _____ that she wasn't interested in our offer.
5 I wouldn't believe a word Mike says – he's a _____ liar you know!
6 I'm not surprised Tim and Sue get on so well – they're totally _____ .
7 Leave me in _____ ! I've had a long day and need to relax.
8 The judge _____ his verdict after a lot of discussion with the jury behind closed doors.
9 Let's _____ the meeting by summarising the action points.
10 I'll be on _____ leave next week – I'm off to Mexico!

2 Complete the sentences with the correct form of a verb from the box.

clarify   come   complete   discontinue   dispose
draw   exchange   publish

1 The train service _____ because not enough people are using it.
2 The sea _____ into sight as we drove over the hill. The holiday could begin!
3 I _____ of my rubbish in the bin. People who drop litter really annoy me.
4 The boss's attention _____ to the fact that half of the staff hadn't come back after lunch and he wondered where they were.
5 The government _____ its plans for the new tax laws and they will be announced next week.
6 Could you _____ what you mean by this instruction? It's not clear to me.
7 The book _____ when the editor noticed a spelling mistake on the front cover.
8 We _____ text messages while the lecture was going on. Then the lecturer realised and took our phones away.

3 Replace the underlined parts of the sentences with an expression using the word in capitals.

1 The ship leaves the harbour at 7 p.m. SET
2 He explained that he had become completely absorbed in the accounts. BOGGED
3 The party was supposed to be a surprise, but somehow Geoffrey heard about it. WIND
4 If you're not careful, both you and Martin are going to be in a lot of trouble! WATER
5 I couldn't cope any more – I had reached the limit of my patience! TETHER
6 Dr Potter is an expert in insect behaviour. AUTHORITY
7 If you have nothing to do, I can give you a few chores. LOOSE
8 Will could have been really annoyed by what happened, but he decided to ignore it. PASS

4 Reading and Use of English, Part 4

For questions 1–6, complete the second sentence so that it has a similar meaning to the first sentence, using the word given. Do not change the word given. You must use between three and six words, including the word given.

1 Instead of finishing the leftovers, I'd prefer to cook something fresh.
   RATHER
   I _____ finish the leftovers.
2 Anthropologists have learnt a lot about human behaviour by studying dolphins.
   SO
   If anthropologists hadn't studied dolphins, they _____ about human behaviour.
3 I'd sooner find out some things about their culture first.
   BETTER
   It _____ out some things about their culture first.
4 Even though he hated cartoons, he agreed to watch it with the kids.
   FACT
   He agreed to watch it with the kids _____ he hated cartoons.
5 No sooner had the lightning struck than all the lights went off.
   WHEN
   Hardly _____ all the lights went off.
6 My dad's pie is far tastier than this one.
   NEARLY
   This pie _____ the one my dad makes.

5 **Complete the collocations with a word or phrase from the box.**

cloud   confirmed   (be) cut off   dispel   drastic   emotional   shock   staple

1 _____ someone out of their ignorance
2 _____ action
3 _____ wreck
4 _____ meat-eater
5 _____ diet
6 _____ my conscience
7 _____ the myth
8 _____ from the rest of the world

6 **Make more collocations by matching the nouns with the words and phrases in the box in exercise 5.**

a time / support
b bachelor / atheist
c mood / mind
d complacency / daydream
e the rumours / the fears
f civilisation / society
g measures / changes
h gun / ingredient

7 **Choose the best word from the options A, B, C or D to complete the sentences.**

1 The human ear is unable to hear the dolphins' signals, but we have developed machinery which can pick _____ up.
A these   C it
B them   D those
2 One area of study that scientists are particularly interested in is _____ of communication between mother dolphins and their offspring.
A such   C that
B what   D one
3 I'd rather you _____ the bus every day instead of driving.
A take   C were taking
B took   D will take
4 _____ you had the chance to do one selfless act. What would it be?
A As if   C Had
B Were   D Suppose
5 _____ the fire, many birds lost their nests.
A Because   C Due to
B Consequently   D As a result
6 _____ it hadn't rained all week, I watered the garden.
A Seeing as   C In case
B Therefore   D Notwithstanding

8 **Reading and Use of English, Part 2**

For questions 1–8, read the text below and think of the word which best fits each gap. Use only one word in each gap.

Saturn runs rings round all the other planets

Why are Saturn's rings so astonishing? It could be that the planet managed to cling on to a moon when all the other gas giants in our solar system had already lost (1) _____ . Today's rings formed when the moon was shattered. Astronomists at the University of Diderot, Paris, suggest (2) _____ was during the 'late heavy bombardment', 700 million years after Saturn formed, (3) _____ a fragment of debris collided (4) _____ one of the planet's moons. Because the moon was orbiting at just the right distance from Saturn when it exploded – within what's known as the Roche limit – the tiny pieces created the rings (5) _____ of dispersing. This could explain (6) _____ other planets don't have rings like Saturn's.

Other astronomists around the world say the French way of showing Saturn's uniqueness among gas giants is interesting, (7) _____ that their hypothesis cannot be proved (8) _____ we have better ways of replicating in model form the evolution of the solar system.

9 **Complete the sentences with a word from the box and a suitable particle.**

ashamed   deficient   derived   eligible   immune   obsessed

1 Lucinda has been _____ _____ this particular rock band for the past three years!
2 Rupert's _____ _____ criticism; you can say what you like, but he won't care at all.
3 If you're _____ _____ vitamin C, you'll suffer from all kinds of problems.
4 This shampoo is _____ _____ various plant oils.
5 My next door neighbours are _____ _____ a building grant from the council.
6 Laura was so _____ _____ her brother's behaviour that she told him to walk home alone.

VOCABULARY ORGANISER 1

1 Getting started, page 10 **Complete the sentences with verbs that mean to *begin* or *start*.**

1 Police in the West Midlands area have _____ an official investigation into the robberies.
2 An estimated six million people watched as the new President was _____ yesterday.
3 We'd better _____ early if we don't want to miss the launch of HMS Victorious at Southampton tomorrow.
4 When I _____ the company, I never expected it to be so successful.
5 The chairwoman _____ a discussion into analysing the failure of the new product.
6 Acupuncture _____ in China over 3,000 years ago.
7 A number of protestors _____ acts of violence, but these were quickly suppressed by the police.
8 At the age of 15, she _____ a promising career in showbusiness.

2 Match the words in exercise 1 with the definitions (a–e).

a to officially introduce someone into an important position with a ceremony
b to start something new, difficult or exciting in your life
c to begin a journey
d to begin to happen or exist
e to cause something to happen as a response or reaction

3 Reading, page 10 **Choose the correct options in italics to complete the sentences.**

1 Charlie Chaplin gained *invaluable / earnest* experience while working as a teenager, which provided ideas for films.
2 His mother suffered from a *distinct / hoarse voice* after working too hard.
3 Chaplin's tramp character was a(n) *auspicious / resounding* success.
4 A barber's shop, printing plant and glass factory were among the various *establishments / institutions* where Chaplin worked as a teenager.

4 Language development, page 12 **Match the phrasal verbs in the box with the definitions (1–8).**

> make for   make into   make it up to
> make off   make out   make something of
> make up   make up for

1 do something to show you are sorry for the problems you caused somebody
2 go towards a particular place or destination
3 invent a new story, song, game, etc.
4 leave quickly, especially in order to escape
5 be able to see or hear something, though not very clearly
6 make a bad situation better, or replace something that has been lost
7 change something so that it has a different use or purpose
8 use the opportunities you have to become successful

ORGANISING VOCABULARY

It's important to record new vocabulary in a notebook in an organised manner, in order to remember it. There are several ways of organising and recording the vocabulary that you learn. Discuss the following methods:

- by theme
- grammatically – phrasal verbs, idioms, collocations, etc.
- word association
- functional use

5 Decide which you think is the most suitable method to record vocabulary from this unit, and start your own Vocabulary organiser notebook.

6 Writing, page 16 **Find a word or phrase in Anneka's letter that means the following:**

1 pleasantly fresh and cold (adj)
2 getting bigger (v)
3 rose, climbed higher (v)
4 something made up of many different parts (n)
5 blowing (v)

BANK OF ENGLISH

Word partnerships

Use a dictionary. Complete the lists below.

1 ***material*** (*Humble beginnings*, page 10)
   Use ***material*** with:
   N COUNT: *building materials*, _____ , _____ , _____
   N UNCOUNT: *reading material*, _____ , _____ , _____
   ADJ: *material things*, _____ , _____ , _____

2 ***matter*** (*The Big Bang*, page 13)
   Use ***matter*** with:
   N UNCOUNT: *waste matter*, _____ , _____ , _____
   N COUNT: *a private matter*, _____ , _____ , _____
   PHRASES: *it's a matter of … , as a matter of fact*, _____ , _____ , _____

VOCABULARY ORGANISER 2

1 Getting started, page 20 **Choose the correct options in italics to complete the sentences.**

1 The boys *waded / clambered* over the rocks on the shore.

2 The lively dog *tiptoed / bounded* up to Peter, wagging its tail in excitement.

3 David and Paul are fighting over that toy again! They're on the floor *wrestling / heaving* with each other!

4 Sally *paddled / waded* across the river to where her friends were waiting for her on the other side.

5 Having stepped on a nail, Tim *hopped / skipped* round the room on one leg.

6 John sat on a plastic bag and, pushing himself along, began to *wander / slide* down the snow-covered slope.

7 The children *paddled / wrestled* at the water's edge, searching for pebbles and shells.

8 Karen *heaved / leaped* her bulging schoolbag on to her shoulder, and headed for the bus stop.

2 Reading, page 20 **Find words in the reading texts which mean the following:**

1 red and healthy looking (adj)
_____

2 people who are the first to do something (n pl)
_____

3 the subjects students study at school (n)
_____

4 unaware of the existence of something (adj)
_____

5 to grow and develop in a healthy way (v)
_____

6 bored and impatient (adj)
_____

7 a poisonous substance (n)
_____

8 without any movement or expenditure of energy (adj)
_____

3 Language development, page 22 **Complete the sentences with one of the body parts in the box.**

| foot   head   mouth   neck   shoulder |

1 She really stuck her _____ out when she supported Tom, because lots of people criticised her for it.

2 I just can't say the right thing to Jake's mum. No matter what I do, I keep putting my _____ in it!

3 The government say they want to improve education, so they should put their money where their _____ is, and do something about it!

4 I can't remember the exact figure, but off the top of my _____ I'd say it was about £500.

5 Dave's got a real chip on his _____; he's always moaning about how unfair life is.

4 **Find idioms on page 22 to mean:**

1 an annoying person

2 very new and so inexperienced

3 light-hearted and not serious

4 in agreement with each other

5 show that you are bothered or worried by something

5 **Draw a word web in your notebook and add the idioms from page 22 to it.**

6 **There are many expressions with *pick*. What do the following expressions mean? Use a dictionary and write example sentences of your own.**

1 pick up the pieces
_____

2 pick somebody's brain
_____

3 take your pick
_____

4 pick holes in something
_____

5 pick your way
_____

6 pick-me-up
_____

7 pickpocket
_____

8 picky
_____

9 pick through
_____

10 pick over
_____

BANK OF ENGLISH

Word partnerships: *play*

Use a dictionary. Find the difference in meaning between the words in the following groups.

N UNCOUNT: *fair play, foul play, horseplay*
N COUNT: *playboy, playmate, playwright*
VERB: *downplay, outplay*
PHRASE: *play on words, plug-and-play*

Add the words in the box to the correct group above.

| airplay   play act   play down   play off   playback   playtime |

VOCABULARY ORGANISER 3

1 Getting started, page 28 **Use the words in capitals to form a word that completes the sentence.**

1 The view from the top of Niagara Falls is
_____ .
AWE

2 Flying in a helicopter was a _____ experience. Never again!
TERRIFY

3 His words were very _____ , and I soon calmed down.
REASSURE

4 Standing at the summit after a long climb is
_____ .
EXHILARATED

5 I found the journey _____ , and needed two days to recover from it!
EXHAUST

2 Reading, page 29 **Complete the sentences with a word or phrase from *A Close Encounter*.**

1 In this competition the _____ are high, as everyone is determined to win.

2 Peter was not sure about his decision to enter the race, and the poor weather conditions did little to
_____ .

3 That was the worst restaurant I've ever been to! The service was _____ , and the food was inedible.

4 Do you know what I had to _____ in order to marry you? My father nearly threw me out and disinherited me!

3 **Find a word or phrase in the text which means the following:**

1 noise (para 1)
2 message asking for help (para 1)
3 freed from difficulty (para 1)
4 stupid (para 1)
5 terrible (para 2)
6 place at risk (para 3)
7 the risks (para 3)
8 make me more determined (para 4)

4 Language development, page 30 **Match the definitions with a phrase with *up* and *down*.**

1 be reduced to
_____

2 misbehave
_____

3 begin to concentrate on doing
_____

4 experience slight depression
_____

5 be not very good
_____

6 be the fault of (someone)
_____

5 List the definitions of the remaining phrases on page 30 in your notebook. Then find the definition for the phrase *we've been having our ups and downs* in your dictionary, and add it to your list.

6 Language development, page 30 **Match the definitions with phrasal verbs with *take*.**

1 mistakenly think one person is another
_____

2 regret having said something
_____

3 resemble someone in your family
_____

4 write something down on paper
_____

5 accept responsibility
_____

6 start a new activity
_____

7 take control from someone else
_____

8 obtain something by applying for it and paying the necessary fee
_____

9 like immediately
_____

10 separate something into pieces
_____

Which of the definitions above can also mean:

11 return something
_____

12 invite someone to go somewhere with you
_____

Look in your dictionary to find more phrasal verbs with *take*.

BANK OF ENGLISH

Word partnerships: *take*
Which of the following phrases do not use *take*?
… *it from me*
… *something lying down*
… *the bright side*
… *it out of you*
… *something as read*
… *a mountain out of a molehill*
… *the bull by the horns*
… *five*
… *your hat off to*
… *it or leave it*
… *or break it*
… *the wind out of somebody's sails*
… *no prisoners*
… *the hard line*
… *it with a pinch of salt*
… *kindly to*

VOCABULARY ORGANISER 4

1 Getting started, page 38 **Match words in the box on page 38 with the definitions.**

1 The study of fossils in order to learn about the history of life on Earth

_____

2 Methods used to solve crimes and find out who committed them

_____

3 The study of space, planets and stars

_____

4 The time in history before any information was written down

_____

2 Reading, page 39 **Find words in the dinosaur book reviews (texts A–E) which mean the following:**

1 obscure, not clear (adj; Text A)
2 connected with the air or flight (adj; Text B)
3 fast (adj; Text B)
4 animals that hunt other animals (n.pl; Text B)
5 disintegrating, dissolving (v; Text C)
6 snakes (n.pl; Text C)
7 developing, growing (v; Text D)
8 able to produce a lot of good ideas (adj; Text E)

3 **Answer the questions with reference to the reading text.**

1 *conjure up* – What's the meaning of this phrasal verb?
2 *a sticky end* – What does this refer to here?
3 *thunder* across the land – Why is the word *thunder* used here?
4 *flutter* among the trees – Why is the word *fly* not used here?
5 *paddle* around the pond – Who or what would you normally expect to paddle around a pond?
6 *under the skin* – What does this expression mean?

4 Language development, page 40 **Use the words in capitals to complete the sentences with colour idioms.**

1 After my first karate lesson, I was _____ all over.
   BLUE
2 After three years heavily in debt, the business is finally in _____ again.
   BLACK
3 The boys were caught _____ stealing Mrs Brown's apples.
   RED
4 Ernie was _____ when he saw the cake Molly got for her birthday.
   GREEN

5 Key word, page 40 **Complete the sentences (1–2) with the correct particle. Then match the sentences to the definitions (a–b).**

| apart   off   on |

1 William was told _____ for speaking during the exam.
2 I find it increasingly difficult to tell the perfumes _____ – they all smell the same to me.
a reprimand, or speak angrily to someone angrily about something they have done
b recognise the difference between different things or people

6 Use of English, page 43 **Match the prefixes (1–8) with the words (a–h).**

1	un-	a	large
2	re-	b	ability
3	il-	c	religious
4	en-	d	media
5	multi-	e	decided
6	ir-	f	consider
7	dis-	g	functional
8	in-	h	legible

BANK OF ENGLISH

Word partnerships: *tech*

Use a dictionary. Find the difference in meaning between the words in the following groups.

> **Nouns**: *technology, technicality, Technicolor, technique, techno, technocracy*
> **Nouns (persons)**: *technician, techie, technical support, technologist, technophobe, technophile, technocrat*
> **Adjectives**: *technical, technocratic, technological*
> **Adverbs**: *technically*

Match a word from the box with the definitions.

1 a person who hates technology
2 a special way of doing something
3 scientific knowledge used for practical purposes
4 a form of modern music with a heavy beat
5 a repair and advice service that some companies offer to their clients
6 a person whose job involves skilled practical work with scientific equipment
7 a system of colour photography used in making cinema films
8 a way of saying that something may be true according to fact, laws or rules, but may not be important or relevant in a particular situation

VOCABULARY ORGANISER 5

1 Reading, page 48 **Write definitions for these words and phrases in connection with computers.**

1 programmer
2 virus
3 crimeware
4 antidote
5 cyber-criminal
6 cyber-crime
7 hacking

2 Language development, page 50 **Replace the underlined words in the sentences below with a suitable verb structure.**

1 Police <u>thought that Larry Jones committed</u> the crime.
2 Sally <u>told Wayne she thought he had stolen</u> her money.
3 Sergeant Vyne <u>caught Jones</u> and took him to the police station.
4 After questioning, Larry <u>said that he had robbed</u> the bank, with help from his girlfriend.
5 Larry's girlfriend <u>said she hadn't helped</u> him.
6 The police <u>officially said that the couple had committed</u> the crime and prepared to take them to court.
7 The court <u>found Larry guilty of</u> robbing the bank.
8 The judge <u>decided he should go to prison for three years</u>.

3 Choose the correct options in italics to complete the sentences.

1 Mandy didn't know what to do, so she turned *in / to* her father for help.
2 Last night, Charlie was tired and turned *in / out* early.
3 The officer asked Maria to turn *out / off* her engine while he wrote the ticket.
4 The business turned *over / down* a profit of $30 million last year.
5 I asked my mum if she'd like to come on holiday with us, but she turned *off / down* the offer and went with my sister instead.

4 Key word, page 50 **Choose the correct phrase to complete the sentences.**

1 The police met with opposition from local youths when they tried to _____ .
   A lay down the new law
   B enforce the new law
   C break the new law
   D take the new law into their own hands
2 James thinks he is _____ and can do what he wants because his father is a friend of Prince Charles.
   A a law unto himself
   B within the law
   C above the law
   D law-abiding

3 It's simple. If you don't _____ , you'll end up in trouble. It's your choice.
   A is law
   B is by law
   C is within the law
   D obey the law
4 _____ agencies around the world are trying to stop drug trafficking.
   A Law enforcement
   B Law and order
5 You are required _____ to show proof of identity when entering this territory.
   A within the law
   B by law

5 Use of English, page 53 **Use prepositions to complete the paragraph.**

I'll always be grateful (1) _____ Connie. She once saved me (2) _____ making a serious mistake, when I nearly got married (3) _____ a man who would have made me unhappy. Later he married someone else, but he was always jealous (4) _____ his wife's ability to make everyone she met feel valued. That was one of her reasons (5) _____ leaving him.

BANK OF ENGLISH

Word partnerships: *cry*

In the text *Of Worms And Woodpeckers*, we learn that computer hacking today is *a far cry from the earliest days of hacking*.

Match the phrases with *cry* in A with the definitions in B.

A
VERB: *cry foul, cry wolf, cry off, cry out for, a shoulder to cry on*
NOUN: *a far cry from, battle cry*
GERUND: *it's no use crying over spilt milk, for crying out loud*
ADJECTIVE: *a crying shame*

B
- phrase used to encourage support for a protest or campaign
- need something desperately
- something very different from something else
- spoken phrase showing annoyance or impatience
- someone to listen sympathetically to your problems
- say you cannot do something you have agreed to do
- ask for help when you don't need it
- protest that something is wrong or unfair
- say that something is very sad or upsetting
- don't waste time feeling sorry about a mistake that cannot be changed

VOCABULARY ORGANISER 6

1 Getting started, page 58 **Complete the sentences in your own words.**

1 On a daily basis I try to consume _____ .

2 Generally it's best to avoid _____ .

3 One way of boosting _____ .

4 Organically grown vegetables are _____ .

5 Your immune system works by _____ .

6 Medication may be prescribed _____ .

7 Yoga is a form of _____ .

8 You should establish the root _____ .

2 Language development, page 60

1 Match the expressions (a–c) with the definitions (i–iii).
   a   a nest egg
   b   an egghead
   c   a bad egg

   i   not a good person
   ii   money you save for a future purpose
   iii an intellectual person (often out of touch with social trends)

2 Which of these words cannot be used to mean *money*?
   a   bread
   b   dough
   c   bacon
   d   butter

3 If you were in a life-threatening situation, you would probably do everything possible to save your
   a   bacon.
   b   meat.
   c   burgers.
   d   chops.

4 A friend of yours picks up a plate and accidentally drops it. What would you call her?
   a   Jelly hands!
   b   Butter fingers!
   c   Oily palms!

3 Key word, page 60 **Complete the sentences with one suitable word.**

1 Unfortunately it's a _____ of life that we all must die one day.

2 I need some chocolate! It's a _____ of life and death!

3 Would you really _____ down your life just to help another person?

4 Use of English, page 63 **Complete the collocations in the sentences with the correct verb.**

1 There are several factors you need to _____ into account if you are considering their offer.

2 Garlic is reputed to _____ wonders for one's health.

3 If you smoke, you _____ a much greater risk of getting cancer.

4 You shouldn't _____ fun of Natalie just because she has to wear glasses.

5 Low levels of vitamin D can _____ rise to a number of problems.

6 After her grandfather died, the house began to _____ into disrepair.

7 They tried to tease Nicole, but she wouldn't _____ for it.

8 Please _____ us know if you decide to visit our town.

BANK OF ENGLISH

Stem word: *heal*

1 How many words can you derive from the stem word *heal*?

2 Which of the words in the box cannot be preceded by *health*?

> bus   care   centre   club   farm   food   provider
> school   visitor

3 Which of the following sentences are incorrect? Correct them.
   a   I've got a sore throat – I'm hoping it will heal by tomorrow.
   b   It's just a little cut – don't worry, it will heal on its own.
   c   Anna says she can heal people just by touching them.
   d   The doctor has given me some pills to heal me.

VOCABULARY ORGANISER 7

1 Reading, page 66 **Complete the sentences with a suitable word from exercise 9 on page 67.**

1 The _____ of the city means that the suburbs are being eaten up.
2 I was totally _____ by the detail in the ceiling paintings of the Sistine Chapel when I visited last year.
3 In any city, the markets are always the most _____ places, full of local traders, shoppers and tourists.
4 Whenever he comes home from a trip overseas, Chris feels a _____ of love for his small rural village and its peaceful way of life.
5 If their campaign for _____ is successful, the new government will have a lot of work to do to establish the state in its own right.
6 I always have a feeling of _____ before I speak in public – it's something I've never got used to.
7 This high street looks exactly the same as all the others – it's full of _____ of shops and restaurants, and nothing is original.
8 I took my husband to my hometown recently and we visited my favourite old _____ , but it didn't feel the same any more. Time has moved on.

2 Language development, page 68 **Do these words have a positive or negative meaning?**

> amazing appealing breathless crumbling
> cosy disgusting dusty eerie grand horrible
> industrious magical passionate remarkable
> run down shoddy sober sparkling unique

Work in pairs and brainstorm other positive and negative words to describe places.

3 **Write definitions for these phrases with *look*. Use a dictionary to help you.**

look ahead
look down on somebody
look forward to
look in on somebody
look into something
look out for each other
look through somebody
look somebody up
look up to somebody
look somebody in the eye

4 Key word, page 68 **Decide whether the following statements are true (T) or false (F).**

1 A *road hog* is a farm animal that has got out into the road.　　　　　　　　　　　T / F
2 *Road rage* is angry behaviour by car drivers towards other drivers.　　　　　　　T / F
3 We say a person is *roadworthy* when they are able to drive a car or motorbike.　　T / F
4 *Road works* are repairs that are being done to a road.　　　　　　　　　　　　T / F
5 A *roadshow* is a type of carnival procession.　T / F
6 A *road block* is an obstacle in the middle of the road that prevents cars from passing.　T / F
7 The *roadside* is the edge of the road.　　　　T / F

Write the phrases in your notebook with their correct definition.

5 Grammar, page 70 **Complete the sentences.**

1 Not only did she go to the party against my wishes
   _____
2 Never before has anyone
   _____
3 No sooner had I got home
   _____
4 On no account must you write
   _____
5 Not once did Winston
   _____
6 Under no circumstances should you call
   _____
7 Not until they arrived at the hotel
   _____
8 Hardly had she walked into the classroom
   _____

BANK OF ENGLISH

Word partnerships: *travel*

Put the phrases in the correct category, according to how the word *travel* is used.

> air travel   on their travels   rail travel   travel agent
> travel by train, car or plane   travel light   travel rug
> travel sickness   travel widely   traveller's cheque
> travel expenses   travelling musician
> travelling salesman   travelogue

VERB:
NOUN:
ADJECTIVE:

VOCABULARY ORGANISER 8

1 Getting started, page 76 **Complete the sentences with the words in the box.**

> awe-inspiring   imposing   massive   peculiar
> unattractive

1 The Sphinx was absolutely _____ – much larger than it looks in pictures.
2 The Great Pyramid of Giza is totally _____ – it just fills you with wonder.
3 Those Easter Island statues are quite _____ really. It's odd that nobody really knows why they made them.
4 Stonehenge is beautiful but rather _____ – it makes you feel ever so small.
5 I think the Great Wall is fairly _____ actually. What's so elegant about miles and miles of solid stone cutting through the landscape?

2 Reading, page 77 **Find adjectives in *Straw Bale Futures* to complete the sentences.**

1 Something that is _____ is new and original. (para 1)
2 Something that is _____ (such as a natural resource) is kept at a steady level and is not likely to be wiped out by overuse. (para 1)
3 If something is _____ to people, they can easily use it or obtain it. (para 2)
4 A _____ substance or object is not stiff, and it bends, stretches, or twists easily. (para 5)
5 Something that is _____ provides you with a feeling of enthusiasm and gives you new and creative ideas. (para 5)
6 Something that is _____ gives you the feeling that you can achieve something, for example by becoming stronger or more successful. (para 5)

3 Language development, page 78 **Match the phrasal verbs in the box with definitions (1–8).**

> bring about   bring along   bring back
> bring down   bring forward   bring off   bring out
> bring up

1 manage to do something successfully
2 cause a government, an aeroplane, or a person to fall
3 take someone or something with you when you go somewhere
4 introduce a new product; cause a particular behaviour in someone
5 arrange for a meeting or event to happen earlier than previously arranged
6 recall a memory, reintroduce a rule or law
7 cause something to happen
8 to mention a subject or to raise children

4 **Complete the sentences with one suitable word.**

1 They're bringing the house _____ every night with the new play at the theatre in town. Let's get tickets!
2 Seeing the farm again brought it _____ to me how happy I had been there.
3 Angela could not bring _____ to sell the old house.
4 He had a difficult illness that almost brought him to his _____ , but he's fine again now.
5 I love walking but I'm so slow! You'll always find me bringing up the _____ .
6 Why don't you use a few good adjectives to bring your description _____ ?

5 Use of English, page 81 **Write the noun form of the verbs. Then write definitions for the nouns.**

1 destroy   2 obsess   3 starve   4 myth

6 Writing, page 83 **Find words on page 83 to match the definitions.**

1 the buildings provided for people to live in (general)
2 the place where someone lives (formal)
3 the place where someone lives (formal address)
4 the place where someone lives (usually indicates simplicity)
5 the place where you live, usually rented
6 the natural environment in which an animal lives or a plant grows

BANK OF ENGLISH

Word partnerships: *house*

Verb forms: *to house someone or something*
Type of house: *boarding house, clearing house, council house, doll's house, full house, open house, opera house, outhouse, public house, Wendy house, White House*
Idiomatic phrases: *get on like a house on fire, eat someone out of house and home, safe as houses*
Fixed phrases: *on the house, get or put one's house in order*
Adjective phrase: *house to house*
House: *arrest, boat, bound, boy, breaker, coat, guest, hold, husband, keeper, lights, maid, master, mate, owner, party, plant, proud, room, warming, wife, work*
House of: *Commons, God, Lords, Representatives, Houses of Parliament*
Housing: *association, benefit, development, estate, project*

Which of the above is ...?

1 an outside toilet or storage room
2 a phrase which means *to have a good relationship*
3 a person who is in charge of the day-to-day running / management of a house
4 the main government building in London
5 money some people receive from the state to help them pay their rent

VOCABULARY ORGANISER 9

1 Reading, page 87 **Read the texts about William Daniels' exhibition again and match the adjectives in the box with the definitions (1–15).**

> alluring   angular   astounding   compelling
> endless   extensive   frustrating   intricate
> meandering   redundant   reflective   rich   shallow
> tedious   understated

1 boring
2 winding
3 large in amount
4 complicated or detailed
5 not needed
6 surprisingly impressive
7 lacking serious ideas
8 shiny because the surface sends back light
9 having sharp corners
10 never finishing
11 powerfully interesting
12 subtle, not obvious
13 annoying because it prevents something from being achieved
14 attractive
15 plentiful

2 **Choose the best adjective from exercise 1 to complete the sentences.**

1 They followed the course of the _____ river as it twisted and turned on its route through the forest.
2 Her figure is quite _____ – all jutting bones and skinny limbs.
3 I'm not keen on bold colours and loud patterns in clothing – I prefer more _____ garments.
4 He made quite a(n) _____ speech about the need for further research into sources of renewable energy. I'll certainly look into some of his ideas.
5 This job has _____ paperwork to complete – I never get home before 9 p.m.
6 Words cannot describe how _____ today's lecture was. I wanted to go to sleep after half an hour!
7 This is so _____ ! My computer keeps crashing and losing my work before I've had a chance to save it.
8 These printers are _____ now we work in a paperless office.
9 What a beautiful design! It's so _____ you see something new every time you look at it.
10 They've carried out a(n) _____ survey into the living conditions of all the poorer people in the area.

3 Key word, page 88 **Choose the correct options in italics to complete the sentences.**

1 Please pay *attention / tribute* to what I am about to say!
2 Sam surprised his mother by paying her *respect / a compliment* about her hair.
3 The underfloor heating system only began paying *its way / for itself* after the first three years.
4 I was forced to pay *the penalty / through the nose* for not studying by failing all my exams.
5 I've come to pay you *my respects / a visit*; I'm so sorry for your loss.

4 Speaking, page 91 **Complete the sentences with words from the box.**

> balance   deceit   happiness   harmony   nostalgia
> rebellious   sophistication   stability   transition
> unique

1 The smell of jasmine arouses feelings of _____ in me, reminding me of times spent at my grandmother's house.
2 Teenagers are sometimes _____ , and refuse to follow rules.
3 I was particularly hurt by her _____ , because I'd thought I could trust her.
4 The teenage years represent a period of _____ from childhood to adulthood.
5 Everything in the room seems to be in _____ , creating a pleasant, relaxed atmosphere.
6 Tom has changed jobs and moved town a lot in recent years, but now he's looking for some _____ in his life.
7 The new baby brought _____ to the family.
8 My father is a _____ man; there's no one like him!
9 Parents nowadays struggle to find a _____ between work and family.
10 Laura has charm and _____ and is able to mix well in any social event.

BANK OF ENGLISH

Word partnerships: *design*

1 **Describe a design feature of your mobile phone or the chair you are sitting on.**
2 **Why is a design fault something undesirable? Give an example.**
3 **Read sentences a–e and explain the use of the phrases in italics.**
   a It is unknown whether the house was set on fire by accident or *by design*.
   b Maria has *grand designs* for her hat-making business.
   c Jason *has designs* on that restaurant in the town centre.
   d Beth is taking a course in *graphic design*.
   e Developments in genetic engineering have given rise to the idea of *designer babies*.

VOCABULARY ORGANISER 10

1 Getting started, page 96 Use a dictionary to find the missing words.

ethical (adj) _____ (definition)
_____ (antonym)
_____ (n pl)
_____ (adv)

2 Reading, page 97 Look back at the text and find words which match definitions 1–5.

1 to leave, or be forced to leave, a place that has been your home for a long time (v)
2 to make something less likely to succeed, especially deliberately (v)
3 an unmarried man (n)
4 fast, energetic but uncontrolled (adj)
5 so bad or so extreme that nobody can bear it (adj)

3 Language development, page 98 Complete the sentences with a suitable phrase. Make any changes that are necessary.

1 Martha started to tell me about what had happened, but her brother walked into the room, just as we were getting down to the _____ .
2 We said we would let Martin come along, as long as he promised not to _____ by mentioning Robert's name to Mary.
3 Fossil fuels and greenhouse gases are beginning to _____ the environment.
4 Elizabeth thought it would be easy to change course in the middle of the year, but she now admits it's been _____ all the way.
5 All the _____ of working in a fast-paced career caused his hair to turn white when he was still only in his thirties.
6 Archie had never looked after his health, so when he got this nasty cough last winter _____ .
7 It was too cold for us in Manchester, so we decided to _____ and move to Florida.
8 _____ is this: if you don't get your act together, you'll be out of a job.

4 Key word, page 98 Replace the underlined parts of the following sentences with a phrasal verb or an expression formed with *pull*.

1 I think Chris was <u>teasing you</u> when he said you'd won the lottery.
2 Mum was always moaning at Dad for not <u>doing his fair share of the work</u>.
3 He managed to <u>succeed at</u> three bank robberies in one week.
4 The factory is going to be <u>demolished</u> to make way for a shopping centre.
5 How long has Lionel been <u>deceiving us</u>?
6 Miriam had been diagnosed with a terminal illness, but she managed to <u>recover</u>.
7 I bet he only got promoted because his father <u>used his influence</u>.
8 <u>Drive to the side of the road and stop</u>. I want to look at the map.

5 Use of English, page 101 Choose the correct options in italics to complete the sentences.

1 I got a *heavy / solid* duty suitcase for my birthday because my old one had fallen to pieces.
2 Martin has hidden *lengths / depths* – he wrote a beautiful poem for Charlotte.
3 We're going to get some new saucepans in the sale because they're really good *value / worth*.
4 Is your ring *solid / hard* gold, or is it mixed with another metal?
5 If you talk about your work to a competitor, you'll be breaking your *position / contract*.
6 I hope we get our pay *packet / wealth* before the holidays.

BANK OF ENGLISH

Words with similar meanings

conscience	dilemma	ethics	morals	scruples

Match the words in the box with the definitions (1–5).

1 _____: the awareness of a moral or ethical aspect to one's conduct, together with the urge to prefer right over wrong.
One of the things that make us different from animals is that we have a _____ .
2 _____: a situation that requires a choice between options that are or seem equally (un)favourable or mutually exclusive.
I found myself in a _____ – what was I going to do?
3 _____: a set of principles of right conduct; a theory or a system of moral values.
According to our society's code of _____ , treating people in this way is wrong.
4 _____: rules or habits of conduct, especially of sexual conduct, with reference to standards of right and wrong.
Historically she was portrayed as a woman of loose _____ , though there is no evidence that this was so.
5 _____: moral principles that stop you doing something bad.
Mike didn't have any _____ about pushing on to the bus first.

VOCABULARY ORGANISER 11

1 Reading, page 105 **Choose the correct options in italics to complete the sentences.**

1 Nancy *ventured / endeavoured* a nervous smile in response to her teacher's words of praise.
2 At the end of the night, the bartender *worked out / totted up* the money in the till.
3 'I have some *troublesome / rudimentary* neighbours in the flat upstairs,' sighed Mandy, as a loud crash made the ceiling shudder.
4 Harry quickly showed them his passport in order to *dispel / exorcise* any suspicions they might have regarding his identity.
5 His excitement mounting, Ian *fleetingly / feverishly* worked out how much a trip to Peru would cost.

2 Language development, page 106 **Decide whether the following statements are true (T) or false (F).**

1 If you feel *out of it*, you feel you don't belong in a group or place.   T / F
2 If something is *out of the question*, it is irrelevant to the discussion in progress.   T / F
3 When something is *out of order*, it is not in the correct position.   T / F
4 We say something is *out of this world* when it is amazing.   T / F
5 When something occurs *out of the blue*, it happens in the sky.   T / F
6 When you are *out of your mind* you are happy. T / F

3 Key word, page106 **Complete the sentences with one of the phrases from the box, making any changes that are necessary.**

> give him a good run for his money
> pump money into
> put your money where your mouth is
> have money to burn   put my money on

1 You want a gold watch and a smartphone for your birthday? Do you think I
_____ ?
2 Well, I may not have beaten James in that match, but I _____ .
3 You keep saying you could do the job better than me, so why not _____ ?
4 I may be wrong, but I'd _____ a woman becoming the next President.
5 Tom wants to develop the company, so he _____ product development.

Word partnerships: *work*

1 Using a dictionary to help you, make a list of example sentences using these phrases.

PHRASES: *work in, work out, work off, work through, work up, have your work cut out, work your fingers to the bone, make light or heavy work of something, work ethic, work in progress* … etc

2 Match the compound nouns (1–10) with their meanings (a–j).

1	workaholic	a	person or machine that does a lot of hard, heavy work
2	workbench	b	total number of people in a country or region who are available for work
3	workbook	c	a heavy wooden table on which people use tools to make or repair things
4	workflow	d	person who works most of the time and finds it difficult to stop
5	workforce	e	the way a project is organised by a company, including who is going to do which part
6	workhorse	f	period of physical exercise, particularly in a gym
7	workmanship	g	book of practice exercises
8	workout	h	skill in making things well
9	worksheet	i	room or building where people use tools to make things
10	workshop	j	piece of paper with questions and exercises for students

VOCABULARY ORGANISER 12

1 Getting started, page 114 **Choose the best option to complete the sentences.**

1 I love a historical drama – the locations are usually stunning and the _____ are always so detailed and accurate.
   a credits   b costumes   c advertisements
2 I don't like horror films which just try to scare you, but I don't mind a good _____ with lots of suspense and adventure every now and then.
   a thriller   b documentary   c film noir
3 The composer's job is to write a good _____ for the film.
   a music   b lyric   c score
4 No matter how good the script is, if you don't have a good _____ it's not going to be worth watching.
   a crew   b cast   c actors
5 The _____ consisted of two or three different storylines which all converge in the final scene, and that's when you finally understand what's been going on!
   a plot   b direction   c production

2 Reading, page 115 **Find each of the words in the box in the film reviews and use them to complete the definitions (1–10).**

> cynical enamoured euphoric gallant
> gargantuan implausible inspired melancholy
> preposterous redundant

1 A _____ person believes the worst of other people. (Text A)
2 If you describe someone as _____ , you mean that they possess or display great dignity or nobility. (Text A)
3 Something that is _____ is no longer needed because its job is being done by something else, or is no longer useful or necessary. (Text B)
4 If you are _____ of something, you like it or admire it a lot. (Text B)
5 If you do something in a _____ manner, you feel very happy or elated. (Text C)
6 If someone is _____ they look and feel sad. (Text C)
7 If you describe something as _____ , you think it is unlikely to be true. (Text C)
8 If you describe something as _____ , you mean it is huge, enormous, bigger than could be expected. (Text D)
9 If you describe something as _____ , you think it is of extraordinary quality, as if it arose from a creative impulse. (Text E)
10 If you describe something as _____ , you think it is extremely foolish. (Text E)

3 Language development, page 116 **Choose one word from A and one word from B to form a collocation to complete the sentences.**

A
> bitterly deeply highly most perfectly
> seriously

B
> amusing disappointed injured kind offended
> simple

1 I thought it was very funny. In fact I found it _____ _____ .
2 I thought the play was a complete waste of money. I felt _____ _____ .
3 Thank you very much for your hospitality. You've been _____ _____ .
4 You shouldn't have said such a terrible thing. He was _____ _____ .
5 He was in an accident. Fortunately he wasn't _____ _____ .
6 It's not complicated at all. In fact it's _____ _____ .

4 Grammar, page 118 **Rewrite the following phrases as participle or compound adjectives.**

1 The clothes were made by hand. They were _____ .
2 The book amused me. It was an _____ .
3 The fruit had been modified genetically. It was _____ .
4 The watch was resistant to water. It was _____ .
5 The river had debris floating on it. There was _____ .

5 Use of English, page 119 **Use a dictionary. Find the words below in the text about screenwriters and write an example sentence of your own. Make a note of any derivatives.**

1 anonymous (adj)
2 embellish (v)
3 tweak (v)

6 Writing, page 120 **What can these adjectives be used to describe when talking about a film?**

1 wooden   4 complicated
2 two-dimensional   5 inspired
3 moving

BANK OF ENGLISH

Humour

1 How many derivatives of the word *humour* can you find? Write an example sentence with each of them.
2 Which one of the following words does not have anything to do with humour?

> amusing comedy comical deadpan
> dehydrated dry farce funny giggle hilarious
> humourist hysterical irony jesting joke
> laughable mirthful prankster uproarious
> sarcasm satire side-splitting slapstick wit

VOCABULARY ORGANISER 13

1 Getting started, page 124 **Complete the sentences with the correct form of a verb related to communicating.**

1 The producer decided to _____ this week's chat show live.
2 The newspaper reporter refused to _____ the source of his information.
3 The research findings are being _____ in this month's *New Scientist*.
4 The town council is running an advert in the local newspaper to _____ the new recycling campaign.
5 The American physicist has agreed to _____ information with a Japanese scientist based in Tokyo.
6 The coach spoke to the team before the match in order to _____ confidence in them.
7 The staff training officer said to the group of new trainees, 'It is my job to _____ knowledge to you about how to sell our products.'
8 The chef _____ the plans for the party to his staff.

2 Reading, page 125 **Find words in the reading text to match the definitions (1–5).**

1 the quality of being complicated and advanced in design (para 3)
2 periods of ten years (para 5)
3 most vague or unclear (para 6)
4 holes in the ground (para A)
5 to start (para B)

3 Language development, page 126 **Complete the table with the words in the box. Use a dictionary if necessary.**

access   admiration   alternative   approach
argument   authority   communication
connection   contact   dispute   effect   matter
product   question   respect   result   search
solution   threat

Nouns followed by	
of	
for	
to	
on	
over	
with	

4 Key word, page 126 **Explain the meaning of the following phrases with *set*.**

1 set a date
_____
2 set a precedent
_____
3 set an example
_____
4 set a trend
_____
5 set in motion
_____
6 set pen to paper
_____
7 set a record
_____
8 set sail
_____

BANK OF ENGLISH

Word partnerships: *co-*

The prefix *co-* is placed at the beginning of verbs or nouns that refer to people doing things together or sharing things.

Verbs	Nouns
co-operate	colleague
collaborate	co-worker
co-exist	co-writer
communicate	co-director
connect	
contact	
converse	

Complete the sentences with one of the verbs from the box in its correct form.

1 Renee and I _____ on writing a book about marine life a few years ago.
2 Have you ever _____ with a parrot? It often has a lot to say!
3 Prisoner 225, if you don't _____ and tell us who sent you, you'll be shot!
4 I just can't _____ with my little brother! He doesn't understand me at all!
5 Have you _____ the doctor yet? Her temperature's gone up to 40 degrees!

VOCABULARY ORGANISER 14

1 Reading, page 135 Match the nouns from *Planet Earth – The Gaia Hypothesis* with the definitions.

> biosphere   diversity   entity   equilibrium
> metabolism   myriad   phenomenon   salinity
> void

1   the saltiness of a liquid or substance
2   the rate at which food is converted into energy
3   something that is observed to happen or exist
4   something that exists separately and has an identity of its own
5   part of a planet's surface and atmosphere that sustains life
6   the different elements to be found within something
7   a large and empty space
8   a very large number or great variety of something
9   balance, harmony

2 Complete the sentences with a verb or adjective from *Planet Earth – The Gaia Hypothesis*. The words in brackets will help you.

1   He was a great philosopher, who came up with many _____ (deep, philosophical) insights into human nature. (para 1)
2   By meditating every day he was able to _____ (reach) a state of absolute tranquillity. (para 1)
3   Some scientists _____ (theorised) that life on Earth had in fact come from outer space. (para 2)
4   The accusations made against him were vague and _____ (not totally accurate). (para 4)
5   His comments about climate change _____ (generated) a negative response from environmentalists. (para 4)
6   Traditional farming methods in the area have created the _____ (most suitable) conditions for biological diversity. (para 4)
7   They learnt how to dry meat and fruit to _____ (support) them during the lean season. (para 4)
8   We were each given our _____ (selected) share of the land to grow our own vegetables. (para 6)

3 Language development, page 136 Which particle follows the groups of adjectives below?

1   aware, capable, conscious, fond, jealous
2   anxious, excited, pleased, sorry, upset
3   incompatible, bored, happy, pleased, connected
4   surprised, bad, annoyed, angry, excellent
5   addicted, attentive, grateful, indifferent, liable
6   baffled, detained, shocked, surprised, ridiculed
7   famous, responsible, liable, ready, sorry
8   experienced, interested, absorbed, disinterested
9   absent, different, missing, safe, distant
10 dependent, reliant, keen, hooked, based

4 Use of English, page 139 Use the words in capitals to form a word that completes the sentence.

1   I couldn't believe the _____ of the situation. **RIDICULE**
2   Do you know how much the _____ is for Australia? **POST**
3   He may be a very small dog, but he's ever so _____ . **COURAGE**
4   Ava is such an _____ little girl – she's always giving me hugs. **AFFECTION**
5   I don't use _____ on my vegetables – I prefer organic gardening methods. **INSECT**
6   Thousands of _____ were trying to get over the border and away from the war zone. **REFUGE**
7   After millions of years of _____ , the variety of species in the forests are beginning to disappear. **DIVERSE**
8   I've decided to switch to _____ light bulbs in an effort to save energy. **ECOLOGY**

BANK OF ENGLISH

Words with similar meanings

Geo- is used at the beginning of words that refer to the whole of the world or to the Earth's surface.

> geography   geographer   geographical   geology
> geologist   geological   geometry   geometrics
> geometrical   geophysics   geophysicist
> geophysical   geopolitics   geopolitical

Bio- is used at the beginning of nouns and adjectives that refer to life or to the study of living things.

> biochemistry   biodegradable   biodiversity
> bioengineering   biographer   biology
> biomedicine   biometric   biopsy   biotechnology
> biosphere

Match words from the boxes with the definitions (1–10).

1   the part of the Earth's surface where there is life
2   the study of the countries of the world, the land, seas, towns etc
3   the science which is concerned with the study of living things
4   the study of the Earth's structure, surface and origins
5   a person who writes an account of someone else's life
6   the mathematical study of lines, angles, curves and shapes
7   the existence of a wide variety of plants and animals in their natural environments
8   something that breaks down or decays naturally in nature
9   a person who uses physics to determine the Earth's structure, climate and oceans
10 affected by a country's position or relationship with other countries

VOCABULARY ORGANISER 15

1 Make a note of …

1 some English words that are used in your language.
2 some words from your language that are used in English.

2 Reading, page 143 **Find words in *Is tradition an obstacle to progress?* that match the definitions (1–6).**

1 something that causes another thing to happen or change (extract A)
2 dull, boring (extract A)
3 harmful, damaging (extract A)
4 intelligent (extract A)
5 progress (extract B)
6 permanently (extract D)

3 Find these words in *Is tradition an obstacle to progress?* and explain their meanings.

Text A

1 obstacle (noun)

_____

2 pitfalls (noun)

_____

Text B
3 non-controversial (adj)

_____

4 disregard (verb)

_____

Text C
5 profound (adj)

_____

6 straitjacket (also spelt *straightjacket*) (noun)

_____

Text D
7 rash (adj)

_____

8 decay (noun)

_____

4 Language development, page 144 **Match a phrasal verb or expression with *pass* with the definitions (1–8).**

1 die
2 give something to someone so they can give it to someone else
3 lose consciousness
4 fail to take advantage of an offer or opportunity
5 convince others that someone or something is someone or something else entirely
6 achieve very high marks in an exam or test
7 to not make a big deal out of a situation but to decide to forget about it
8 to cast blame or responsibility on someone else

5 Use of English, page 147 **Find words in *Body language and gestures* that match the definitions.**

1 An adjective that means *unaware* or *not knowledgeable* about something.

_____

2 An adjective that means '*rude*'.

_____

3 A word for a person who is lower in rank than his superiors.

_____

4 Two verbs of movement with the body.

_____

BANK OF ENGLISH

Culture
culture (noun)
1: activities such as the arts and philosophy, literature and music which are considered important for the development of civilisation;
2: a particular society or civilisation that exists or existed in history;
3: the habits, attitudes and beliefs that are shared by a particular society or civilisation;
4: bacteria or cells that are grown in a laboratory for scientific purposes.
cultural (adj)
1: belonging to a particular society and its ideas, behaviour and customs;
2: relating to art, literature, music etc.
culturally (adv)
cultured (adj)
intelligent, educated and sophisticated, with an interest in the arts.
cultural awareness (n phr)
someone's understanding of the differences between themselves and people from other societies or backgrounds.
culture shock (n phr)
a feeling of anxiety or discomfort that people experience when they visit a foreign country with very different customs.

Use your dictionary to find an example sentence for each of the definitions above.

VOCABULARY ORGANISER 16

Organise your vocabulary for examination revision!

1 **Reading, page 153** Circle the odd one out in the following word groups.

1 **obese** chubby, stout, overweight, skinny, plump, well-built
2 **relegate** demote, downgrade, promote, lower
3 **dormant** inactive, sleeping, useless, undeveloped, hidden
4 **treadmill** trial, daily grind, routine, slog, grindstone
5 **clinch (it)** settle, confuse, seal, decide, determine
6 **profess** admit, confess, acknowledge, teach, recognise
7 **forsake** abandon, provide, leave, disown, give up, sacrifice
8 **agonise** worry, be in pain, dwell on, brood, torment yourself
9 **heed** listen to, take note, involve, follow

Final revision tip Group synonyms and words of similar meaning together, to help you create variety in your use of language in writing tasks.

2 **Language development, page 154** Complete the sentences with a suitable phrase.

1 After his divorce, Paul felt the need to make some _____ in his life.
2 Going through a divorce and then losing her mother was a very _____ for Sarah, but she's feeling a lot happier these days.
3 In order to _____ that she was leaving the school, Mrs Scoones told the students of her decision to stay.
4 'Sorry, Mum!' said Ian, 'I'm a _____ , so don't expect me to ever get married!'
5 I thought I'd be working in that factory for the rest of my life, so the news of its closure really _____ .
6 Rice is a _____ in the Chinese diet.
7 When I first moved to the Isle of Skye, I felt lonely and _____ .
8 Yes, I eat meat, and I simply don't allow the knowledge that animals are killed to feed me to _____ .

3 **Key word, page 154** Match the sentence beginnings (1–5) with the endings (a–e).

1 I made a mistake in my calculations, and found myself on
2 Stephen cheated people all his life, but he came to
3 I had no idea what they'd been talking about, because I came in on
4 Heidi helped me
5 So you didn't do well in your geography test! It's hardly the

a no end, by taking the kids out for the day so I could work.
b end of the world!
c a sticky end, when someone shot him.
d the receiving end of my boss's anger.
e the tail end of the conversation.

4 **Use of English, page 156** Complete the sentences with a word or phrase from the options in *Time travel possibilities*. Make any changes necessary.

1 A lorry had overturned and blocked the road, and as a result the traffic was _____ .
2 Being an editor is a _____ job, but Sue loves it.
3 My sister's a _____ shopper; she just can't stop herself!
4 Mobile phones have _____ from telephones to pocket computers faster than we could ever have imagined.
5 We were very disappointed when our biggest client decided to _____ of the deal.
6 The river _____ alongside the railway line for about five miles.
7 Chris was _____ to receive his long service award of £1,000 from his company.
8 I've got a _____ cold so I won't be coming to the party tonight.

BANK OF ENGLISH

Word partnerships: *re-*

The prefix *re-* is used before many words to give the meaning of 'doing something again'.

Categorise the words in the box: noun, verb or adjective.

> rebuild   reconsider   reform   reformist   regain
> regenerated   reintroduction   rejuvenate   relapse
> remake   remix   renewal   reorganise   repeatable
> replay

Speaking video worksheet

1 **Look at the flowchart and read the sentences (1–16) taken from _Cambridge English: Advanced_ Speaking test.**

1 Which part of the exam does each sentence come from?
2 Who said each sentence: the interlocutor (I) or a candidate (C)?

> ### _Cambridge English: Advanced Speaking test_
>
> #### Part 1
> A short conversation between the interlocutor and the two candidates. This part focuses on general interaction and social language. (2 minutes)
>
> ⬇
>
> #### Part 2
> Each candidate speaks for a minute about three pictures. The other candidate follows up with a 30-second response. (4 minutes)
>
> ⬇
>
> #### Part 3
> The two candidates discuss a topic with each other and make decisions about a given topic. (4 minutes)
>
> ⬇
>
> #### Part 4
> The interlocutor asks the candidates additional questions about the topic in Part 3. This part focuses on expressing opinions, agreeing/disagreeing and speculating. (5 minutes)

2 **Watch a _Cambridge English: Advanced_ Speaking test with two real students. As you watch, look at the materials that the interlocutor uses and the material that the candidates are given.**

1 Where are you from? Part _1_ (_I_)
2 It's your turn first. Here are your pictures. They show people working in different environments. Part _2_ (_I_)
3 Some people think it becomes more difficult to study as you get older. What is your opinion? Part ___ (___)
4 I'm a student – I'm currently studying English at King's College. Part ___ (___)
5 I'm not sure, but everyone has a different personality, so we all do things in different ways. Part ___ (___)
6 Why do you think some people are better at time-management than others? Part ___ (___)?
7 I'd like you to compare two of the pictures, and say what difficult decisions these people are making, and how the people might be feeling. Part ___ (___)
8 What do you enjoy most about learning English? Part ___ (___)
9 Now talk to each other about what people can do to be more environmentally friendly. Part ___ (___)
10 I'm going to compare this one, where the person is wearing very formal clothes, and this one, which shows someone dressed very casually. Part ___ (___)
11 I like being outdoors – cycling or walking. Part ___ (___)
12 OK, so which one do we think is the best solution? Part ___ (___)
13 I'm not sure what this person is thinking – he looks quite sad, but that might be because he's tired. Part ___ (___)
14 That's an interesting question. I think it's because cars are generally much more convenient. Part ___ (___)
15 Thank you. Now you have about a minute to decide which type of job would be the hardest. Part ___ (___)
16 I see your point, but I think this one – having a baby – changes people's life the most. Part ___ (___)

Part 1

Good morning / afternoon / evening. My name is ....
and this is my colleague ....

And your names are?

Can I have your mark sheets, please?

Thank you.

First of all, we'd like to know something about you.

Select one or two questions and ask candidates in turn, as appropriate.

- **Where are you from?**
- **What do you do here / there?**
- **How long have you been studying English?**
- **What do you enjoy most about learning English?**

Select one or more questions from the following, as appropriate

- **What free-time activity do you enjoy most? (Why?)**
- **What sort of work would you like to do in the future? (Why?)**
- **Do you think you spend too much time working or studying? (Why? / Why not?)**
- **Do you like using the Internet to keep in touch with people?**
- **Have you celebrated anything recently? (How?)**
- **If you could travel to one country in the world, where would you go? (Why?)**
- **How important is it to you to spend time with your family? (Why? / Why not?)**
- **Who do you think has had the greatest influence on your life? (Why?)**

Part 2

In this part of the test, I'm going to give each of you three pictures. I'd like you to talk about **two** of them on your own for about a minute, and also to answer a question briefly about your partner's pictures.

(Candidate A), it's your turn first. Here are your pictures. They show different types of meals.

I'd like you to compare two of the pictures, and say what is good and bad about each choice of meal and what kind of person you think would typically choose each type of meal. All right?

(Candidate A speaks for about 1 minute.)

Thank you.

(Candidate B), which of these meals would you prefer to eat?

(Candidate B speaks for about 30 seconds.)

Now, *(Candidate B)*, here are your pictures. They show different holiday locations.

I'd like you to compare two of the pictures and say why people might choose to spend their holidays in places like these, and which one you think is the best holiday location. All right?

(Candidate B speaks for about 1 minute.)

Thank you.

(Candidate A), which of these places would you most like to go to on holiday?

(Candidate A speaks for about 30 seconds.)

Thank you. (Can I have the booklet, please?)

Part 3

Now, I'd like you to talk about something together for about two minutes.

Here are some ways people use to stay in touch with family and friends and a question for you to discuss. First you have some time to look at the task.

Place Part 3 booklet, open at Task 3, in front of the candidates. Allow 15 seconds.

Now, talk to each other about how effective each of these ways are for keeping in touch.

(Candidates speak for about 2 minutes.)

Thank you. Now you have about a minute to decide which two ways are the most effective for keeping in touch.

(Candidates speak for about 1 minute.)

Thank you. (Can I have the booklet please?)

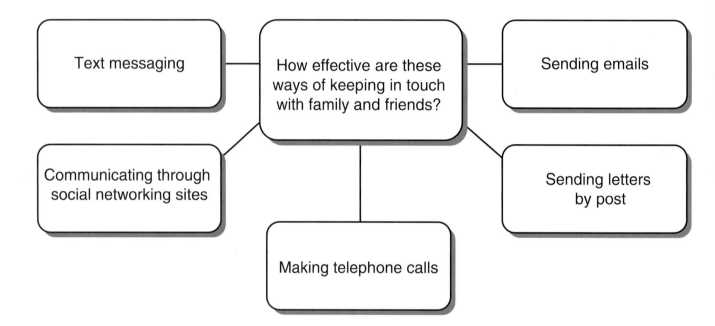

Part 4

Use the following questions, in order, as appropriate:

- **Do you think social networking sites are important in modern life? (Why? / Why not?)**
- **Many people using social networking sites are not careful about what they post online. Why might this be a problem?**
- **How do you think parents and teachers can help younger people to understand the dangers of the Internet?**
- **What kinds of subjects do you think are important for young people to learn at school nowadays?**
- **Some people think that earning money is more important than job satisfaction. What do you think?**

Select any of the following prompts, as appropriate:

- **What do you think?**
- **Do you agree?**
- **How about you?**

Thank you. That is the end of the test.

3 ⊙ **Look at the advice in the table. Watch the Speaking test again and score how well the two students followed the advice.**

1 = They did this very well.
2 = They did this quite well.
3 = They need to improve this part of the exam.

Part 1	Score		
talk about yourself and general topics	1	2	3
make sure you answer the interlocutor's questions	1	2	3
give full answers with reasons	1	2	3
speak naturally and fluently	1	2	3
Part 2			
select and describe two photographs	1	2	3
speculate and express opinions about the photographs in relation to the question	1	2	3
speak fluently and clearly for up to one minute	1	2	3
answer the interlocutor's supplementary question	1	2	3
Part 3			
exchange ideas with your partner, inviting each other's opinions where necessary	1	2	3
express and justify your opinions	1	2	3
speculate on each of the options available	1	2	3
reach a decision through polite negotiation	1	2	3
Part 4			
express a view towards the interlocutor's questions	1	2	3
collaborate with your partner to share your opinions	1	2	3
agree or disagree with your partner's views	1	2	3
use a wide range of language and structures	1	2	3

4 **Work in groups of three. Practise the Speaking test using the exam extracts on pages 178–180.**

Students A and B: you are the candidates. Answer the interlocutor's questions.

Student C: you are the interlocutor. Ask the questions for the Speaking test Parts 1–4. Time each part of the test and stop the candidates when they have spoken for the correct length of time.

Change roles and repeat the exam.

EXAM SPOTLIGHT

PAPER 4 Speaking test

In the *Cambridge English: Advanced* Speaking test, the two examiners mark the following areas of your speaking performance:

Grammar and vocabulary

The examiner wants to hear a wide range of grammatical forms and vocabulary used appropriately and flexibly.

Discourse management

The examiner will give marks for well-structured responses and clearly organised ideas.

Pronunciation

The examiner should be able to understand everything you say, and wants to hear how you express mood, meaning and new information using appropriate intonation.

Interactive communication

You will also receive marks if you interact well with the other people and actively develop the conversation throughout the test.

Practice test answer sheet: Reading and Use of English

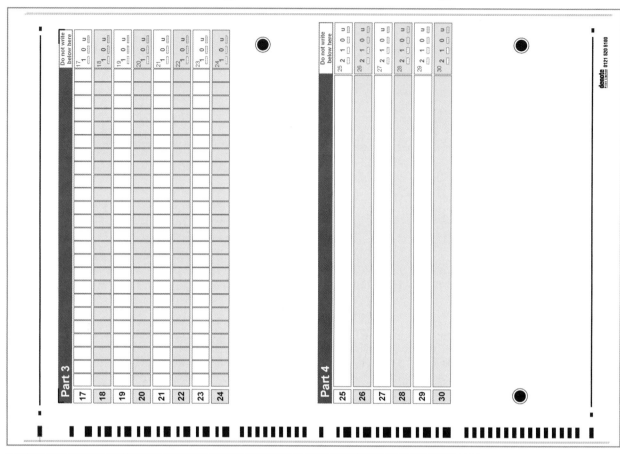

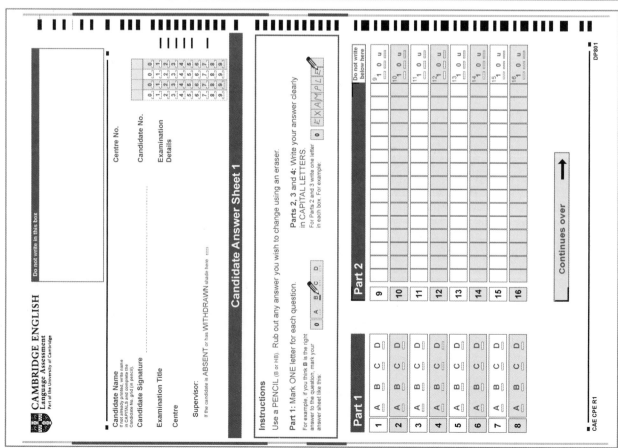

CAMBRIDGE ENGLISH
Language Assessment
Part of the University of Cambridge

Candidate Name
If not already printed, write name
in CAPITALS and complete the
Candidate No. grid (in pencil).

Candidate Signature

Examination Title

Centre

Supervisor:

If the candidate is ABSENT or has WITHDRAWN shade here

Centre No.

Candidate No.

**Examination
Details**

0	0	0	0
1	1	1	1
2	2	2	2
3	3	3	3
4	4	4	4
5	5	5	5
6	6	6	6
7	7	7	7
8	8	8	8
9	9	9	9

Candidate Answer Sheet 2

Instructions

Use a PENCIL (B or HB).
Rub out any answer you wish to change
using an eraser.

Parts 5, 6, 7 and 8: Mark ONE letter for
each question.

For example, if you think B is the
right answer to the question, mark
your answer sheet like this:

| 0 | A | B | C | D |

Part 5

31	A	B	C	D
32	A	B	C	D
33	A	B	C	D
34	A	B	C	D
35	A	B	C	D
36	A	B	C	D

Part 6

37	A	B	C	D
38	A	B	C	D
39	A	B	C	D
40	A	B	C	D

Part 7

41	A	B	C	D	E	F	G
42	A	B	C	D	E	F	G
43	A	B	C	D	E	F	G
44	A	B	C	D	E	F	G
45	A	B	C	D	E	F	G
46	A	B	C	D	E	F	G

Part 8

47	A	B	C	D	E	F
48	A	B	C	D	E	F
49	A	B	C	D	E	F
50	A	B	C	D	E	F
51	A	B	C	D	E	F
52	A	B	C	D	E	F
53	A	B	C	D	E	F
54	A	B	C	D	E	F
55	A	B	C	D	E	F
56	A	B	C	D	E	F

CAE R2

denote
Print Limited 0121 520 5100

DP800

Practice test answer sheet: Listening

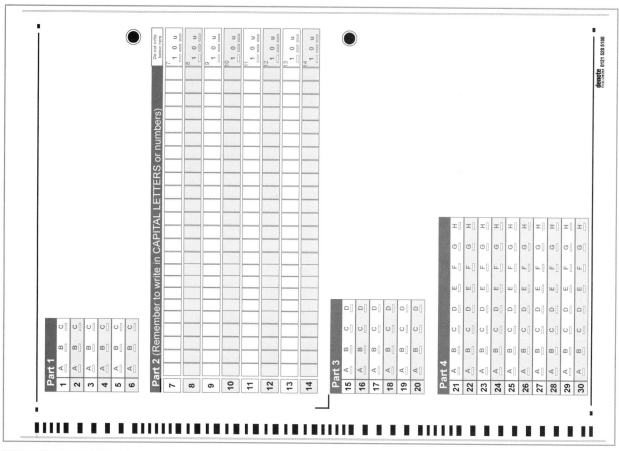

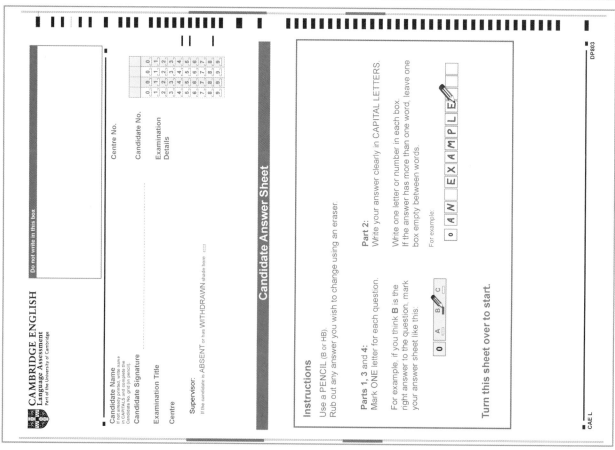

Cambridge English

Advanced

Practice test

Reading and Use of English

Part 1

For questions **1–8**, read the text below and decide which answer (**A, B, C** or **D**) best fits each gap. There is an example at the beginning (**0**).

Mark your answers **on the separate answer sheet**.

Example:

0 A goes   **B** makes   **C** causes   **D** leads

0	A	B	C	D
	A	B	C	D

Scientific progress

Progress is generally thought of as a process which (**0**) ...... to improvements. Nowadays, it is in the (**1**) ...... of science where progress is most in evidence. Science has made the world a far more comfortable and interesting place to live in, (**2**) ...... us to do things that in the past would have been regarded as completely impossible. Indeed, it is sometimes taken for (**3**) ...... that science will always (**4**) ...... improvements. But is this actually so? The answer has to be 'No' as it is scientific progress that has given us the atom bomb and ever more lethal weapons of war.

Science is neither good nor bad; it is how science is (**5**) ...... that is good or bad. It is, therefore, vital that scientific progress be accompanied by moral progress. Moral values must be taken into (**6**) ...... when deciding how scientific developments are to be used; only when this happens can we feel (**7**) ...... that science is being used for the (**8**) ...... of humanity, not for its destruction.

1	**A** field	**B** line	**C** matter	**D** topic
2	**A** supporting	**B** allowing	**C** admitting	**D** letting
3	**A** understood	**B** convinced	**C** granted	**D** accepted
4	**A** carry out	**B** bring about	**C** turn up	**D** pass off
5	**A** accomplished	**B** performed	**C** exercised	**D** applied
6	**A** consideration	**B** view	**C** assessment	**D** mind
7	**A** positive	**B** secure	**C** confident	**D** definite
8	**A** provision	**B** gain	**C** profit	**D** benefit

Part 2

For questions **9–16**, read the text below and think of the word which best fits each gap. Use only **one** word in each gap. There is an example at the beginning (**0**).

Write your answers **IN CAPITAL LETTERS on the separate answer sheet.**

Example:

0		I	T	S																

Impressionism

The artistic movement now known as Impressionism had **(0)** …… beginnings in France in the middle of the

nineteenth century. The Impressionist painters used bright colours and made nature and contemporary life the

subject of their paintings. **(9)** …… of working in a studio, they often worked in the open air so as to capture the

effect of light on their subjects.

Their paintings came **(10)** …… for harsh criticism from the leading figures of the art establishment, **(11)** ……

disliked the bright colours and considered everyday life an unsuitable subject for serious art.

It was in fact a critic, Louis Leroy, who gave these artists the name 'Impressionists'. Leroy wrote a newspaper article

in **(12)** …… he said the paintings were little **(13)** …… than sketches and called the artists 'Impressionists' because

one of the painters, Claude Monet, **(14)** …… called one of his paintings 'Sunrise, Impression'. **(15)** …… the term was

meant to be an insult, the painters liked it and adopted it **(16)** …… the name for their group.

Part 3

For questions **17–24**, read the text below. Use the word given in capitals at the end of some of the lines to form a word that fits in the gap **in the same line**. There is an example at the beginning (**0**).

Write your answers **IN CAPITAL LETTERS on the separate answer sheet.**

Example: | 0 | P | L | E | A | S | U | R | E | | | | | | | | |

Taste in music

Music can give (**0**) ...... to almost everyone. However, people's tastes   **PLEASE**

vary; what one person considers to be a masterpiece, another person may

regard as (**17**) ....   **DREAD**

Many classical music (**18**) ...... feel that there is no music that is   **ENTHUSIASM**

(**19**) ...... to a symphony played by a large orchestra of skilled musicians.   **COMPARE**

Inevitably, this is not the way people who do not like classical music feel;

they claim that symphonies are too long and (**20**) ...... boring. Lovers of   **EXCEED**

classical music, of course, (**21**) ...... ; they claim that symphonies are in no **AGREE**

way boring and put a high value on the (**22**) ...... of a symphony as they   **LONG**

believe that this (**23**) ...... them to have a better understanding of how the   **ABLE**

composer has developed his theme.

We all have our personal tastes in music but we can gain by listening to

types of music with which we are not familiar. We may find that we like

them and, thus, (**24**) ...... our tastes and increase our enjoyment of music.   **BROAD**

Part 4

For questions **25–30**, complete the second sentence so that it has a similar meaning to the first sentence, using the word given. **Do not change the word given.** You must use between **three** and **six** words, including the word given. Here is an example (**0**).

Example:

0 Why don't you follow his suggestion?

WISH

I .... he suggested.

The gap can be filled by the words 'wish you would do what', so you write:

Example: | **0** | WISH YOU WOULD DO WHAT |

Write **only** the missing words **IN CAPITAL LETTERS on the separate answer sheet.**

---

25 People say that the hall was built in 1745.

SAID

The hall .... in 1745.

26 'Would you mind helping me to carry these boxes upstairs?' said my brother.

LIKE

My brother said that .... him carry some boxes upstairs.

27 John didn't think that anybody would be interested in his opinions.

HAVE

John thought that .... in his opinions.

28 I thought that her fluency in English was really impressive.

HOW

I was really .... in English.

29 It seems that Claire is the only one who isn't keen on going to university.

THOUGH

It looks .... from Claire is keen on going to university.

30 Cinema tickets are ten per cent more expensive than they were last year.

INCREASE

There .... ten per cent in the price of cinema tickets since last year.

Part 5

You are going to read a review of a book about letter writing. For questions **31–36**, choose the answer (**A**, **B**, **C** or **D**) which you think fits best according to the text.

Mark your answers **on the separate answer sheet**.

To the Letter, by Simon Garfield, reviewed by Kathryn Hughes

Over the last few years Simon Garfield has made it his job to remind us of what we risk losing in the rush towards a virtual world. *Just My Type* explored the historical nooks and crannies of printing fonts at the moment everyone was tipping towards e-readers. *On the Map* arrived just as sat navs made battered street maps redundant. Now Garfield turns his attention to letters, yet another cultural form that looks as though it might soon be going the way of all paper.

There are no surprises in the pageant of epistolary superstars that Garfield summons to celebrate the deckle-edged past. Still, the nice thing about letters is that they lend themselves to rereading, and Garfield provides us with substantial extracts over which to pore. In the process you find yourself wondering how the 15th–16th century scholar Erasmus managed to reform the world while knocking out scores of communiques a day (at the end of his life the Dutchman reckoned he had spent over half of it writing to people, an annoying number of whom didn't bother to write back). And why does novelist Jane Austen's emotional elegance take a holiday whenever she sits down to write her letters, which taste as sharp as pear drops?

Cantering through two millennia of letters with Garfield as our guide, it's fun to spot the things that never change. Whether the setting is Roman Britain or Renaissance Italy, correspondents are always whining about not getting back as many letters as they send. Elders fret constantly that young people's spelling and grammar is dropping off a cliff. And it's comforting to learn that the whole Hello/Goodbye thing has always got people in a tizz. Err on the side of formality and you sound cross, go chummy and you sound like a stalker. It's for that reason that letter-writing manuals emerged in the 16th century, supplying specimen sign-ons and sign-offs for every ticklish situation.

Garfield is as transfixed by the touch and smell of letters as he is by their tone. He starts with some thin tablets excavated from Roman Northumberland in the 1970s. In the lee of Hadrian's Wall soldiers regularly received slivers of birch and alder sent from home, on which were scratched urgent details about bedspreads and spare underwear. During the late 16th century paper cost a fortune, and the show-off Earl of Essex made a point of leaving boastfully big margins, just because he could.

Garfield pings about his subject like an early-morning business email fuelled by the first caffeine of the day. He knocks on John Mullan's professorial door for an emergency tutorial on Jane Austen before scooting over to the Harry Ransom library in Texas where the archives of most famous British writers come to rest. The challenge for the curators here is how to store and manage material that increasingly arrives in pixel form rather than in a series of old exercise books. Finally, Garfield participates in an international initiative to revive the art of letter-writing between strangers. In this sprawling narrative, Garfield includes a historical correspondence that turns out to be the most compelling part of his book: between Signalman Chris Barker and Bessie Moore during the closing years of the Second World War, until they were able to get married.

Garfield predicates his love letter to the letter on the assumption that there is something intrinsically superior about committing your thoughts to paper rather than pinging them through the web. With a letter, he suggests, you think a bit harder, write a bit slower and the result is a richer thing. He's right, up to a point, but what he never considers fully is that letter-writing is always a kind of performance. Every time we sit down to write we make up a new self to show the world – one that is cleverer, wittier, stronger, kinder or crosser than we actually are. That makes letters cathartic to write and intriguing to read, but it doesn't automatically qualify them as the ultimate in self-expression. Just like emails, letters are only as good as the people who write them.

31 What does the reviewer say about Garfield's previous books?

    A   They reveal his attitude towards the modern world.
    B   They focus on aspects of life that are disappearing.
    C   They tend to be about subjects that are generally unpopular.
    D   They show he knows more about the past than the present.

32 According to the reviewer, the extracts from letters that Garfield includes in the book

    A   stimulate questions about the writers.
    B   were mostly written by well-known novelists.
    C   sometimes reveal more than Garfield realises.
    D   are not the ones that the reviewer would have chosen.

33 The reviewer refers to 16th century letter-writing manuals to show that

    A   the nature of letters has changed considerably since then.
    B   attitudes towards letter-writing have changed since then.
    C   concerns about writing correctly are not limited to the present day.
    D   the reasons for writing letters are the same now as they were then.

34 Why did the Earl of Essex leave wide margins in his letters?

    A   to show that he had a personal style of writing
    B   to hide the fact that he had very little to say
    C   to make his letters easier to read
    D   to demonstrate his wealth

35 According to the fifth paragraph, what is the reviewer's opinion of the book?

    A   It would benefit from having a more focused structure.
    B   It contains a great deal of carefully chosen material.
    C   It relies too heavily on quoting the views of experts.
    D   It is good at comparing different types of communication.

36 According to the sixth paragraph, Garfield

    A   fails to identify the differences between letters and emails.
    B   ignores letters that do not fit with the view he wants to present.
    C   believes letter writers deliberately present themselves in a good light.
    D   sees letters as revealing their writers more accurately than they really do.

Part 6

You are going to read four reviews of a book about language. For questions **37–40**, choose from the reviews **A–D**. The reviews may be chosen more than once.

Language and mobility: unexpected places

by Alastair Pennycook

A

Language and Mobility: Unexpected Places is itself rather unexpected. It is unusual in the way Pennycook draws on literary texts and personal stories and letters to support his theories – some of which this reader, at least, has not previously encountered. He uses these sources to shine a fresh and fascinating light on the relationship between language and cultural identity, including the common belief, or misconception, that each language has its own supposedly appropriate location. Pennycook raises a number of questions about fundamental concepts in language and linguistics, such as the notion of the native speaker and what it means to be bilingual. The narrative is at times clumsy, but this only slightly detracts from the author's challenge to professional linguists to analyse our assumptions about language. In so doing, the book invites a welcome debate around some long-held beliefs. In some respects, however, *Language and Mobility* seems not to have been written with the general reader in mind, which is disappointing.

B

The globalisation of modern life, in terms not only of business but more significantly of human mobility, is having a profound impact on languages. This impact is extensively examined in both sociolinguistics and literacy studies, leaving me unconvinced that Pennycook's approach adds much to the discussion. Nevertheless, I believe he asks questions that will inspire many academics to engage in further investigations into the many ways that language functions in a globalised world. I must mention Pennycook's engaging way of writing, to which his extensive quotations from literature and letters make an attractive contribution. He uses these to bridge the divide between academic analysis and the choices made in their writing by the common man and woman, who, as well as specialists, are likely to find that *Language and Mobility* has much to offer them.

C

Pennycook's discussion of unexpected uses of language in unexpected places certainly gives food for thought. Alongside theoretical analysis, he takes the reader on a journey as he explores his own family history, in order to illustrate concepts of language and location. He also backs up his ideas – some of which come as a breath of fresh air – with a wide range of letters and literature from a range of sources. The drawback of this approach, though, is that the book ends up lacking a consistent voice: the reader is sometimes brought up short by an abrupt change of gear. I was left wondering who Pennycook envisaged as his intended readers: academics could be put off by the personal nature of his enquiry, while non-specialists may find some of the linguistic concepts hard going. I would have welcomed a discussion of different types and levels of unexpectedness, though there is probably insufficient mileage in this to provide material for another book.

D

Reading *Language and Mobility* sensitises one not only to the relative unimportance of some of the traditional sociolinguistic classifications, but also to the obstacles they can place in the way of understanding how people use their linguistic resources, in the places where they happen to be. Pennycook explores these ideas within the context of 'cultures of mobility', through examples such as the unexpected presence of England's 'extinct' Cornish language in places as diverse as South America and Australia. His explanations of the unexpected breathe new life into the debate, and will undoubtedly encourage future investigations in the field. Pennycook has a good ear for telling a story in a way that engrosses the reader, who in my view is likely to be anyone with a mild interest in language, whether or not they are professional linguists.

Which reviewer

has a different opinion from the others on the originality of the arguments in the book? **37** ☐

disagrees with reviewer D about whether the book is likely to stimulate further research? **38** ☐

shares reviewer B's opinion of the appeal of the author's writing style? **39** ☐

has a different view from reviewer D of the book's likely readership? **40** ☐

Part 7

You are going to read a newspaper article about a ski resort in Canada. Six paragraphs have been removed from the extract. Choose from the paragraphs **A–G** the one which fits each gap (**41–46**). There is one extra paragraph which you do not need to use.

Mark your answers **on the separate answer sheet**.

The Shames Mountain story: are ski co-operatives the way forward?

Skiers in Canada are forming co-operatives to buy their local slopes – reconnecting with the true spirit of the sport

'Whatever happened to that simple joy?' asks the narrator of the ski film *Valhalla*. The film features a fictional ski community who shun fast chairlifts and expensive mountain restaurants in favour of a purer, gentler life in harmony with the mountain. It is rich in nostalgia – for a time when being in the mountains in winter was about freedom and adventure. Yet, in one sense, *Valhalla* is located firmly in the 21st century: it will resonate with anyone who has ever winced at the cost of a week's lift pass in a big resort, or stood in a 30-minute chairlift queue before descending a piste packed with skiers, dodging cannons making artificial snow.

41	

Shames is no ski resort: it has no hotels, no glitzy bars, no restaurants or shops selling the latest gear. It boasts two chairlifts and one tow bar, and a base lodge where you can buy food and drink and hire equipment.

42	

Until recently there was just one flight a day from Vancouver up to Terrace; Air Canada now runs 34 each week, making the hill more accessible to visitors. 'People generally only come to us when it's foggy somewhere else,' says Jephson. 'But once they ski here, they're like, "This is awesome!"'

43	

General manager Christian Theberge is sure of the explanation. 'Community ownership of ski areas allows for a certain pride,' he says. 'People tend to take better care of what's theirs. It also allows members to actively participate in the improvements and really understand what makes the magic happen.'

44	

One of its key features is that these new ski destinations don't expect to compete with large resorts; what they offer is simpler, more affordable, friendly skiing. And they're usually much more individual.

45	

In fact, talking about the environment is a controversial pastime when your chosen activity is skiing. However, Shames' visitor numbers and their associated impact – including waste disposal and travel infrastructure – is a fraction of that of the big hubs: 20,000 skiers a season come to Shames, and two million go to Whistler. The emphasis is on small-scale, and keeping it that way, to preserve the environment.

46	

Their approach might suggest a similarity with the mythical Valhalla of the movies. However, Shames and the other hills run in the same way are no-frills, hardworking, for the most part bare-bones ski mountains that depend on community support to survive. And, in that sense, as in others, they tap into the simple joy of skiing.

A That special quality is spreading. The co-op model is generating interest among other mountain communities, with *My Mountain Co-op* receiving enquiries monthly about how to replicate the model.

B Some visitors might agree with him that this could be a drawback, but are drawn nonetheless by the idea of avoiding the more commercial, developed resorts.

C Has it ever occurred to you that it doesn't have to be this way? It occurred to the residents of Terrace, British Columbia, who not long ago became the proud owners of their local hill, Shames Mountain, making it Canada's first not-for-profit ski co-operative. *My Mountain Co-op* took ownership of the mountain (which had been for sale for a decade), saving it from otherwise certain closure. Local businesses, individuals and families bought memberships to the co-op and, through various other fundraising schemes, managed to raise the C$360,000 (£216,000) needed to meet the purchase price.

D 'Destination ski areas try to offer the same experience – different snow and terrain, perhaps, but in general they are mostly clones of each other,' says Theberge. 'Small community areas are unique.' They also, he might have added, have far better green credentials.

E Not a reaction that every ski area can count on. Visiting skiers stay in Terrace and drive the 20 minutes each day to ski. The mountain is maintained by volunteers, who do everything from painting boundary lines to servicing machinery. And the co-operative model tends to raise standards.

F It also has plenty of snow each year – in fact, slightly more than Canadian mega-resort Whistler. 'We're pretty spoilt,' says David Jephson, a member of *My Mountain Co-op*. 'We don't have fast chairs or fast tow bars, but we have world-class skiing, a huge amount of snow, and it's beautiful here.'

G Theberge explains: 'The co-op got a great deal on buying the mountain, but that was because there was a lot of work to be done. Our goal is to fix and improve all facets of the mountain's infrastructure. Expansion only makes sense with growth in the community.' And Jephson adds, laughing: 'We almost don't want more people to come.'

Part 8

You are going to read extracts from an article about being a member of a team at work. For questions **47–56**, choose from the extracts (**A–E**). The extracts may be chosen more than once.

Mark your answers **on the separate answer sheet**.

In which extract does the writer mention each of these qualities of effective team players?

being flexible enough to cope with experimentation	**47**
fully understanding what the team as a whole needs to achieve	**48**
being prepared to express opinions that may not be supported by other team members	**49**
an ability to create an effective working relationship with other team members even when they disagree	**50**
a readiness to carry out all the tasks they are given	**51**
being willing to take the initiative in order to deal with problems	**52**
a wish for recognition as a contributor to the success of the team	**53**
a willingness not to persist in a course of action that might hold the team back	**54**
an ability not to respond to other people's ideas without considering them	**55**
understanding the feelings of other team members	**56**

Qualities of an effective team player in business

A

You can count on effective team members to pull their weight when there's a job to be done, to work hard and to meet commitments. They follow through on assignments. You can rely on them to uniformly deliver good performance, not just sporadically. Teams need people who speak up and express their thoughts and ideas clearly, directly, honestly, and with respect for others and for the work of the team. Such a team member does not shy away from making a point that might be unwelcome to others, but makes it in the best way possible – in a positive, confident, and respectful manner.

B

Good listeners are essential for teams to function effectively. Teams need team players who can absorb, understand, and give due thought to suggestions and points of view that they are presented with, to listen with an open mind before speaking, so that meaningful dialogue results. Such a team member can also receive criticism without reacting defensively. Good team players come prepared for team meetings and listen and speak up in discussions. They're fully engaged in the work of the team and do not sit passively on the sidelines. They are proactive in helping to overcome sticking points, and they volunteer for assignments.

C

It is second nature to effective team players to work with others and collaborate in order to accomplish a job. Good team players, despite differences they may have with other team members concerning style and perspective, figure out ways to co-operate to solve problems and get work done. Strong team players have a degree of emotional investment in their work and the team's work. They show up every day with this commitment up front. They want to make a strong effort, and they want other team members to do the same.

D

Good team players don't complain or get stressed out because something innovative is being tried or some new direction is being set. In addition, good team members can consider different points of view and compromise when needed. They don't stick rigidly to a point of view and argue it to death, especially when the team needs to move forward to make a decision or get something done. Strong team players are firm in their thoughts yet open to what others have to offer.

E

Team players treat fellow team members with courtesy and consideration – not just sporadically but consistently. In addition, they empathise with them and provide appropriate support, to help get the job done. They don't place conditions on when they'll provide assistance, when they'll choose to listen, and when they'll exchange information. Good team players also have a sense of humour and know how to have fun (and all teams can use a bit of both), but they don't have fun at someone else's expense. Quite simply, effective team players deal with other people in a professional manner.

F

Team players who show commitment don't come in any particular style or personality. They don't need to be cheerleader types. In fact, they may even be soft-spoken, but they aren't pushovers. They contribute to the work of the team without needing continual urging. Team players with commitment look beyond their own piece of the jigsaw and see the big picture, the purpose of the team's overall task. In the end, their commitment is about winning – not in the sports sense of beating your opponent, but about seeing the team reach its goals and knowing they have played their part in this. Winning as a team is one of the great motivators of employee performance. Good team players have and show this motivation, and are happy to share the credit for the team's achievement.

Writing

Part 1

You **must** answer this question. Write your answer in **220–260** words in an appropriate style on the separate answer sheet.

---

1   Your class has attended a lecture on job satisfaction in the workplace. You have made the notes below:

Which factors contribute to job satisfaction?

- a clear description of what the job involves

- a pleasant office or other working environment

- opportunities for training and professional development

Some views expressed in the lecture:

'A job description should highlight the most important duties.'

'Employers may not be able to improve the work environment.'

'Training is only useful if it is relevant to the job.'

Write an essay for your tutor discussing **two** of the factors in your notes. You should **explain which factor you think is more important** for employers to focus on for their staff, **giving reasons** in support of your answer.

You may, if you wish, make use of the views expressed in the lecture, but you should use your own words as far as possible.

Part 2

Write an answer to **one** of the questions **2–4** in this part. Write your answer in **220–260** words in an appropriate style on the separate answer sheet. Put the question number in the box at the top of the page.

---

2   You see this notice in the staffroom of the restaurant where you work part-time.

> Customer numbers have been falling over the past few months and we need to reverse this trend if all staff are to keep their jobs.
>
> As the restaurant proprietor, I am inviting staff to send me a written proposal explaining why you think we have fewer customers and suggesting ways of encouraging more people to eat in the restaurant.

Write your **proposal**.

3   You have recently moved to another country to study. A close friend in your home town is keen to hear about your new experiences.

Write an email to your friend. In your email you should describe your first days in your new accommodation, say what you like and dislike about the area you live in, and compare studying in the new country with studying at home.

Write your **email**.

4   You see the advertisement below on the website of your university music club.

> **Help needed!**
>
> Running the music club takes a lot of time and none of the organisers is able to review the performances that we feature each month. Would you like to write our online reviews?
>
> Send in a review which describes one of the musicians you have seen recently and explains why you attended their performance. We'll offer the job to whoever writes the best review.

Write your **review**.

Listening

Part 1

You will hear three different extracts. For questions **1–6** choose the answer (**A**, **B** or **C**) which fits best according to what you hear. There are two questions for each extract.

Extract One

You hear two friends talking about a workshop that the woman wanted to attend.

1   Why didn't the woman know the workshop had been postponed?

    A   The college didn't inform the people who had registered.

    B   She hadn't read the text that she had received.

    C   Her friend wasn't able to send her the information.

2   What did she do instead of attending the workshop?

    A   She went to see some friends who lived nearby.

    B   She went to a café with someone.

    C   She went straight home.

Extract Two

You hear two students discussing the possibility of studying in France.

3   The man is unsure about studying in France because he doesn't want to

    A   change the nature of the contact he has with friends.

    B   live in a country where he can't speak the language.

    C   give up any of the leisure activities he does at home.

4   By mentioning her visit to Spain, the woman is explaining that she

    A   needed to have all the relevant information before making a decision.

    B   thought it important to spend time on a decision.

    C   found it difficult to make a decision.

Extract Three

You hear two friends discussing the business that the man intends to set up.

5   Which activity do the friends disagree about the need to finish before the man starts his business?

    A   creating a full product range

    B   researching the competition

    C   finding suppliers

6   What does the woman advise the man to do to promote his business?

    A   advertise in trade magazines

    B   join an organisation for small businesses

    C   make it possible to place orders on his website

Part 2

You will hear part of a talk about dangers threatening the oceans. For questions **7–14**, complete the sentences with a word or short phrase.

Threats to the oceans

The speaker describes the oceans as the **(7)** .... of the planet.

Damage to fish species might have an impact on what the speaker describes as **(8)** '................' for humans.

Fish species such as **(9)** .... are threatened.

Apart from fish, several other species that live in the sea, including **(10)** .... , are at risk because they get caught accidentally.

One way in which marine habitats are being destroyed is through the use of **(11)** .... in fishing.

Some substances used in **(12)** .... are damaging the oceans.

Unsuitable **(13)** .... poses a threat to coral reefs.

Damage to coral reefs reduces the appeal of **(14)** ....

Part 3

You will hear two friends, Johnny and Lindsey, talking about a school reunion. For questions **15–20**, choose the answer (**A, B, C** or **D**) which fits best according to what you hear.

15 What was Johnny's initial feeling when he read the email about the school reunion?

    A   regret that he had lost touch with most people from school

    B   surprise at how much time had passed since he left school

    C   relief that he had been invited to the reunion

    D   determination not to attend the reunion

16 Johnny's chief motive for attending the reunion was a wish

    A   to show the other students they had been wrong about him.

    B   to find out what the other students were like now.

    C   to prove that the other students were just like him.

    D   to feel he was accepted as part of the group.

17 Johnny mentions the English teacher to make the point that at school

    A   she had made fun of him in class.

    B   he had been better at other subjects.

    C   he had liked making the other students laugh.

    D   she had made the other students feel sorry for him.

18 At the reunion, Johnny made the English teacher

    A   regret the way she had treated him at school.

    B   sympathise with him for his lack of success.

    C   admire him for something he hadn't done.

    D   disbelieve the story of his achievement.

19 What was Johnny's state of mind when he left the reunion?

    A   He had more positive feelings towards the school.

    B   He was sorry not to have talked to more people.

    C   He was disappointed at how he was treated.

    D   He had mixed feelings about attending.

20 Johnny and Lindsey agree that school friendships are

    A   usually closer than friendships formed later.

    B   based on shared experiences.

    C   likely to have a lasting effect.

    D   the most important aspect of being at school.

Part 4

You will hear five short extracts in which people are talking about going to university.

TASK ONE

For questions **21–25**, choose from the list (**A–H**) the reason each speaker gives for choosing their course.

TASK TWO

For questions **26–30**, choose from the list (**A–H**) how each speaker feels about their studies.

While you listen you must complete both tasks.

A	They wanted to understand themselves better.	**A**	relieved that the course was not harder
B	It would lead to a career they are interested in.	**B**	surprised that the course is not more popular
C	They wanted to meet other people with a similar interest.	**C**	pleased that they have found the course easy
D	They wanted to study with people they knew.	**D**	excited by the people they have met during the course
E	They wanted to prove that they could succeed academically.	**E**	optimistic about their prospects of doing a higher degree
F	They wanted to learn more about their hobby.	**F**	enthusiastic about topics they were not expecting to study
G	They were encouraged to study it by their parents.	**G**	satisfied that they have done their best
H	It provided the opportunity to study with a particular expert.	**H**	sorry that the course is about to come to an end

Speaker 1 | 21 |

Speaker 2 | 22 |

Speaker 3 | 23 |

Speaker 4 | 24 |

Speaker 5 | 25 |

Speaker 1 | 26 |

Speaker 2 | 27 |

Speaker 3 | 28 |

Speaker 4 | 29 |

Speaker 5 | 30 |

Speaking

Part 1
2 minutes (3 minutes for groups of three)

Select one or two questions and answer as appropriate.

- Where are you from?

- What do you do?

- How long have you been studying English?

- What do you like most about studying English?

Select one or two questions and answer as appropriate.

- What has been the most challenging aspect of learning English for you? (Why?)

- What did you enjoy most about the place where you grew up?

- Who do you most admire among your friends or family? (Why?)

- Do you prefer to keep in touch with people face-to-face or online? (Why?)

- Do you ever wish you could go and live in another country?(Why?)

Part 2
4 minutes (6 minutes for groups of three)

Interlocutor

In this part of the test, I'm going to give each of you three pictures. I'd like you to talk about two of them on your own for about a minute and also to answer a question briefly about your partner's pictures.

Candidate A, it's your turn first. Here are your pictures. They show **people who have chosen to have a new experience.**

(Turn to page 205, look at Task 1)

I'd like you to compare **two** of the pictures and say why the people might have chosen to have these new experiences and what might be memorable about the experiences.

(one minute)

Candidate B, which experience do you think would be the most exciting?

(30 seconds)

Candidate B, here are your pictures. They show **people wearing protective clothing.**

(Turn to page 205, look at Task 2)

I'd like you to choose **two** of the pictures, and say why the people might be wearing protective clothing, and how the people might be feeling about wearing this clothing.

(one minute)

Candidate A, in which situation do you think it is most important for people to wear protective clothing?

(30 seconds)

- Why might the people have chosen to have these new experiences?
- What might be memorable about the experiences?

- Why might the people be wearing protective clothing?
- How might the people be feeling about wearing this clothing?

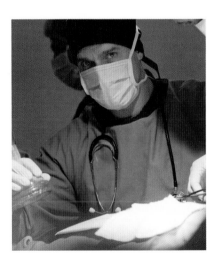

Part 3
4 minutes (5 minutes for groups of three)

Now, I'd like you to talk about something together for about two minutes. (*3 minutes for groups of three*)
Here are some things that people of all ages can do to help them stay fit and healthy and a question for you to discuss. First you have some time to look at the task.

(15 seconds)

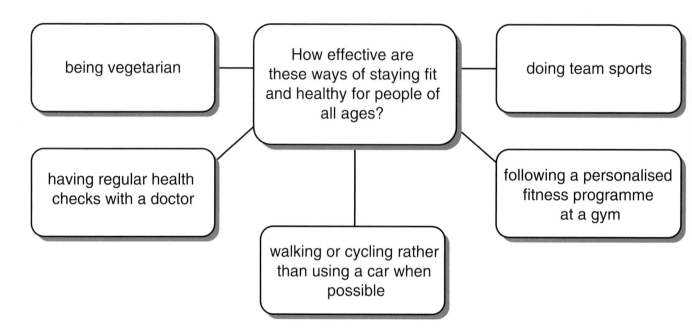

Now, talk to each other about **how effective these ways of staying fit and healthy might be for people of all ages.**

(2 minutes)

Now you have a minute (*two minutes for groups of three*) to decide **which way of staying fit and healthy would be most effective for people of all ages.**

(1 minute)

Part 4

5 minutes (8 minutes for groups of three)

For both candidates

- In your opinion, how important is it to keep fit and healthy?
- Do you think people are more or less healthy now than in the past? (Why?)
- What do you think can motivate people to exercise regularly?
- To what extent does the advertising of fast food influence people's diets?
- What could educational establishments do to encourage healthy lifestyles?

Grammar reference

Index

Unit 1 Beginnings

1 Review of tenses (past and present)

The present simple is used to talk about:

• habits and routines • permanent situations • scientific or natural facts	I **always walk** the dog after breakfast. She **lives** in Sweden. Water **boils** at 100 degrees Celsius.

The present continuous is used to talk about:

• actions happening now • temporary situations • annoying habits (with *always, forever* etc)	She's **talking** to someone. I'**m staying** with Jenny until I find a place of my own. He's **always** being mean to me.

The past simple is used for:

• a sequence of actions that happened in the past • complete past actions • actions that happened in the past at a stated or definite time • past habits or general past states	First she **picked** up her umbrella, then she **opened** the door. She **walked** to the train station. Edward **went** on holiday last month. She **went** to bed at 8 o'clock. She always **had** porridge for breakfast.

The past continuous is used for:

• an action in progress in the past that was interrupted by another action • parallel actions happening at the same time in the past	She **was getting** on the bus when someone stole her bag. While she **was having** a lesson, the children **were making** a noise.

The present perfect is used for:

• actions that happened in the past but the time is unknown or not stated • actions which began or happened in the past but relate to the present • actions that have happened in a period of time that has not yet finished	I think I **have been** here before. They **have lived** in this town for several years. They **have been woken** by the neighbours shouting three times this week.

The present perfect continuous is used to:

• focus on the duration of an action that started in the past and continues up to the present	The universe **has been expanding** for over 13 billion years.

The past perfect is used for:

• an action that happened before another action or time in the past	When I arrived at the airport, the plane **had** already **landed**.

The past perfect continuous is used to:

• focus on the duration of an action that started and finished before another action or time in the past	We **had** already **been waiting** for over an hour, when they informed us that the train to Brighton had been cancelled.

Unit 2 A child's world

2 Passive forms

The passive

The passive voice is *not* a tense. We form it by using a suitable tense of the verb **be** and a past participle.

	Active voice	Passive voice
Present simple	He writes a letter.	A letter is written.
Present continuous	He is writing a letter.	A letter is being written.
Simple past	He wrote a letter.	A letter was written.
Past continuous	He was writing a letter.	A letter was being written.
Present perfect	He has written a letter.	A letter has been written.
Past perfect	He had written a letter.	A letter had been written.
Going to future	He is going to write a letter.	A letter is going to be written.
Modals in present	He can/should/will write a letter.	A letter can/should/will be written.
Future perfect	He will have written a letter.	A letter will have been written.

◁ **REMEMBER**

The present and past perfect continuous do not have a passive form (except in rare cases). The passive cannot be used for intransitive verbs, such as *appear, disappear* etc.

The passive voice is used:

- when we are more interested in the action than who or what did it or caused it (the agent)
- when the agent is obvious, unimportant, or unknown
- to avoid saying *they, someone* etc
- for formal situations and events

Helen **was robbed** last night.
Andy **was made** redundant yesterday.
Cars **are not permitted** in the centre of Zurich.
Our house **was broken** into last night.
You **are** kindly **requested** not to smoke.

The causative *have* and *get*:

- **have something done** usually describes an action or service that someone else does for us
- it can also be used to describe unfortunate incidents or accidents
- **get something done** can be used in a similar way to **have**
- **get** is sometimes more emphatic than **have**, and is used to create a sense of urgency or obligation in some cases

We**'re having** our living room decorated.

Officer, I**'ve had** my bag stolen!

I **got** the leak in the bathroom **repaired**.
I must **get** this work **finished** by lunchtime.
Get your homework **done**!

As a passive:

- **get** can also replace **be** in a passive sense

After the party, the house was a mess, but it eventually **got cleaned** up.

Passive with auxiliary verbs: *can, will, may/might, should* are used to signify:

- certainty about the effect of an action
- possible effect of an action

- advice on how an action should be viewed or treated
- occasional reaction to an action or event

The new law **will be regarded** as a restriction on freedom of speech.
Katie's marriage to Tom **may be viewed** unfavourably by some members of the family.
This new approach **should be implemented** with caution.
This new approach to teaching literature **can be regarded** as too radical.

need can be used:

- with a passive sense, to signify when something has to be done without saying who should do it

The plants **need watering**. (passive sense: gerund)
The plants **need to be watered**. (passive infinitive)

Impersonal passive with *say, consider, believe, think, assume, suppose, report*

Reporting verbs are often used in the passive in news broadcasts or newspaper articles to report widely held views, which may or may not have been proven. There are two forms.

It **is thought** that the victim knew her attacker.
It **is said** that Mr Cole's tomatoes are the largest ever recorded in the UK.

The victim **is thought to have known** her attacker.
Mr Cole's tomatoes **are said to be** the largest ever recorded in the UK.

Let and **make**
Let does not have a passive form, but needs to be replaced with **allow**:
Mum won't let me go to the party.
I**'m not allowed to go** to the party.
Make is followed by a passive infinitive form:
John's father made him wash the car and cut the grass before he could go out on Saturday.
John **was made to wash** the car and cut the grass before he could go out on Saturday.

Unit 3 Are you game?

3 Modal auxiliaries (1)

Form

The modal auxiliary verbs are generally followed by the bare infinitive of the main verb (with the exception of **ought to**):

It must be …; It may be …; It might be …; It could be …; It can't be …

The past form takes the bare infinitive of **have** and the past participle of the main verb:

It must have been …; It could have been …; It can't have been … etc

Speculation and suggestion

• We use **may**, **could** and **might** to talk about possibility, speculate or suggest, when we are not sure of an answer, or a reaction.	*Who's that talking to Mark? – I'm not sure. It **may be** his new secretary. When's your mum coming to visit?'– It **could be** Tuesday or Wednesday of next week.*
• We use **must** when we are fairly certain that something is true.	*That **must be** Anna's new car! She said she was getting an Audi.*
• We use **can't** when we are fairly certain that something is not true.	*Isn't that Tony over there?– It **can't be**! He's in Tunisia this week.*
• We use **could have, might have, must have** and **can't have** to speculate about the past.	*It **could have been** young Henry who broke the kitchen window. Fred's car's a write-off! He **must have been** doing 100km when he drove off the road! The concert **can't have been** last night! It says here that it's on the 25th!*

Deduction

• We use **must** to talk about deduction, when we are certain that something is true, based on the information we have.	*The murderer **must have known** that his victim went along that route every evening, as he knew exactly where to attack her. This must be the right house as it's the only one with a red wooden gate.*
• We use **can't** and **couldn't** to talk about negative deduction, when we are certain that something is not true, based on the information we have.	*The number nine **can't go** in that square, as there's one in the box directly above it. You **couldn't have done** anything to stop him from leaving, as he'd made up his mind a long time ago.*

Assumption

• We use **will** or **would** to make an assumption, when we think something is true without having evidence.	*There's the doorbell! That **will be** John. If you'd told him, he **would have been** angry. You know what he's like!*

Refuting a comment and qualifying criticism

• We use **may** or **might** … **but** when we want to refute someone else's argument or comment, or qualify someone's criticism of us.	*I **may** not talk a lot, **but** I'm not stupid!*

Unit 4 Eureka!

4.1 The future

Future form	Use	Example
Present simple	programmed / scheduled events	*The plane **leaves** at 4pm.*
will / shall + infinitive	statements of fact	*The sun **will rise** tomorrow.*
will / shall + infinitive	predictions	*You **will win** some money.*
will / shall + infinitive	promises	*I **will** never **leave** you.*
Present continuous	prearranged events	*I'm **going** to the doctor tomorrow.*
going to + infinitive	intentions / plans	*I'm **going to make** an appointment with the doctor tomorrow.*
going to + infinitive	statements based on present evidence	*It looks as if it's **going to** snow.*
Future continuous	actions in progress at a certain time in the future	*He **will be taking** his French exam this time tomorrow.*
Future perfect	actions which will be finished by a given future time	*He **will have retired** by then.*
Future perfect continuous	the duration of an action or state at a given future time	*On the 11th March, she **will have been working** here for 30 years.*

Other ways of talking about the future

The following expressions can be used to introduce the future, or future ideas.

be about to do something	*I'm about to put* the kettle on. Do you want a cup?
be on the point of do*ing* something	Peter*'s on the point of resigning* from his job.
be bound / certain / sure to do something	Lucile *is bound to pass* her French exam.
should + infinitive	You *should be* promoted!
it's (about) time somebody *did* something / something *happened*	*It's about time* you *were promoted*!
there's a good chance that	*There's a good chance that* Laurence *will get* the job.
I doubt whether / if / that	*I doubt that* Vicky *will get* the job.

4.2 Future time in subordinate clauses

With certain time reference words, a different tense is sometimes used in the subordinate clause to the one used in the main clause.

	Main clause	Example
While is used to link two clauses in which two actions are happening simultaneously.	subject + future *will* / *while* + [subordinate clause] subject + simple present	*I'll open the wine while you find some glasses.*
By the time is used to link two clauses in which one action happens after another action has happened.	*By the time* + subject + simple present + [subordinate clause] subject + future / future perfect.	*By the time the rest of the group arrive, it will have started to rain.*
As soon as is used to link two clauses in which one action happens immediately after another.	*As soon as* + subject + simple present + [subordinate clause] subject + future.	*As soon as the film starts, I'll sit down.*
Until is used to link two clauses in which one action is completed before another one happens.	subject + future *will / won't* (usually negative) *until* + [subordinate clause] subject + simple present / present perfect	*I won't leave the house until Martha calls.*

Unit 5 Safe and sound?

5 Verbs followed by infinitive or *-ing*

Please note: the list below is not exhaustive. These are simply among the most common examples.

Normally followed by infinitive with *to*:		Normally followed by infinitive without *to*:	Normally followed by *-ing*:
agree to do	advise somebody to do	hear somebody do	appreciate somebody doing
ask (somebody) to do	arrange to do	let somebody do	avoid doing
attempt to do	dare to do	make somebody do	consider doing
choose to do	decide to do	see somebody do	contemplate doing
expect to do	encourage somebody to do	watch somebody do	deny doing
order somebody to do	fail to do		enjoy doing
persuade somebody to do	need to do		face doing
pretend to be	threaten to do		hate doing
refuse to do	want to do		like doing
			involve doing

Problematic items

There are many verbs which can be followed by more than one structure. This can alter the meaning considerably, so be careful about which structure you use!

• **Like doing** refers to somebody's attitude towards something	*I like **swimming** and **playing** basketball.*
• **Like to do** refers to habitual preferences	*We **like to go** to the cinema on Fridays.*
• **Not like to** or **hate to** means to think something is wrong	*I **hate to disturb** you at home, doctor, but it's rather urgent.*

remember, forget

• **Remember doing** and **forget doing** refer to past events	*I **remember putting** my keys in my bag before I left the house.*
• With **to** both verbs refer to some kind of obligation	*I don't **remember telling** you that at all.*
	*I'll never **forget dancing** with Brad Pitt at that wedding last month!*
	*He was supposed to phone me but he **forgot to do** so.*
	*Will you **remember to water** the plants on Sunday?*

go on

• **Go on doing** refers to the continuation of an action, sometimes for too long	*He **went on working** until midnight.*
• **Go on to** refers to the next thing someone does	*She **went on talking** for an hour.*
	*The Headmaster **went on to praise** the school football team for winning the cup.*

mean

• **Mean doing** refers to what is involved in performing an action	*If we take that flight, it'll **mean getting up** at 5am!*
• **Mean to do** refers to intend to do	*I **meant to tell** you earlier, but we're having a meeting at 4 o'clock.*

stop

• **Stop doing** refers to the ending of an activity	*Kevin **stopped smoking** a month ago.*
• **Stop to do** refers to the interruption of one action in order to do something else	*As she was walking along the High Street, Sara **stopped to look** in the shop windows.*

regret

• **Regret to do** is usually used in formal letters, when the writer is sorry about what he is going to say	*We **regret to inform** you that your application to join the army has been unsuccessful.*
• **Regret doing** refers to a regret about an action in the past	*I **regret arguing** with him over such a silly matter.*

watch, see, hear

• With **-ing**, these verbs refer to an action that is still in progress when the speaker stops paying attention to it	*I **saw** someone **coming** out of the bank, but then I turned away to talk to my friend.*
• With the bare infinitive, these verbs refer to an action that is complete	*We **watched** David Beckham **score** a goal against Juventus.*

consider

• **Consider doing** means think about doing	*I **considered becoming** a doctor, but didn't want to have to study so hard.*
• **Consider** + object + **to** refers to an opinion	*This piece of music is **considered to be** one of Mozart's finest works.*

Unit 6 Hale and hearty

6 Conditionals

Type	Use	Form	Example
Zero conditional	What is always true	Present + present	*If I **eat** sweets, I **feel** awful afterwards.*
1st conditional	What is likely or probable	Present + future	*If you **take up** Pilates, you**'ll** soon **lose** weight.*
2nd conditional	Hypothetical situations	Past + **would**	*If I **found** the time, I**'d join** a gym.*
3rd conditional	Hypothetical past situations	Past perfect + **would have**	*If I **hadn't eaten** so much, I **would have had** some cake.*
Conditional with modal	Possible situations	Present, past or past perfect + **should, could, can, may, might (have)**	*If you **don't feel** well, you **should see** a doctor.* *If you **hadn't woken** me, I **might have missed** the meeting.*
Mixed conditional	Possible or hypothetical situations in the past, present or future (when the time reference in the conditional clause is different from that in the main clause)	Past perfect + **would** Past + **would have** Past + future	*If I**'d looked** after my health better, I **wouldn't feel** so sick now.* *If I **were** a different person, I **wouldn't have put** up with your behaviour for so long!* *If you **slept** well, **you'll do** well in the exam.*
False conditional	A sentence with **if** but the meaning is not a condition or a hypothesis	Present + present Past + past	*If you **hate** sailing, why **are you getting** on the boat?* *If we **ate** all our dinner, we **had** dessert.*

Other types of conditionals

Conditional phrase	Use	Example
unless	means *but not if* (and only if)	I'll cook chicken, **unless** Jackie doesn't eat meat.
on condition that / provided / providing / as long as / so long as	can be used as alternative to *if*	I'll cook **if / as long as / on condition that / provided** you wash up afterwards.
even if	emphasises the conditional clause	**Even if** you miss the wedding, you should still get them a present.
but for	can be used to mean *if it hadn't been for*	**But for** Malcolm's insistence, I would never have applied for the job.
supposing / suppose	can be used to introduce a hypothetical situation; can be used to mean *if you were to* …	**Supposing** you saw a UFO, would you tell anyone?
otherwise / or else	used to introduce an alternative situation	You'd better not be late, **otherwise** you'll be in trouble.
in case / lest	used as a conditional when the speaker does not know the future outcome	I'll take an umbrella **in case** it rains.

More formal or less likely conditionals

were to	used to make an event more formal or hypothetical	If I **were to** apply for the position, do you think I would stand a chance?
should	used when you do not expect something to happen	If you **should** see my keys anywhere, do let me know.
happen to	as above: used when something is unlikely or unexpected; sometimes used with *should*	If you **should happen to** see my keys anywhere, do let me know.

Inverted conditionals

If he were to eat all his dinner, he could have an ice cream.	**Were he to eat** all his dinner …
If you had come when I called you, you'd have seen the eagle!	**Had you come** when I called you …
If you should get a part in the film, I want to be the first to know.	**Should you get** a part in the film …

Unit 7 Wish you were there …

7 Inversion

REFRESH YOUR MEMORY

Function

We tend to use inversion in the following ways.

1	In formal situations	*Not only is our guest speaker tonight an accomplished scientist, he is also a musician of considerable talent.*
2	To emphasise a point, especially in official or political speeches	*Never before has the community been in such desperate need of change!*
3	To make a statement more convincing or interesting	*No sooner had she walked in than the phone rang, and it was him!*
4	To make a recommendation more persuasive	*Not only can this new vacuum cleaner save you time, but also money, as it uses only 40% of the electricity that other cleaners use.*
5	To make a narrative more dramatic	*No sooner did she say his name, than he appeared.*
6	To make conditional sentences more emphatic	*If I had known it would cause so much trouble, I would never have told him the truth.* *Had I known it would cause so much trouble, I would never have told him the truth.* *If she contacts you, please call me.* *Should she contact you, please call me.*

We can invert certain negative adverbs and adverbial phrases by placing them at the beginning of the sentence for emphasis, in the following ways:

We may invert a sentence by inserting **do / did** as in the question form	*Nicole hardly ever speaks to Tom.* *Hardly ever does Nicole speak to Tom.*
When an auxiliary is present, we reverse the auxiliary and the subject	*You can use this mobile phone to access the Internet and also watch videos.* *Not only can you use this mobile phone to access the Internet, but also to watch videos.*
It can be used with negative adverbs of frequency	*I've never been treated so badly before!* *Never before have I been treated so badly!* *Rarely have we seen such a magnificent performance of this play!* *Seldom has the President given such a moving speech.*
With time expressions: **no sooner**, **hardly**, **scarcely**, **barely** (when one event quickly follows another in the past)	*No sooner had I shut the front door, than I realised I had left the keys inside.* *Scarcely had he walked into the room, when the lights went out.* *Hardly had she sat down, when a stone came flying through the window.* *Barely had she finished answering her emails, when more started coming in.*
After **not**	*Not only did he forget to lock the door, but he left several windows open!* *Not until we got home did we realise we had forgotten to pay the bill!*
After certain phrases with **no**	*Under no circumstances are you to touch that wire!* *On no condition must you contact me while I'm away.* *On no account will you open my briefcase!* *At no time did I imagine he would jump.*
After **only**	*Only when I saw him did I realise how much we had both changed.*
After **little**, to express a lack of awareness of something	*Little did she realise how much he cared for her.*
After **so** and **such**, used to emphasise the strong effect of something	*So catastrophic was the earthquake that it will take years to rebuild the town.*
Such followed by **be**	*Such was the force of the wind that the fire quickly swept across the forest.*

Unit 8 Making our mark

8.1 Relative pronouns

To talk about people	• who / that / whom / whose • all / some / many / both / neither / none + of whom • to / for / about + whom • someone / anyone / everyone + who	*Ali and Mike, **neither of whom** had been abroad before, thought it was great.* ***Who** were you talking to just now?*
To talk about things, animals, etc	• which / that / whose • all / some / many / both / neither / none + of which • something / anything / everything + that	*The play **which / that** I saw was Hamlet.* *He examined the reports, **some of which** had quite shocking results.*
To talk about places	• where • in / at / on etc + which	*That was the hospital **where / in which** my mother was born.*
To talk about time	• when • by which time, at which point etc • by / since / until + when	*He got there after 6 o'clock, **by which time** the doors had been closed.*
To talk about situations	• in which case • as a result of which	*She said she might bring a friend, **in which case**, I'd better cook a bit extra.*
To talk about reasons	• why / that • which was why	*Her car broke down, **which is why** she was late for the lecture.*

8.2 Defining and non-defining relative clauses

A defining relative clause • contains essential information that must be included. • is not surrounded by commas.	*The people **who / that had insulated their houses** had much lower fuel bills that winter.* → *Only the people who had insulated their houses had lower fuel bills.*

◁ **REMEMBER**

We can omit the defining relative pronoun if it is an object.
*She's the woman (**who / that**) I gave my money to!*

A non-defining relative clause • adds extra information which is not essential to the main clause. • is surrounded by commas.	*The people, **who had insulated their houses**, had much lower fuel bills that winter.* → All the people had insulated their houses and had lower fuel bills.	◁ **REMEMBER** We cannot omit the relative pronoun. ***That*** cannot be used in non-defining relative clauses.

Reduced relative clauses

A relative clause in the present or past continuous can be 'reduced' to just the present participle clause (*-ing*).	*The men **who are building** that house over there are friends of mine.* *The men **building that house** over there are friends of mine.*
A passive relative clause can be 'reduced' to a past participle.	*The film, **which was written** and directed by an Asian woman, was a box-office hit.* *The film, **written and directed** by an Asian woman, was a box-office hit.*
Some relative clauses can also be reduced by using the infinitive with **to**.	*The last person **who crossed** the line was given a consolation prize.* *The last person **to cross** the line was given a consolation prize.*

Unit 9 Brushstrokes and blueprints

9 Changing sentence structure: change in emphasis, or different meaning?

REFRESH YOUR MEMORY

Altering emphasis and meaning

Inverting the word order generally alters the emphasis.	*It was Bryan who broke the kitchen window.* *It was the kitchen window that Bryan broke.* [See also Unit 7, Inversion]
Changing the position of the comma, or adding and omitting words in a sentence can alter the meaning.	*John admired that photograph of Heidi.* → Heidi is the subject of the photograph. *John admired that photograph of Heidi's.* → Heidi took the photograph (of a landscape). *We went to the taverna which was owned by a Greek couple.* → We went to that particular one because it was owned by a Greek couple. *We went to the taverna, which was owned by a Greek couple.* → The fact that the taverna was owned by a Greek couple is extra information.

Position of the comma

Relative clauses

a Defining relative clause: *We bought the house in Boston which was close to a school.*	The reason we bought it was because it was close to a school.
b Non-defining relative clause: *We bought the house in Boston, which was close to a school.*	We bought the house in Boston, not New York. The fact that it was close to a school is simply extra information, and not important.

Numbers of people mentioned

a *The boys, Will and Harry, had a great time together.*	There are two boys, and their names are Will and Harry.
b *The boys, Will, and Harry had a great time together.*	There are four boys or more. *The boys* refers to boys who are well known to the speaker, possibly family, and Will and Harry are two extra boys who have joined them. The extra comma makes it clear that Will and Harry are not *the boys*.

it or *what*

Sarah crashed into my car last night. *It was Sarah who crashed into my car last night.*	I'm making a simple statement. I'm emphasising the fact that Sarah, not Diana or Elizabeth, crashed into my car.
I was surprised that Charles didn't call to say that he wouldn't be coming. *What surprised me was that Charles didn't call to say he wouldn't be coming.*	I'm surprised that Charles didn't come. I might not have been surprised that he didn't come, but I was surprised that he didn't *call*.

The position of a clause

As I'd expected, George didn't pass his driving test. *George didn't pass his driving test as I'd expected.*	I knew he would fail. I believed he would pass.

Unit 10 The good life

10.1 Direct and reported speech

1 Tense changes: to report something said in the past using a past tense reporting verb, we use a tense one step back in the past.

Words spoken	Reported speech with backshift
'I **like** sport.'	She said (that) she **liked** sport.
'He **is reading** a book.'	She said (that) he **was reading** a book.
'I **have been** to Spain twice.'	He said (that) he **had been** to Spain twice.
'I**'ve been** running.'	He said (that) he **had been running**.
'Angela **went** home.'	I said (that) Angela **had gone** home.
'I **was listening** to music.'	She said (that) she **had been listening** to music.

We do not backshift

- when the reporting verb is in the present tense
- when the reporter sees the past events from the same point of view as the speaker
- with the past perfect simple and past perfect continuous
- when we report modals: **would**, **should**, **might**, **could**, **ought to**

'I**'m going to** quit my job.' → She **says** she**'s going to** quit her job.
'We **are** very happy about your engagement.' →They said they **are** very happy about my engagement.
'The show **had** already **started**.'→ He said the show **had** already **started**.
'You **ought to** study harder.'→ She said I **ought to** study harder.

> **REMEMBER**
> When **shall** refers to the future we use **would**; when it is a suggestion, we use **should**. For example, 'We shall have to leave soon,' means that they said they ◁ **would** have to leave soon – but 'Shall I pick you up at seven?' means that he asked if he **should** pick me up at seven.

We can choose whether to backshift or not

- when present and future events are still true

'The moon **orbits** the earth.' → He said the moon **orbits** the earth.

2 Changes of pronouns and adverbs: these change only if the person, place or time of reporting is significantly different from the words in the direct speech.

'I'm meeting **your** sister **here tomorrow**.'	Reported the same day in the same place: He said he's meeting **my** sister **here tomorrow**. Reported three days later somewhere else: He said **he** was meeting **my** sister **there the next day**.

3 Word order in reported questions: to report questions, we use the same order as in statements.

'**Where is** the supermarket?' '**Would you** like a lift home?'	He asked **where** the supermarket **was**. He asked me if **I would** like a lift home.
'**Which is** your first choice?'	She wanted to know **which was** my first choice / **which** my first choice **was**.

> **REMEMBER**
> With **what / who / which** questions + **be** + complement, be can go ◁ before the complement.

10.2 Patterns after reporting verbs

Verb + *that* clause

verb + that
add, admit, agree, announce, answer, argue, claim, complain, confess, decide, deny, expect, explain, hope, promise, realise, remember, repeat, reply, swear, suggest, think, threaten, warn

She **confessed (that)** she had got on the wrong bus without noticing.

verb + that clause (+ should)
advise, beg, demand, insist, prefer, propose, recommend, request, suggest

> ◁ **REMEMBER**
> in more formal contexts we can omit should. For example, *He demanded that he be released from prison.*

I **propose (that) we should** all listen to what Garry has to say.

> ◁ **REMEMBER**
> In less formal contexts, we use an ordinary tense. For example, *He demanded that he was released from prison.*

Verb + *to*- infinitive

agree, ask, claim, decide, demand, expect, hope, intend, offer, promise, refuse, swear, threaten

She **swore to leave** if he ever did it again.

Verb + *object* + *to*- infinitive

advise, ask, beg, command, encourage, expect, forbid, intend, invite, order, persuade, recommend, remind, tell, urge, warn

He **begged her not to break** off their relationship.

Verb + -*ing*

admit, deny, mention, propose, recommend, regret, report, suggest

She **suggested going** for a walk.

Verb + (object) + preposition (+ object or genitive) + -*ing*

accuse (somebody) of, apologise (to somebody) about / for, blame somebody for, complain (to somebody) about, comment on, confess to, insist on, object to

She **apologised to** him **for crashing** the car.

Unit 11 Making ends meet

11 Modal auxiliaries (2)

Making plans	
will and **would** can be used for making decisions about future plans	*I think I **will** go for a swim later.* *He decided he **would** take his girlfriend out for a romantic meal.*
Making predictions	
will and **would** can also be used to make predictions	*Mr Bond **won't** be available today, as his wife's having a baby.* *Jennifer thought it **would** be a great party.*
Criticism	
might and **could** can be used to express criticism or annoyance	*You must be careful! You **might** have cut yourself with that knife!* *You **could** at least explain to me why you didn't turn up last night!*
should have and **ought to have**	*You **should have** told her you were getting married.* *They **ought to have** gone to see the doctor.*
Annoyance	
will and **would** can also be used to express annoyance	*She **will** keep taking to me while I'm trying to work!* *He **would** call now, just when we've sat down to eat!*
Resignation	
may as well and **might as well** can be used to express acceptance of a situation when there is no better alternative	*You **may as well** go home, because Angelina Jolie's not coming.* *It's getting dark, so we **might as well** go inside.*

REFRESH YOUR MEMORY

Need

1 Remember that **need to** is not a modal: *Do you need to phone home?*
2 **Need** is a modal auxiliary, but is used mainly in question and negative forms: *Need you use all the hot water every time you have a shower?*
3 **Needn't have** refers to an unnecessary action that was done: *You needn't have prepared all that food.* [but you did]
4 **Didn't need to** refers to an unnecessary action that was not done. *I didn't need to go to the supermarket after all.* [so I didn't go]

Unit 12 Behind the silver screen

12 Participle clauses

The present participle can be used:	
• as an adjective	*boring, exciting*
• to form continuous tenses	*He is **watching** you.*
• after verbs of sensation	*I heard him **moving**. I saw him **talking** …*
• after **catch** or **find** + object	*She **caught** him **stealing**.*
• after **have** + object	*I'll **have** you **dancing** again in no time.*
• after **spend** or **waste**	*She **spends** two hours **commuting** every day.*
• after **be busy**	*He **was busy working** in the garden.*
• to introduce a statement in indirect speech	***Apologising** for his lateness …*

A present participle can replace a sentence or main clause:	
• when two actions by the same subject occur simultaneously	***Holding** the dogs in one hand, he tried to unlock the door with the other.*
• when one action is immediately followed by another and is performed by the same subject	***Hanging** up the phone, she turned and faced us.* *He pushed past me, **knocking** over a priceless vase.*
• when the second action is caused by, or is a result of, the first action	

A present participle can replace:			
• a subordinate clause with **as / since / because** + subject + verb	◁ REMEMBER It is possible to use two or more participles one after the other. For example, **Being** interested in music, and not **wanting** to change anyone's plans, I agreed to go to the concert.	***Realising** that he would be late, he decided to call a taxi.*	◁ REMEMBER Note – the subject of the participle clause can be different from the subject in the main / subordinate clause. For example, **The weather** being lousy, **we** decided to stay at home.
• a relative clause (= reduced relative clause)		*Anyone **needing** assistance should call the supervisor.*	

The perfect participle (active) can be used:	
• to more clearly show that one action had finished before another began	*Having failed* his driving test twice before, he lacked confidence.

The perfect participle (passive) can be used:	
• to emphasise that an action expressed by the participle happened before the action expressed by the next verb	*Having been laughed* at before, he decided not to make the same mistake again.

The past participle can be used:	
• as an adjective • to form the perfect tenses / infinitives / passive voice • to replace a subject + passive verb	a *broken* bottle, the *scared* cat he had *fallen*, to have *slept*, it had been *stolen* *Made* by the finest Italian shoemakers …

Unit 13 Getting the message across

13 Text references: *this, that, it, such, these, those*

REFRESH YOUR MEMORY

Reference words may

1	refer to something that has already been mentioned	*There is now a new method of extraction.* ***This method*** *is called …*
2	point forward to something about to be mentioned	*The point is* ***this****: you must work harder.*

Text references	
We generally use reference words to avoid repetition when explaining or describing something.	*Janet decided to leave her job and go to live in Kenya.* ***This*** *was to change her life dramatically.* *Paul wrote his first novel at school, with encouragement from his English teacher.* ***That's*** *how he became a writer.* *Laura had a bad accident when she was 10, and* ***it*** *affected her for the rest of her life.* *John said that the local council were irresponsible in their attitude towards energy conservation.* ***Such*** *open criticism will cost him his seat in the next election.* *I have with me today two very special people, Mary and Peter.* ***These*** *two are responsible for setting up a charity organisation to help old people in the local area.* *I realised that I couldn't fit any more clothes in my wardrobe. So, I decided to throw out* ***those*** *that I didn't wear any more.*
We can also avoid repetition in a number of other ways.	*He liked the film, and* ***so did I****.* *Sally doesn't want to go to Paris, and* ***neither does*** *Jenny.* *She asked me to finish the report, but I'd already* ***done so****.* *'Are you ready?' 'I* ***think so****.'* *'Do you think he'll break down on the stage?' 'I* ***hope not****.'* *I'm hoping Ian will be able to come on Saturday.* ***If not****, we'll arrange it for another date.* *They say it's going to be hot at the weekend.* ***If so****, let's go to the beach.*

Unit 14 Gaia's legacy

14 Unreal tenses

The unreal past is used to express:		
Unfulfilled or impossible conditions (*If …*) Present and past	If you *were* to listen, you'd know what I mean. *Were* I to go back in time, I would probably visit the Jurassic era. If I *had passed* the exam … / *Had I passed* …	◁ **REMEMBER** The unreal past is also sometimes called the past subjunctive.
Wishes and regrets (*wish / if only*) Present and past	I wish I *were* rich enough to buy my own house. If only we *had been* more careful. I wish I *had paid* more attention in class.	
Unreal comparisons (*as if / as though*)	The Earth looked as if it *were* a single living being. It looked as though the whole forest *had been* destroyed.	

| Advice, suggestions and complaints (*it's time*) | It's time we **did** something about global warming.
It's high time the polluters **were held** accountable.
It's about time you **took** responsibility for your actions. |
| Preference (**would** + **rather** / **sooner** / **prefer**)* | I'd rather / sooner you **left** / **didn't leave** / **hadn't left**.
I'd prefer it if you **left** / **didn't go** / **hadn't left**. |

◁ **REMEMBER**
With **would** + **rather** / **sooner**, when the subject is the same in both clauses, we use the bare infinitive. For example, I **would rather** / **sooner live in the country**.
With **would** + **prefer**, when the subject is the same in both clauses, we use the full infinitive. For example, I would prefer **to go** out.

| **Suppose** and **imagine** | Imagine you **won** the lottery!
Suppose you **met** someone you really liked!
Imagine **I'd never met** you. |

Unit 15 Our global village

15 Adverbial clauses

REFRESH YOUR MEMORY

Types of adverbial clauses
Adverbial clauses give information about the circumstances of the event described by the verb in the main clause. There are many different types of adverbial clause: clauses of time, clauses of place, clauses of manner, clauses of comparison, clauses of cause or reason, clauses of purpose, clauses of result, clauses of condition and clauses of concession.

Time	I'll meet you **when** I've finished.	Purpose	She smiled **so that** I'd feel welcome.
Place	She wanted to know **where** I'd been.	Result	It got **so** hot **that** I couldn't concentrate.
Manner	She asked me **how** I had done it.	Condition	**If** I'd known you'd be late, I'd have started without you.
Comparison	It was as bad **as** I'd feared.	Concession	She won the game **although** she'd never played before.
Cause / reason	I walked fast **because** it was late.		

Clauses of time

after, since, ever since, once, before, now	**After** leaving the house, she went straight to the station. **Once** she got on the train, she relaxed. **Before** the train left, she looked out of the window.
while / whilst, as	**While** the train was moving, she felt safe.
immediately, as soon as, on, the minute, the moment	**As soon as** the train arrived at the station, the detective got on.
until / till	He searched the carriages **until** he spotted her.
when, whenever, by which time	**When** she noticed him it was too late.
hardly ... when, no sooner ... than	**Hardly** had he moved towards her **when** the train screeched to a halt.

◁ **REMEMBER**
The future perfect becomes present perfect in a time clause. **By the time I have found** her it may be too late. (Not *by the time I will have found her …*)

Note on tenses: Future forms and conditionals are not used in time clauses. We use the present simple when talking about the future, or the present continuous if we need to show that an action is continuous.
When I **get** on the train I will give her your message. (not *When I will get …*)
While I am travelling I will be careful. (not *While I will be travelling …*)

Clauses of result

Consequently, therefore, as a result, so	I overslept and **therefore** / **consequently** / **as a result** / **so** I missed the bus.
So that / **such that** (**so** and **such** can be used in very formal sentences with inverted forms to precede that clauses of result)	It is **so** hot **that** I'd rather stay at home. It was **such** a hot day that I preferred to stay at home. **Such** is the damage **that** I'll need a new car. **So** badly damaged was the car **that** I had to replace it.
Clauses of result are often preceded by the expressions **so much / little** + noun, or **so many** / **few** + noun.	He's got **so little** money (**that**) he can't come out. She's got **so many** children (**that**) I feel sorry for her.
otherwise / **or else** (used to mention a consequence or result that we wish to avoid)	You'd better clean that up, **otherwise** I'll tell Mum. Give me your money **or else** you'll be sorry!

Clauses of concession

Although, though, even though, even if, despite the fact that, in spite of the fact that, notwithstanding the fact that + clause	**Although** she knew how to swim perfectly well, she was still afraid of the water.
While / whilst + -ing / subject clause ◁ REMEMBER **Whilst** is formal or old-fashioned.	**While** believing / I believed her story, I wasn't very interested in it.
In spite of / Despite / Notwithstanding (one's) + noun / **-ing**	**In spite of** his lack of interest / his not being interested in the subject, he decided to attend the lecture.
but, yet ◁ REMEMBER **Yet** is slightly more formal and is sometimes preceded by a semi-colon rather than a comma.	I have been listening to the radio, **but** I'd rather read a book. I have been reading the book all morning; **yet** I have failed to understand a word.
however, nevertheless	Sandra has been researching her novel for over a year; **however**, she still hasn't started writing.
No matter how, however	**No matter how** hard I work, I never seem to finish my chores.
Adjective / adverb + **as / though**	**Tall though** he is, he can't reach the top shelf.
even so, all the same, (but) still	Yves is very smart; **even so**, he must study if he wants to do well.

Clauses of reason

The reason (why) + clause **The reason for** (object) + **-ing**	**The reason why** I dropped out of college was that I wanted to see the world. **The reason for** (my) dropping…
Due to / because of (the fact that)	**Due to the fact that** it was raining, we cancelled the picnic.
as / since / for / because	He gave me a bonus **as / since / because** I'd worked / **for working** hard.
in that / insofar as	Checking your work helps **in that / insofar** as it helps avoid mistakes.
in case	I took some extra money **in case** I needed to catch the train home.
Present participle **(that)** + clause	**Realising (that)** it was almost nine o'clock, I ran all the way to the theatre. **Being** the only person who could speak French, I ordered the meal. **Seeing as** it's a lovely day, let's go out.

Clauses of purpose

Full infinitive (can't be used to express negative purpose)	He stayed up all night **to complete** his project.
In order (not) to, in order that, so as (not) to	He stayed up all night **in order to / so as to** complete his project. **In order not to / So as not to** fail, he worked extra hard.
so that (+ subject + **could / would**)	He stayed up all night **so that** he could complete his project.
to avoid + gerund, **to preven**t + noun / pronoun + gerund	I have set three alarm clocks **to avoid oversleeping**. The rabbits were placed in different boxes **to prevent fighting / their fighting / them (from) fighting**.
in case, for fear of, for fear that, lest (formal or rare)	He wore a disguise **in case** he was followed / **for fear of** being followed / **for fear that** he might be followed / **lest** he were / was / be followed.
for + gerund / **for** + noun	Aromatherapy is good **for strengthening** the immune system. We had a water-fight **for fun**.
with a view to, with the aim of	We decided to go to Paris **with a view to / with the aim of** visiting the Louvre.

Unit 16 Endings – and new beginnings

16 Making and intensifying comparisons

Making comparisons

We can make comparisons in the following ways: *Life is **easier now than** it used to be.*
*It was **more difficult** saying goodbye to friends **than** to places. I try to be **less critical** of my son **than** I used to be.*

There are also other ways of making comparisons either more descriptive, or more emphatic.

Comparing past situations with the present	*She **now** has **more** time to enjoy the simple things in life.* ***Instead of** parkland, there is now an ugly shopping centre.* ***Where once** she had to drive 50 miles to work, she **now** walks 10 metres from the kitchen to the computer in her study.* *They find life **far more** enjoyable **than ever before**.*
Qualifying comparisons	*Computer technology has made it **considerably** easier to work or study at home.* *Petrol is **significantly** more expensive than it was six months ago.* *Pollution levels in the town are **slightly** lower than they were last year.* *Life is a **lot more** stressful than it used to be.* *There are **far fewer** families living in the villages than before.* *There aren't **quite** as many cars on the road as before.* ***The more** fruit and vegetables you eat, **the healthier** you will be.*
Emphatic comparisons	***By far the hardest** thing about changing jobs is fitting in with your new colleagues.* ***Nothing compares to / with** the joy of having your first child.* *The journey up the mountain was exciting enough, but **that was nothing compared to / with** skiing down it.* *Your mobile phone is **nowhere near** as impressive as mine.* *Fran's painting was the best in the class, **by a long way**.*
so and such	*I'd never seen **such a** big garden as that one.* *The show wasn't **so** spectacular **as** we'd expected.* *When choosing a place to live, it's **not so much** the position that's important **as** who your neighbours are going to be.*

◁ **REMEMBER**
How is **so** used in the second sentence below?
*Her house is **as** spacious as John's.*
*My new curtains are **not so** well made as the old ones.*

Forms of comparison for adjectives and adverbs

comparative + **than**	*Bob is **cleverer than** Jim.*
the** + superlative + **in / of	*... **the most expensive** in the shop.*
the superlative to mean *very*	*Her decision was **most** irregular!*
-er and **-er / more and more** + adjective	*I wake up **earlier** and **earlier**.*
***the** + comparative, **the** + comparative*	*... **the longer** you wait, **the harder** it will be.*
as ... as	*Sally is **as** spoilt **as** Matthew.*
less ... than, more ... than, not so / as ... as	*Paul is **not so** relaxed **as** his brother.*
***any / no** + comparative*	*You aren't **any smarter** than me.*
prefer, would prefer, would rather, would sooner	[See unit 14]

too / enough / very

too + adjective / adverb	*This exercise is **too hard** for me to do on my own.*
much too + adjective / adverb	*You've been working **much too hard**! Have a rest!*
too much + noun	*The neighbours are making **too much** noise. I can't sleep!*
adjective / adverb + **enough**	*It isn't **warm enough** to go swimming in the sea today.*
enough + noun	*Is there **enough room** in the car for one more?*
very + noun	*He is the **very person** I want to talk to.*

like / as

like for similarities	*He swims **like** a fish.*
as	*He works **as** a nurse.* *You should do **as** you're told.*

Qualifying / intensifying comparisons

a bit / a little	*James is **a little** less shy than his sister.*
slightly	*This cake is **slightly** sweeter than the last one you made.*
much	*Katie's **much** friendlier than Karen.*
a lot	*It's **a lot** hotter in the Bahamas than here.*
far	*The owners of this hotel are **far** less welcoming than the last one I stayed in.*

Writing guide

A *Cambridge English: Advanced* essay may be written for a teacher and it may follow up on a classroom activity. It should be well-organised, with an introduction, clear development and appropriate conclusion.

You have recently listened to a radio discussion programme about the effects of cars on people and the environment. You have made the notes below.

What do cars affect most?	Some opinions expressed in the discussion:
• people's daily lives • society as a whole • the environment	'For lots of people, cars are the only way of visiting friends and going shopping.' 'If people work close to their home, they can get more involved in their local community.' 'Traffic emissions make it very hard to breathe in some cities.'

Write an essay discussing **two** of the categories of effects in your notes. You should **explain which category is more badly affected** by cars, **giving reasons** in support of your answer.

You may, if you wish, make use of the opinions expressed in the discussion, but you should use your own words as far as possible.

Write your **essay**.

PLANNING AN ESSAY

1 **Brainstorm ideas:** What points can you make to answer the question?
2 **Write an outline or paragraph plan:** What will you say in your main body paragraphs? Think about your introduction and conclusion also.
3 **Write your essay:** Use linking words and examples if necessary to make your argument stronger or your points clearer.
4 **Check your work.**

The effects of cars

For thousands of years, people have lived without cars. Yet in the century since the car was invented, our lives have been transformed – on the whole, for the better. However, we are becoming far more conscious of the negative impact that cars have.

Our current dependence on cars affects the society we live in. Cars encourage individualism, as they enable us to travel around whenever it suits us. That means fewer people use public transport, which therefore becomes less viable financially. Buses and trains are then cut, and people without cars suffer as a result.

Cars also affect society by allowing us to work at a distance from our homes. Consequently, many people have so little time at home that they can't be active in their local community. As a result, many areas turn into 'dormitory towns', where nobody knows anyone else.

With regard to the environment, the carbon monoxide emissions of cars are disastrous, polluting the air – which makes breathing difficult for many people – and killing plants and trees. In addition, the construction of roads and massive motorway junctions destroys the countryside.

Cars have a major impact on both society and the environment, but on balance I believe the effects on the latter are more significant. After all, if our environment is harmed, we won't survive: the air pollution in many cities makes life extremely hard for many people, such as asthma sufferers. If the situation continues to deteriorate, this can only be bad news for the human race.

USEFUL LINKING PHRASES

To introduce
It is often said that …
Many people believe / claim that …
Everyone often says / mentions / claims / goes on …

To add points
Also, Moreover, Furthermore, Secondly, On the one hand …

To contrast points
However, Alternatively, Nevertheless, In contrast, On the other hand, whereas, while, Despite the fact that

To introduce a result
For which reason, Subsequently, which is why, As a result of this / which …

To conclude
Therefore, To sum up, On balance, To conclude, In conclusion, Consequently, Finally …

INFORMAL LETTER OR EMAIL

Part 2: 220–260 words

A letter or email in *Cambridge English: Advanced* involves answering according to a situation outlined in the question you are given. You must reply in a way which is appropriate for your (imagined) reader.

A friend of yours is looking for a summer job and has asked you to suggest a good job based on your experiences.

Write a letter to your friend describing a temporary job you had and saying why you would recommend it.

Write your **letter**. You do not need to include postal addresses.

USEFUL LETTER-WRITING PHRASES

Opening
Dear Maria, Hi Jim, [to a friend, family member]
Dear Editor, Dear Sir, [to the editor of a newspaper or magazine]
Main paragraphs
Thanks for your letter / email …
I'm just writing to let you know …
I thought you might like to know …
It was nice to hear from you again …
In answer to the newspaper article in your last edition …
Ending
Look forward to hearing from you / seeing you.
Bye for now / All the best / Best wishes / Talk soon / Write back soon.
Yours sincerely / Sincerely / Yours faithfully

PLANNING A LETTER

1 **Brainstorm ideas:** Try to come up with several possible answers.
2 **Write an outline:** Make sure you answer all parts of the question.
3 **Paragraph plan:** Make sure you link ideas appropriately.
4 **Write your letter:** Remember to include descriptive vocabulary.
5 **Make sure you write in an informal style, if that is appropriate.**
6 **Check your work:** for spelling, punctuation and grammatical errors.

Dear Jeanette,

Thanks for your email. I'm glad to hear that you've decided to get some work experience this summer before you start university. I found it was very useful and I started my university studies the following year feeling refreshed and enthusiastic!

If you remember, I worked last year on a sailing yacht. I've always loved the sea, so it wasn't difficult for me to decide what I wanted to do. I didn't have much experience but it didn't matter. I completed a basic sailing course and learnt how to be a useful member of a ship's crew. Then I got myself a job on a sailing yacht in the Caribbean!

I can't say the money was great, but I did benefit from the experience and made a lot of friends. I also got to see a part of the world I probably wouldn't have seen otherwise, and most of the time it was like a working holiday! We saw dolphins and once we even saw whales! On the whole it was an unforgettable experience. By the end of the summer I had learnt so much about sailing that I did a course when I got home, got my skipper's certificate, and now I can charter a sailing yacht whenever I want, anywhere in the world!

So my recommendation to you would be to do something similar if you are looking for good experiences and plenty of laughs! But only if you don't get sea-sick!

Let me know how it goes. All the best,

Jimmy

ALTERNATIVE QUESTION

An aunt of yours wants to buy a nice present for your parents, whose wedding anniversary is coming up soon. She has asked you to suggest a suitable present and to say why you think it would be appreciated by both of them. Write a letter to your aunt describing a possible gift and saying why you would recommend it.

Write your **letter**. You do not need to include postal addresses.

A review in *Cambridge English: Advanced* is usually written for an English-language website, magazine or newspaper. You usually need to describe an experience or express a personal opinion about something. You need to give your reader a clear impression of what the item described is like.

A tourist agency is updating its website, and has asked its customers to send in reviews of holidays they have had. You decide to write about a holiday you went on recently. Describe the place and type of holiday, what you really enjoyed about it, and if there was anything you disliked. Then say who you would recommend the holiday to, and why.

Write your **review**.

PLANNING YOUR REVIEW

1 **Brainstorm ideas:** Which holiday are you going to write about? What aspects of it did you particularly enjoy? Did anything unexpected or unpleasant happen? Who would you recommend it to and why?
2 **Style and register:** Check who the target reader is to decide whether your review should be formal or informal, and whether your style should be lively or remain fairly neutral.
3 **Paragraphs:** Use the points mentioned in the question to help you organise your answer into paragraphs.
4 **Check your work.**

One way of really relaxing and getting away from it all is to take a canal boat along the Canal du Midi, in the south of France. My family and I did just that this summer, and discovered how pleasant it can be to travel in the slow lane for a while.

Introduction. State what you're going to write about.

Being inexperienced boaters, my parents felt uncomfortable about trying to manoeuvre a large boat, and opted for a 30-foot canal cruiser. In fact, they needn't have worried, because the company provided us with excellent instruction before we set off, and it was a lot easier than we'd expected. Even my brother and I had a go!

We spent a wonderful week gliding along the beautiful waterways of Languedoc and the Camargue. The facilities on board were excellent, and any worries we'd had of getting bored were soon forgotten about, as every day proved to be an adventure. We'd spend three to four hours cruising each day, before stopping to explore places inland. We passed through pretty little villages, practised our appalling French on the amused locals, and saw some fascinating wildlife. The highlight of the holiday, however, was the nautical jousting tournament held in the seaside port of Sete. This was great fun, and the town was buzzing with excitement.

Use a range of descriptive vocabulary to convey your attitude.

Looking back, I think we'd all agree that we should have booked a bigger boat. Thirty feet for four people can be rather cramped. Nevertheless, I'd definitely recommend this trip to anyone who really needs to unwind for a while.

Remember to include a recommendation in your concluding paragraph.

ALTERNATIVE QUESTION

Your local bookshop wants to run a special promotion of children's books. The manager has asked customers to send reviews of their favourite children's book, to appear on the shop's website. You decide to write a review of the book you most enjoyed reading as a child, saying why you enjoyed it so much and who you would recommend should read it.

Write your **review**.

FORMAL LETTER
Part 2: 220–260 words

> The advertisement below appeared in an English language magazine.
>
> > **Writers!**
> > We are updating our popular *Connections* website, and need writers to contribute regularly to our blog, presenting articles of interest to young people worldwide. Successful candidates will have some writing experience, and show an awareness of young people's interests and concerns.
> > Send us an application, electronically, or by post, explaining why you think you are suitable, and describing two or three subjects you would like to write about.
>
> Write your **letter** of application. You do not need to include postal addresses.

PLANNING A FORMAL LETTER

1 **Analyse the question:** Who is the target reader? What is your reason for writing? What information must you include?
2 **Style and register:** Make sure your language is appropriate for the specific question, and that your tone remains fairly neutral and polite.
3 **Write your answer:** Make sure you address all the points in the question.
4 **Check your work:** Make sure you haven't written too little or too much.

Dear Sir / Madam,

I am writing in response to your advertisement in the 'English Today' magazine, asking for people to contribute to the blog on your website, 'Connections'.

I am a student in my final year at school, and have written various articles for our school magazine, on such subjects as child safety on the Internet, exam stress and bullying, samples of which you will find in the attachment I've included. I feel quite strongly that these issues need to be addressed, not only by teachers and parents, but by the student body as a whole. We need to take more active responsibility for our actions and those of our peers. I should mention that I have received a considerable amount of positive feedback from readers, including people who have no connection with the school I attend.

For this reason, I feel that your blog could offer young people the opportunity to reach out to people in other countries, and would welcome the opportunity to contribute to promoting greater understanding between multinational groups. One of the issues I would like to address on the blog is the problems which sometimes arise in the multicultural classroom, and I would also like to examine the possibility of setting up a regular environmental feature.

I would therefore be grateful if you could consider my application, and accept me as a contributing writer. I look forward to hearing from you.

Yours faithfully,

Razia Azad

USEFUL FORMAL LETTER WRITING PHRASES

Opening
Dear Sir / Madam …
Dear Mrs Smith …
To whom it may concern [usually for writing a reference]

Main paragraphs
I am writing in response to your advertisement / announcement, etc …
I am writing with regard to …
I am interested in applying for the post of …
I would like to enquire about / apply for, etc …
I feel strongly that not only is this …

Ending
I would therefore be grateful if you could …
I would appreciate it if you could …
I look forward to hearing from you.
Yours sincerely / Yours faithfully

REPORT

Part 2:
220–260 words

A report in *Cambridge English: Advanced* is usually written for a superior, such as a line manager, or a peer group, such as colleagues. You'll need to give some factual comments as well as make suggestions.

You are an independent business consultant. The owner of a bookshop has asked you to investigate why sales are falling. You have examined various aspects of the business, including the interior design of the premises and the threat of competition in the area.

Your report should make recommendations for improvements based on your findings.

Write your **report**.

PLANNING YOUR REPORT

1 **Analyse the question:** As for a proposal, you should take care to make a list of all the points you need to include.
2 **Plan your answer:** Decide on suitable headings for each paragraph, and the points you want to include in each.
3 **Write your answer:** Remember, the main content of a report is to analyse certain problems of a current situation, and make suggestions for improvement. You may leave your recommendations for improvement until the final paragraph.
4 **Check your work.**

Introduction

This report presents the findings of my research into why business in the Tawny Owl bookshop is declining, and makes some recommendations for improvement.

The competition

Although the shop is ideally located in the centre of the town, it has suffered losses as a result of the opening of a large discount bookstore almost directly opposite. To combat this, one solution would be to create a series of promotions involving special-interest authors, aimed at attracting a particular section of the market each time. Book signing sessions by well-known authors are also an effective way to attract customers.

The shop premises

The shop is housed in an old building, and decorated in an old-fashioned, rather plain style. Although the shop has a wide range of books on offer, these are placed in rows of tightly packed bookshelves throughout, creating a rather dark atmosphere, and making it difficult to browse. A solution to this problem would be to remove some of the bookshelves, and open up space to create a reading area, where customers could examine books at leisure. A children's corner would also encourage busy mothers to enter the shop. The interior could be redecorated, and the shop front redesigned to create a brighter atmosphere.

Conclusion

With some investment and careful planning, the Tawny Owl could attract more customers, by offering them something different to its competitors. The key lies in offering them quality, and creating a pleasant, welcoming atmosphere.

PROPOSAL

Part 2:

220–260 words

In a *Cambridge English: Advanced* proposal, you're expected to give factual information and make a recommendation to be followed by your readers.

> You are a school teacher. You have received an email from the school principal, regarding the question of raising funds to build a new science laboratory. Using the information given, write a **proposal** for a fundraising event.

> From: Phil
> To: Hannah
> Hannah,
> As we discussed at this morning's meeting, we need to raise money to help build the new science lab. Suggestions included a sponsored walk, a 60's disco and a lottery.
> Could you write a proposal outlining these three possibilities, and making your recommendation, so that I can present it at the parents' meeting on Thursday?
> Thanks
> Phil

PLANNING YOUR PROPOSAL

1 **Analyse the question:** Consider what you are being asked.
2 **Plan your answer:** Decide on suitable headings and points for each paragraph.
3 **Write your answer:** Remember to make, support and summarise suggestions.
4 **Check your work.**

Introduction

The aim of this proposal is to present the Parents and Teachers Association with suggestions to raise money for the school's new science laboratory.

A sponsored walk

One idea put forward is to organise a sponsored walk. A ten-mile route would be sufficient for younger students, and could be clearly marked out around the town. Also, to make the walk more fun, students could be dressed in fancy dress. Under careful supervision, this could be a very enjoyable fundraising event.

A disco

Another suggestion is to hold a disco. This has certain advantages over the walk, in that it is held indoors, so would not be affected by bad weather, and would be easier to both organise and monitor. One possible drawback, however, is that shy students may feel too inhibited to participate.

A lottery

Possibly the easiest way to raise money would be to hold a lottery. Several local businesses have kindly offered prizes to support our efforts, and so this would need little input on the part of the students.

Recommendation

I recommend organising all three fundraising events, to ensure that all students in the school can be involved in the scheme in some way. Although this would clearly require a great deal of work, with careful planning and organisation, it could prove rewarding for everyone. It would also be the way to raise the greatest amount of money.

ALTERNATIVE QUESTION

> You are a representative of your school council. You have received an email from the school principal, regarding the forthcoming visit of a group of foreign students.
> Read the email and write a **proposal** for offering the visitors a warm welcome.

> Duncan,
> As we discussed at yesterday's meeting, we'd like to do something special to welcome Mrs Chan and her students next Friday. Suggestions included holding a disco and buffet reception, an introductory talk with video on things to do in the town, and a performance by the school orchestra.
> Could you draw up a proposal outlining the value of these ideas, so I can present it to the school governors?
> Thank you
> Mrs Brodie

A   Building a coherent answer

Cambridge English: Advanced writing tasks need to be carefully planned and written so that they include
- paragraphs with clear themes or topics
- logically ordered sentences within paragraphs
- clear links within and between sentences

1   **Read the review of an unusual sport called Octopush. The writer should have divided the answer into four paragraphs. Mark where each new paragraph should begin.**

A few weeks ago, I was invited to watch one of the strangest sports I've ever come across: Octopush. I must admit that when I first heard the name, I thought it must have something to do with eight-legged sea creatures. However, Octopush is basically an underwater game of hockey – and what an amazing game it is! All you need to take part in a game of Octopush is a mask, a snorkel, a protective glove to stop your hands getting scratched on the bottom of the pool, a small, specially designed stick and a puck, which is a lead disc, rather like those used in ice hockey. There's an underwater goal at each end of the pool, and the object of the game is for one of the six players in each team to flick the puck into the opposition's goal. From where I was sitting with my friends, it looked almost impossible for the players to tell who their opponents were, apart from the fact that the sticks were black for one team and white for the other. As they thrashed around underwater, we found ourselves amused but engrossed in the display and amazed at how long some players managed to stay underwater before rising to the surface for another lungful of air and then diving back down again. Clearly, this isn't a game that most people would enjoy playing, but it's dramatic stuff and strongly recommended for anyone who enjoys watching a fast, physically demanding competition, with a touch of difference.

2   **What is the topic of each of the four paragraphs?**

3   **Put the following sentences into the correct order to form a coherent paragraph.**

a   Similarly, the orchestra had a professional sound and seemed to be note-perfect.

b   Every year, the sixth-form college in my city puts on a musical that would be worthy of London's West End – and this year's was no exception.

c   Receiving a standing ovation seemed to take the participants by surprise, but I can assure you it was well deserved.

d   Even though many of the dancers who took part in it were first-year students, with relatively little real stage experience, they put on an amazing, seamless show.

e   Like the rest of the audience, I was overwhelmed by such incredible talent and was on my feet at the end, clapping as hard as I could.

4   **Consider which links helped you decide the order.**

5   **Complete the paragraph from a book review with the reference words in the box.**

his	it	one	others	such	that	their	this
which							

One of the best books I have read recently is entitled 'The Last Exhibit' by David Parrin. Although I don't usually enjoy books by (1) _____ author, I must say that this (2) _____ surprised me. I suspect this is because, unlike his (3) _____ , it was written from the perspective of an ordinary person on the street, and so (4) _____ lacked much of the detailed material on criminal law that (5) _____ novels often contain. (6) _____ is not to say that writers shouldn't include (7) _____ own professional knowledge in a work of fiction, but there is a point beyond (8) _____ the reader loses patience and, unfortunately, Parrin usually oversteps this. In the case of 'The Last Exhibit', however, there is no (9) _____ indulgence.

B Structuring an essay

In addition to ensuring that paragraphs are coherent and sentences well linked, an essay should have clear links between paragraphs so that the reader can follow the line of argument.

1 Read the essay on the importance of protecting old buildings and underline the following.

1 a sentence that expresses the writer's main argument
2 two sentences that express the key ideas supporting the main argument

Today, there are many buildings around the world that are in danger of being destroyed because of our desire to 'modernise'. However, I believe that some of these could be renovated or rebuilt, with significant benefits to the community.

Our obsession with updating cities tends to be driven by the need to create homes, restaurants and shops for increasing numbers of residents. Thus, traditional buildings may be knocked down in order to provide construction space. Yet this seems to be a short-sighted approach. In fact, if developers renovated these buildings instead and turned them into characteristic apartments or cafés, local citizens would have a much more attractive environment to live in. This, in turn, would enhance their sense of well-being since they would appreciate their neighbourhood more fully and not see important cultural elements being destroyed.

Maintaining a city's architectural history is also vitally important if you live in one that wishes to encourage visitors. Nothing destroys the look of an area more than the construction of featureless low-rises. They have no historical value and can quite rapidly deteriorate, detracting from an otherwise interesting or popular region. On the other hand, a place where traditional styles have been not only preserved but improved upon can boost tourism and bring money into the local community. This can then be used to fund important local projects.

Despite the demands of a growing population, I would argue that there are several reasons why preservation should be considered as a first priority. Admittedly, it may not always be practical or feasible but there are clear advantages if it is successfully achieved.

2 Underline the links between the paragraphs.

3 What is the function of the following words and phrases?

1 *some of these* (paragraph 1)
2 *Thus* (paragraph 2)
3 *Yet* and *this* (paragraph 2)
4 *one* (paragraph 3)
5 *On the other hand* (paragraph 3)
6 *it* (paragraph 4)

C Levels of formality

Most *Cambridge English: Advanced* writing answers should be written in a neutral or formal tone. It is only appropriate to use an informal style in letters to family and friends. The general rule is that the more authority the reader has, the more formal the writing should be.

1 Read the extract from a proposal to a local council about youth activities and change the highlighted words and phrases into a more formal register.

I think we should set up a youth centre so that kids can mess about there outside school hours. It's hopeless expecting young people to entertain themselves, when there is nowhere for them to do this. The centre could cater for teenagers up to the age of 17, while anyone under 12 could also go if they were with mum or dad. It would be great to offer table tennis, snooker and darts as activities. There would still be a need for some supervision during these activities so how about three attendants on full-time duty, which the council should be able to splash out on easily.

Formality is not just about avoiding slang and idiomatic expressions. Precise, advanced language also helps in developing a formal tone.

2 Read the extract from a letter of application. Find six verb phrases that could be improved using the correct form of one of the options in the box.

be (interested in)   enquire   find   inform
observe   specialise

I am studying sociology at Goldsmiths University and I am writing to check whether you have any job opportunities for undergraduates during the holiday period. I've been a student for two years now and I do mostly child protection. This has included working with the local authority and seeing some case trials at court. It's all been really helpful and I would love to work in this area in my spare time. Could you let me know if you have anything available?

D Spelling

You should always leave a few minutes at the end of the test to proofread your work. Spelling mistakes can spoil an otherwise good answer, so ensure that you check:

- singular / plural forms – ensuring nouns and verbs are consistent
- words that include the addition of suffixes and prefixes
- double / single consonants
- commonly misspelt words such as *necessary*
- homonyms such as *principle* and *principal*
- words that you know you find difficult to spell

1 Write the noun and adjective forms of the verbs in the table. Sometimes there is more than one possible answer.

Verbs	Noun form(s)	Adjective form(s)
affect		
appeal		
correspond		
enquire		
prefer		
specify		
vary		

2 Correct the spelling mistake in each of the sentences.

1 My course involves a lot of academic reaserches.
2 Many works by contempory artists were incorporated into the show.
3 The producers used some tecniqes that were quite unique.
4 Too many avoidable accidents have ocurred in the local area.
5 Like many people, I think euthanasia is a controversal issue.
6 People prefer to work in a harmonyous atmosphere.
7 Deciding weather politicians are being genuine can sometimes be difficult.
8 Cars which are stationery should be made to turn their engines off.

E Punctuation

Accurate punctuation is important because it makes your writing clear and easy to follow, and improves the overall presentation of your answer.

Areas of punctuation that you should check when you proofread your work include:

- **capital letters** for proper nouns and to open sentences
- **full stops** to end sentences
- **commas** to separate lists, phrases and clauses
- **apostrophes** for contractions and possessives
- **dashes** to add extra information (brackets or commas also)
- **colons** to introduce a list or an explanation
- **semi-colons** to separate two closely connected sentences
- **inverted commas** to highlight special names or terms
- **question marks** after questions

1 Read the paragraph from an article on video games and find six punctuation errors.

Many young people enjoy playing video games because they allow you to take part in a story give you some control over events and let you interact with other characters. Video games stretch your imagination so that you can exist for a while in a fantasy world a world that is more immediate than a good allegorical novel, such as orwell's 'Animal Farm'. Tests have shown that playing video games from an early age actually strengthens handeye co-ordination and stimulates brain development. Many video games require the player to make logical decisions which help to develop brain function in a way that watching television never can this can only be a good thing.

2 Punctuate the sentences.

1 a recent survey has shown that video games are very popular especially with young people
2 the best video game I have ever played is rachet and clank it's fast paced exciting colourful and hugely imaginative
3 with the exception of extreme cases is there any evidence to support the criticism of video games
4 however not all video games are good for everyone and not everyone enjoys them
5 parents most of whom have concerns about the length of time their children spend using technology often limit their childrens exposure to video games
6 if the game is good whats the problem
7 psychologists have reached the following conclusions video games have educational value utilise various skills simultaneously and help some children perform better at school
8 there is increasing evidence that the elderly are enjoying games on tablet devices these days too which is a recent development

Speaking reference files

Unit 2

USEFUL EXPRESSIONS

I think / I believe / I strongly feel that …
It could be said … / It can be argued that …
One of the main arguments in favour of / against …
Young people under the age of 18 are often thought to be …
However, in my opinion …
If you ask me, I would say that …

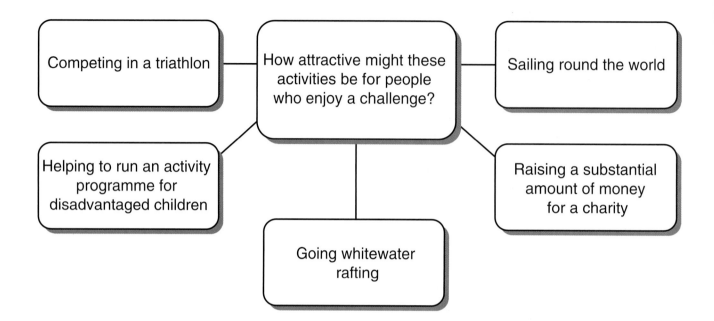

Competing in a triathlon

How attractive might these activities be for people who enjoy a challenge?

Sailing round the world

Helping to run an activity programme for disadvantaged children

Going whitewater rafting

Raising a substantial amount of money for a charity

USEFUL EXPRESSIONS

MAKING SUGGESTIONS AND RESPONDING TO IDEAS

Try to vary your language when discussing ideas. Avoid repeating phrases your partner uses. Use the following to help you.

Suggestions
It might be a good idea for them to …
One possibility is for them to …
Another interesting challenge is …
What about …

Responding
Competing in a triathlon may be popular, but I'm not sure about …
Going whitewater rafting might be attractive to some people, but most people who enjoy a challenge probably want …
While it's good to raise money for charity, I really don't think …
I'm not sure that'll be challenging enough …
Yes, but don't you think it would be more appealing to …
While it's a good idea to raise money for charity, I really don't think …
That's a great idea, and they could also …

Unit 6

- Can food affect our mood?
- How might these people be feeling?

- How can exercise help people to stay healthy?
- How might these people be feeling?

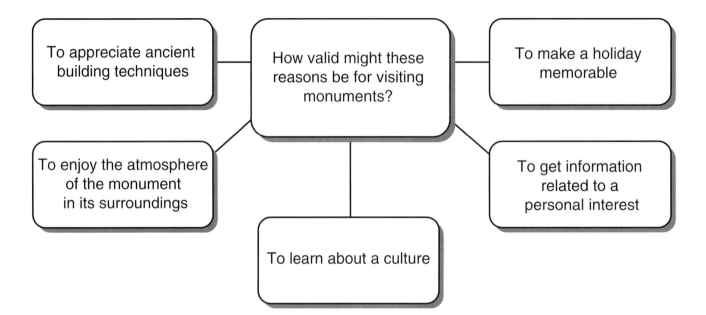

Unit 10

A How might these methods of food production affect people's health and the environment?

B How might these methods of energy production affect people's health and the environment?

USEFUL EXPRESSIONS

I think / I believe / I strongly feel that …
It could be said … / It can be argued that …
One of the main arguments in favour of / against …
However, in my opinion …
If you ask me, I would say that …

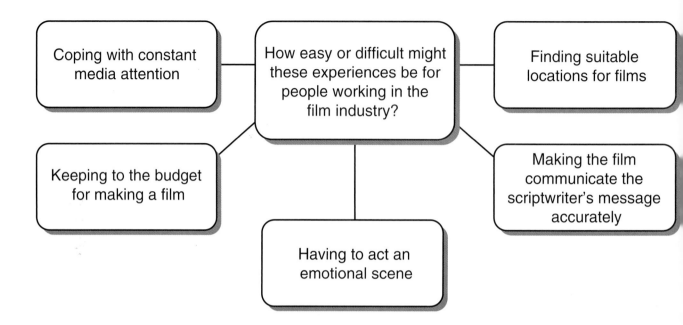

10 **Work in pairs and discuss the questions.**

1   In what ways can film and television influence our lives? Is this a good or bad thing in your opinion? Why?

2   Sometimes millions of dollars are spent on a film. With so much poverty in the world, what's your view on this?

3   Do you think films should be used as a vehicle for expressing political or religious beliefs? Why? / Why not?

4   Some people say that violence on television and in film has contributed to the violence in the world today. What do you think?

5   Some people watch a film to escape from reality for a while and feel better. To what extent do you think this works?

6   How important is film as an art form when compared with painting, novels, music, etc?

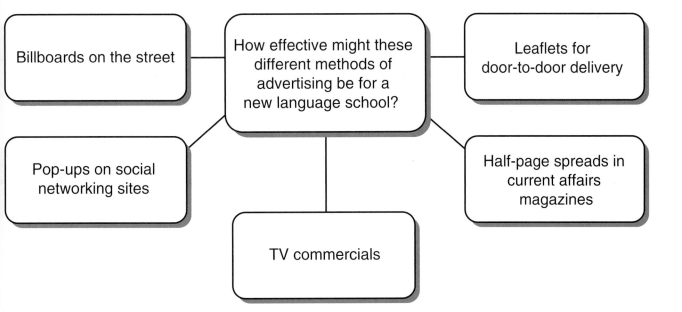

STATUS: CRITCALLY ENDANGERED

Yangtze River dolphin: the most endangered cetacean, probably already extinct; population: between one and ten individuals, although none have been seen for several years.

Long-beaked echidna: one of the most primitive egg-laying mammals; population: 30,000 individuals. One species already thought to be extinct.

Sumatran rhinoceros: smallest and most endangered of all rhino species; population: around 300 individuals are thought to remain.

Bactrian camel: probably the ancestor of all domestic two-humped camels; population: fewer than 1,000 individuals live in the world's most hostile desert.

Mediterranean monk seal: considered the world's most endangered marine mammal; population: 400–500 individuals.

California condor: classified as a member of the order *Falconiformes* (eagles, hawks and vultures), the condor is classified as a critically endangered species due to an estimated population of fewer than 50 mature individuals.

THINKING OUT LOUD

One of the reasons I'd prefer to save certain animals is that …
At first glance, I'd say that we should save animals that …
Personally, I'd prefer to save animals that … because …
I believe we can't afford to let animals that … die out because …
We shouldn't ignore the fact that …
Although it's difficult to choose just one reason, I think …
There's no doubt in my mind which category of animals should be saved; it's ones that … because …
In what way do you think this type of animal is important?
Would you agree that if we saved animals that … , the world would be a better place because … ?
Well, taking everything into consideration, I would have to say …

Yellow-tailed woolly monkey: thought to be extinct until its rediscovery in 1974; population: fewer than 250 individuals are thought to survive today.

Blue whale: the largest mammal ever known to have lived; population: approximately 5,000 individuals.

Unit 16

Student A

Information files

UNIT 2 page 20, exercise 6, File 1

A Their unusual uniform was chosen by the local education authority for being the most practical solution in these circumstances. The boys seem to like it and so there are plans to market it and have it in the shops by the time school starts in September.

B These two boys, wrapped up like seafarers against the squally autumn weather that often drenches their corner of Scotland, are about to be pioneers in a nursery education experiment. And it is a project that could make many urban parents fearful.

C Both boys felt cold and irritable and had demonstrated a marked disinclination to get involved with any of the team projects, despite Cathy's intention to introduce them to the rigours of outdoor living.

UNIT 3 page 28, exercise 4, File 2

How Game Are You?

1 What would you do if you saw someone stealing an old lady's purse?
   a Ignore it and carry on with what you were doing.
   b Shout 'Stop, thief!' and chase after him.
   c Telephone the police.
2 You are offered a free lesson in kite land-boarding. Do you …
   a say 'Thanks, but no thanks'?
   b immediately accept?
   c find out a little more about it before accepting?
3 You see some boys bullying a smaller boy. Do you …
   a do nothing and walk away?
   b go to help him?
   c go and get someone to stop them?
4 You are offered a place on an expedition to the South Pole. Do you …
   a politely decline?
   b start packing your bags?
   c ask for some time to think about it?

Answers

If you answered all b, you are very daring, and a little reckless!
If you answered all c, you are game, but more cautious, thinking about safety.
If you answered all a, you are not daring at all, and try to avoid trouble at all costs.
If you answered with a combination of b and c, you are daring, but consider safety occasionally.
If you answered with a combination of a and c, you only take risks in certain situations.

UNIT 5 page 48, exercise 3, File 3

A They have been working solidly for the last ten hours, developing some of the world's most sophisticated crimeware to date.

B Inspired by such impressive surroundings, these young people are engrossed in their task, creating a new computer game for the American market.

C In a former life it was a nuclear research facility at the heart of the cold war. Now this dark skyscraper is home to a different kind of power struggle.

UNIT 14 page 134, exercise 5, File 4

1 The first astronauts in space were
   A surprised by the colours they saw on Earth.
   B forced to adjust their perspective of their place in the cosmos.
   C astonished by the size of the Earth.
   D made aware of the life-forces operating on Earth.
2 Dr James Lovelock had originally
   A been an astronomer in Britain.
   B been employed to compare Mars with Earth.
   C been looking for Martian life.
   D identified similarities between Mars and Earth.
3 Lovelock's hypothesis was that
   A Earth's inconstant atmosphere was a by-product of life on the planet.
   B the chemical condition of the Earth had come about by accident.
   C the imbalance of gases on Earth had created life.
   D life had evolved to survive in Earth's planetary conditions.
4 Research carried out since the publication of Lovelock's book has shown that
   A the various systems on our planet are regulated by different mechanisms.
   B clouds are formed by metabolic chemical changes in the sky.
   C the saltiness of the seas is due to the presence of oceanic algae.
   D the way that organisms regulate their systems is evolving.
5 In the fifth paragraph, what point does the author make in relation to Gaia theory?
   A The planet uses mechanisms that have been found on other planets.
   B The temperature of the oceans is affected by the atmosphere.
   C The rainforests are being destroyed by pollution.
   D Each species on Earth has a part to play in the planet's survival.
6 According to the final paragraph, what are we recommended to do?
   A focus on improving our standard of living
   B try to minimise the damage we cause to the planet's systems
   C carry out research into how animal species affect the planet
   D reduce the differences between the way of life in different parts of the world

Audioscripts

Unit 1 Track 1

Husband: Mandy! This one sounds good for Joey.
Mandy: Go on, then. What have you found?
Husband: 'A Child's First Clock … Most children don't learn how to tell the time until they are in first grade, or beyond, but with this lovely 'no-numbers-needed' clock, even toddlers can learn the basics of timekeeping.'
Mandy: Mm. Sounds interesting. Tell me more …
Husband: 'Developed by two mothers – a children's television presenter Noni Anderson and artist Alison Perrin – the woodland clock features a slow painted turtle for the hour hand, a faster grey rabbit for the minute hand, and a speedy red-breasted robin on the second hand' … Blah, blah, blah. 'You can assemble a clock much like ours by printing out the art materials attached, and applying them to a clock from a do-it-yourself kit.' So, Mandy, what do you think? Shall we download the attachment?

Track 2

Woman 1: So, what's brought this on, then?
Woman 2: Yeah, well, Bill's just had enough of living in the city. It's all the stress, you know. Not only at the office itself, but when he's to-ing and fro-ing in all that traffic! He's just sick of it. So, he suddenly decided to pack it all in, and make a fresh start. So, we're off to the Isle of Man, in the middle of the Irish Sea. Middle of nowhere, if you ask me! Still, at least it's not like moving abroad. He's taking up sheep farming, of all things! God knows if it'll work. But you know Bill, when he sets his mind to something, there's no stopping him.
Woman 1: Well, I never! It seems a bit drastic, though.
Woman 2: He reckons it'll be good for us, like starting over. All I can think of is sitting alone, with the wind howling outside. I mean, how many people stay there in the winter? We're used to the noise of the traffic. But, I've told him I'll give it a go. Who knows, it may be the making of us!

Track 3

Oliver: So, what do you think of our ideas, Jane?
Jane: Well, overall, quite acceptable, Oliver, but I'm not happy about some of the omissions. I mean, ignoring the details in the first two chapters means that members of the audience who haven't read the book will be left in the dark. They won't understand the reasons behind the protagonist's actions in the film.
Oliver: Yeah, but most people have read the book! It was a blockbuster, after all!
Jane: We shouldn't take that for granted, though. I feel that, as it stands, your proposal threatens to focus too much on action and special effects, leaving little room for character development.
Oliver: Huh! Yeah, well, you know, this is only a rough outline of the scenes, as yet …
Jane: OK. But, personally, I would prefer the opening scene to include some sense of Jim's confusion and fear about what he's about to do.
Oliver: OK! … But don't you think hitting the audience with the murder straight away creates suspense?
Jane: Perhaps. But it also looks like a cold-blooded, calculated murder rather than … Look, I don't know what you got out of the book, but I wrote a psychological thriller, Oliver, and I'd like some element of the psychology to come through in the film, and not just the thriller aspect! Jim's character is a complex one, and your plans for him threaten to reduce it to a wooden stereotype!

Track 4

Teacher: OK, let's brainstorm some ideas. What new experiences have you had that you clearly remember?
Student A: I tried bungee jumping once. I'll never forget that!
Student B: Really? That must have been terrifying. I don't even like heights. But I did travel to America – a totally new experience for me.
Teacher: Good – don't forget you also need to tell us why it was memorable or significant for you.
Student B: I was very impressed by the lifestyle there and I decided I wanted to improve my English enough to go and study over there.
Teacher: Excellent! What about you Vasilis?
Student C: I've been swimming with dolphins in the water. It was amazing. I would love to write about that, because it made me respect animals and nature.

Teacher: How wonderful! I can't wait to read about it. Massimo, what about you?
Student D: I, er, haven't had any new or exciting experiences that I can think of.
Teacher: Well … maybe you could make one up?
Student D: Mm, well I suppose I could say I have been to a rock concert.
Teacher: Yes, and why would that have been memorable or significant to you?
Student D: Er – I could say that it changed my life and made me want to become a rock star.
Student A: Oh, I almost forgot. I have flown in a helicopter too.
Teacher: Well, we've certainly got a few ideas there.

Track 5

Teacher: OK, so you've brainstormed some ideas for your writing and chosen one. Now we need to outline the structure. What's the best way of doing that?
Student D: With paragraphs?
Teacher: That's right, Massimo. But you need to have an idea about what to say in each paragraph, and they should link together well. What's an easy way to do that?
Student D: You need to decide what the main purpose is of each paragraph.
Teacher: Good. Claudine, what would be the main purpose of the first paragraph?
Student A: Um, I think I would have to write about what made me decide to go bungee jumping in the first place.
Teacher: OK, so for planning purposes, we could say: 'What led to the experience.' What else could you call that … Svetlana?
Student B: I would talk about how I prepared for my journey to America, and the hopes and fears I had.
Teacher: Good, so you could write about the preparations and the background to the experience then. Right, now, what about the main body of our piece? What would we need to focus on?
Student C: It would have to be about the experience itself. Describing it, our feelings, what happened.
Teacher: Very good Vasilis, and very important too. And what mustn't we forget?
Student B: An ending? And the reason why it was significant.
Student D: I would say what happened afterwards, and how I felt about it later, and why it changed my life.
Teacher: Excellent – so a good, strong concluding paragraph. Now we're getting somewhere.

Unit 2 Track 6

We still don't fully understand how or why human language came about, although there are certainly a good number of theories. One main theory suggests that when men became hunters, they needed to develop a language in order to share hunting tactics with one another during the chase, despite the fact that most carnivorous animals – even those that hunt in packs – find silence to be a distinct advantage. And yet historians are agreed that the first spoken languages must have been very crude. How then could they have been of any practical use? There is, however, one theory that proposes that it wasn't men who first used language. It wasn't even women. It was in fact children who invented it, and taught it to their parents. The truth is that fully grown adults actually lack the ability to learn to speak. Only children can do it. People that have never been exposed to any kind of spoken language before the age of five (and there are a handful of documented cases) have never been able to learn to speak at all, despite concerted efforts to teach them. Similarly, children that are born deaf may have difficulty learning to make verbal sounds because they've never heard them. Children's natural propensity for learning languages is taken as read. They don't have to be taught their first language – they only have to hear it spoken around them. During the first four or five years of life a child can learn several languages simultaneously, without being taught, without any apparent effort.

Newborn babies all over the world have their own repertoire of involuntary sounds which are useful for communicating to the mother their most basic needs – hunger, pain or the need for attention. This is true of the young of most mammals. However, between three and four months of age the human baby begins to emit new sounds and before long, will start to 'babble'. This baby talk varies from country to country, suggesting that the baby is responding to, and trying to imitate, the sounds around him. Before long, he learns to control the sounds. He gets a response. He says 'ma' and mother responds. This could be the reason why the word for mother is so similar in almost every language. It's one of the first syllables a human child can voluntarily produce. Can we be so sure that baby is really imitating mum or could it be the other way round? Next, he is inventing his own words for objects and his mother is using them too. Language is born. Perhaps this is why girls often learn to speak sooner and more fluently than boys, because at one time the ability to develop language was essential to the mother-infant relationship.

Unit 3 Track 7

Speaker 1: So, I said, well, I'm game, if you are. But I wish I hadn't. It was terrifying! The water flows so fast, with rocks appearing out of nowhere … There's no time to think. I was petrified! Never again!

Speaker 2: Well, the long hours without sleep were exhausting, and the loneliness got me down occasionally, but I was determined not to give up, and would keep myself busy, by repairing sails and ropes, or sending faxes to folks back on dry land. Also, listening to music had a way of relaxing me, and was quite reassuring.

Speaker 3: That was awesome! Absolutely incredible! A real adrenalin rush! Everything happens so fast, you've got to be on your toes, and, like, keep control of both the board and the kite, otherwise you'll overturn … and … Man, it was so exhilarating!

Track 8

Man: … Right! That's everything. Are we ready to go?

Woman: Jane still hasn't arrived. It's not like her to be so late.

Man: She might have missed the bus.

Woman: I don't think so. She would have phoned to say she'd be late.

Man: She may have forgotten to take her mobile phone with her. You do that all the time!

Woman: Yeah, much to your annoyance! No, Jane's so organised. She wouldn't have forgotten her mobile, and even if she had, she would still be able to use a payphone! No. Something must have happened.

Man: Oh, come on, love. Don't worry so much. There's always a first time for forgetting things, you know. I'm sure it's … There! That'll be her now!

Woman: Hello, Jane, is that you? … Oh, sorry … Yes … Oh no! When? How did it happen? Yes, I'm on my way.

Track 9

Speaker 1: Well, naturally, I was disappointed, but … nothing I could do about it. Just one of those things, I suppose.

Speaker 2: Honestly, you could have told me about it beforehand. Then I wouldn't have gone to all that trouble, not to mention expense!

Speaker 3: Who? James? Well, I wouldn't like to say, really. I mean, I don't know him all that well … Why are you asking?

Speaker 4: Oh, don't let him worry you! He's just a nobody. Don't take any notice of him, dear.

Track 10

Interviewer: … Right! My next guest is someone who I personally admire very much. Tom Masefield has done it all! Whether it be climbing the highest peaks, such as Everest, trekking to the South Pole or kayaking along the coast from Alexandroupolis, on the Greek-Turkish border, to the town of Agria in Central Greece, where he now lives … a mere 505 kilometres … You name it, he's probably done it! Tom, welcome. Tell me, how did all this start?

Tom: Well, Tracy, I started rock climbing ten years ago, near the town where I now live. Agria is at the foot of Pelion mountain, so there are lots of places to climb there. I trained as a PE teacher, and I'm not only a climbing instructor for the town council, but I also teach handball and skiing for them, and watersports such as kayaking and swimming in the summer months. Two summers ago, we took a group of nine teenagers and kayaked down the coast from Alexandroupolis to Agria. That was an amazing experience for all of us.

Interviewer: Wasn't it a little dangerous, being on the open sea in a canoe?

Tom: Well, um, I suppose it was a little risky, but we were all experienced, and the kids did really well.

Interviewer: Did you see any interesting sea life on your voyage?

Tom: We saw lots of dolphins. They liked swimming alongside us, but from a distance. Then one day, the leader thought he saw what looked like a sunken ship floating under the surface, but as we approached for a closer look, we realised it was a huge sea turtle. The guys in front were so surprised by the size of it they nearly overturned! It was an amazing feeling.

Interviewer: So, is the sea your true love?

Tom: I enjoy being on the water, certainly … but climbing is what I

really love. The feeling when you're hanging from a rope, 300 metres from the ground … There's nothing like it. It's the closest we can get to being a bird.

Interviewer: Is it easy being a member of an international team, Tom?

Tom: Not always. At Everest, I was with a Kuwaiti, an American woman, two Belgians and two Japanese. That often caused misunderstandings, obviously, some amusing, some frustrating. But on the whole, we got on well and became good friends. You're in close proximity with each other 24 hours a day, under extreme conditions … There's going to be friction, but also you form strong bonds. Climbing is about teamwork – you have to rely on the next person holding the rope. Every mountaineer understands that, and everyone is working towards a common goal.

Interviewer: Did you experience any difficulties during the climb?

Tom: Well, the worst thing that happened was that two of the team got very bad frostbite, and had to have the ends of two of their fingers chopped off. That meant returning to base camp for a while. But, they recovered and carried on. It's one of the recognised hazards of mountaineering. Experienced climbers accept it as a risk they take.

Interviewer: I wouldn't like to have been in their shoes, though! Now, the trip to Everest was just part of a bigger project, wasn't it?

Tom: Yes. We've just managed to complete the ascent of the 'Seven Summits', as it's known. These are the highest peaks in each continent, including Everest. The last one we attempted, Carstensz Pyramid, Papua New Guinea, proved the most difficult to climb, due to problems beyond our control. We had a struggle to raise enough sponsorship money, but then we had to abandon an attempt because of helicopter failure. The next time we planned to climb it, there was an earthquake shortly before we were due to arrive! However, we succeeded in March of this year, and it was a special achievement for me, as not that many people have ever climbed all seven summits. This time, we had a tough climb in a snowstorm, but when the Belgian climber, Robert Huygh, and I reached the top, it was a moment neither of us will ever forget. The culmination of a lifetime dream …

Interviewer: Very impressive! And I believe you've written a book …

Unit 4 Track 11

Kate: Hi Sally. I wanted to tell you about what happened to me yesterday, but I don't want you to think I'm being a tell tale.

Sally: Tell you what, why don't you tell me about it and I promise I won't kiss and tell.

Kate: I'll try. But I don't want you to say 'I told you so'!

Sally: Well, you never can tell …

Kate: I can't tell you how much it means to me that you're my friend.

Sally: As far as I can tell you're my friend too!

Kate: Yes, but only time will tell!

Track 12

Interlocutor: In the future, do you think it will be essential to know how to use a computer to get a job in your country, Fernando?

Student A: No, I think there will always be a need for people who don't know how to use a computer. Computers cannot do everything – for example, we still need bus drivers, and shop assistants, farmers, erm … craftsmen, and, although technology may help them, it's not an essential aspect of those jobs.

Interlocutor: What do you think, Maria?

Student B: I agree with that point. Er …

Student A: And … erm, I also think that at some point, technology will have given us all it has to offer, and after that, people will be looking for alternatives. I mean, even today, you see that more and more people actually want to cycle to work instead of driving, or go to the gym more instead of watching TV. Technology has taken over our lives so much, we are almost fed up with it. What do you think?

Student B: Yes, er … that sounds like an interesting point. Erm …

Interlocutor: Thank you. That is the end of the test.

Track 13

Speaker 1: Well, I don't know where I'd be without it, to tell the truth. There's just no other way to get around these days, unless you want the stress and pollution brought on by driving in the city centre.

Speaker 2: At first, I hated them. Only the rich and pretentious seemed to have them – do you remember what they were like then? Great big unwieldy things, almost the size of a briefcase. Now of course, they fit in the palm of your hand and I'd be lost without one.

Speaker 3: It's probably the greatest invention of all time because just imagine where we'd be without it. I mean, there wouldn't be vehicles of any kind – except monorails perhaps.

Speaker 4: It's amazing – and great fun too. First time I've actually enjoyed doing the housework. Marjory can get on with her writing and I just zoom round the house with my new toy!

Speaker 5: As far as my family is concerned, it's the best invention there's ever been, because it's really made a difference to our lives. It gives us so many opportunities for research, plus we use it all the time for communication, and the kids can do their homework without having to go to the library. But I know not everyone feels the same way.

Track 14

Speaker 1: Well, I don't know where I'd be without it, to tell the truth. There's just no other way to get around these days, unless you want the stress and pollution brought on by driving in the city. I live out in the suburbs, so it's good exercise. And of course, ecologically speaking, I know I'm doing my bit to save the planet. I'm setting an example for the kids I teach as well, although you do occasionally get one of them shouting out something clever as their teacher goes by. Just because they're stuck on a double-decker bus in rush hour traffic. I know which one I'd rather use.

Speaker 2: At first I hated them. Only the rich and pretentious seemed to have them – do you remember what they were like then? Great big unwieldy things, almost the size of a briefcase. Now of course, they fit in the palm of your hand and I'd be lost without one. I have to spend so much of my day visiting sites, negotiating with clients, co-ordinating workers and then back to the office to go over designs, or tweak a plan. I use it to check the time, do quick calculations, store reminders. And then of course wherever I am, Harry or the kids can find me if they need to tell me something or to find out what time I'll be home for dinner. In the old days they would just have had to leave messages all over the place.

Speaker 3: It's probably the greatest invention of all time because just imagine where we'd be without it. I mean, there wouldn't be vehicles of any kind – except monorails perhaps. Boats would be OK, but planes wouldn't be able to take off. We'd all be riding horses – good for the environment, maybe, but not very convenient these days. In fact, it's quite obvious that we'd still be stuck in the dark ages if some bright spark hadn't come up with it. I know most people would probably say the most important invention was television, or the computer, or something, but I don't think we would even have them if this hadn't come first.

Speaker 4: It's amazing – and great fun too. First time I've actually enjoyed doing the housework. Marjory can get on with her writing and I just zoom round the house with my new toy. Compared to our old one, this has loads of advantages. For one thing, you don't have to carry a heavy load around the house with you; secondly, there are no bags to change – you just empty the bin every now and then; thirdly, it doesn't smell out the house because the actual engine is down in the basement; and fourthly, it's quieter too. There are several outlets in the house that automatically switch on when you plug in, but the hose is nine metres long anyway, so it reaches every corner.

Speaker 5: As far as my family is concerned, it's the best invention there's ever been, because it's really made a difference to our lives. It gives us so many opportunities for research, plus we use it all the time for communication, and the kids can do their homework without having to go to the library. It provides entertainment as well as knowledge, and they enjoy it too. It keeps them off the streets, off the TV and I think they learn a lot. OK, granted, there is a downside, because you don't always know how accurate the information is, and some people seem to get a kick from being abusive, but we try to teach the children how to deal with all that.

Unit 5 Track 15

… The three main types of forensic DNA testing, then, are all extremely useful, but each has its own limitations. The first type, RFLP testing, requires large amounts of DNA from a recent sample. Therefore, old evidence from a crime scene is quite unlikely to be suitable for RFLP testing. Furthermore, warm and moist conditions usually cause DNA to become degraded quicker, so samples from crime scenes near water are unsuitable. The second type, STR testing, can be used on smaller amounts of DNA, but is still subject to the same limitations as the first type.

The third type, PCR-based testing, has certain advantages over the other two, in that it requires smaller amounts of DNA, and the sample may be partially degraded. However, it still has limitations which must not be ignored. PCR testing can easily become contaminated, both at the crime scene and in the lab. This can affect the test results, particularly if lab regulations are not strict.

Track 16

Personally, I see the idea of a national DNA database with everyone's DNA on record as a necessary evil. Yes, it has its risks, and there would need to be strict legislation to protect people, but if it were universal, surely it would eliminate the possibility of suspects being picked out at will.

More importantly, the risk of almost certain detection would act as a powerful deterrent to first-time offenders, and so reduce the risk of innocent people becoming the victims of a violent crime.

Track 17

Since the mid-1980s, when Sir Alec Jeffreys first discovered that every human being has his or her own unique genetic make-up, DNA profiling has replaced fingerprinting as the chief forensic tool in criminal investigations. Technological advances enable new techniques for testing DNA to be developed all the time, and forensic scientists are now able to solve cases from years ago. The recent conviction of John Lloyd, who attacked a number of women between 1983 and 1986, is a case in point.

As a result of all the media attention, the discipline has come to be seen as glamorous, with forensic scientists now occupying centre stage in TV detective series, rather than detective inspectors. Many people assume that DNA testing provides unquestionable proof of a person's guilt or innocence, leaving no room for error. Yet the controversy now surrounding the case of Barry George, convicted in 2001 for the murder of TV presenter Jill Dando, brings to light a number of problems with this idealistic point of view. One of the jurors expressed doubt about the conviction, and gained support from several forensic experts who believe the forensic evidence presented in the case should be regarded as 'unreliable' and therefore inconclusive. And this is not the only example where forensic evidence has led specialists to the wrong conclusion.

Don't get me wrong, I'm not trying to suggest that DNA profiling has no place in criminal investigations! But what we need to clarify from the outset is not simply the merits of DNA profiling – and they are indeed many – but also its limitations. We must dispense with the idealised, glamorous view presented on TV, and rather examine in an objective manner exactly what DNA testing can and cannot do. The processes involved in DNA testing are complex.

The most effective DNA testing procedure to date is STR analysis. It has a greater ability to distinguish differences than the earlier type of testing, RFLP analysis, yet can be used on a smaller sample. This method analyses a DNA sample in greater detail, so there is less chance of two individuals giving the same results. STR analysis is now used together with the 'polymerase chain reaction', or PCR, as it is commonly known, a process which enables DNA contained in a degraded sample to be analysed. The present technology allows scientists to find DNA matches with odds estimated at 1 in 37 million, but this does not mean that it is not possible for individuals to have similar matches.

For this reason, strict rules must be maintained within the laboratory, and while technology has enhanced the level of accuracy, it is not perfect, nor should we rule out the possibility of human error during the process. Forensic scientists are often under pressure to produce results quickly, and this can lead to errors in judgement.

Track 18

Interlocutor: Hello. My name is Jill Simpson, and this is my colleague, Helen Jones. And your names are …?

Juan: Juan.

Beret: Beret.

Interlocutor: OK. First of all, we'd like to know something about you. Where are you from, Juan?

Juan: Spain.

Interlocutor: And you, Beret?

Beret: I'm from a small village on the edge of the Norwegian fjords.

Interlocutor: And what are you doing here in England, Beret?

Beret: I'm studying Accountancy at the London School of Economics, and generally having a good time!

Interlocutor: And you, Juan?

Juan: Er, I'm working, and trying to improve my English.

Interlocutor: So, how important is sport and exercise to you, Juan?

Juan: I play football every Saturday, and I train twice a week.

Interlocutor: And how about you, Beret? Is sport and exercise important to you?

Beret: Oh yes, very important. I think we all need to do some form of exercise to stay healthy. Personally, I do aerobics at a gym three times

a week, and also I cycle to my lessons every day … I wear, um a … how do you say, scarf over my nose and mouth, to stop breathing the smoke from the cars.
Interlocutor: If you had the opportunity to take up a new activity, what would you like to do … er, Beret?
Beret: Well, there are lots of things I'd like to do if I had more time … and money, of course! … But, I think I'd really love to go horse-riding. I love horses, and I like being out in the fresh air. It's difficult here in London, though, and very expensive.
Interlocutor: Yes, indeed. How about you, Juan? What would you choose to do?
Juan: Er … Can you repeat the question, please?
Interlocutor: What new activity would you like to do, if you had the chance?
Juan: I'd like to play water polo.
Interlocutor: That's interesting. Why?
Juan: Er … because I like swimming.
Interlocutor: … OK. Now, in this next part of the test, I'm going to show you …

Track 19

Now, I think we'd all agree that prevention is better than cure, particularly in the case of fire. So, it is vital to establish a fire safety plan in your school. Teaching staff must be instructed on what to do in case of fire. Fire alarms and fire exits must be clearly marked, and all teachers should be aware of their location. Teachers must know where the nearest fire exit is at all times, and must be able to evacuate students efficiently. Therefore, it is advisable to hold regular fire drills for the whole school, so that students can also be made aware of procedures.
In case a fire does break out, teachers should always sound the alarm at the first sign of smoke or flames. Even if it turns out to be nothing, you will have ensured the safety of everyone in the building. Instruct your students to leave the room in an orderly fashion, and move towards the nearest fire exit. If you are able to, use the nearest fire extinguisher to put out the fire. If you are unable to control the fire, leave immediately, and close all doors behind you, to prevent smoke from spreading. Once outside the building, teachers must check that all students are accounted for. Students must stay in their classroom groups, to avoid confusion.
Teachers should learn how to use the fire extinguishers in the school, and all equipment should be checked regularly by the local fire department. Doorways and fire exits must be clearly marked, and kept clear at all times. This last point is most important. Now, I'd just like to demonstrate how …

Unit 6   Track 20

Speaker 1: Well, my old man was always going to the doctor for this, that or the other reason, but never for any life-threatening cause. Whatever the doctor said was gospel. No questions asked. Didn't have a clue what he was putting into his system, poor man. If the doc said it was the thing to take, you can bet he believed it. Sometimes it worked, but more often than not the problem just got worse. I've read up quite a bit about conventional medicine since then and discovered that prescription meds, more often than not, just tend to treat the symptoms, never the root cause. 'Course, that's what made me interested in holistic medicine and the like, right.
Speaker 2: We live in an age where synthetic compounds surround us on a daily basis, from the solvents in our woodwork, to the ingredients in our shampoo. I read somewhere that we are exposed to over 70,000 different chemicals every single day. Did you know the same ingredients in our toothpaste can be found in car engine oil? Some of these have of course been classified as carcinogens, so it's hardly surprising that the more domestic products we use in the home, the more we see an increase in cancer rates. If you're worried about your health there are alternatives to chlorines and bleaches. In pre-industrial eras, our grandmothers used vinegar and lemon juice, salt and bicarbonate of soda to clean the house! You can do the same.
Speaker 3: I first started doing it about three years ago when I heard about how it can reduce stress and therefore decrease heart rate and blood pressure. I also read about how, in some cases, simple visualisation exercises have caused the regression of cancer. It is said to boost the immune system and is often used in hospitals with patients who are terminally ill. The medical community tends to agree that if mental factors such as stress are significantly reduced, a person's physical health would be much better. There's a growing movement in mainstream science to fund research into this kind of exercise. Personally, I do it because I find it so relaxing on both my mind and

body, and because it keeps me fit and healthy. I don't need any equipment, just a quiet room or a spot in the garden where no one will disturb me.

Track 21

1
Man: I found a box of abandoned kittens by the side of the road the other day.
Woman: Oh no! That's terrible! What did you do?
Man: Well, I took them to the cat rescue centre of course. They were a bit hungry but basically OK.
Woman: Well that was good of you. Anyone worth their salt would have tried to give them a chance. But what heartless person could have left them there in the first place?
2
Young woman: Did Sally tell you that she's been having a hard time at work?
Older woman: No, why? What's been happening?
Young woman: She's been putting in all this overtime and is just fed up of being taken for granted. Everyone expects her to run around for them all the time.
Older woman: Why doesn't she complain to her supervisor?
Young woman: She'd never do that. She's the next in line for promotion so she knows which side her bread is buttered!
Older woman: Yeah, I suppose you're right.
3
Man: Emily got into trouble at school yesterday.
Woman: No! You're joking? Whatever for?
Man: Well apparently she was accused of breaking a window.
Woman: No! I don't believe it. What did she say?
Man: She denied it of course and I think the headmaster believed her story.
Woman: Well of course he did. How could anyone suspect Emily of lying? She looks as if butter wouldn't melt in her mouth! And it's true. It wouldn't.
4
Woman: Hello Bob! How's business?
Man: Not so bad. Pretty good in fact.
Woman: Really? That's fabulous. I always knew you'd make a good salesman.
Man: It's not me – it's the book. Everyone just wants a copy. The first 1,000 sold like hotcakes. I'm already half way through the second shipment. How about you? Why don't I try and interest you in …
Woman: Oh no you don't! I certainly don't need any more books, thank you!

Track 22

Raw foods, such as fresh fruit and vegetables, nuts and seeds, are foods which contain enzymes, the living energy of plants. Enzymes are of vital importance to our health because without them we would get sick and many of our bodily systems wouldn't be able to function properly. We need enzymes to digest our food, to strengthen our immune systems, to flush out toxins and to regenerate our cells. In fact, clinical tests have shown that enzyme-rich diets can even help people suffering from some serious illnesses.

Track 23

Interviewer: Today we are in the studio with Dr Maureen Cunningham whose latest book, *Raw Power*, has raised a few eyebrows. Dr Cunningham, your book advocates that a diet rich in raw fruit and vegetables is the healthiest diet of all. Can you tell us a little bit more about it?
Maureen: Raw foods, such as fresh fruit and vegetables, nuts and seeds, are foods which contain enzymes, the living energy of plants. Enzymes are of vital importance to our health because without them we would get sick and many of our bodily systems wouldn't be able to function properly. We need enzymes to digest our food, to strengthen our immune systems, to flush out toxins and to regenerate our cells. In fact, clinical tests have shown that enzyme-rich diets can even help people suffering from some serious illnesses.
Interviewer: I think most people are aware that fresh fruit and vegetables are good for us. But in your book you mention that eating too much cooked food can actually be bad for us and this has caused some strong reactions. Can you tell us why you advocate reducing our intake of cooked food?
Maureen: I'm certainly not suggesting that anyone should suddenly switch to a strictly raw food diet, but most of us do rely far too heavily

on cooked meals to fulfil most of our nutritional requirements, which it simply can't do because cooking destroys so many of the nutrients. Obviously, if we're always eating cooked food, then we can't be eating enough raw plant food.

Interviewer: In your book, you cite a famous experiment involving about 900 cats I think.

Maureen: Yes, that's right. Half of the cats, which were studied over four generations, were fed a diet of raw meat (which is of course the natural diet of cats), while the other half were fed cooked, processed meat (tinned cat food). Within only one generation this second group had started to develop a variety of pathological problems, similar to the health problems that so often afflict even humans today. The second generation of cats suffered even more and with each subsequent generation, the problems increased so that by the fourth generation the cats were displaying all kinds of problems. Conversely the majority of cats in the first group lived healthy long lives in each generation, with very few of them developing serious illnesses.

Interviewer: But surely humans are not cats – and our bodies react differently to cooked foods?

Maureen: Yes, but we all need enzymes to digest our food, which unfortunately suffer complete and total destruction by cooking. This means we have to draw on our own limited reserve of enzymes, which puts enormous strain on our bodies. Similarly, as most people are aware, much of the vitamin content of foods is destroyed by cooking. But that's not all; a great deal of protein is damaged or destroyed when we cook our food, so that it becomes either completely useless or worse still, toxic to us.

Interviewer: Well, how are we supposed to get enough protein then?

Maureen: Well – fortunately most raw foods contain protein in easily digestible form. All nuts and beans are rich in protein, and in fact the richest source of protein is found in sprouted seeds and beans.

Interviewer: So does that mean that we don't need to worry about eating two square, home-cooked meals every day, as long as we eat a salad or some fruit?

Maureen: Well, basically, I would recommend eating plenty of raw food salads and vegetables with every meal. Further evidence is showing that the majority of our health problems are related to an ineffective immune system that has been weakened by a bad diet: too much junk food, not enough raw plant food. In fact, it is has been shown that the body's response to cooked food is to suddenly increase the number of white blood cells in our blood, something that usually happens when our bodies are attacked by alien invaders. By mixing our cooked food with at least 50% raw, we can reverse this reaction and keep our immune system on standby for when it's needed.

Interviewer: So your advice to anyone who hates boiled carrots, as I do, would be …?

Maureen: That's simple. Eat them raw!

Unit 7   Track 24

Well, I think you're going to see airship hotels. You know, like cruise ships, but in the air. That's likely to be big business, because it'll be affordable for most people. Space hotels are a possibility, but they'll be pricey, so accessible only to the few. What's really taking off are eco-friendly holidays, as people are becoming more concerned about how they affect the environment. They're going to be really big, I reckon. Another thing in the offing is your holiday down under. Hydropolis is being designed for an area off the coast of Dubai, an underwater paradise, but again, this is not going to do your bank balance a lot of good. Also, we shouldn't forget that you're still going to get the traditionalist tourist who wants to see the world as it is at ground level, who still yearns to walk the streets of cities of old. You know what I mean. What I can't see happening is this so-called virtual tourism being popular. I mean, you like travel because you want to leave home for a while. That's the whole point, isn't it? I don't think computers will ever be able to really capture that feeling of excitement you get as you climb on board a plane or a ship to go somewhere new, do you?

Track 25

Nick: …You know, I think of all the places we've been to, Edinburgh was my favourite.

Fiona: Really? It's certainly one of my favourites, but compared to Prague, and Amsterdam … I don't really think I've got one particular favourite.

Nick: No? Well, for me, Edinburgh's got it all. Amazing architecture, culture, great shops and this warm, friendly air about it.

Fiona: I have to agree with you on that point. You feel safe walking about. Perhaps because it's a small city, and everything's easy to get

to. Personally though, I found the architecture rather intimidating. All those tall, stark buildings and dark stone. You can really believe all the ghost stories that come out of Scotland!

Nick: That's exactly what's so amazing about it! The setting and buildings make you feel you've walked onto a Charles Dickens film set, with their medieval and Georgian facades. Then, you walk inside, and you're hit with vibrant colours and the innovative designs of modern life.

Fiona: Umm … I think what I liked about the place most were the coffee shops and art cafés. As you say, they were colourful, but I was struck by the friendliness of the people. Did you notice how chatty everyone was? And the laughter … I seem to remember lots of animated conversation and laughter. Fantastic!

Nick: Yes, they were very helpful, too, weren't they? And I remember the aroma of fresh coffee and bread in the shops, while outside, the crisp sea breeze left a faint taste of salt in my mouth.

Fiona: Yes … Definitely worth a return visit, possibly around Festival time …

Track 26

Speaker 1: I've been fascinated by the universe and our place in it for as long as I can remember! As a property developer I built up a real empire here in sunny California, all the time keeping a close eye on developments in the space programme. The current race to create spaceflights for tourists is particularly exciting, but no sooner had NASA announced plans for a space station than I decided I had to have a piece of that pie. Space tourism is just moments away, so why not be the first to build an orbiting space hotel? Wild, huh!? We're almost there, though!

Speaker 2: To be honest, studying the space science modules in my physics course here at university has put me right off the idea of going into orbit in a spacecraft in this day and age. Not only are there risks involved in launching, but there's also the danger of space debris … surely that's more than enough to make me feel just fine looking at the stars with my feet placed firmly on the ground!

Speaker 3: Astronaut passengers will come to the spaceport three days prior to their flight for pre-flight training. This is to prepare them mentally and physically for the spaceflight experience, and enable astronauts to become acquainted with the spacecraft and their fellow passengers. As we speak, doctors and spaceflight specialists are developing the training programme, which will include g-force training.

Speaker 4: Space tourism, I ask you! No sooner do they make it to the moon than they start talking about commercialising space travel! Has anybody really stopped to consider the effects this is going to have on the environment? Not only on Earth, but in space, too! I recently interviewed an astro-environmentalist for an article I was writing, who stressed the need to avoid making the same mistakes in space as we have on Earth. What I want to know is, does anybody in authority really care about these issues, or are the potential profits to be made from commercial space travel too great?'

Speaker 5: It's been my dream since I was small, really. I used to look up at the night sky and think about what it must be like to be up there, among the stars … And the money? Well, I know it's a lot, and I've heard all the ethical arguments about what better use it could be put to, and I agree with them all, but I think it'll be worth it. I've worked hard all my life, and it's my money! Rarely do people of my generation get the chance to fulfil such a dream. At my age, don't I have the right to have this once-in-a-lifetime experience?

Unit 8   Track 27

Here are seven great reasons why you should consider building your next house with straw bales.

Reason number one: Energy efficiency. A well-built straw bale home can save you up to 75% on heating and cooling costs. In fact, in most climates, we do not even install air conditioning units into our homes as the natural cooling cycles of the planets are enough to keep the house cool all summer long.

Reason number two: Sound proofing. Straw bale walls provide excellent sound insulation and are superior wall systems for home owners looking to block out the sounds of traffic or aircraft in urban environments.

Reason number three: Fire resistance. Straw bale homes have roughly three times the fire resistance of conventional homes. Thick, dense bales mean limited oxygen which, in turn, means no flames.

Reason number four: Environmental responsibility. Building with straw helps the planet in many ways. For example, straw is a waste product that is either burned or composted in standing water. By using the straw instead of eliminating it, we reduce either air pollution or water consumption, both of which impact the environment in general.

Reason number five: Natural materials. The use of straw as insulation means that the usual, standard insulation materials are removed from the home. Standard fibreglass insulation has formaldehyde in it, which is known to cause cancer. Bale walls also eliminate the use of plywood in the walls. Plywood contains unhealthy glues that can off-gas into the house over time.

Reason number six: Aesthetics. There is nothing as calming and beautiful as a straw bale wall in a home. Time and time again I walk people through homes and they are immediately struck by the beauty and the 'feeling' of the walls. I really can't explain this one, you'll just have to walk through your own to see what I mean.

Reason number seven: Minimise wood consumption. If built as a 'load bearing assembly', which can support a roof, the wood in the walls can be completely eliminated, except for around the windows. The harvesting of forests is a global concern and any reduction in the use of wood material is a good thing for the long-term health of the planet.

Track 28

Interviewer: So what interests you most about your work?
Man: Well, being able to create something that has real value is the main thing. I mean, it's great to be an artist or a sculptor and I'm certainly not belittling the value of fine art in society, but it's a totally different feeling knowing that what you create will have real practical value. I mean, people actually live in your creations! And of course, egotistically speaking, it's a chance to make a real mark on the landscape, something that can probably be seen for miles around.
Interviewer: Sometimes that's not such a good thing though. There are some undeniable monstrosities in the landscape which somebody must have thought was beautiful.
Man: Well, that's the second reason I love my work. My philosophy is to design structures that blend into the landscape, using natural materials and organic shapes. My clients come to me for that reason. I am confident that no one would call any of my designs an eye-sore and that gives me a real feeling of satisfaction.

Track 29

Extract 1
Interviewer: So what interests you most about your work?
Man: Well, being able to create something that has real value is the main thing. I mean, it's great to be an artist or a sculptor and I'm certainly not belittling the value of fine art in society, but it's a totally different feeling knowing that what you create will have real practical value. I mean, people actually live in your creations! And of course, egotistically speaking, it's a chance to make a real mark on the landscape, something that can probably be seen for miles around.
Interviewer: Sometimes that's not such a good thing though. There are some undeniable monstrosities in the landscape which somebody must have thought was beautiful.
Man: Well, that's the second reason I love my work. My philosophy is to design structures that blend into the landscape, using natural materials and organic shapes. My clients come to me for that reason. I am confident that no one would call any of my designs an eye-sore and that gives me a real feeling of satisfaction.

Extract 2
Woman 1: When I first saw it I didn't realise quite how important it would turn out to be, although my first thought was that I was probably looking at something very old indeed.
Woman 2: It must have been very exciting.
Woman 1: I suppose it was, but I didn't know then that it would be a turning point for the project, and for me. I mean, the dig had been turning up very little, and our sponsors were threatening to pull our funds, so it was significant in more ways than one.
Woman 2: When did you realise the significance of the find itself?
Woman 1: Well, more or less at once. I called over Professor Hargreaves, and we carefully brushed out the piece in order to define it more clearly. It appeared to be man-made, but of course we couldn't date it until we submitted it for radio carbon testing, but from the level of the dig, we knew we must have been looking at something pre-Egyptian, possibly 10,000 years old.

Extract 3
Interviewer: So it was ambition that drove you, from an early age?
Angel: Yeah, I suppose you could say that. I knew I wanted to be famous when I was little. I used to tell all my parents' friends and say: 'I'm gonna be dead famous one day!'

Interviewer: And what did they say?
Angel: Well they laughed mostly. They thought I was being cute but that just made me more and more determined, see, so that's all I thought about all through school. I wrote my own songs and got a band together, even though my teachers kept telling me I'd never achieve anything the way I was going.
Interviewer: And do you think that your fame will last? Are you more concerned about being the flavour of the month, or creating a legacy in music that has your name on it?
Angel: Well, I've since realised that being famous isn't all roses. I mean, I love the media attention, and the money ain't bad either, but there comes a point where you think 'OK, that's enough for today, can you leave me alone now!' and they don't. It just keeps going on and then you start to cherish your privacy and you put dark glasses and hats on and try to achieve anonymity like you had before – well, some of the time anyway.
Interviewer: It must be a tough life!

Track 30

Between 1200 and 1600 AD, the people of Easter Island built and erected around 400 enormous statues, or 'moai' as they are called, and another 400 were left unfinished in the quarries where they were made. Up to ten metres tall and weighing up to 75 tonnes, the enigmatic statues raise a host of questions – not least, why did the islanders build them, how did they move them and why were so many left unfinished? One theory is that different groups competed against each other, striving to build the most impressive moai.

Some researchers have suggested that this 'moai mania' was a disaster for the society. Yet others point to mounting evidence that prehistoric occupants made a success of life on the island and state that there is in fact painfully little archaeological evidence for the fundamental claims that underpin the self-destruction theory.

When the Dutch explorer Jacob Roggeveen 'discovered' the island on Easter day in 1722, he was stunned at the sight of monumental stone statues lined along the coast. He could see few trees, and he wondered how this apparently small, primitive society had transported and erected such monoliths without timber or ropes. Later on, pollen and soil analysis revealed that the island had once been home to flourishing palm forests with an estimated 16 million trees. Deforestation seems to have begun as soon as the settlers arrived around 1200, and was complete by about 1500. The reason why the islanders wiped out their forest has long nagged at researchers and is still open to dispute. Some palms may indeed have been cut down to assist in moving the statues, though, with their very soft interiors they would not have been ideal for the job. Other trees were used for firewood, and land was cleared for agriculture. Still, the blame for the disappearance of the palms might not rest entirely with people. Recent genetic research suggests rats, which love to eat palm nuts, were introduced to the island in the canoes of the original colonisers. Most of the evidence for starvation and cannibalism comes from oral histories, which are extremely contradictory and unreliable. Some researchers suspect that stories of cannibalism, in particular, could have been invented by missionaries. Very few of the remains of prehistoric islanders show any signs of personal violence. True, the 17th and 18th centuries saw an increase in artefacts identified by some as spearheads, but many believe the artefacts are agricultural implements.

The story of ecocide may usefully confirm our darkest fears about humanity but, for every society that self-destructs, there is another that does the right thing. It is far from clear that the Easter Islanders made their situation much worse for themselves, but only more evidence will resolve the issue.

Unit 9 Track 31

Joe: Will ya look at this? The amount of work that's gone into it! It's amazing!
Clare: Ummm … But seriously, Joe, would you really want that hanging on your wall?
Joe: Yeah, why not? So, OK, it's bulky, but it's powerful, and I love the symbolic effect of all those lyrics scrawled across the glass background. Set within the boat like that, it creates the effect of a window on the world as you travel on your voyage through life.
Clare: Wow, Joe! That's a bit deep for you! Personally, I find the colours rather garish for my tastes.
Joe: Well, ya see, Clare, I think they're meant to be. I mean, it's boat paint … No, I really like it!

Track 32

Interviewer: Now, Kapodistrias's kind of art is rather unusual, isn't it, so can you start by giving us a brief description of what he does?

George: He does a lot of different things, really, because he loves experimenting with materials, and he's certainly innovative. He isn't just interested in the look of something, but in how it feels to the touch, if you know what I mean. So I suppose his work is a combination of three-dimensional painting and sculpture. He's been influenced by the work of Kostas Tsoklis, a popular Greek 3D artist, who he admires a great deal.

Interviewer: Would you say Tsoklis was the reason Kapodistrias became interested in producing his own work?

George: Tsoklis certainly influenced the direction in which his art developed. But in fact he's always had an interest. His father painted for a hobby, too – landscapes, mainly – and Kapodistrias talks about how as a boy, he went out on painting trips with his father, and sometimes he drew, as well. Then, at university, it was photography that intrigued him for a while, and he gradually moved on to painting watercolours, and then using acrylic. It was some time after his university days that he grew interested in working in three dimensions.

Interviewer: What materials does he use?

George: At first, he used cardboard, and then plaster. Here his professional work helped. As a dentist, he uses plaster, glues and materials for making dentures, wire for braces, and so on. So it seemed natural to experiment with such materials to develop his hobby. Now he's keen on polystyrene and fibreglass for their strength and durability. And because fibreglass is used in boat building, there's a link with a major theme in his art – the sea. He loves boats, and they appear in a number of his works.

Interviewer: Isn't polystyrene a rather difficult substance to work with?

George: Yes, and not very healthy, either! But it's versatile, and easy to mix with other materials to create different textures. Kapodistrias has an interesting approach to his work. He hasn't followed any art courses, and claims not to know much about particular techniques. He just, as he puts it, follows his heart in a painting. When he's creating a new piece, he feels he participates in it, but the materials gradually take on a life of their own, and seem to mould themselves. He finds that exciting – and many people would say the same about his work.

Interviewer: He's produced a lot of work, yet he hasn't held an exhibition yet. Is there any particular reason?

George: What Kapodistrias has said is that the symbolism in his work is increasingly reflective, and in a sense quite private. For instance, many of his backgrounds contain the lyrics from songs or poems that have a special meaning for him, one that isn't apparent to anyone looking at the painting. On top of that, he doesn't see himself in a professional light, and has never sold anything. It's hard to put a price on a work, since he spends months on each one. He's also rather shy of publicity.

Interviewer: And finally, George, what do you think of Kapodistrias's work?

George: He's not regarded as a major modern artist, admittedly, but I would stick my neck out and argue that he's underrated. His best work is expressive without spelling everything out. It encourages viewers to use their imagination. I find I can gaze at one of his works for a long time, and go into a reverie. I may not feel I understand the painting, but it certainly evokes ideas and feelings.

Interviewer: George Buckingham, thank you very much for coming to talk to us today.

George: Thank you.

Track 33

1a: I don't know where she finds the time to do all those activities.
b: Where she finds the time to do all those activities, I don't know.
2a: Although this exercise may seem boring, it is useful.
b: Boring though this exercise may seem, it is useful.
3a: You need a complete break from the office.
b: What you need is a complete break from the office.
4a: They are creating unnecessary waste.
b: What they are doing is creating unnecessary waste.
5a: Don't get upset. You just need to go and talk to your teacher about the problem.
b: Don't get upset. All you need to do is talk to your teacher about the problem.

Track 34

Vincent Van Gogh cut off his ear after a quarrel with his good friend Gauguin.

Vincent Van Gogh **cut off** his ear after a quarrel with his good friend Gauguin.

Vincent Van Gogh cut off his *ear* after a quarrel with his good friend Gauguin.

Vincent Van Gogh cut off his ear after *a quarrel* with his good friend Gauguin.

Vincent Van Gogh cut off his ear after a quarrel with his good friend *Gauguin*.

Unit 10 Track 35

Speaker 1: Nowadays, everyone's suddenly jumping on the ecological bandwagon and talking about sustainable living. But really, my walking to the shops instead of driving is hardly going to make much difference, is it? I find it easy enough to do, but I suspect all it achieves is to make me feel virtuous. People think concern about the environment is something new, but when I was a child, we used to get told off if we left a light on when we went out of a room, and wearing your elder brother's or sister's handed down clothes to save money was just a fact of life. You didn't expect to have new clothes until you were an adult.

Speaker 2: I suppose most people have one thing that they really try hard with. I can remember my mum and dad being obsessed with water. They saved water from the kitchen for the pot plants, as long as it didn't have detergent in it. They also attached water-butts to the drainpipes around our house, to collect rainwater for the garden. That's had quite a powerful influence on me, because they still seem like natural things to do. I wish I could get the rest of my family to do the same, though – they just laugh at me, and refuse. Yet they're all very concerned about not wasting food. It's illogical, really!

Speaker 3: Where I live, the council can recycle certain materials, but in other districts they do far more. It's really annoying – I've contacted the council a couple of times about it, but they say they haven't got the facilities to recycle anything else. My target is to only buy things in packaging that can be reused, like cardboard, but it isn't easy. And of course we produce so much more waste these days. When I was young, we didn't have much money to spend, so a lot of my clothes were homemade. I remember my mother knitted me itchy pullovers that didn't fit. When they wore thin, they were patched, and patched again. It was pretty embarrassing, I can tell you!

Speaker 4: I travel by train rather than car, whenever possible, and I haven't flown for years. But it's surprising how many other people regard me as eccentric, which makes me feel uncomfortable. So to avoid awkward situations, I don't mention it – I say I don't *like* flying, or I prefer looking out of a train window. I wouldn't try to change people's minds. My concern about the environment came from my parents. I can remember everything organic from the kitchen got composted. It was the only household chore I enjoyed doing, taking potato peelings, egg shells, coffee grounds and so on out to the compost bin in the garden. It made excellent fertiliser for the plants.

Speaker 5: When I was a teenager, I wanted to start buying make-up, but my parents wouldn't let me. As a joke, my father said why didn't I make my own. I decided to take him seriously and rubbed beetroot juice into my lips to make them pink. I was very excited the first time I went out like that, and my friends thought I looked great! I do a lot more for the environment now, like cycling instead of driving a car. But it has an impact on my children. They'd love to go ice skating, but the only way to get to the nearest skating rink is by car, so it's impossible.

Track 36

Dave: We love *Freecycle*. My girlfriend Helen enforces a policy of household recycling as much as possible and it was her idea to join, because we were about to move in together and had a lot of stuff lying around that was doubled up. We've also used the site to help furnish our new flat. We had absolutely no furniture so it was a big challenge for us. But our *Freecycle* group seemed to offer everything we needed, from three-piece suites to the kitchen sink. After bagging some great stuff in the first few weeks, we were completely hooked. We managed to wangle a bathroom cabinet, a set of bookshelves, a laundry basket and loads of kitchen utensils and crockery. Helen seemed to have more success at claiming things than I did – maybe it was the female touch or maybe it was the sheer speed of her email responses, I don't know. I have shifted, among other things, an old chair, some speakers, and Helen's old curling tongs. It is so much more rewarding to have people pick up the goods from you than just putting things in the bin. The pinnacle of our *Freecycle* success has got to be claiming a huge shelving unit and a lovely sofa. Helen then requested a sewing machine, which she used to make a cover for the new sofa. We have been able to put other people's unwanted (but perfectly good) furniture to new use. It has also made the cost of decorating an entire flat far easier to stomach. I am now offering a lot more stuff on the site. I'm well and truly converted, and use it more than Helen! I check the site all the time for new offers – come summer, I'd love a garden table and chairs.

Julia: I found out about *Freecycle* when my colleague posted up loads of our ancient office furniture that would been dumped otherwise. I've been hooked since.

When I drive past the dump, the amount of wonderful stuff I see that's going to waste seems criminal. I'm tempted to give out flyers for *Freecycle* when I go past, to tell people they don't have to throw good things away. There are three main benefits to *Freecycle*. First: people can get things for free. I've got a massive list of things I'm really happy with: shower doors, a sewing machine, a farm gate, a china umbrella stand. I've actually taken more than I've been able to give. Second: people usually post up stuff that they think isn't worth selling, which makes *Freecycle* good for avoiding landfill. Third: people come and collect what you've advertised, so it's very convenient for you. I once offered a broken lawnmower, which somebody snapped up! *Freecycle* in Oxford has quite strict guidelines, because everything on the forum should be stuff that could end up on the dump otherwise. People accept the rules, but they also love the community feel of the group, so in order to avoid clogging up the Freecycle forum, a subgroup has been set up called the Oxford *Freecycle* Café. The café is more chatty and people offer all kinds of things on it, such as wind-fallen apples or spare firewood. It really shows the demand for free community networks.

Anna: My partner and I moved to a smallholding here just over a year ago with the aim of setting up a more sustainable lifestyle. We provide for ourselves by growing produce, raising and eating our own poultry and meat and using our own fuel. We found out about our local *Freecycle* group from an article in our daily newspaper (recycled for composting and firelighting), and its philosophy seemed to go hand-in-hand with our own, so we thought there would be no better way of offloading some of the excess chicks we had at the time. We instantly got involved with this wonderful system of free exchange, and have since taken many items that have been incredibly useful. Since we started out we have found homes for two cockerels, and we took someone's vacuum cleaner which is now in my son's flat, and we have given away some lovely 'eggs for sale' signs written on slate.

One of the great things about *Freecycle* is that you can choose whom to give things to. You are encouraged to give items to charities if they request it, but otherwise choosing a recipient is entirely up to you and no explanations are necessary. In our *Freecycle* group, there are the usual postings for items like sofas, TVs, computers and cots, all of which are extremely useful to members, but there are also postings which probably would not be found in groups in cities; requests to re-house dogs, geese, a sow and her piglets and sheep. These latter items reflect the fact that here *Freecycle* has become a real aid to those of us who value the idea of sustainability while being part of the farming community.

Unit 11 Track 37

As you may know, there's an international classification system for household spending, called the Classification of Individual Consumption by Purpose. If we look at the figures for household expenditure in the UK in 2011, average weekly expenditure was £483.60, a rise of £10 from 2010's £473.60. Total expenditure generally increases from year to year, partly because of inflation and partly because incomes tend to rise. However, the 2009 figure of £455 was in fact lower than in 2008. If we now break down that total into categories, the highest area of spending in 2011 was transport, which accounted for £65.70 a week. Most of that was related to purchasing and running cars and other vehicles, with only £10.20 a week being spent on public transport. Slightly less – £63.90, in fact – was spent on recreation and culture, which was the second largest category. Just under £19 of that was spent on package holidays – mostly holidays abroad – while the remaining £45.10 went on computers, TVs and other leisure activities.

Track 38

The credit card is a 20th century invention, but the concept of credit goes back over 3,000 years. Basically, it means providing somebody with money or goods, and trusting them to repay or return those resources at some later date.

It's sometimes said that before the emergence of money, the earliest farming communities exchanged goods or services in a barter system. It now seems more likely that a form of credit called a 'gift economy' was in operation, where people helped others without receiving anything in exchange. Instead, there was an expectation that if they later needed help, they would get it.

The earliest records of a form of credit date back to around 1300 BC, among the Babylonians and Assyrians of present-day Iraq. And by 1000 BC, the Babylonians had devised a system of credit that simplified payments in trade between distant places. A merchant who bought from one supplier might be asked to pay a third party who had given the supplier credit.

In ancient Egypt, grain functioned as both food and money, and was stored in granaries, whose administration was effectively a government bank. This became a trade credit system, with payments transferred between accounts without money changing hands. Egyptians also sold real estate with payment being made in instalments.

The vast area of the Roman Empire 2,000 years ago, encouraged widespread trading and the use of credit, particularly among traders on the shores of the Mediterranean. Then, as the empire declined, and transferring money became both dangerous and difficult, credit was widely used to get round the problems.

During the Middle Ages, from about 500 to 1500 AD, credit was essential to the trading activities of the prosperous Italian city-states. Lending and borrowing, as well as buying and selling on credit, became commonplace among all social classes, from peasants to nobles.

In a common form of investment and credit, especially in Italy, a capitalist might help to finance a merchant's trading expedition, and share the risk. If the voyage was a success, the creditor recovered his investment plus a large bonus; however, if the ship was lost, the creditor could lose his entire investment.

Trading centres of the Middle Ages held fairs at regular intervals, and here another form of credit developed. A merchant who was short of cash could secure goods on credit by writing a letter promising to pay on a certain date. Before repaying the money, he had time either to sell the goods he'd brought with him, or to take home and sell the goods that he'd purchased on credit.

The first English settlers in North America, in the early 17th century, used credit to finance their voyage. Before they set sail, negotiations to raise the funds they needed lasted for three years. A wealthy London merchant organised a group of investors to finance the trip. Although these investors were supposed to be repaid in seven years, it was 25 years before they received their money in full!

Now I'll go on …

Track 39

Interlocutor: Some people say that having any job is better than no job at all. What do you think?

Fernando: Well, I think it depends on the kind of job we're talking about, and the kind of person you are. A university graduate, for instance, would not want to clean the streets for a living! I mean, he'd expect something better than that!

Katrina: Yes, but if there was no other job available, what then? Would you rather be unemployed?

Fernando: I think I would try to create a job for myself. Now, with the Internet, an imaginative person can find a way to earn a living.

Katrina: I'm afraid I don't agree with you. Perhaps you can do that, but it's not always so easy. For me, I would find it frustrating to be unemployed, so I think I would get a job cleaning rather than not work at all. I hate sitting around doing nothing.

Fernando: I think there are certain jobs I would find it embarrassing to do, so I cannot say the same for me. Also, if you are looking for a specific career, you need to be available for interviews, etc. So, remaining unemployed until you find what you are looking for is not always bad.

Katrina: Maybe, but that becomes a problem when you are out of work for … six months! I think a potential employer will be more impressed by someone who shows a general willingness to work.

Fernando: Yes, but … !

Interlocutor: Thank you. That is the end of the test.

Unit 12 Track 40

a I think it's time Roger retired. Yes, well, *quite!*
b Gillian is *quite* a little troublemaker isn't she!
c I think it's *quite* a good idea to take her advice.
d It's *quite* clear to me that you weren't listening.
e After the accident, he was never *quite* the same.
f I thought the script was *quite* ridiculous.

Track 41

Extract 1

Interviewer: So Richard, tell us about what got you started as an independent filmmaker.

Richard: From an early age I was obsessive about film, about directing and cinematography but it never occurred to me that I could do it myself until one day I picked up my dad's 8mm camera and started recording family life. I used to watch films all the time too. My local video shop had a section of 'unclassifiable' films that didn't belong in any section, and these were all my favourite films. They were totally unique, they made up their own rules and they always left me feeling as if something inside me had changed. These films proved that the medium of film had the power to change someone's perception of the world, and that just made me more determined.

Interviewer: And yet you claim that you don't make 'arty' films.

Richard: While I knew I wanted to work in this genre, I also knew how easy it was for experimental films to turn into pretentious rubbish. I wanted to express my message through film, using abstraction and music, but not some over-the-top art piece. I'm just not interested in art films where I watch ten minutes and know what's going to happen in the next hour.

Extract 2

Woman: I went to see the latest *Narnia* film last night. Have you seen it?

Man: No, I haven't. What was it like?

Woman: It's got great special effects and everything, but you know how sometimes an adaptation brings a book to life, and you think 'this is exactly right'? Well this one couldn't have been more different from my childhood memory of it. I sat there getting more and more annoyed! But that reminded me of why I loved the book in the first place, so as soon as I got home, I went and dug out my old copy and started reading it again.

Man: And did you enjoy it?

Woman: I certainly did.

Man: I just don't think I'll ever be satisfied by an adaptation. I'm sure they're made with the best intentions, but every time I read good reviews and go and see one, I'm disappointed. With books I grew up with, I feel I inhabit them – every character and every scene means something very specific to me, and I don't want the film to interfere with that.

Woman: Mm.

Man: Obviously there's an audience for these films, though, and if they introduce the book to some people who don't know it, that can't be bad.

Woman: Absolutely.

Extract 3

Woman 1: I think it's depressing that women film directors are in such a tiny minority. There are some that *have* done well commercially, like Jane Campion with her film *The Piano*, or Gurinder Chadha's *Bend It Like Beckham*, and Nora Ephron – she had several big successes, like *Sleepless In Seattle*. But, really, how many films can you actually think of that were directed by women? I'm sure that if this imbalance were to occur in any other profession, there'd be a major outcry. Why is it that film-making continues to be the most unbalanced career in the arts?

Woman 2: Well, obviously there are the difficulties of working in a male-dominated industry. Women need role-models – like the two women you just mentioned. And if they're raising children, they may not be able to make the most of the opportunities that present themselves. And there's no easy solution to that. But the truth is that, whether you're male or female, it's really hard to make films. Creativity is stifled because film-makers have to spend far too much time fundraising. And women are not generally used to asking for money – it seems to come more easily to men.

Track 42

Speaker 1: Well it's about a pirate, Jack Sparrow, played by Johnny Depp, who used to be captain of a ship called The Black Pearl, but now that ship's been commandeered by a zombie pirate called Captain Barbosa. He has been cursed with living death until he can find the living heir of old 'Bootstrap' Bill Turner, who is actually played by Orlando Bloom and, to that end he has kidnapped the beautiful Elizabeth Swann …

Speaker 2: It's an animated film about an ogre who lives in a swamp. Coming home one day he finds that all these fairytale characters have moved in, which he is not very happy about, to say the least. Accompanied by a talking donkey that irritates him greatly, he sets off on a fairytale adventure of his own, and comes face-to-face with dragons, princesses and even happy endings …

Speaker 3: It's a musical actually, and it's about two brothers, Jake and Elwood, who are on a mission from God to save a convent orphanage from closure. In order to legitimately raise the money they need, they have to put their old blues band back together, no mean feat in itself, despite the fact that the police and all their old enemies are all in hot pursuit. What I love is the wonderful performances by John Lee Hooker, James Brown, Aretha Franklin, Ray Charles, to name but a few …

Speaker 4: The film is based on an actual historical event of course, but the main story is a romance, told in flashback by the old woman, Rose, remembering Jack, whom she met on board the ship for the first time. He is a penniless artist who won his ticket to America in a game of cards; she is an attractive young lady engaged to marry a wealthy aristocrat to pay off her family's debts …

Speaker 5: I love this film – even though it's quite spooky really. I think the actor who plays the scared little boy with psychic abilities is excellent, and Bruce Willis is great as the failed child psychologist who wants to make sure he gets it right second time around. You really need to see it twice because only then do you really appreciate all the details leading to the final twist.

Unit 13   Track 43

Interlocutor: Now, I'd like you to talk about something together for about two minutes. Here are some different methods of advertising a product or service. Talk to each other about how effective these different methods might be for advertising a new language school.

Carlos: Yes … Well, I think the billboard is a very effective way of advertising, as it can be seen by everyone in the area. Also, people are not so angry at seeing billboards, whereas they get annoyed when people push leaflets under their door. Do you agree, Magda?

Magda: Yes, you're right. They don't like leaflets … erm … not at all …

Carlos: Er … I know I usually throw leaflets away without looking at them! But I think it depends on what product you want to advertise. Leaflets might be a good idea for a new language school, because you can include information on courses, and photos of the classrooms and facilities in the school … and a bold advert in the local newspaper is a good idea, as most people read the newspaper, and so they will see it. But I still think the billboard is the best idea, don't you?

Magda: Yes, I agree with you. It will be seen by the largest number of people, and so will be most effective … erm … That's all.

Track 44

Speaker 1: Communication seems to be absolutely non-stop these days. You can even receive emails and text messages in the middle of the night. But though the quantity is increasing, quality seems to be going downhill. At least we were more careful when we used a pen or typewriter for letters, because changing anything could look a mess, so they were much more accurate. It was while I was discussing this with a friend that we came up with the idea of setting up a training firm. We know there's a demand for training in all types of communication skills, so potentially it could be very profitable. And we've both got a lot of relevant experience.

Speaker 2: What I find fascinating is how delicate a tool language is. You can express tiny nuances of meaning through the choice of words, or, in speech, your intonation, or by putting in a pause. It's such a pleasure to listen to someone who has really good communication skills – some stand-up comics, for example, and one or two people I've heard giving presentations. I've decided to develop this interest of mine further by writing a series of children's books. This will involve quite a lot of work. First, I'll enrol on a creative writing course, and improve what I've already produced, and during the course I intend to contact several publishers, to find out how best to get my work published.

Speaker 3: The organisation I belong to monitors the press, TV and radio, and our aim is to challenge anything that we consider harmful to children. And believe me, there's a great deal that worries us, particularly some of the things that are shown as acceptable behaviour for children. We want to make journalists think carefully about the potential effects of what they write on young readers. Now, we're all volunteers, so our work is unpaid. However, we have numerous expenses, not least of which is the cost of postage on letters. So I'm here today to ask for your financial assistance. Even a small contribution from each of you would be greatly appreciated, and will be put to good use.

Speaker 4: We've had a lot of feedback from the public pointing out mistakes in the information sheets and leaflets we produce. Most of them contain grammatical mistakes or spelling errors, or don't make the meaning clear. And there's really no excuse. It harms the image of the whole organisation, and anyway, what's the point of having information sheets that aren't fit for purpose? So could each of you try to set aside some time to look through the materials you've produced yourself, and classify them as being fine as they are, needing some quick and easy improvement, or requiring a major rewrite? It would certainly help us to improve our materials.

Speaker 5: We have quite a few communication difficulties at work, with clashes between people that can get out of control. One of the other managers, Stephen, is very good at handling that sort of thing. When it happens, he chats to each person individually, to find out how they see what's going on, and usually he can defuse the situation before it gets too serious. And I try to learn from him. So I really don't think there's any need to worry about Stephen's style of management. He always encourages people to make up their own mind, and to play an active role in the running of the department. I think that's far more effective than giving orders to everyone.

Unit 14   Track 45

The earliest multi-celled animals might have been sponges, which although they look like plants are actually animals. They most likely appeared around 700 million years ago. Invertebrates, which are the first animals that could get around, such as flatworms and jellyfish, are believed to have evolved around 570 million years ago. And then, about 500 million years ago, vertebrates, the group which includes fish and other animals with a backbone, suddenly appeared.

About 470 million years ago, the first plants began to grow out of the water, and this is when life on land established itself. Insects originally appeared on land about 380 million years ago and were followed, relatively soon after that, by the first amphibians, which surfaced from the water to become land animals approximately 350 million years ago. Essentially, they were fish that evolved lungs to breathe air. They employed their fins to crawl from one pond to another and these gradually became legs. The next group to emerge, about 300 million years ago, were the reptiles.

For the next 50 million years, life on Earth prospered – but about 250 million years ago, the Earth experienced a period of mass extinction, which meant that many species disappeared. Around this time, one group of reptiles, called 'dinosaurs', started to dominate all others. Their name means 'terrible lizard'. They were the commonest vertebrates and they controlled the Earth for the next 150 million years.

Throughout this time, a new type of animal began to evolve. These animals were the mammals. They gave birth to live young, which they nourished with milk from their bodies, and they first appeared about 200 million years ago.

The closest living family to the dinosaurs is believed to be birds. The first known bird, Archaeopteryx, appeared about 150 million years ago. It existed for around 70 million years before becoming extinct, and was replaced by the group which includes modern birds, believed to have appeared around 60 million years ago, at the same time that the dinosaurs became extinct.

The group of mammals to which humans belong – the primates – emerged from an ancestral group of animals that ate mainly insects, around 50 million years ago. But it wasn't until about three million years ago – about the time the last ice age started – that intelligent apes, with the ability to walk on their back legs, appeared in southern Africa. Simultaneously, their brains evolved and they learnt to make and use tools. Although called *Homo habilis*, meaning 'handy man', these creatures were more like apes than men. About two million years ago, *Homo habilis* evolved into the first people called *Homo erectus*. Their bodies were like ours, but their faces were still ape-like. They evolved in Africa and spread as far as South-East Asia. Modern people (*Homo sapiens*) appear to have evolved in Africa about 100,000 years ago (although the date is far from certain).

Track 46

We all take for granted the air we breathe and the oxygen essential for our survival. But the Earth's atmosphere didn't always contain oxygen! In fact, for most of its history there wasn't really any oxygen in the air at all! It's only been during the last 600 million years that there's been enough to support life, which, as it happens, is how long there has been life on land. The amount of oxygen in the atmosphere has swung wildly between tiny amounts – as little as 12% compared to today's 21% – to huge proportions – up to 30% during one particular period. This variation has of course had a massive impact on the animals living on Earth at any particular time. Animals have either taken advantage of

the sudden increases in oxygen in order to evolve and colonise the land, or they have faced being made extinct during the periods when oxygen was scarce.

Palaeontologists have always had an interest in the occurrences that may have caused species to become extinct. The leading causes have been identified as meteors, ice ages, climate change, and so on, but fascinatingly enough, it's now clear that each mass extinction on Earth coincided with times of reduced oxygen. These periods have usually been followed by bursts of much higher oxygen levels, which again have coincided with a time of incredibly fast evolution in animal species. In most cases it appears that the most successful animals to inhabit the land during these times were those that developed more advanced respiratory systems. For example, invertebrates appeared on land for the first time around 420 million years ago – at a time when oxygen levels were higher than today's. Yet soon after that, approximately 400 million years ago, oxygen levels suddenly fell dramatically and most of these animals disappeared: either becoming extinct or returning to the ocean. Oxygen levels didn't increase again for another 50 million years or so, during which time only a small number of animals could survive on land. Then, 350 million years ago, oxygen levels started to rise, reaching their highest ever levels around 280 to 300 million years ago. This is when reptiles appeared, and they thrived in this rich atmosphere, but as oxygen levels started to fall once more over the next 50 million years, animals had to make some swift adjustments, or they suffocated for lack of air.

The animals that adjusted most efficiently were the dinosaurs. What they did was to add another pair of air sacs next to the lungs. This enabled them to extract even greater amounts of oxygen from the thinning air. Because of this evolutionary adaptation, it appears that they were the only animals that managed to do well during the mass extinction of 200 million years ago, the time with the lowest recorded oxygen levels. We can still see these air-sac adaptations in their descendants today – the birds – and it's actually this which then allows some birds to fly at altitudes with little oxygen.

Track 47

Interlocutor: Now, I'd like you to talk about something together for about two minutes. Here are some of the ecological issues that need attention. First, you have some time to look at the task. Now, talk to each other about how serious each of these issues is.

Elisabeth: OK … well, at first glance I would say that deforestation is probably the most important ecological issue. What do you think?

Giovanni: Yes, I agree. It's terrible that they're cutting down the rainforests so fast. These forests are important because they're the home to so many species of animals and plants. If they're all cut down, it'll cause lots of problems.

Elisabeth: Yes, and the forests also affect the weather and the Earth's temperature, I think, don't they? However, we shouldn't ignore the issue of pollution. That's another very serious issue.

Giovanni: Yes, you're quite right. Pollution is dangerous for our health and it's also dangerous to wildlife. Some species may disappear for ever because their habitats have been destroyed by pollution. On the other hand, the extinction of species is a very serious issue. I've read that if we don't do something now, over half the Earth's species could be extinct in the next hundred years.

Elisabeth: Yes, and that's a frightening idea! […]

Interlocutor: Thank you. Now you have about a minute to decide which is the most serious issue.

Elisabeth: I don't know about you, Giovanni, but taking everything into consideration, it seems to me that climate change is the most urgent issue.

Giovanni: Why do you think that?

Elisabeth: Well, if the world's temperature rises by even a couple of degrees, it'll almost certainly have a catastrophic effect on nearly everything. For example, if the Greenland ice cap melts, sea level will rise, causing flooding in lots of places around the world.

Giovanni: That's true, and of course that would destroy a lot of habitats, possibly resulting in the loss of species living there. Yes, I would agree with you.

Interlocutor: Thank you. Can I have the booklet, please?

Unit 15   Track 48

Interviewer: Today we're here to discuss the subject of kissing and its origins. With me in the studio are two anthropologists: Professor Rosemary O'Bryan and Dr Andrew Peters. Professor O'Bryan, is kissing learnt or instinctive behaviour?

Rosemary: Affectionate kissing is a learnt behaviour that most probably originated from a mother gently touching or nibbling her child's body with her lips, to cement the bond between them, or it may have arisen from premasticating food to make it easier for her child to swallow. From there it developed into a way of showing affection towards family members, close friends or other members of society and as a sign of respect to older, senior group members.

Interviewer: And yet, according to some anthropologists, kissing is an echo of an ancient form of communication that was necessary for the healthy and successful continuation of the species. Dr Peters.

Andrew: Yes, kissing in humans is an instinctive behaviour which most likely evolved from grooming behaviour common in mammals. However, recent research has indicated that this kind of behaviour had a much more serious biological function than just social bonding. Kissing, or rubbing noses, actually allows prospective mates to smell or taste each other's pheromones …

Interviewer: You mean the chemicals which give off information about our biological make-up?

Andrew: Correct, and thus we get more information about our biological compatibility. Women are more attracted to men who are more genetically compatible to them, and a woman picks this up by breathing in his pheromones. Any resulting offspring will have better resistance to a greater number of diseases, and will consequently have a better chance of survival. That's why we still like to kiss – to maximise our chances of sampling each other's aroma.

Interviewer: So that's why couples are more likely to bond if they have the right 'chemistry'.

Andrew: Yes, and it's not just a mating tool. Chimpanzees, for instance, use it for reconciliation, by kissing and embracing after fights, providing good evidence that kissing in the higher primates has the function of repairing social relationships.

Interviewer: So when did the romantic act of kissing one's sweetheart on the mouth as a form of affection actually develop?

Rosemary: Well, not until comparatively late in the evolution of love in fact. In antiquity, kissing – especially on the eyes or cheek – was mainly a form of greeting, but there's no evidence of it being romantic. One of the earliest descriptions of kissing as a form of love and affection comes from the sixth century, in France. Around that time it seems to have become fashionable for a young man to give his betrothed a kiss on the lips as a seal of his affection.

Interviewer: But the rest of the world did not practise kissing as a sign of affection?

Rosemary: In the years before cinema the lovers' kiss was largely a western habit – unknown in other parts of the world. By the the end of the Second World War, western motion pictures had carried the image of romantic couples engaged in a kiss to many other parts of the world. Until quite recently, it was only in North America and Europe that kissing was an important aspect of courtship, which puts paid to the notion that kissing must be instinctive in all people. For instance, the Chinese and the Japanese never kissed on the lips.

Andrew: Yes, but in other cultures affection was expressed in a number of ways – for instance, in Samoa, lovers would express affection by sniffing the air beside each other's cheek; in Polynesia affection was shown by rubbing noses together. The same goes for Eskimos and Laplanders, as with many animals who smell each other or rub noses to smell each other's pheromones. This indicates that it's still instinctive …

Rosemary: It's hardly the same thing …

Andrew: What about monkeys? Bonobos? They'll kiss each other on the lips for just about any excuse at all. They do it to make up after fights, to comfort each other, to develop social bonds, and sometimes for no clear reason at all – just like us.

Track 49

Speaker 1: I was born in Britain, and my family came to Japan when my father was transferred here 15 years ago – he works for an engineering company that's a Japanese-British joint venture. I was only five at the time, and my memories of Britain have faded – it's almost as though I've never been there. Originally my father planned to stay here for three years, but the whole family liked living here so much, we stayed. There are people from lots of different countries in Tokyo, where we live, and that's great. I have plenty of friends, both Japanese and other foreigners, so I feel I fit in pretty well, even though I don't speak perfect Japanese.

Speaker 2: My parents are Greek Cypriots, and moved to Britain before I was born, so I grew up there. We used to go to Cyprus on holiday every year to see the relations, and I've always been just as comfortable here as in Britain – both places are special to me. For events like my grandmother's 80th birthday, all my 35 cousins were here – most had

flown in from other countries for the celebrations. I can understand why not everyone would want to have so many cousins and aunts and uncles, but I love it! In fact, that's one reason I came to live in Cyprus after university. Now I spend my holidays in Britain, to see my friends there.

Speaker 3: I grew up in a tiny community in Britain where you had to behave in certain ways, and believe certain things, and if you didn't, there was no place for you. Well, I couldn't stand it, and by the age of 18, I was desperate to get away – the further the better. I didn't want to study or work anywhere in Britain. I spent a year travelling round the world, and ended up in Thailand. And at last I'm beginning to find out what sort of person is the real me, and to realise that I can be that person just as easily in Britain as in Thailand. So maybe one day I'll go back to Britain – but not yet.

Speaker 4: It's quite difficult to say how British I am, because although the language within my family is English, I've spent all my life in Germany: my parents settled here before I was born. So, I'm bilingual. I've been to the UK on holiday, of course, with my parents. They intend to move back when they give up work, but I'll probably stay in Germany and just go over on holiday. I expect I'll settle down with a German wife, and if we have a family, this will be their home. Britain will be somewhere that we visit from time to time, because of my parents, but it won't be any more than that.

Speaker 5: When I finished my French and business degree in Britain, I wanted to do an MBA at a French business school. I applied, and was accepted, but at the last minute, both my parents fell ill, and I stayed at home to look after them. They eventually recovered, but by then I didn't feel like becoming a student again, though I still fancied using my French. So I came to France as a sales rep for a British food exporter. I thought my French was quite good, but living here soon showed me how wrong I was. I'm trying very hard to improve. After all, you can't really become part of the culture if it's a struggle to communicate.

Unit 16   Track 50

James: Here you are, Sally. I've finished it.

Sally: Hmm? Oh, *The Last Will*! Thanks, James. What did you think of it? Great, wasn't it?

James: Actually, I found it rather disappointing in comparison with his other books. Not so believable, if you know what I mean.

Sally: Really? I find that hard to believe. I thought it was by far his best ever! Far superior to *Waiting to Die* and *A Just Cause*, for instance.

James: I feel just the opposite. Compared to his first novel, the plot in this one is far-fetched and unrealistic, to say the least.

Sally: You're joking! For a start, we see a lot more courtroom drama in this book, which is lacking from his others. They tend to focus purely on lawyers playing detective, which is not always very convincing.

James: It keeps things interesting, though, wouldn't you say?

Sally: Perhaps. But you have to admit that the courtroom drama in this novel lends weight to it, makes it even more believable.

James: Well, admittedly, the courtroom scenes are the most exciting in the book, quite gripping in places in fact, but the rest of the book is often slow and boring. I mean, all that description during the search in South Africa – I practically fell asleep!

Sally: But the protagonist is significantly more rounded and better developed here, wouldn't you say? The way we are led through his drug-induced self-pity to his struggle to redeem himself is cleverly created.

James: It was exactly this that I found just too good to be true! Our hero goes from being a total waster to becoming a knight in shining armour, against a background of support characters who are singularly wooden in their weakness and selfishness. They're nowhere near as realistic as the cast in *A Just Cause*, where good and bad qualities are more evenly shared out.

Sally: Funny! I didn't feel that way at all when I read it, and I thought you'd like it more than that. A pity …

Track 51

Extract 1

Man: For a while, it felt like we were on a second honeymoon. But then the quiet started getting to us.

Woman: Well, I won't say I don't miss Mike, but frankly I was glad when he went to university. It was as if the house was no longer big enough for the two of us. We both like our independence, and I think the pressure was getting us both down.

Man: But don't you feel lonely in the house?

Woman: Well, that's just it. I like having the house to myself, but I can see Mike when we both feel like it. And it's good for him to know that I'm not waiting by the phone for his every call. That puts a lot of pressure on any child.

Man: Too right! Jan gets frantic if more than three days go by without a phone call from one of the boys, and I know that bugs Davy, in particular! I try to tell her to relax about it, that 'no news is good news', and all that.

Woman: Mmm, at their age, it can be restrictive to have to account for their movements all the time. They don't want to be thinking about us right now, but about enjoying themselves as much as possible.

Track 52

Extract 1

Man: For a while, it felt like we were on a second honeymoon. But then the quiet started getting to us.

Woman: Well, I won't say I don't miss Mike, but frankly I was glad when he went to university. It was as if the house was no longer big enough for the two of us. We both like our independence, and I think the pressure was getting us both down.

Man: But don't you feel lonely in the house?

Woman: Well, that's just it. I like having the house to myself, but I can see Mike when we both feel like it. And it's good for him to know that I'm not waiting by the phone for his every call. That puts a lot of pressure on any child.

Man: Too right! Jan gets frantic if more than three days go by without a phone call from one of the boys, and I know that bugs Davy, in particular! I try to tell her to relax about it, that 'no news is good news', and all that.

Woman: Mmm, at their age, it can be restrictive to have to account for their movements all the time. They don't want to be thinking about us right now, but about enjoying themselves as much as possible.

Extract 2

Interviewer: So, how did you feel when you first retired?

Man: Guilty, basically.

Interviewer: Guilty? About what?

Man: The fact that I wasn't going to work. As the weeks went by, I became bored and irritable. The change was hard on my wife as well, because I started making demands on her time. I'd expected to do more things together, while she thought that she would go on as before, meeting up with her friends for coffee, going on shopping sprees, all without me. That was difficult for both of us. I had to find my own interests, and she had to make some room for me.

Interviewer: So how do you feel now?

Man: Well, I wonder how I ever had the time to go to work! I find I'm busy nearly all the time now. I think the secret to enjoying your retirement is firstly, health, and then having enough money to do the things you really want to do. Those two elements prevent you from being a burden on your children. Having a good circle of friends has helped. We see the kids when we can, of course, but we're not under their feet, and they're not under ours, either! So, life's fairly good now.

Extract 3

Woman: My decision to start my own business was all about money. I was stuck in a poorly paid job, with virtually no prospects. I saw an opportunity and grabbed it. However, I knew I'd need some kind of routine to my working day, and that there'd be too many distractions at home! Difficult to ignore the pile of washing up in the sink, and the ironing waiting by the ironing board! So, I opened an office, and I think that was the key to making it work – keeping work and home separate.

Man: Yes, I can see that. Working at home just didn't work for me. I also found it stressful having to rely on myself for all the decision-making. Sometimes, I wanted to share ideas with someone, to get some feedback before putting things into operation, and there was no one. That began to get to me. Now, I'm back in an office, with other people around me, and I feel part of the team again.

Woman: That's it, though I've never really been a team player, so as I said, that isn't my reason for the way I work. I like the independence of making my own decisions. I won't say it always works, though!

Videoscripts

Unit 1 Profiles in exploration

Alexandra Cousteau: So there's nothing I would rather be than a National Geographic explorer and I'll tell you why. Coming from a family of explorers and growing up travelling all over the world, I learned to dive with my grandfather when I was seven years old, I got to go snorkelling in tide pools, I've gone swimming with dolphins and diving with whales and I've made films about sharks in Tahiti. And all of these things are … it's like Christmas every day.

There's nothing more exciting than being able to go out, and seeing a wild place or a wild creature or a new kind of culture, or food. The smell of every new place is always a revelation and you learn so much and you're free; you're free to explore anything you want and to talk about anything you want, with anybody – because that's your job. Your job is to explore the unknown and to bring those stories back and share them with your friends and your family and people who are excited and inspired by what you do.

Johan Reinhard: I'm probably best known for having discovered the Ice Maiden. This is on a mountain summit of about over 20,000 feet high. An Inca child had been sacrificed, but later we returned and found several more mummies. And then, eventually, on some other mountains, including up to 22,000 feet on the Argentine border, we found three perfectly preserved Inca mummies.

Probably the things that most excited me for discoveries weren't so much the mummies per se, but what they told us about the past because they were so well preserved. The point that I realised just how important the discovery of the Ice Maiden was, was the moment I saw her face. I realised then that it was indeed a mummy because we weren't a 100% sure what was inside this kind of a dusty covered bundle, an ice-covered bundle. And my companion Miguel Zárate turned it on its side to get a better grip on it to try and lift it up, and all of a sudden we saw this face of this Inca mummy staring at us.

But, in a way, it was tinged with disappointment because the face had dried, and the real moment came when we tried to lift the mummy and realised that it weighed nearly 100 pounds. And that meant that the body itself was frozen, so even though the face had been exposed and dried out, the rest of the body probably was frozen. And what that means is that, we're not only going to get all the textiles and all the other things in, in context, (this is the key thing for archaeology) but we're also going to be able to get DNA studies, and I knew that she was … a she.

Dr Sylvia Earle: The best part of my job is that you never know what you're going to find. It's the joy of … of discovery. It's finding, not just new things but new ideas, to begin to connect the dots. When you spend a lot of time actually in the ocean, as I do, after a while you begin to see things that you might have missed the first time. But, over a period of hours, days, weeks, years, you really begin to understand something about how systems work. You get to see the behaviour of fish, it's not just a fish that swims by, but a fish that has a life, and trying to understand how they spend their days and nights, how long it takes for them to grow.

I think the best part is, just the excitement of … discovery. It's something anybody can do, everybody should do. To look around, see the natural world, and try to understand not only how it works, but where do we fit in to the systems that keep us alive.

Unit 3 Frozen search and rescue

Narrator: The unforgiving weather and terrain means time is running out to find a man who has been lost on the mountain overnight.

State trooper (ST)1: OK, let's go find this guy now.

Narrator: In the air, Helo 1 scours the terrain for any signs of Dave. But with no leads, the possibilities of where he could be are endless.

ST 1: Did John give you guys a pretty good idea of where he might be?

Rescue Base: He has no idea whatsoever.

Narrator: To make matters worse, Dave's tracks could be covered by last night's snow storm, making it impossible to track him.

Rescue Base: He said the wind was covering up the tracks as fast as they'd made 'em.

Narrator: From the air, they can easily mistake the trees and rocks for a human, or, just as easily, overlook him entirely.

ST 1: There's a few dark spots up there.

ST 2: Got 'em.

ST 1: They're just some rocks sticking out.

ST 2: Yeah, pretty small.

Narrator: Then, Helo 1 spots a set of faded tracks. But they lead up the crest of the mountain. If Dave went over the edge, it would mean a fall to almost certain death.

ST 1: If he got turned around he could easily have dropped down in there.

ST 2: They wouldn't have wanted to drop down into any of this.

ST 1: What's that to the left there?

ST 2: I think that's his snow-machine right there.

ST 1: Rescue Base to Helo 1. Helo 1, come in. We've located a second snow-machine at the following co-ordinates. – North 6, 1 …

Narrator: Dave has seemingly abandoned his snow-machine. But spotting footprints from the air will be nearly impossible. Now, rescuers hope he hasn't strayed too far.

ST 1: Subject is on foot, but not with machine.

Rescue Base: So confirming, you saw the machine, but not the subject, over?

ST 1: That's affirmative.

ST 2: Nothing out there?

ST 1: No, I don't see anything out there.

ST 1: What's that out there?

ST 2: Got one dark spot over to the left there, see it? Right here.

ST 1: There he is, there he is.

ST 2: Rescue Base, Helo 1. We have the subject in sight.

Rescue Base: Is subject vertical and moving?

ST 1: That's affirmative.

Rescue Base: Team 3, Base, do you copy?

Team 3 leader: Go for Team 3.

Rescue Base: Do you copy the Helo is going to be picking up our subject?

Team 3: Roger, Roger.

ST 1: Rescue Base, we're landing at this time.

Rescue Base: Roger.

ST 2: Dave? Dave? Dave, how you doing?

Dave: Tired.

ST 1: You doing OK?

Dave: Any word from John?

ST 1: Yeah, we've got him down at the …

ST 2: He's back at the truck.

Dave: I tracked him for, last night, picked up his trail this morning; it came to the point I had to get the hell out of here.

ST 2: Yeah, you guys were kind of chasing each other round from the looks of the tracks.

Dave: You couldn't see anything.

ST 2: I understand. Yeah, it was a white-out last night. How you doing?

Dave: Well, last night wasn't no party.

ST 1 and ST 2: Yeah.

Dave: It was blowing so hard.

ST 1 and ST 2: OK, yeah.

Dave: I was up on that ridge; did you see where I camped?

ST 2: I didn't see where you camped but we were looking.

Dave: I couldn't get off that ridge. You get on the edge and it was just – phew!

ST 2: OK this is it, we'll get you out of here.

Dave: We tried coming out, couldn't see five feet in front of you going up the hill.

Dave: Well, that wasn't no party last night, that's for sure. Wind blowing like … man it was cold. It was cold.

Narrator: Dave is finally on his way home. If not for the Alaska state troopers and volunteers, he may not have made it off this Talkeetna mountain top alive.

Unit 5   The world in a station

Narrator: There are seven billion people around the globe, from many different backgrounds. But we're more similar and more connected than you might think. Who were our ancestors? Where do we come from? And how did we get here? In April 2005, National Geographic and IBM worked together on a joint project to find out.

Spencer Wells: I wanted to draw people together, to make people realise that we're all part of an extended family and that our DNA connects all of us.

Narrator: National Geographic and IBM wanted to conduct a study to show that, as a human species, we're all part of one big family and that our DNA connects all of us. So they started the Genographic Project. The goal was to trace our human DNA back tens of thousands of years to our first ancestors in East Africa.

National Geographic and IBM are working with hundreds of thousands of people around the world and gathering DNA samples, so they can learn about our human history. They need to create the world's largest database of DNA. To do this, they have to get samples from hundreds of thousands of people around the world.

There's no better place to show that we're all connected than here at Grand Central station, a huge train station in the middle of New York city. Here, you can find people from all over the world.

Wells: My name is Spencer Wells.

Dee Dee: Hello, Spencer.

Wells: I work with National Geographic. I direct a project for them called the Genographic Project.

Frank: Yeah?

Wells: And we're using DNA as a tool to study how people all over the world are related to each other. Would you be interested in maybe giving us a sample and becoming a part of it?

Cecile: Oh definitely, yes, I'd love to contribute my DNA.

J.W.: Absolutely.

Wells: Maybe getting yourself tested?

J.W.: 100%

Wells: What do you think you might find out? What is your family history?

Cecile: Well, I have a lot of questions because my last name is not common in the country where I was born.

Frank: We have Aztec Indian in ours. Because my basic heritage is Mexican as far as I'm concerned, but we traced it back to Spain.

Wells: Fascinating. So you'd be interested in maybe getting yourself tested?

Narrator: Wells explains that the test is very simple. People swab the inside of their cheek to get some DNA cells. Then, they send the cells to a lab anonymously. The lab analyses the DNA and puts the results on a website in a few weeks.

Wells: Well let's get you started swabbing.

Dee Dee: Don't look at any of my fillings!

Narrator: Wells explains that the DNA research shows all people are related. Humans all started out in Africa about 50,000 years ago. They only started separating and moving to other parts of the world about 2,000 generations ago.

Wells: What do you know about your family history?

J.W.: I know a lot of my relatives. Some of them look as you do and then I have, like, for example, my mother's father was very dark.

Wells: We all started off in Africa around 50,000 years ago. So you are African, I'm African.

Dee Dee: So, like, you and I are related?

Wells: We could be related. How do you feel about that?

Dee Dee: Oh, fantastic! I can't wait for my Christmas present!

Narrator: In just a few weeks, Cecile, J. W., Frank and Dee Dee will get the results of their DNA tests and learn about the mysteries of their past. So far, the Genographic Project has collected over 200,000 samples. Dr Ajay Royyuru is Computational Director at IBM. He is helping analyse the results.

Dr Ajay Royyuru: This is our first chance in the history of human civilisation to look within and learn something that actually was not knowable before.

Narrator: Analysing this DNA helps us understand how we're all connected. Like our four participants from Grand Central station. They are about to learn about their distant past.
Dee Dee lives near Minneapolis, Minnesota.

Dee Dee: Oh hi Spencer the scientist, from National Geographic!

Wells: Hi Dee Dee. How's it going? It's good to see you again!

Dee Dee: Nice to see you. Great! How are you?

Wells: You start off in Africa …

Narrator: Wells explain that Dee Dee's ancestors, like all other humans, started out in Africa. Around 45,000 years ago, a small group of her ancestors left Africa. They moved north to the Middle East. It was very cold and dangerous.

Wells: Suddenly you're living in this icy wasteland with things like that walking around, and you've got to figure out a way to kill them to make a living and survive.

Dee Dee: Mmm.

Wells: What would you have done?

Dee Dee: Well, I would have killed him. No, I would've found a guy to do it for me. Yeah!

Narrator: Frank lives in Southern California. He discovers that his ancient relatives were the first humans in the Americas. He might really have Aztec ancestors.

Frank: It's quite interesting. Up to the last 15–20,000 years, our ancestors were extremely adaptable, who survived by hunting large mammals. It kind of makes me understand why I feel I'm such a survivor. Because I am, I can create, you know, things out of nothing. I've always been that way.

Narrator: Cecile Nepal's results show that her ancestors were some of the first humans to live in South-East Asia. Now Cecile lives and works in New York city. But she still feels connected to her Philippine roots.

Cecile: There's something that we still have, that we carry on. And it's something to be proud about.

Narrator: J. W. is a police officer in New York City. He lives there with his wife and son. His DNA results show that he has Puerto Rican, Spanish and ancient African ancestors. But that isn't all. J.W. finds that some of his early ancestors were probably the first farmers.

J.W.: Coming from grandparents who were farmers themselves, I kind of see the relation there so, pretty interesting.

Wells: Everybody that we met at Grand Central that day ultimately traces back to an ancestor in Africa.

J.W.: I feel connected because we all have one common place of origin. East Africa.

Wells: The cool thing that comes out of this research is obviously that we're all connected to each other and that we scattered to the wind, if you will, to populate the world over the last 60,000 years.

Unit 7   Our ATM is a goat

Lemarti: After a long flight from Africa, we wanted to get out and stretch our legs. And Rene said, 'I'll show you around my village'.
Rene: Follow my lead, follow my lead.
Lemarti: Yes, boss!
Lemarti: Village? This is not what I call a village.
Rene: Check it out.
Lemarti: Some people are living on top of that?
Rene: Yeah, the apartment bit on top. That's the second floor, third floor, fourth floor. So we live on top of each other.
Lemarti: Because there's no place to live, or what? Why do people go up there?
Rene: There's no land so you have to live on top of each other. So you keep building and building and building, up, up, up, up.
Lemarti: One very important thing we need to do first. If you want to walk on the street, you must have dollar.
Rene: Here we go guys, ATM. This is where I get my money. Voilà.
Boni: What's voilà? Have you taken someone else's money?
Rene: There you go. I'm not taking it, this is my money.
Boni: So you always put your money in here?
Rene: It's from my bank account.
Boni: […] and get your money here?
Rene: Yes.
Boni: Why do you put your money here?
Lemarti: Where Boni and I come from, we trade things to get money. Our ATM it's a goat. We take the goat to the market, we sell it, we get money from it. No dollars coming from the wall. I think dollars talk in America very much, you know. You have no dollar, you have no voice.
Rene: Yeah, I wish I could fully explain it to you, but I can't.
Boni: That was easy money, easy!
Lemarti: What's this place, Rene?
Rene: This is Washington Square Park.
Lemarti: We're walking to the park. It's a lot of people sitting around, eating, drinking, chilling. You know, people eat a lot here. People graze like cows man, you know. Non-stop; every corner you go, you see somebody sitting down, eating. Rene said 'Hey, let's grab something to eat, guys'.
Rene: Alright, so we're going to order a hot dog.
Boni: What kind of a dog's that ... that they sell?
Rene: Hot dogs!
Boni: Beef?
Seller: Yes.
Rene: Can we have one hot dog please, with mustard and ketchup on it.
Boni: You can't even tell if this is meat or what.
Lemarti: Rene, what's inside this hot dog? What's that, inside the hot dog?
Rene: It's a smushed up cow.
Lemarti: Boni just like, to the hot dog and says 'Oh yeah'. I'm going to take one home to show people what Boni ate.
Boni: Are you sure any of this is a cow? Is that New York style?
Rene: That's New York style. Let's hear you ...

Unit 9   Aboriginal rock art

Narrator: Far in the Australian outback, in the Arnhem Land Plateau, ancient ceremonial sites offer an unprecedented glimpse into the fascinating culture of the Aborigines. Lost for generations, these sites were only recently found.
Wade Davis: So are there like dozens and dozens of sites out through here?
Adam McPhee: There are hundreds of sites, most of which they still haven't discovered.
Narrator: The ceremonial sites are home to rock paintings older than the pyramids. They are tens of thousands of years old, from before the last ice age. Adam McPhee, a local anthropologist, is our guide.
Adam McPhee: Talking about art that possibly goes back 40,000 years or more, probably some of the oldest art in the world. And the world doesn't know about it, that's the other thing.
Narrator: Aborigines settled in Australia about 55,000 years ago. Their ceremonies were performed here for millennia, all the way up to the 20th century. This was, in essence, a living museum.
Adam McPhee: This is an example of what I mean by a master artist. You can only imagine the detail that's missing here but this is very, very fine work. Very, very fine indeed.

Narrator: The drawings depict images of the Dreaming, a time when the world as we know it was created. Its rivers and mountains, human beings and the social order.
Adam McPhee: Come up here and have a look. There's a baby hanging on the breast here. Here are the feet, travel up the legs, the head.
Narrator: One of the most important stories of the Dreaming is that of the Rainbow Serpent, the creator of everything we see.
Wade Davis: What is the story of the Rainbow Serpent?
Margaret Catherine: It's really special, the Rainbow, and it stays underneath the water. It's their spirit that looks after the river and the country. If I die, my spirit will be there.
Narrator: These mythical stories are passed down, from generation to generation. And the drawings have no meaning without them. Together they create a link to the ancestors. And they are all part of the land.
Margaret Catherine: I feel really, really good when I come back to the land because I can always feel the presence of my great-great-grandfather. And he's there.
Narrator: Sadly there are fewer and fewer tribal elders like Margaret Catherine who speak the languages and know the ancient stories. For the aborigines, to tell the story of The Dreaming is to create the world anew. When the stories die, so do we.
Margaret Catherine: Don't forget your culture and live on with it forever in your heart and mind.

Unit 11   Rainy day flea market

Natalia: I have no idea how we're going to sell all this stuff and make our goal.
Natalia's mother: But we have time. It's so cold now.
Natalia: Hello.
Jimmy: How's it going?
Natalia: I'm cold.
Natalia's mother: Tired.
Natalia: Getting tired.
Jimmy: Where's the chairs?
Natalia: The chairs?
Jimmy: Yeah, the ch ...
Natalia: I decided to keep them at home.
Jimmy: Oh, I mean, I knew you weren't going to sell them but, you didn't even want to bring them?
Natalia: No, no.
Jimmy: OK.
Natalia: I … yeah, I wasn't ready to let them go.
Jimmy: I told Natalia to bring the folding chairs, the big brass ones. You know, even if she didn't want to sell them, they bring people into the booth. You know, they see it, they're drawn to it, they come in, you sell them something else. She should've brought the chairs; she should've listened. Big mistake.
Natalia: First it was really, really cold and now, in the last five minutes, it's starting to rain badly and I can see people are leaving. I feel pretty bad. So far, we've just made money for my mom to take a cab to the airport and back. We'll see, I guess it's just my luck.
Jill: I could not care less about the rain because people are still coming here in droves.
Jill's friend: Jill, I think, is doing a lot better since we started early this morning. There were a couple of missteps, I think, when she was just so eager to make a sale, and Jimmy's really kind of helped her figure out, you know, how to get more for what she's trying to sell. And so, so far we're doing really good.
Male buyer: Do you know who this is? That's Fred Packer. He did Mavis advertisements in 1920 and *Ladies Home Journals*.
Jill: Oh, OK.
Male buyer: He did women similar to this.
Jill: As you can see, it's in excellent condition.
Male buyer: Yeah, I can see what it is, yeah. How much are you asking?
Jill: It's authentic, it's in the original frame and it's in great condition, which is why I'm asking $100.
Male buyer: OK.
Jill: Please, take a look. Yeah.
Male buyer: Yeah. No problem. I have the larger print, the one that's 15 x 30. So I'm looking for the medium. OK, I'll do it.
Jill: Fabulous! Fantastic, thank you. OK.
Male buyer: Thank you. I like Fred Packer, I like the deco. I have the large print and I was always looking for the medium one. So, now I've found the medium one. It's the hunt. I can say that's what I like the best. Once you find it, move on to something else.
Jill's friend: High five!
Jill: This is great.
Jimmy: So Jill learned another valuable lesson and that is, she's

learning to keep her mouth shut, she's letting the buyers do the talking. Sometimes it's best to let somebody educate you. Even if they buy it or not, you'll learn more about it than you knew when you brought it.
Jill: It is raining money. Like, like raindrops from heaven! As is my money! Love it! Yes!

Unit 13 The Braille Hubble

Narrator: From the endless reaches of space, images that delight the eye are admired in a most unlikely place – the Colorado School for the Deaf and Blind.
Female student 1: Are these stars?
Narrator: Where students have the universe at their fingertips.
Nimer Jaber: I've got Jupiter.
Male student 1: That one shows the arms of the galaxy.
Male student 2: Let's see, I see those moons and I see, like, those stars.
Narrator: Images taken by the Hubble Space Telescope have found their way into a classroom for students with different levels of vision loss. These are the critics who were chosen to review a new book that displays some of the most spectacular space images ever produced.
Male student 1: Now it says red for sulphur, green for hydrogen and blue for oxygen. Yeah. But the problem with that is, I can't tell the different coloured gases, these lines are all the same.
Narrator: The book is called *Touch the Universe: A NASA Braille Book of Astronomy*. Each photo comes with a transparent plastic sheet overlay, covered with raised dots and ridges, giving visually impaired readers a feel for the limitless reaches of space.
Nimer Jaber: I've always wondered about space. You know, what it feels like, you know, how big it really was.
Noreen Grice: I mean, you can't just reach out and touch the stars, nobody can. But we can bring it to people's fingertips, we can bring images that people might have only imagined. And we can bring it close to them so people can understand what these objects are in the universe and I think better understand their place within the universe.
Narrator: When asked to feel test prototypes of the book, the students were happy just to be involved. Then they realised that their opinions would shape the way the book was presented to people who were blind around the world.
Ben Wentworth: Then they started tearing the images up.
Narrator: Part of the problem with early versions of the plastic overlays is that they had touch-points for everything in the photograph. Fingers got lost in the galaxy of dots and ridges. Later versions of the book provided more room to manoeuvre.
Nimer Jaber: It has great pictures. I can, you know, you could feel them better; you could, you know what their shapes are.
Narrator: Revisions were duly noted.
Noreen Grice: Alright, I can make that change in the plate.
Male student 1: Yeah, that's all the really suggestions I have.
Noreen Grice: OK.
Narrator: Exactly what these students see in their mind's eye remains a mystery for sighted people.
Female student 1: This one reminds me of onion rings.
Narrator: Still, it's clear that with each raised ridge and dot, an image of space that makes sense reveals itself.

Female student 2: That's pretty cool.
Ben Wentworth: To get the kids to say 'Oh, that's what you're seeing', and I ... think that's what's so unique about the Hubble book.
Narrator: The images provided by the Hubble Space Telescope continue to astonish and amaze, and provide a window on the wonders of space, no matter how you see them.

Unit 15 The Hadzabe tribe

Narrator: *Homo sapiens* have been around for about 200,000 years and our various languages and cultures have been evolving for just as long. But our links to the past are becoming more and more fragile. Anthropologists estimate that 50% of human languages will disappear by the end of this century. And our ancient traditions are increasingly kept alive mainly for the sake of tourists.
However, in North Central Tanzania, in the Serengeti plateau, one tribe is resisting the pressure: the Hadzabe. A small group of them continue to live as hunter-gatherers, much as their ancestors have for 60,000 years.
Spencer Wells: They are one of the last groups of hunter-gatherers on Earth, essentially using fairly primitive technology to survive. And that's the way we lived for most of our history.
Narrator: In fact, as you will see, our collective history is tightly linked to the Hadzabe. Geneticist Spencer Wells is working with Chief Julius Endiyo to record and preserve their ancient traditions.
Julius: You take branches, the leaf, you are crush and then you are going there for three times per day and then two days, coughing is gone.
Wells: Julius can read the forest, the savannah that we're walking through as though it's a book. It's like walking through a library with him and he'll pull a volume from the shelf and he'll fan it to page 45 and read some passage to you.
Julius: This here is poison, very poisonous. But is, the roots is very nice medicine for stomach.
Narrator: It is precisely these skills, accumulated knowledge, advanced tools and language that helped human beings survive the bleakest period in their history. About 130,000 years ago, an ice age froze most of the northern hemisphere but turned the lush African lands into desert. There was no rain, and people were forced to move in search of food and water. Such harsh conditions lasted thousands of years. It was truly survival of the fittest. And scientists believe that human population numbered as few as 2,000 members.
Wells: If you take that at face value, our species is hanging on by its fingernails. We were on the verge of extinction. It wasn't until we went through that climate crunch that you really needed those skills in order to survive.
Scientist: Really this climatic variability is what's driven us. It's forced us to be inventive and made one particular population so inventive that they've managed to cope with all this, and with a bit of luck, here we are.
Narrator: With a bit of luck, here we all are. Because one choice made by the ancient ancestors of the Hadzabe affects us all. They decided to leave Africa. Little did they know that their descendants would come to populate the whole planet. So, whether you are European, American, Asian or Australian, we are all related to those ancient ancestors of the Hadzabe.

The publisher would like to thank the following sources for permission to reproduce their copyright protected images and videos:

Cover photo: Raul Touzon/National Geographic

Inside photos: 4 a (STACY GOLD /National Geographic Image Collection), 4 b (GIANLUCA COLLA /National Geographic Image Collection), 4 c (Christophe Launay/Getty Images), 4 d (LOOK Die Bildagentur der Fotografen GmbH/Alamy), 4 e (Jochen Tack/Alamy), 4 f (THOMAS J. ABERCROMBIE /National Geographic Image Collection), 4 g (KEENPRESS/National Geographic Image Collection), 4 h (Heeb Christian/Prisma/Superstock Ltd.), 6 a (GIPSTEIN, TODD/ National Geograp/National Geographic Image Collection), 6 b (MIKE THEISS/National Geographic Creative/National Geographic Image Collection), 6 c (Erik T Witsoe/Getty Images), 6 d (VOLKMAR WENTZEL /National Geographic Image Collection), 6 e (B. Wylezich/Fotolia), 6 f (O. LOUIS MAZZATENTA /National Geographic Image Collection), 6 g (XPACIFICA /National Geographic Image Collection), 6 h (Image Source Plus/Alamy), 10 b (Mary Evans / Grenville Collins P/Mary Evans Picture Library), 10 t (STACY GOLD /National Geographic Image Collection), 11 (UniversalImagesGroup/Getty Images), 12/13 (Sergii Tsololo/Alamy), 13 t (NASA/ National Geographic Image Collection), 14 (David Noton Photography/Alamy), 15 t (Victor Paul Borg/Alamy), 15 b (JaySi/Shutterstock), 15 c (FRANS LANTING / National Geographic Image Collection), 17 (DEREK VON BRIESEN/National Geographic Image Collection), 18 (STEPHEN ALVAREZ/National Geographic Image Collection), 20 (GIANLUCA COLLA /National Geographic Image Collection), 22 (Charles O'rear/Corbis UK Ltd.), 25 (Blend Images/Alamy), 26 (Nathalie Louvel/ Getty Images), 27 (PhotoDisc/Getty Images), 28 (Christophe Launay/Getty Images), 31 (amana images inc./Alamy), 32 t (BOBBY MODEL /National Geographic Image Collection), 34 (LOOK Die Bildagentur der Fotografen GmbH/Alamy), 35 (PAUL CHESLEY /National Geographic Image Collection), 36 (MARK COSSLETT / National Geographic Image Collection), 38 (LOOK Die Bildagentur der Fotografen GmbH/Alamy), 39 (National Geographic Image Collection/Alamy), 40 (TODD GIPSTEIN/National Geographic Image Collection), 43 (Ancient Art & Architecture Collection Ltd/Alamy), 44/45 (Jose Luis Pelaez Inc/Blend Images/Corbis UK Ltd.), 48 (Jochen Tack/Alamy), 50 (epa european pressphoto agency b.v./Alamy), 51 (Scanrail/Fotolia), 52/53 (Science Photo Library/Alamy), 54 (STUART FRANKLIN /National Geographic Image Collection), 56 (IRA BLOCK /National Geographic Image Collection), 57 l (Corepics VOF/Shutterstock), 57 c (michaeljung/ Shutterstock), 57 r (Iakov Filimonov/Shutterstock), 58 (THOMAS J. ABERCROMBIE /National Geographic Image Collection), 59 (incamerastock/Alamy), 60/61 (ALISON WRIGHT /National Geographic Image Collection), 62 (© Pixelbliss/Fotolia), 64/65 (Terry Mathews/Alamy), 66 b (noel moore/Alamy), 66 t (KEENPRESS/ National Geographic Image Collection), 68 (JAMES FORTE /National Geographic Image Collection), 70 (REX A. STUCKY /National Geographic Image Collection), 73 (KENNETH GARRETT /National Geographic Image Collection), 74 (ROBIN MOORE/National Geographic Image Collection), 76 (Heeb Christian/Prisma/ Superstock Ltd.), 78 (fazon/Fotolia), 81 (Gavin Hellier/Alamy), 82 (MasterLu/Fotolia), 83 (2010 Ulrich Baumgarten/Getty Images), 86 (GIPSTEIN, TODD/ National Geograp/National Geographic Image Collection), 88 tl (Vasilis Kapodistrias), 88 r (Vasilis Kapodistrias), 88 bl (Vasilis Kapodistrias), 89 (Vasilis